Zombie Capitalism

Zombie Capitalism

Global Crisis and the Relevance of Marx

Chris Harman

Haymarket Books
Chicago, Illinois

First published in July 2009 by Bookmarks Publications.
Copyright © Bookmarks Publications.

This edition published in 2010 by Haymarket Books
P.O. Box 180165
Chicago, IL 60618
773-583-7884
www.haymarketbooks.org
info@haymarketbooks.org

ISBN: 978-1-60846-104-2

Distributed to the trade in the US through Consortium Book Sales and
Distribution (www.cbsd.com) and internationally through Ingram Publisher
Services International (www.ingramcontent.com).

This book was published with the generous support of Lannan Foundation
and Wallace Action Fund.

Special discounts are available for bulk purchases by organizations and
institutions. Please call 773-583-7884 or email info@haymarketbooks.org for
more information.

Cover design by Josh On.

Printed in the United States.

Entered into digital printing November 2019.

Library of Congress Cataloging in Publication data is available.

Contents

About the Author

Chris Harman (1942–2009) was a leading member of the Socialist Workers Party (www.swp.org.uk). He was the author of numerous books including *A Peoples History of the World* (Bookmarks 1999 and Verso 2008), *Revolution in the 21st Century* (Bookmarks 2007), *The Fire Last Time: 1968 and After* (Bookmarks 1988), *The Lost Revolution: Germany 1918 to 1923* (Bookmarks 1982). He was the editor of *International Socialism*, a quarterly journal of Marxist theory (www.isj.org.uk).

The Socialist Workers Party is linked to an international network of organisations, for further information go to www.swp.org.uk/international.php

Introduction

An unstable world

We live in an unstable world, and the instability is going to increase. It is a world where a billion people feel hungry every day, and the hunger is going to increase. It is a world which is destroying its own environment, and the destruction is going to increase. It is a violent world, and the violence is going to increase. It is a world where people are less happy, even in the industrially advanced countries, than they used to be,[1] and the unhappiness is going to increase.

Even the most craven apologists for capitalism find it hard to deny this reality any longer, as the worst economic crisis since the Second World War continues to deepen as I write.

The world's best known banks have only been saved from going bust by vast government bail-outs. Thousands of factories, stores and offices are closing across Europe and North America. Unemployment is shooting upwards. Twenty million Chinese workers have been told they have to return to the villages because there are no jobs for them in the cities. An Indian employers' think tank warns that ten million of their employees face the sack. A hundred million of the world's people in the Global South are still threatened with hunger because of last year's doubling of grain prices, while in the richest country in the world, the United States, three million families have been dispossessed from their homes in 18 months.

Yet just two years ago, when I began this book, the message was very different: "Recent high levels of growth will continue, global inflation will stay quite subdued, and global current account imbalances will gradually moderate," was the "consensus" among mainstream economists, reported the Bank of International Settlements. The politicians, industrialists, financiers and commentators all agreed. They toasted the wonders of free markets and rejoiced that "entrepreneurial genius" had been liberated from regulation. It was wonderful, they told us, that the rich were getting richer because that provided the incentives which made the system so bountiful.

Trade was going to obliterate hunger in Africa. Economic growth was draining the vast pools of poverty in Asia. The crises of the 1970s, 80s, 90s and 2001-2 were memories we could put behind us. There might be horrors in the world, wars in the Middle East, civil wars in Africa, but these were to be blamed on the short-sightedness of essentially honest politicians in Washington and London who may have made mistakes but whose humanitarian intervention was still needed to deal with psychopathic maniacs. The words of those who saw things differently were ignored, as the media poured out candyfloss layers of celebrity culture, upper middle class self-congratulation and senseless nationalist euphoria over sporting events.

Then in mid-August 2007 something happened which began to sweep the candyfloss away to provide a glimpse of the underlying reality. A number of banks suddenly discovered they could not balance their books and stopped lending to each other. The world's financial system began grinding to a halt with a credit crunch that turned into a crash of the whole system in October 2008. Capitalist complacency turned to capitalist panic, euphoria to desperation. Yesterday's heroes became today's swindlers. From those who had assured us of the wonders of the system there now came one message: "We don't know what has gone wrong and we don't know what to do." The man who not long before had been treated as the supreme genius overseeing the US economic system, Alan Greenspan, of the Federal Reserve, admitted to the US Congress that he still did "not fully understand what went wrong in what he thought were self-governing markets".[2]

Governments have been throwing hundreds of billions to those who run the banks—and tens of billions to those who run the multinational car firms—in the hope that this will somehow stop the crisis. But they cannot agree among themselves how to do this and even whether it will work or not.

Yet one thing is certain. The moment any part of the global economy begins to stabilise they will forget the hundreds of millions of lives that have been shattered by the crisis. A few months when banks are not collapsing and profits are not falling through the floor and the apologists will be pumping out candyfloss once again. Their futures will seem better and they will generalise this to the world at large with renewed talk about the wonders of capitalism and the impossibility of any alternative—until crisis hits again and throws them into another panic.

But crises are not some new feature of the system. They have occurred at longer or shorter intervals ever since the industrial revolution established the modern form of capitalism in Britain fully at the beginning of the 19th century.

The poverty of economics

The mainstream economics that is taught in schools and universities has proved completely unable to come to terms with such things. The Bank of International Settlements recognises that:

> Virtually no one foresaw the Great Depression of the 1930s, or the crises which affected Japan and South East Asia in the early and late 1990s, respectively. In fact, each downturn was preceded by a period of non-inflationary growth exuberant enough to lead many commentators to suggest that a "new era" had arrived.[3]

Nothing sums up the incomprehension of those who defend capitalism as much as their inability to explain the most significant economic episode in the 20th century—the slump of the 1930s. Ben Bernanke, the present head of the US Federal Reserve and supposedly one of mainstream economics' most respected experts on economic crises, admits that "understanding the Great Depression is the Holy Grail of macroeconomics"[4]—in other words, he can find no explanation for it. Nobel economic laureate Edward C Prescott describes it as "a... pathological episode and it defies explanation by standard economics".[5] For Robert Lucas, another Nobel Laureate "it takes a real effort of will to admit you don't know what the hell is going on in some areas".[6]

These are not accidental failings. They are built into the very assumptions of the "neoclassical" or "marginalist" school that has dominated mainstream economics for a century and a quarter. Its founders set themselves the task of showing how markets "clear"—that is, how all the goods in them will find buyers. But that assumes in advance that crises are not possible.

The implausibility of the neoclassical model in the face of some of the most obvious features of capitalism has led to recurrent attempts within the mainstream to bolt extra elements onto it in an ad hoc way. None of these additions, however, alter the basic belief that the system will return to equilibrium—providing prices, and especially wages, adjust to market pressures without hindrance. Even John Maynard Keynes, who went further than anyone else in the mainstream in questioning the equilibrium model, still assumed it could be made to work with a degree of government intervention.

There were always challenges to such complacency. The Austrian economist Joseph Schumpeter derided any idea of equilibrium as incompatible with what he saw as the great positive virtue of capitalism, its dynamism. Some of Keynes's disciples went much further than he did in breaking with neoclassical orthodoxy. Cambridge economists tore apart the theoretical basis of the neoclassical school. Yet the orthodoxy is as strongly entrenched in the universities and schools as ever, pumping into the heads of each new generation a picture of the economic system that bears little relationship to reality. The pressure on students to study the books putting forward such views as if they were scientific texts has led to Paul Samuelson's *Economics* and Lipsey's *An Introduction to Positive Economics* selling millions of copies.

It is hardly surprising that the economics profession has difficulty coming to terms with those aspects of the capitalist system that have the greatest impact on the mass of people who live within it. The obtuse theorems that fill economic textbooks and academic journals, with their successive algebraic calculations and geometric figures, assume stability and equilibrium, and so have little to say to people worried by the system's propensity to crisis. One of the founders of the neoclassical school, Alfred Marshall, observed nearly a century ago that the economic theory he believed in was of little use in practice and that "a man is likely to be a better economist if he trusts his common sense and practical instincts".[7]

Yet what is involved is not just abstract academic scholasticism. The orthodoxy is an ideological product in the sense that it operates from the standpoint of those who profit from the market system. It presents their profiteering as the supreme way of contributing to the common good, while absolving them of anything that goes wrong. And it rules out any fundamental critique of the present system, in a way that suits those with commanding positions in educational structures, connected as they are to all the

Introduction

other structures of capitalism. The radical Keynesian Joan Robinson summed up the situation:

> The radicals have the easier case to make. They have only to point to the discrepancies between the operation of the modern economy and the ideas by which it is supposed to be judged, while the conservatives have the well nigh impossible task of demonstrating that this is the best of all possible worlds. For the same reason, however, the conservatives are compensated by occupying positions of power, which they can use to keep criticism in check... The conservatives do not feel obliged to answer radical criticisms on their merits and the argument is never fairly joined.[8]

But even most of the "radicals" usually start by taking the existing system for granted. The arguments of the radical Keynesians like Joan Robinson have always been in terms of amendments to the system, through greater state intervention than that envisaged by the mainstream. They have not seen the system itself as driven by an inner dynamic whose destructive effects are not restricted to purely economic phenomena. In the 21st century it is producing wars, hunger and climate change as well as economic crises, and doing so in ways which threatens the very basis of human life.

Capitalism transforms society in its entirety as its sucks people by the billions into labouring for it. It changes the whole pattern by which humanity lives, remoulding human nature itself. It gives a new character to old oppressions and throws up completely new ones. It creates drives to war and ecological destruction. It seems to act like a force of nature, creating chaos and devastation on a scale much greater than any earthquake, hurricane or tsunami. Yet the system is not a product of nature, but of human activity, human activity that has somehow escaped from human control and taken on a life of its own. Economists write that "the market does this" or "the market demands that". But the market is only the coming together of the products of many disparate acts of human creative activity, labour. What the economists' talk disguises is that somehow these have turned into a machine that dominates the humans that undertake such activity, hurling the world in a direction that few people in their right mind would want. Faced with the financial crisis that began in 2007, some economic commentators did begin to talk of "zombie banks"—

financial institutions that were in the "undead state" and incapable of fulfilling any positive function, but representing a threat to everything else.[9] What they do not recognise is that 21st century capitalism as a whole is a zombie system, seemingly dead when it comes to achieving human goals and responding to human feelings, but capable of sudden spurts of activity that cause chaos all around.

A world turned against ourselves

There has only been one serious tradition of analysis to attempt to provide an account of the system in these terms. It is that which originated in the writings of Karl Marx and his long-time colleague Frederick Engels.

Marx came to adulthood in the early 1840s, just as industrial capitalism began to make its first, limited, impact on southern Germany where he was born. Engels was sent by his father to help manage a factory in Manchester, where the new system was already flourishing. They shared with almost the whole of their generation of German intellectual youth a desire to overthrow the oppressive Prussian feudal system of class rule presided over by a monarch with despotic powers. But they soon began to grasp that the industrial capitalism that was supplementing feudalism contained oppressive features of its own. Above all it was characterised by an inhuman subordination of the mass of people to the work they did. What Marx was beginning to discover about the functioning of this then-new system led him to undertake a critical reading of its most eminent proponents, political economists like Adam Smith and David Ricardo. His conclusion was that, although the system vastly increased the amount of wealth humans could produce, it also denied the majority of them the benefits of this wealth:

> The more the worker produces, the less he has to consume. The more values he creates, the more valueless, the more unworthy he becomes... [The system] replaces labour by machines, but it throws one section of workers back to a barbarous type of labour, and it turns the other section into a machine... It produces intelligence—but for the worker, stupidity... It is true that labour produces wonderful things for the rich—but for the

worker it produces privation. It produces palaces—but for the worker, hovels. It produces beauty—but for the worker, deformity... The worker only feels himself outside his work, and in his work feels outside himself. He feels at home when he is not working; when he is working he does not feel at home.

In his early writings Marx called what was happening "alienation", taking up a philosophical term developed by the philosopher Georg Wilhelm Frederich Hegel. Marx's contemporary Ludwig Feuerbach had used the term to describe religion. It was, he argued, a human creation that people had allowed to dominate their lives. Marx now saw capitalism in the same way. It was human labour that produced new wealth. But under capitalism that wealth was turned into a monster dominating them, demanding to be fed by ever more labour.

The object that labour produces, its product, stands opposed to it as something alien, as a power independent of the producer. The more the worker exerts himself in his work, the more powerful the alien, objective world becomes which he brings into being over against himself, the poorer he and his inner world become, and the less they belong to him... The worker places his life in the object; but now it no longer belongs to him, but to the object...[10]

As Marx put it in his notebooks for *Capital* in the early 1860s:

The rule of the capitalist over the worker is the rule of the object over the human, of dead labour over living, of the product over the producer, since in fact the commodities which become the means of domination over the worker are... the products of the production process... It is the alienation process of his own social labour.[11]

But Marx did not simply record this state of affairs. Others had done so before him, and many were to continue to do so long after he was dead. He also set out, through a quarter of a century of grinding intellectual labour, to try to understand how the system had come into being and how it created forces opposed to itself.

His works were not just works of economics, but a "critique of political economy", of the system which other schools of economics took for granted. His starting point was that capitalism is a historical product, arriving where he found it as a result of a dynamic which drove it ever onwards in a process of endless change with "constant revolutionising of production, uninterrupted disturbance of all social conditions, everlasting uncertainty and agitation".[12] The economic studies of the mature Marx aimed to grasp the nature of this dynamic, and with it the trends in the development of the system. They are the indispensable starting point for anyone who wants to try to grasp where the world is going today.

His method was to analyse the system at different levels of abstraction. In the first volume of *Capital* he set out to delineate the most general underlying features of capitalist production. The second volume[13] deals with the way in which capital, commodities and money circulate within the system, and the third volume[14] integrates the process of production and circulation to provide more concrete accounts of things like profit rates, the crisis, the credit system and rent. Marx's original intention had been to produce further volumes, dealing among other things with the state, foreign trade and world markets. He was unable to complete these, although some of his work towards them is contained in various notebooks by him.[15] *Capital* was, then, an unfinished work in some respects. But it was an unfinished work that accomplished the goal of unveiling the basic processes of the system, integrating into its account the very things ignored by the static equilibrium analysis of the neoclassical mainstream: technical advance, accumulation, recurrent crises and the growth of poverty alongside the growth of wealth.

Using Marx today

For these reasons, any account of the world system today has to begin with basic concepts developed by Marx. I try to outline these in the first three chapters of this book. Some readers from a Marxist background might regard the account as redundant. But the concepts have often been misunderstood within the Marxist camp as well as outside it. They have been seen as competing with the neoclassical to provide an equilibrium account of price formation and then faulted for failing to do so.[16]

One reaction has been to drop key elements in Marx's own analysis, keeping it only as an account of exploitation and of the anarchy of competition. Another, apparently opposed, reaction has been an almost scholastic approach in which competing interpretations pore over texts by Marx and Hegel. It is often as if Marxist theory had been ambushed by its opponents and retreated into a theoretical bunker of its own, just as detached as they are from the real world. For this reason I have felt it necessary to expound the basic concepts in a way which is (I hope) easy to follow, showing how they describe the interaction of the underlying forces that determine the direction of capitalist development. I have left detailed discussion of other interpretations to footnotes. I have, however, felt it necessary to deal with the most common objections to Marx's account from mainstream economists in Chapter Two, since anyone who studies economics at school or university will have their views inflicted on them. Readers who have been lucky enough to escape that fate are welcome to skip this chapter.

Where the incompleteness of Marx's own account does matter is in coming to terms with changes in capitalism since his death. Things he only refers to in passing in *Capital*—the growth of monopolies, the intervention by states in capitalist production and markets, the provision of welfare services, war as an economic weapon—have become massively important. Marxists in the first decades of the 20th century were forced by circumstances to debate some of these matters, and there was a new burst of creative thinking in the 1960s and early 1970s. I attempt to draw from such discussions the concepts needed to "go beyond *Capital*" and fill in gaps in Marx's own account of the system (Chapters Four and Five). The rest of the book then tries to come to terms with the development of capitalism over the last 80 years, from the great slump of the inter-war years to the crisis causing turmoil across the world as I write. The account must be not simply one of economic processes, but at every stage of how the interaction of capitals and states on a world scale gives rise to wars and civil wars, hunger and environmental disaster, as well as booms and slumps. Nuclear weapons and greenhouse gases are as much a product of alienated labour as car factories and coal mines.

A note on the book

The instability of the capitalist economy has had its impact on the writing of this book. I set about writing the first draft when what I call "the great delusion"—the belief that the capitalism had found a new way of expanding without crises—was at its height in late 2006. I viewed another economic crisis as inevitable, in much the same way that someone living in a city built on a seismic fault line knows it is at some point going to suffer an earthquake. But I did not pretend to be able to predict when this would happen, or how destructive it would be. My aim, rather, was to update my *Explaining the Crisis* of 25 years ago, taking into account changes in the system since, but repeating the basic conclusion that its blind rush forward would have devastating repercussions for people's lives through the rest of this century, creating immense social and political crises with potentially revolutionary implications.

But one of these blind rushes had its effect as I was finishing a 150,000-word draft. The credit crunch of August 2007 turned into the great crash of September-October 2008, leading one apologist for the system, Willem Buiter, to write of "the end of capitalism as we knew it".[17] Many details about the system which I treated as part of the present were suddenly in the past, and everywhere there was an urgent demand for an explanation as to what brought this crisis about. I had no choice but to update and restructure what I had written, shifting the emphasis in some of the chapters towards the end of the book from what was going to happen over the decades to come, to what was happening in the here and now. In the process I cut about a third of the words out of the draft, removing a good deal of empirical detail in an effort to make the whole book more accessible. Anyone interested in greater detail can find some in the 15 articles on economics I have written for the journal *International Socialism* over the last two decades, while some of the theoretical arguments are articulated more fully in *Explaining the Crisis*.

Acknowledgements

I owe thanks for reading and making comments on my excessively long and disorganised draft to Tobias Brink, Joseph Choonara, Alex Callinicos, Neil Davidson, Jane Hardy, Mike Haynes, Rick Kuhn, Matt Nichter and Mark Thomas. Thanks are also due for comments on some of the preparatory material that appeared in *International Socialism* to Tom Bramble, Sam Friedman, Mehmet Ufuk Tutan, Thomas Weiss and others, and for information on profit rates to Robert Brenner and Andrew Kliman. I also have a huge intellectual debt to many other people. Pride of place goes to what I learnt in my youth from Mike Kidron and Tony Cliff. Along with that there has been the stimulus over the years from the works of dozens of others who have maintained the tradition of Marxist economic analysis from the late 1960s to the present—Riccardo Bellofiore, Henry Bernstein, Dick Bryan, Terry Byers, Guglielmo Carchedi, François Chesnais, Gérard Duménil, Alfredo Saad Filho, Ben Fine, John Bellamy Foster, Alan Freeman, David Harvey, Peter Gowan, Claudio Katz, Jim Kincaid, Costas Lapavitsas, István Mészáros, Fred Moseley, Geert Reuten, Anwar Shaikh, and many others. Some I have been able to listen to and converse with, most I have never met, and a few I disagree with strongly. But all in one way or another have helped shape my conclusions.

A note on figures and terms

Anyone attempting to explain economic changes has little choice but to use the statistical information provided by governments, business organisations and international institutions like the Organization of Economic Cooperation and Development (OECD), the United Nations Conference on Trade and Development (UNCTAD), the World Trade Organisation (WTO), the World Bank and the International Monetary Fund (IMF). This book is no exception. But readers should be warned that some of the most commonly used figures can be misleading in important respects.

Figures for economic growth, in particular, are not as clear cut as they sometimes seem. The growth they usually measure is of marketed output. But a lot of the human labour that adds to people's well-being is not marketed. This is true of the domestic labour of women and, to a considerably lesser extent, men. It has also been true historically of much of the family labour on peasant land. The result is that there is a false impression of increasing wealth as households begin to pay for things they used to produce outside the market—when a housewife gets a job and buys ready to cook meals, or when a peasant family pays someone else to build a shed on their land where previously they would have done the job themselves.

Such changes lead the usually provided figures to give an increasingly distorted picture with growing marketisation and the feminisation of paid labour in recent decades. The officially provided figures also exaggerate the real rate of growth of the things that satisfy human need by counting in output things like financial services which merely move wealth from one pocket to another—again a particularly marked phenomenon in recent decades.[18] Finally measurements of output per head cannot be equated, as they are all too frequently, with human welfare, since the output is always unevenly distributed between classes. Nevertheless, for want of anything better, I have had to use such figures.

A brief explanation of some of the terms I use. Generally "West" and "East" are used in the way they were in the Cold War decades of the last century, with "the West" including Japan. "Third World" and "Global South" refer to the poorer parts of the world which were relatively unindustrialised for most of the 20th century, as do the phrases "developing" or "underdeveloped countries" used with some of the statistics. The "Communist countries" are those with systems similar to that of the USSR before 1991. "Productive capital" is that employed in industry or agriculture, as opposed to that in finance and commerce. Finally, capitalists are assumed to be male, since 99.99 percent of them were until only a couple of decades ago, while the workers they exploit have always been of both genders. I provide a glossary in an attempt to make the material more accessible both to those fortunate enough not to have studied mainstream economics and to those who are not yet familiar with Marxist writings.

Part One

UNDERSTANDING THE SYSTEM: MARX AND BEYOND

CHAPTER ONE

Marx's Concepts

A world of commodities

The most obvious feature of the economic system in which we live is that it is centred around the buying and selling of goods of all sorts. We have to pay for food, shelter, clothing, energy to light and heat our homes, transport to move around, everything we need to keep ourselves and our families alive. And in order to buy we have to sell, even if all we have to sell is our capacity to work for others. Our very lives depend on the movements of commodities. Hence Marx's starting point in *Capital*:

> The wealth of those societies in which the capitalist mode of production prevails, presents itself as an immense accumulation of commodities.

Marx was writing at a time when market relations had still not penetrated large parts of the world. There were still societies in which all production was for people's immediate needs, whether in "primitive communist" societies based on hunter-gathering or light agriculture,[1] where people agreed freely among themselves how and what to produce, or in peasant societies where a local lord or ruler dictated to them from above. Even in most of the societies where the market already existed, the majority of the population were still subsistence farmers, producing most of the things they needed to keep their families alive, with only a small proportion bought or sold. Today we can extend Marx's words to say that "the wealth of the whole world, with a few exceptions, presents itself as a mass of commodities". And the exceptions— the provision, for instance, of free health and education in a number of advanced countries—are increasingly subject to forces seeking to commodify them. This near universality of commodity production marks society today off from anything that has ever happened before. To understand what is happening to the world we have to begin by understanding the workings of commodity production.

Marx was not the first to try to understand such workings. He was preceded by the classical political economists—early supporters of capitalism who tried to understand its basic dynamics as it struggled to break through, in a Europe still dominated by landowning classes. Two were of special importance: Adam Smith, who wrote in the 1770s at the time when the first modern factory, a spinning mill, was opening at Cromford in Derbyshire; and David Ricardo, who defended the interests of the early industrialists against the big landowners 40 years later in the aftermath of the Napoleonic wars.

Use value and exchange value

Smith is often treated as the patron saint of present day capitalism and of its neoclassical economic theorists. But he made an important point, developed further by Ricardo, which has been completely obliterated by nearly all those mainstream economists who claim to follow in his footsteps. He noted that once society is based on production for the market, every commodity can be seen from two completely different points of view:

> The word value…has two different meanings, and sometimes expresses the utility of some particular object, and sometimes the power of purchasing other goods which the possession of that object conveys. The one may be called "value in use"; the other, "value in exchange". The things which have the greatest value in use have frequently little or no value in exchange; and on the contrary, those which have the greatest value in exchange have frequently little or no value in use. Nothing is more useful than water: but it will purchase scarce any thing; scarce any thing can be had in exchange for it. A diamond, on the contrary, has scarce any value in use; but a very great quantity of other goods may frequently be had in exchange for it.[2]

Marx's *Capital* took up and developed this insight, removing certain ambiguities found in Smith's work:

Understanding the System: Marx and Beyond

The utility of a thing makes it a use value... Being limited by the physical properties of the commodity, it has no existence apart from that commodity. A commodity, such as iron, corn, or a diamond, is therefore, so far as it is a material thing, a use value, something useful. This property of a commodity is independent of the amount of labour required to appropriate its useful qualities.

But commodities are also:

the material depositories of exchange value [which] presents itself as a quantitative relation, as the proportion in which values in use of one sort are exchanged for those of another sort, a relation constantly changing with time and place.[3]

This distinction is not made by today's mainstream neoclassical economists.[4] The only sort of value they see is "marginal utility", based on people's subjective appreciation of use values. Nor is it made by some of those dissident economists who claim to be in the tradition of Ricardo (the so-called "Sraffians").[5] Their model is based on the inputs and outputs of physical objects, in other words, again on use values. Finally there are some present day Marxists who argue the distinction is not relevant, since the important point Marx was making was about exploitation, not value.[6]

In erasing the distinction made by Smith, Ricardo and Marx, all such theories miss something essential to a system based on commodity production: everything that happens in it is subject to two different sets of scientific laws.

On the one side there are the laws of the physical world—of physics, chemistry, biology, geology and so on. It is these which determine the ways in which different things have to be combined to produce goods (the different components of a machine, the material structure of a factory, the techniques used in a surgical operation and so on) and also the usefulness of those goods to those who finally consume them (the nutritional value of food, the warmth provided by fuels and electricity, the number of children who can be accommodated in a school or patients in a hospital, etc).

On the other side, there is the way things relate to each other as exchange values. These often behave in a very different way to use values. The exchange value of something can fall while its use value remains unaltered. This has happened to the price of computers in recent years—the computer I used to write my last book was twice the price of the much more powerful one I am using now. What is more, exchange values are infinitely divisible while use values are usually not; you might say that a bicycle is worth one twentieth of a car, but if you cut a car up into twenty parts it is of nil use to anyone. This matters immensely when it comes to things which are important for modern capitalism like factories, oil wells, airliners, schools and hospitals. The market treats these as exchange values that can be infinitely divided into parts (worth so many pounds, pence, etc); but they have a physical existence that cannot usually be divided in that way.

The exchange values of commodities are also infinitely fluid. In the form of money they can move from one part of the economy to another, from one part of the world to another, be spent on one item or any other of the same price. But the fluidity of use values, like their divisibility, is restricted by their physical make up. You can move £100 million in cash from Britain to India overnight, but you cannot move a factory worth £100 million at anything like the same speed. Use values and exchange values operate according to different, often contradictory, logics and a failure to see this leads to a failure to understand the most basic thing about a commodity producing economy. It does not operate smoothly, just through the flow of exchange values, but is always subject to bumps, to stopping and starting, due to the embodiment of exchange values in use values with physical properties that limit their fluidity.

Labour and money

Smith and Ricardo were not content just with seeing the double nature of commodities. They went on to argue that it was only possible to ascribe exchange values to objects with very different physical properties because they have one thing in common—they are all products of human labour.

As Smith wrote:

> The real price of every thing, what every thing really costs to the man who wants to acquire it, is the toil and trouble of acquiring it. What every thing is really worth to the man who has acquired it, and who wants to dispose of it or exchange it for

something else, is the toil and trouble which it can save to himself, and which it can impose upon other people. What is bought with money or with goods is purchased by labour, as much as what we acquire by the toil of our own body... They contain the value of a certain quantity of labour which we exchange for what is supposed at the time to contain the value of an equal quantity.

Labour was the first price, the original purchase-money that was paid for all things. It was not by gold or by silver, but by labour, that all the wealth of the world was originally purchased; and its value, to those who possess it, and who want to exchange it for some new productions, is precisely equal to the quantity of labour which it can enable them to purchase or command.[7]

This understanding Marx also incorporated into his own analysis:

The exchange values of commodities must be capable of being expressed in terms of something common to them all, of which thing they represent a greater or less quantity. This common "something" cannot be a geometrical, a chemical, or any other natural property of commodities... If then we leave out of consideration the use value of commodities, they have only one common property left, that of being products of labour.

But Marx refined the analysis of Smith and Ricardo in a very important way. It was not the particular concrete exertions of labour as such that determined exchange value. For different people with different skills take different amounts of time and use different amounts of effort to produce particular commodities:

Some people might think that if the value of a commodity is determined by the quantity of labour spent on it, the more idle and unskilful the labourer, the more valuable would his commodity be, because more time would be required in its production.[8]

Rather the exchange value of a commodity depends on the "socially necessary labour time":

that is required to produce an article under the normal conditions of production, and with the average degree of skill and intensity prevalent at the time...[9]

It is social labour that has transformed nature to create the means that humans depend on for a livelihood. So it is the amount of social labour incorporated in it that constitutes the underlying value of a commodity. The concrete labour of individuals is transformed through exchange in a commodity-producing society into a proportionate[10] part of "homogenous", "social" labour—or "abstract labour". Marx calls this abstract labour the "substance of value". It finds expression in exchange value and determines the level around which the commodity's price will fluctuate on the market:

> Every child knows that any nation that stopped working, not for a year, but let us say, just for a few weeks, would perish. And every child knows, too, that the amounts of products corresponding to the differing amounts of needs demand differing and quantitatively determined amounts of society's aggregate labour... And the form in which this proportional distribution of labour asserts itself in a state of society in which the interconnection of social labour expresses itself as the private exchange of the individual products of labour, is precisely the exchange value of these products.[11] All the different kinds of private labour, which are carried on independently of each other...are continually being reduced to the quantitative proportions in which society requires them.[12]

Neoclassical economists tried to develop a notion of value out of people's subjective judgements, with some even trying to incorporate labour as "disutility". Marx, by contrast, saw value as something objective, as indicating the proportion of total social labour "embodied"[13] in it. But what that value is only comes to light as a result of the continual, blind, interaction of commodities on the market.[14] The system as a whole forces its individual components to worry about how the individual labour they employ relates to labour elsewhere.[15] He calls this process the operation of "the law of value".

Values, however, are not unchanging. All the time there is the introduction of new techniques or new methods somewhere in the system. This results in a change in the amount of socially necessary labour needed to produce certain commodities—and that changes their exchange value. The use values of objects remain fixed until natural processes of wear, tear and decay damage them. But the exchange value of things—the value that matters for the system as a whole—declines every time the technical advance somewhere in the system decreases the amount of labour required to make them.

This leads Marx to a "counter-intuitive" conclusion which distinguishes his account of the system—and it is one which even some Marxists have difficulties coming to terms with. A rise in productivity reduces the value at which things exchange. It seems absurd on the face of it. Yet there are numerous examples of increased productivity causing some goods to fall in price compared to others. Marx provided one from his own time:

> The introduction of power-looms into England probably reduced by one-half the labour required to weave a given quantity of yarn into cloth. The hand-loom weavers, as a matter of fact, continued to require the same time as before; but for all that, the product of one hour of their labour represented after the change only half an hour's social labour and consequently fell to one-half its former value.[16]

Thousands more examples could be given today. For we are living in a period in which technical advance is much faster in some industries (especially those involving microprocessors) than others, and so the prices of things like DVDs, televisions and computers produced by industries using the most technologically advanced equipment are tending to fall while those in other industries using older techniques remain fixed or tend to rise. This is something of central importance as we shall see later when we discuss the dynamics of 21st century capitalism.

Once commodity production is generalised across a society, one particular good comes to be used to represent the value of all others—money (Marx calls it "the universal equivalent"). In Marx's day it was usually in the form of gold (or sometimes silver), and a certain quantity of gold (say an ounce), produced by a certain amount of average labour time, could act as a measure of the value for all the other goods that were bought and sold. As capitalism developed as a system, banks and then governments found that they could use paper notes to stand in for gold in many transactions and eventually to dispense with reliance on it at all, so long as people believed others would accept those notes (known technically as "fiat money") for goods. Credit from banks could also function in the same way, so long as people continued to trust the banks.

The development of commodity production had one important effect. It systematically distorted people's understanding of reality through what Marx called the "fetishism of commodities":

The...relation of the producers to the sum total of their own labour is presented to them as a social relation, existing not between themselves, but between the products of their labour... A definite social relation between men assumes, in their eyes, the fantastic form of a relation between things. In order to find an analogy, we must have recourse to the mist-enveloped regions of the religious world. In that world the productions of the human brain appear as independent beings endowed with life, and entering into relation both with one another and the human race. So it is in the world of commodities with the products of men's hands.[17]

People speak of "the power of money", as if its power did not come from the human labour for which it is a token; or of the "needs of the market", as if the market was anything more than an arrangement for linking together the concrete acts of labour of different human beings. Such mystical attitudes lead people to ascribe social ills to things beyond human control—the process which the young Marx had called "alienation" and which some Marxists since Marx have called "reification". Simply seeing through such mysticism does not in itself deal with the social ills. As Marx noted, simply arriving at a scientific understanding of the character of existing society leaves it intact just as "after the discovery of the component gases of air, the atmosphere itself remained unaltered".[18] But without seeing through the fetishism, conscious action to transform society cannot take place. Hence the importance of grasping the distinction between use value and exchange value and of grounding value in socially necessary labour.

Exploitation and surplus value

We do not only live in a world of commodity production. We live in a world where control of most of that production is concentrated in relatively few hands. In 2008 the sales of the world's biggest 2,000 companies equalled about half of total world output.[19] If we assume that around ten directors sit on the board of each of the multinationals, then the out of a world population of over six billion, a mere 20,000 people exercise decisive control over the creation of wealth; in fact, the figure will be considerably lower than that because most of the directors will sit on the boards of more than one firm. Production, of course, is not carried out simply by the multinationals. Alongside them are a mass of nationally based medium-sized firms that have not achieved multinational status, and alongside them exist an even larger number of small firms, some little more than family operations employing perhaps a couple of people. But, even taking all these into consideration, only a small percentage of the world's population control the means of production responsible for producing the major portion of its wealth.

Those who do not own and control such means of production have no choice if they are to make a livelihood, beyond the minimum provided by welfare programmes, other than to try to sell their ability to work to those that do. They get paid a wage, while their labour produces goods that are the property of those who control the means of production. Some of the value of these goods is used to cover the wages of the workers, some to pay for the materials used in production, some to cover the wear and tear of means of production. But some forms an excess which is the basis of the profits of the owners—what Marx called "surplus value" and some non-Marxist economists simply call "the surplus".

Adam Smith had already suggested where this surplus came from (although he did not stick consistently to this view):

> In the original state of things, which precedes both the appropriation of land and the accumulation of stock, the whole product of labour belonged to the labourer... But as soon as the land becomes private property, the landowner demands a share of the produce... The produce of almost all other labour is liable to the like deduction of profit. In all arts and manufactures the greater part of the workmen stand in need of a master to advance them the materials of their work, and their wages and maintenance till it be completed. He shares in the produce of their labour, or in the value which it adds to the materials upon which it is bestowed; and in this share consists his profit.[20]

Profit, then, arises when the land, tools and materials required for production become the private property of one section of society. This section is then able to get control of the labour of others.

Ricardo took up and developed Smith's ideas. In doing so he pointed to a central ambiguity in Smith's own writings. Smith mixes with the view that labour alone creates value another approach, in which profits and rent as well as labour contribute to the final value of goods. Ricardo rejected this latter view. But soon after his death in the 1820s it became the orthodoxy among pro-capitalist economists. It was much more palatable to defenders of the existing system than implying that profits were parasitic on labour.

Marx, however, saw that the development of Smith's views by Ricardo could alone provide the basis for a scientific account of how capitalism functioned. Like Ricardo, he recognised it was absurd to say that profits somehow created value when they were part of value that had already been created. But he went much further than Ricardo had in clarifying the issues and working out the implications of the theory.

The first important advance he made was to differentiate clearly two different meanings given to "the value of labour" by Smith. On the one hand it meant the amount of labour required to keep the labourer for the time during which he or she worked. Adam Smith had argued:

> There is…a certain rate below which it seems impossible to reduce for any considerable time the ordinary wages of even the lower species of labour. A man must always live by his work, and his wages must at least be sufficient to maintain him. They must even upon most occasions be somewhat more otherwise it would be impossible for him to bring up a family, and the race of such workmen would not last beyond the first generation.[21]

From this point of view, the "value of labour" was the value of the wage of the labourer.

But Smith also used the term "labour" to refer to the amount of labour actually performed by the worker. And, Marx stressed, the two amounts were by no means the same. Labour, he pointed out, was like all other commodities in that it was bought and sold. But it differed from them because it had the peculiar property that when put to use it performed more labour than required to produce it.

In the 1850s he introduced a new term designed to make the distinction between the two uses of the concept of labour in Smith and Ricardo (and in his own earlier writings) absolutely clear. He said that what the capitalist paid for when he employed someone

Understanding the System: Marx and Beyond

was not labour as such but "labour power"—the ability of someone to work for a certain period of time. The value of labour power depended, like that of any other commodity, on the amount of labour needed to produce it. Workers could not provide labour power unless they had adequate food, clothing, housing, a certain amount of relaxation, etc. These were their requirements if they were to be fit and capable of working. Their wage had to cover the cost of these things—that is, to correspond to the amount of social labour needed to produce them. This determined the value of labour power.

It should be noted that Marx did not see the minimal level of subsistence alone as determining the value of labour power. There was also the need to make minimal provision for the upbringing of the workers' children, since they would constitute the next generation of labour power. And there was a "historical and moral element" which depended on the "habits and degree of comfort" which the workers were accustomed to. Without it they would not apply their full faculties to their labour and might even rebel against it. In this way the cumulative effect of workers' struggles could influence the value of labour power. Marx was not, as he is sometimes presented, a believer in an "iron law of wages" whereby only a fixed portion of national output could go to the workers.[22]

Be that as it may, the labour people could perform was greater than the amount of labour needed to provide them with at least a minimal livelihood—to replenish their labour power. It might, for instance, take an average of only four hours work a day to provide the level of consumption necessary for someone to be able to perform a day's work. But they could then perform eight, nine or even ten hours work a day. The extra labour went to the employer, so that the value of the goods turned out by his factory was always greater than his investment. It was this which enabled him continually to get surplus value, which he could keep for himself or pass on to other members of the capitalist class in the form of interest and rent.

The relation between the employer and the worker had the appearance of being between equals. The employer agreed to give the wage and the worker his or her labour. No coercion was involved. On the face of it the situation was very different to that between the slave owner and the slave, or between the feudal lord and the serf. It was compatible with a juridical system based on "the rights of man", of equality before the law of all citizens. Even if actually existing bourgeois societies were tardy in granting this, it seemed engraved on their structure. Yet the surface appearance of equality hid a deeper inequality. The employer possessed the prerequisites for the workers engaging in social production and getting a livelihood. The workers were "free" in the sense that they do not have to work for any individual firm or capitalist. But they could not escape having to try to work for someone. As Marx put it:

> the worker can leave the individual capitalist to whom he hires himself whenever he likes... But the worker, whose sole source of livelihood is the sale of his labour, cannot leave the whole class of purchasers, that is the capitalist class, without renouncing his existence. He belongs not to this or that bourgeois, but to the bourgeois class.[23]

The difference between the value of the worker's labour power and the value created by the labour done was the source of the surplus value. Once the employer had got this surplus value, it could be kept directly as profit, it could be used to pay off interest on any money borrowed to build the factory, or as rent to the owner of the land on which the factory stood. But however surplus value was divided up into profits, interest and rent, its source remained the excess work done by the workers—the exploitation by those who owned the means of production of those who did not. Once the owner had got the profit, he could use it to build new means of production, increasing still further his capacity to blackmail workers into labouring for him on his terms if they were to get a livelihood.

It was this process which made the employer a capitalist. It also gave a special meaning to the word "capital". The word is used by mainstream economists and in everyday life simply to mean long-term investment as opposed to immediate consumption. But it has a deeper significance once the means of production are in the control of one group of society, compelling others who want a livelihood to work for them. It is now a product of past labour which is able to expand through the exploitation of current labour. It is, as Marx put it, not a thing, but a relation:

> Value-creating and value-enhancing power belongs not to the worker but to the capitalist... All the development of the productive forces of labour is development of the productive forces

Understanding the System: Marx and Beyond

of capital. By incorporating into itself this power, capital comes alive and begins to work "as if its body were by love possessed". Living labour thus becomes a means whereby objectified labour is preserved and increased...[24]

The fetishism of commodities now takes the form of making it seem that creativity does not lie with living human beings but with the products of their labour, so that people talk of capital creating wealth and employers "providing people with work", whereas in reality it is labour that adds to the value of capital and the worker who provides labour to the employer.

Absolute and relative surplus value

Marx distinguished between two ways in which firms could raise the ratio of surplus value to wages. One was by the crude method of lengthening the working day. He called this "absolute surplus value". This method of forcing up profits was very widespread in the early days of industrial capitalism, and Marx in *Capital* provides many examples of it. But Marx also noted in *Capital* that prolonging the working day over much could be counterproductive for the capitalist:

A point must inevitably be reached, where extension of the working day and intensity of the labour mutually exclude one another, in such a way that lengthening of the working day becomes compatible only with a lower degree of intensity.[25]

So it was that, after putting up massive opposition to successive attempts to provide a legal limit to the working day for children, major capitalist interests gave way to working class pressure—and sometimes found that production actually increased once hours were shorter. For much of the 20th century the method of prolonging the working day seemed to belong to the past. In the advanced industrial countries, at least, workers' resistance had forced capitalists to concede a shorter working week and holidays with pay. The 72-hour week of Victorian times had become the 48-hour week and then the 44-hour week.

But there was another range of methods for increasing the amount of surplus value to be obtained from each worker, which

Marx called "relative surplus value". It relied on reducing the proportion of the work time that went into covering the cost of replenishing worker's capacity to work, that is, their labour power.

This took three forms. The first was to introduce new machinery into the workplace, so as to increase productivity and reduce the amount of time it took for the workers to produce goods whose sale would cover their wages. In effect, instead of, say, four hours work covering the cost of their labour power, two hours would do so—with two hours extra going to produce surplus value.

Marx saw this as the method of increasing exploitation capitalists turned to as they faced difficulties in extending the working week any further in the mid-19th century. The productivity of the workforce per hour became central, rather than extending the number of hours worked.[26] But it was in itself only a short-term expedient for the capitalist. The first capitalist to introduce new machinery would be able to produce the same amount of value with less hours of labour. Once other capitalists also introduced new machinery, the socially necessary time needed for production fell and with it the value of the goods he sold and the excess surplus value he obtained.

The second form it took was increased productivity in the consumer goods industries and agriculture. This would reduce the amount of labour time needed to produce their output and the prices workers had to pay for their means of livelihood. This meant that the cost to the capitalists everywhere of providing workers with their accustomed living standard (of paying for their labour power) fell, and the amount of surplus value extracted could be increased without cutting real wages or extending the working day.

The third method was to intensify the pressure on workers to work harder. As Marx puts it, the only way to "change the relative magnitudes" of the working day going to the capitalist rather than the worker without cutting real wages was to "change either the productivity of labour or its intensity".[27] There was a drive to impose "on the workman increased expenditure of labour in a given time, heightened tension of labour-power, and closer filling up of the pores of the working-day."[28] Or again, "What is lost by shortening the duration is gained by the increasing tension of labour power".[29]

The drive for increased productivity became an obsession for big business, as was shown by the movement for "scientific management" founded by the American F W Taylor in the 1890s.

Taylor believed that every task done in industry could be broken down into individual components and timed, so as to determine the maximum which workers could accomplish. In this way, any breaks in the tempo of work could be eliminated, with Taylor claiming he could increase the amount of work done in a day by as much as 200 percent.

"Taylorism" found its fullest expression with the introduction of the assembly line in Henry Ford's car plants. The speed at which people worked now depended on the speed at which the line moved, rather than their individual motivation. In other industries the same pressure on people to work flat out was achieved by increasing surveillance by supervisors, with, for instance, mechanical counters on machines indicating the level of work achieved. And today a similar approach is being attempted in a variety of white collar occupations with increased use of assessment, attempts at payment by results, the use of key stroke counters on computers, and so on.

Accumulation and competition

A world of commodity production is a world of competition between producers. It is this element of competition which distinguishes a society based on commodity production and exchange value from one where individuals or groups decide on what use values to produce for their own consumption. Through exchange the effort put in by those working in one unit of production is linked to those of millions of other individuals in other units, but the link only takes place through competition between those taking the decisions about production in the individual units. In Engels' phrase there is "social production but capitalist appropriation".[30]

The capitalist firm which exploits the worker is therefore, necessarily, in competition with other capitalist firms. If it cannot out-compete them, eventually it will be forced out of business. To out-compete means keeping ahead in developing new, more productive techniques—only in that way can it ensure that it is not going to be driven out of business by rivals producing and selling goods more cheaply than it can. It cannot guarantee being able to afford new equipment using such techniques unless its profits are as high as possible. But if it raises its profits in order to be able to reinvest, so must its rivals. The fact that each firm is involved in exploiting wage labour means that none of them dare rest on its laurels.

However successful a firm may have been in the past, it lives in fear of a rival firm investing profits in newer and more modern plant and machinery. No capitalist dare stand still for any length of time, for that would mean falling behind the competitors. And to fall behind is eventually to go bust. It is this which explains the dynamism of capitalism. The pressure on each capitalist to keep ahead of every other leads to the continual upgrading of plant and machinery.

So it is that capitalism becomes not merely a system of exploiting "free" wage workers, but also a system of compulsive accumulation. The *Communist Manifesto*, which Marx wrote with Engels early in 1848, insisted:

> The bourgeoisie, during its rule of scarce one hundred years, has created more massive and more colossal productive forces than all the preceding generations put together.

It emphasised the continual transformation of industry under capitalism:

> The bourgeoisie cannot exist without constantly revolutionising the means of production... Constant revolutionising of production...distinguishes the bourgeois epoch from all earlier ones.

In *Capital* Marx sees the continual drive to build up ever bigger industry as the characteristic feature of capitalism:

> Fanatically bent on making value expand itself, he [the capitalist] ruthlessly forces the human race to produce for production's sake... Accumulation for the sake of accumulation, production for production's sake![31]

The work's first volume begins with analysing production for the market ("commodity production"), then looks at what happens when wage labour arises and labour power becomes a commodity, and finally culminates in showing how production using wage labour brings about a process of compulsive accumulation that ignores human need and individual desires.

Capital is not then defined just by exploitation (which occurred in many precapitalist societies), but by its necessary drive to self-expansion. The motivation for production and exchange is increasing the amount of value in the hands of the capitalist firm—a process for which some Marxist writers use the (in my view confusing) neologism "valorisation".[32]

So the system is not just a system of commodity production; it is also a system of competitive accumulation. This creates limits to the action possible not only for workers, but also for capitalists. For if they do not continually seek to exploit their workers as much as is practically possible, they will not dispose of the surplus value necessary to accumulate as quickly as their rivals. They can choose to exploit their workers in one way rather than another. But they cannot choose not to exploit their workers at all, or even to exploit them less than other capitalists do—unless they want to go bust. They themselves are subject to a system which pursues its relentless course whatever the feelings of individual human beings.

Surplus value, accumulation and the rate of profit

Machines and raw materials do not themselves create value. Only the exercise of human labour has added to the natural wealth that existed in a state of nature and only continued human labour can increase it still further. Machines and raw materials exist because human labour has been applied in the past and they cannot substitute for it in the creation of new value. But they are necessary if labour is to achieve the average level of productivity prevailing in a particular society at a particular time. The final value of goods produced has to include an element covering the cost of the machines and materials used.

When a company produces cloth by employing workers to work on power looms that weave wool, the price of the final product has to cover not only the cost of providing the labour power of the workers (their wages) and the profit of the company, but also the cost of the wool and the wear and tear to the power looms. If the power loom can keep going for ten years, then in each year one tenth of its cost has to be covered by the annual sales of the cloth—this is what accountants refer to the depreciation costs of capital. Or, to put it another way, the labour incorporated in the value of the cloth includes not only the new socially necessary labour expended by the workers, but also the "dead labour" used to produce the wool and one tenth of the power loom.

For these reasons, Marx argued that the investment made by the capitalist could be divided into two parts. One was the expenditure on paying wages to hire the workers. This he called "variable capital"—because it was capital that by putting labour power to work expanded value to create surplus value in the course of production. The other part was expenditure on the means of production. He called this "constant capital" because its existing value passed into the value of the goods produced without growing any bigger—its value was simply transferred to the final product. In the case of fixed constant capital (factory buildings, machinery etc) this took place over several production cycles; in the case of circulating constant capital (raw materials, energy, components) in a single production cycle.

Marxists usually use the letter v to stand for variable capital (wages that purchase workers' labour); c to stand for constant capital (plant, equipment and raw materials); s to stand for surplus value. The ratio of surplus value to variable capital (wages) is the ratio of the length of the working day the worker gives to capital compared to that which provides for themselves—sometimes called the rate of exploitation. It can be represented by s/v.

But for the capitalist, the ratio of surplus value to wages is not the only thing that matters, since his investment is bigger than simply what he has spent on wages. He is interested in making his total capital expand, not just that which goes into wages. What matters, therefore, is the ratio of surplus value to total investment—that is, expenditure on instruments and materials of production as well as on wages. This is the "rate of profit", which Marx depicted as s/(c+v).

It is affected not only by the ratio of surplus value to wages, but also by the ratio of expenditure on instruments and materials of production (constant capital) to wages (variable capital). Marx called this last ratio (c/v) the "organic composition of capital". This varies from industry to industry and over time. Different production processes can use the same amount of labour but different amounts of plant and equipment; the cost of equipment in a factory employing 1,000 people to sew cloth into clothes is less than that to employ the same number to smelt iron ore into steel. This has important implications for the dynamic of capitalism. It is

Understanding the System: Marx and Beyond

driven forward not only by concern with the ratio of surplus value to wages, but by the drive to maintain and increase the ratio of surplus value to different levels of total investment. It is a point we will have to return to repeatedly.

Primitive accumulation

Today we take the buying and selling of labour power for granted. It seems as "natural" as the rising and setting of the sun. Yet nowhere was it more than a minor feature of any society until a few hundred years ago. So in Europe in the late Middle Ages, or in Africa and Asia at the time of European colonisation in the 18th and 19th centuries, most people had at least some direct access to the means of getting a livelihood—even if they had to hand over a slice of what they produced to a parasitic landlord. Peasants could grow food on their own land and craftsmen make goods in their own little workshops.

What changed this, according to Marx, was a primeval act of robbery—the use of force to remove masses of people from any control over the means of production. This was often carried through by the state at the behest of some of the most privileged groups in society. In England and Wales, for example, the rise of capitalism was accompanied by "enclosures"—the forcible driving of peasants from common land they had cultivated for centuries. Laws against "vagrancy" then compelled the dispossessed peasants to seek work at whatever wage they could get. In Scotland the "clearances" had the same effect, as the lairds drove the crofters (small farmers) from the land so as to replace them first by sheep and then by deer. As Britain's rulers carved out an empire for themselves throughout the rest of the world, they took measures to bring about the same separation of the mass of people from control over the means of gaining a livelihood. In India, for example, they granted complete ownership of the land to the already highly privileged *zamindar* class. In East and South Africa they usually forced each household to pay a fixed sum of money, a poll tax, which it could only raise by sending some of its members to seek employment with European ranchers or businessmen.

Marx called this process of creating the conditions for the growth of capitalist production "the primitive accumulation of capital". Marx tells how:

The discovery of gold and silver in America, the extirpation, enslavement and entombment in mines of the aboriginal population, the beginning of the conquest and looting of the East Indies, the turning of Africa into a warren for the commercial hunting of black skins, signalised the rosy dawn of the era of capitalist production...[33]

But by itself this could not lead to *capitalist* production. There had, after all, been pillage of one sort or another throughout the history of class society, going back to Babylonian times, without it leading to the rapid accumulation that characterises capitalism. The forcible separation of masses of people from any control over the means of production—and so from any possibility of making a livelihood without selling their labour power—was indispensable. "The expropriation of the agricultural producer, of the peasant, from the soil, is the basis of the whole process".[34] For this reason, it can be misleading to refer to any forcible seizure of wealth by capitalists as "primitive accumulation".[35]

In Marx's writings it has two aspects: on the one hand the "freeing" of the mass of population from any direct access to the means of making a livelihood; on the other the accumulation of wealth by a class that can use economic necessity to make such "free labour" toil for it.

Once capitalism had established itself, its own economic mechanisms pushed the process of separating people from control over the means of production even further, without necessarily needing intervention by the state or the use of force to bring it about. Thus in Britain in the late 18th century there were still hundreds of thousands of handloom weavers, who worked for themselves weaving cloth to sell. Within 50 years they had all been driven out of business by capitalist firms using power looms. In Ireland in the 1840s a terrible famine caused by the requirement that hungry peasants pay rent to (mainly British) landlords led a million to die of hunger and another million to abandon their holdings and seek work in Britain and the US. The market could achieve such horrors without the direct help of the state (except, of course, in protecting the property of the landlords). Capitalism had become a self-sustaining and self-expanding system destined to absorb the whole world into its workings.

Understanding the System: Marx and Beyond

CHAPTER TWO

Marx and His Critics

The neoclassical critique of his theory of value

Marx's theory of value has been under attack ever since *Capital* was first published. The most common form this attack takes is to claim that capital as well as labour creates value. After all, it is said, a worker using a machine produces much more than a worker without one, and all the time workers are being replaced by machines that do the same job. It is even possible to conceive of an economy in which all work is done by machines. So neoclassical economists argue that not only labour but also capital is involved in producing things which satisfy human need. And just as labour gets paid according to what it contributes to wealth creation, so does capital. Each "factor of production" gets a "reward" equal to its "marginal output".

There is a central fallacy in this argument against Marx. It rests of a static picture of the economy, in which capital and labour simply exist alongside each other. It ignores the palpable reality that the means and materials of production themselves have been produced. Machines and factory buildings are not things that exist in their own right. They are the product of previous human labour. The wheelbarrow which aids the toil of the labourer is itself the product of the toil of the metal worker. That was why Marx called the means of production "dead labour" (as opposed to present work, which is "living labour"). They are the products of labour that has taken place previously—and can, if necessary, be replicated by the application of labour today. The amount of socially necessary labour needed to reproduce them determines their current worth.

The failure of neoclassical theory to take into account the creation of the means of production by labour is no accidental failing. Its founders in the late 19th century—the Austrians Carl Menger and Eugen von Böhm-Bawerk, the Englishmen W Stanley Jevons and

Alfred Marshall, the Frenchman Léon Walras, the Italian Vilfredo Pareto, and the American John Bates Clark—built the assumption of a static system into their theory. They viewed the whole economy as like a street market where the buyers calculate what combination of goods gives them the best value for the money they have got in their pockets, while the stallholders calculate the best price they can get for each of their goods. The mutual adjustment of the price each seller is willing to accept and each buyer is willing to pay leads to all the goods being sold. And, since each seller is in turn the buyer from someone who has bought from someone else, a whole network of prices is set up which ensures that what is produced is exactly what people want. Walras claimed to show how this works for a national economy with hundreds of pages of equations and graphs.

Inbuilt into the whole approach was a very unreal view of capitalism. For, whatever else capitalism is, it is not static. In a real street market, people do not agree instantaneously on the prices for buying and selling. But neoclassical theory assumed that through the mediation of a central auctioneer they could arrive at agreed prices instantaneously. Real life haggling often takes quite a long time, with prices across the market as a whole being arrived at through a process of successive adjustments. Once that is taken into account divergences open up between the actual prices of goods and those presupposed in the theory. The actual production of goods that are to be sold is always a process taking place in time. "Price signals" do not tell you what *will* be wanted when production is finished, but what was wanted before it began. The simultaneity of the theory is a myth, and the simultaneous equations developed on the basis of its assumptions bear little relation to really existing capitalism.

Faced with the reality that production occurs over time, how did the founders of neoclassical economics react? They did not allow it to affect their theory one iota. Walras, for instance, recognised that "production requires a certain lapse of time". But he then wrote he would deal with the "difficulty purely and simply by ignoring the time element at this point";[1] and when he returned to the issue it was to assume that "data" remained "constant for a given period of time",[2] as if the transformation of the whole productive apparatus with economic growth would not mean continual transformation of the structure of supply and demand. Marshall went as far as to admit that "time is the source of many of the greatest difficulties in economics",[3] since "changes in the

Understanding the System: Marx and Beyond

volume of production, in its methods, and its costs are ever mutually modifying one another." This did not, however, stop him teaching the theory and a whole generation of mainstream economists taking it as proof of the efficacy of market capitalism. An updated version of Walras's mathematical model was produced in the early 1950s by Kenneth Arrow and Gerard Debreu which attempted to take time into account. But Arrow himself recognised that the model only works "if you assume no technological progress, no growth in population and lots of other things".[4]

The refusal of the neoclassical school to grasp the basic point that capitalism is a system undergoing continual transformation that disrupts the old price structure and prevents any settled equilibrium means that it provides at best an apologetic description of things as they exist at any moment in time, not an account of economic developments and dynamics.

The neoclassical school's own theory of value, which it counterposes to the theories of Smith, Ricardo and Marx, is in terms of the utility which a commodity gives—that is, how individuals evaluate the commodity compared to other commodities. But this leaves completely unresolved the basis for measuring the utility for one person compared to another. How do you measure the "utility" of a glass of water to someone in the desert with the "utility" of a diamond tiara to a princess? The most you can do is list the preferences of individuals. But to explain why the preferences of some individuals matter more than the preferences of others you have to explain why some are wealthier than others—and that depends on factors to do with the structure and dynamic of capitalist society which "utility" theory ignores.

Pareto replaced the term "utility" by "ophelimity"[5] because, as his American contemporary Irving Fischer put it, "the great untutored and naïve public... find it hard to call an overcoat no more truly useful than a necklace, or a grindstone than a roulette wheel".[6] Some later neoclassical theorists dropped any notion of value altogether—although "marginal utility" continues to be taught in school and college textbooks to this day as the "modern" answer to the labour theory of value.

Neoclassical economists have not succeeded in giving an objective basis to their theory of value, despite more than a century of effort. Of course, ultimately, someone must want to use something (or, at least be able to sell it to someone else who will use it) if they are going to pay for it. But it is not use that determines price.

Nor can "marginal output" as defined by the neoclassical school provide an answer. This is measured, they argue, by the value of the capital used up in producing it; but when they define the value of that capital they do so in terms of the marginal output. They end up saying, in effect, that "the marginal value of capital equals the marginal value of capital", or "profit equals profit". Statements of this sort cannot explain anything. All they do is to state that if something exists, it exists.

Orthodox economics in fact does no more than state that certain things are bought and certain things are sold at present, without explaining why these things are produced and not others, why some people are rich and some poor, and why some goods pile up unsold while people who desperately need them go without, or why sometimes there are booms and at other times slumps.

These points were made against marginal economics more than 80 years ago by the Austrian Marxist Rudolf Hilferding and the Russian revolutionary Nicolai Bukharin. They have been put across more recently in a rigorously logical form by dissident academic economists known as the "Cambridge School".[7] But the capacity of dissident economists to point out the absurdities in neoclassical theory has not weakened its hold on academic economics. It has simply led to ever more obtuse mathematical models being used to provide an appearance of scientific rigour. As Joan Robinson pointed out half a century ago:

> Quantitative utility has long since evaporated but it is still common to set up a model in which quantities of "capital" appear, without any indication of what it is supposed to be a quantity of. Just as the problem of giving an operational meaning to utility used to be avoided by putting it into a diagram, so the problem of giving a meaning to the quantity of "capital" is evaded by putting it into algebra.[8]

Recognition of the difficulties with their own theory has, on occasions, forced those who otherwise accept the neoclassical system to try to reinforce it with elements from the labour theory of value. So Marshall suggested there might occasionally be merit in using a labour theory of value: "the real value of money is better measured for some purposes in labour rather than in commodities", although he hastened to add, "This difficulty will not affect our work in the present volume..."[9] John Maynard Keynes also half grasped the limitations of the very neoclassical system whose postulates he took for granted. At one point in his most famous work, the *General Theory of Employment, Money and Interest*, he recognised that you cannot simply add together different sets of physical commodities at one point in time and compare them with a different set at a later point.[10] To make such comparisons involves "covertly introducing changes in value".[11] To deal with this problem, he dropped the usual assumptions of neoclassical theory and made half a turn to a labour theory of value,[12] suggesting that output could be measured by "the amount of employment associated with a given capital equipment".[13] He explained later:

> I sympathise with the pre-classical [sic] doctrine that everything is produced by labour, aided by what used to be called art and is now called technique, by natural resources...and by the results of past labour, embodied in assets..."[14]

Neither Marshall nor Keynes was prepared to go further and jettison the neoclassical system as a whole. But if they had taken their own observations of these points seriously, they would have been compelled to do so.

The failings of the neoclassical system provide at least a partial, negative, proof of Marx's approach. For his theory of value avoids such a subjective and static approach. Marx's theory is objective because it is not based on individual evaluations of a commodity, but on the necessary amount of labour needed to produce it given the level of technology existing in the system as a whole at a particular point in time—both the direct living labour of the worker and "dead labour" embodied in the equipment and materials of production used up in the production process. For Marx, it is the pressure different capitals exert on each other, not the evaluations of individuals, that matters, since any capitalist who prices a commodity at a level higher than the amount of socially necessary labour needed to produce it will soon be driven out of business. The law of value is therefore an external force operating on every capitalist through the interaction of all capitalists once there is the general production of commodities for exchange mediated by money. Since the "individual capitalists", writes Marx, "confront one another only as commodity-owners, the 'inner law' enforces itself only through their competition, their mutual pressure upon each other, whereby the deviations are mutually cancelled".[15]

The relation between capitals cannot be understood as something fixed and unchanging. It is a dynamic process, based on the interaction through time of different capitals, so that the average "socially necessary labour" at any point is the result of individual processes of production organised independently of each other with different, often changing, amounts of concrete labour. The first capitalist to introduce a new technique in any section of industry will be able to produce goods with less than the amounts of labour prevailing in the system as a whole, and will be able to capture markets from others. But once other capitalists adopt the technique, this advantage is lost. Only a capitalist who controls a very large part of the market for particular commodities, or who can exert political pressure to impede others accessing his markets, will be able to get away for longer or shorter periods of time with charging prices which reflect amounts of labour higher than those that are socially necessary. The law of value only operates as the result of the pressures these different capitals exert on each other through time. Any still photograph from the moving film of capitalist development will always show discrepancies—and sometimes large ones—from the law of value. But the film itself will show the discrepancies eventually disappearing under the pressure of inter-capitalist competition even as other discrepancies arise.

Value and prices

It is this dynamic aspect to Marx's theory that enables it to deal with a problem that beset the attempts by Smith and Ricardo to base value on labour. This is that the ratio of labour to investment varies from industry to industry. Yet in practice the rate of profit (the ratio of the surplus value to investment) does not vary in the same way, even when wages are more or less the same level and the rate of exploitation must be about the same. The prices of goods seem to depend not on the amount of socially necessary labour needed to produce them, but on a mark up on the cost of capital investment. The bigger the capital investment the bigger, it seems, is the mark up. A capitalist selling something produced by one person working on an expensive machine will expect a bigger mark up than for something produced by one person working on a cheap machine. The fact that some industries are more "capital intensive" than others implies that prices have to diverge from values in terms of labour if profitability is not to be much lower in some cases than others.

This is what led Adam Smith to dilute his labour theory of value with another, contradictory approach. The sale of goods produces a payment that is divided up into different "revenues"—wages for the workers, profit for the industrialist, interest for the banker who lent the industrialist money, and rent for the landlord. Smith contradicts his own initial labour-based theory of value by arguing that each of these revenues adds to value. David Ricardo was more consistent than Smith and tried to stick to the pure labour theory. But this left a gap in his theory that economists who came after him could not solve—one which eventually opened the way to the neoclassical abandonment of the labour theory of value.

Marx could, however, deal with the problem—usually called the "transformation problem"—precisely because his model is a dynamic one that operates through time. His solution depends on looking at how firms will react to the emergence of different profit rates. Those with lower profit rates will begin to move their capital elsewhere. This will cause a potential shortage in what they have been producing, leading to a rise in prices above their value in labour terms. Other firms who use those products as inputs to their own production (either directly or through paying their workers to buy them to replenish their labour power)[16] are forced to pay the higher prices, in the process effectively handing over some of the surplus value in their own hands. The equalisation of the rate of profit takes place through the redistribution of surplus value within the capitalist class.

This does not in any degree alter the fact that the surplus value came from the exploitation of workers in the first place, and that every change in the socially necessary labour time needed to produce a commodity has an effect on its price. It is the flow of already produced surplus value from one capitalist to another through time that equalises the rate of profit[17]—which is also why there can be big differences between the rates of profit in different parts of the system when there are impediments to the flow of value through the system (for instance, when firms have very large amounts of investment tied down immovably in certain sorts of fixed capital or when states prevent investment moving out of what they see as priority industries).

Marx's solution to the problem posed in Smith and Ricardo was attacked within two years of it appearing in Volume Three of

Capital by the marginalist Böhm-Bawerk. The same arguments he used have been employed repeatedly every since. They have often thrown Marxists onto the defensive, with many accepting the core of the criticism and retreating from the attempt to understand the dynamics of capitalism using Marx's concepts. This happened, for instance, soon after the revival of interest in Marxism after the events of 1968. Figures on the left such as Ian Steedman and Geoff Hodgson took up arguments essentially the same as those used against Marx by Böhm-Bawerk (although they did not accept the marginalist theory of value) and his successors like Samuelson.[18] Marxist scholarship, already on the defensive for political reasons inside university economics faculties, often retreated into scholastic debates over texts or into obtuse mathematical calculations as remote from the real world as those of their mainstream colleagues. The result overall was, as Ben Fine has put it, "an increasingly and exclusively academicised Marxism"[19] and "limited engagement with the world of capital as opposed to that of *Capital*".[20]

The criticism of Marx's approach centres around the contention that simply looking at the movement of value between capitals after production has taken place cannot explain final prices, since it does not explain the prices of the inputs into production (the means of production and labour power). For the inputs themselves are commodities with prices different to their values. So Marx's method, it is claimed, explains prices in terms of prices, not in terms of labour values.[21]

The Ricardian, Ladislavs von Bortkiewicz, attempted in 1907 to solve the problem of deducing prices from labour values mathematically, using simultaneous equations. He used a model in which there is no change in the amount of capital investment from one cycle of production to the next (what is called "simple reproduction"). His equations supposedly showed that any attempt to provide a generally applicable way of transforming labour values into prices led to one of the "equalities" taken for granted by Marx not working. Either *total price did not equal total value*, or *total profit did not equal total surplus value*.

Every attempt to deduce prices from values for most of the 20th century ran into the same problem. The response of Marxists was either to abandon the central feature of the labour theory of value or to conclude, as for instance Paul Sweezy did in 1942, that "the Marxian method of transformation is logically unsatisfactory" but that the "patterns of development" of value and price "will differ

Understanding the System: Marx and Beyond

only in minor details".[22] A somewhat similar conclusion was arrived at by Miguel Angel Garcia and Anwar Shaikh among others in the late 1970s using models that were much less mathematical and easier to follow than von Bortkiewicz's.[23] Shaikh showed that total price could equal total value, but total profit would not always equal total surplus value. Garcia claimed to prove that both equalities could hold. But he could only do so by allowing a change in the rate of exploitation from one production cycle to the next, since the shift in prices caused by the movements of value between sectors caused changes in the relative prices of wage goods and capital goods.[24]

Since then, however, a number of Marxists have been able completely to rescue Marx's position by challenging the fundamental assumption made by von Bortkiewicz, Sweezy, Shaikh and many others—the reliance on simultaneity.[25] The method of simultaneous equations assumes that the prices of the inputs to production have to equal the prices of the outputs. But they do not. The outputs are produced after the inputs have gone into production. Or, to put it another way, the value of the inputs for a process A will differ from that of the same inputs for a later process B—even if in terms of their physical composition as use values they are identical. The value of a ton of steel used to make a machine today will not be the same as the value used to make an identical machine next week.[26]

But, argue the critics of Marx, this still leaves the inputs into production as prices, not as values, and to reduce them to labour values involves an infinite regress. The investment need to produce the inputs needs to be broken down into labour values, but that is not possible without breaking down in turn the investment needed to produce it, ad infinitum.

There is a simple response to those who pose the problem like this: Why? Why do the investments needed to produce the inputs have to be broken down in terms of their labour value when they themselves were produced?[27]

The starting point for looking at any cycle of production is the money price of the inputs needed to undertake it. The exercise of labour in the production process then adds a certain amount of new value, which forms the basis of the new commodity, the price of which in turn is formed through the movement of surplus value from capitalists who would otherwise get a higher than average rate of profit to those who would get a lower one.

There is no need to go back in history to decompose into labour values the prices of things which were paid for at the beginning of the production round, in order to understand the impact of creating new value and surplus value on the dynamics of the system. It is no more necessary than it is in physical dynamics to decompose the momentum of an object that strikes another into all the forces that have previously acted on it to create that momentum, going right back to the foundation of the universe with the big bang; or than it is necessary in biology to know the whole history of the evolution of an organism, going right back to the first formation of organic life forms, in order to see what the effect of a genetic change will be in the present.

As Guglielmo Carchedi has pointed out, "If this critique were sound, it would mean the bankruptcy not only of Marx's transformation procedure but also of social science in all its versions" including those that criticise Marx:

> This critique, in fact, would have to apply to any social phenomenon inasmuch as it is determined by other phenomena, both present and past. Social sciences, then, would become an endless quest for the starting point of the inquiry.[28]

It would never be possible to analyse how some current actions related to the cumulative products of past actions.

Skilled and unskilled labour

The same dynamic character of Marx's model also dispels what has been presented from Böhm-Bawerk onwards as another problem for the labour theory of value. This is how the contribution of skilled labour to value creation is to be measured. Marx seems to see this as easily solved. He writes that:

> skilled labour counts only as simple labour intensified, or rather, as multiplied simple labour, a given quantity of skilled being considered equal to a greater quantity of simple labour... The different proportions in which the different sorts of labour are reduced to unskilled labour as their standard, are established by a social process that goes on behind the back of the producers and, consequently, appear to be fixed by custom.[29]

Understanding the System: Marx and Beyond

This explanation is fully adequate when the same job is done by a skilled worker and unskilled worker, with the skilled worker doing it much more quickly. An hour of the skilled labour will be worth more than one hour of the average "socially necessary" labour in the system as a whole, while the unskilled labour will be worth less than that.

There is a problem, however, when it comes to skilled labour that cannot be replaced by a greater quantity of unskilled labour. It does not matter how many unskilled labourers a capitalist employs, they will never be able to do the same task as a skilled toolmaker or a systems analyst. How then can the value produced by the second group be measured in terms of hours of labour of the first group? It seems that any attempt to do so must involve an arbitrariness that undermines the basic theory. Böhm-Bawerk argued that when Marx writes that "a social process" explains the measurement, he is taking for granted that which he is trying to explain. For Böhm-Bawerk this proved that it is not the amount of labour in goods which determines their prices, but the way people evaluate them in relation to other goods (their "utility") and that this deals a death blow to the labour theory of value.

However, the problem for the theory evaporates once the law of value is seen as something working through time. The development of technology again and again leads to jobs emerging that can only be carried out by those with particular skills. At first there is no objective measure of the amount of socially necessary labour time needed to produce them, and those in possession of such skills or the goods produced by them can receive payments which bear no obvious relation to labour time. In effect, value flows to those controlling a monopoly of these skills from the rest of the system. But this is only a transitory phase, even if sometimes a long one, as capitalists elsewhere in the system will do their utmost to try to gain control of some of the benefits of the new skills for themselves.

There are two ways they can do this. They can train new groups of workers to acquire the skills. This effectively amounts to using one sort of labour to create new labour power capable of doing the skilled work, so that the final labour is in fact composite labour, made up of the living labour of the immediate workers and a form of dead labour embodied in their labour power as skills. The capitalists can get this extra element in labour power directly by on the job training for workers (as with apprenticeship systems), they can leave its provision to the workers themselves (when workers pay to go through courses to get skills qualifications) or they can rely in part on the state providing it through its training courses. But in each case, dead labour is embodied in the enhanced labour power and then transferred into the products of the labour process, as with the dead labour embodied in means and materials of production.[30]

But this still leaves a question unresolved. Who trains the trainers? Skilled trainers cannot themselves get their skills from unskilled workers. If their skills are monopoly skills and they produce goods that cannot be produced by unskilled workers, however many work together at the job, then those who own those goods will be able to charge monopoly prices that do not reflect labour values, but simply how much people are prepared to pay.

This will be true of certain skills and certain goods at any particular point in time. But over time this labour too will be reduced to some objective ratio of other labour. Capitalists elsewhere in the system will actively seek out new technologies that undermine such skill monopolies by enabling the tasks to be done by much less skilled labour. In this way, the reduction of skilled labour to unskilled labour over time is a never ending feature of capitalist accumulation. If enough unskilled labour is trained up to the level of skilled labour needed to produce particular commodities, those commodities will cease to be scarce and their value will fall to the level that reflects the combination of the labour needed to reproduce average labour power and the extra cost of the training.

As Carchedi puts it:

> Due to the introduction of new techniques in the labour process, the level of skills required of an agent is lowered. The value of his or her labour power is then devalued. We can refer to this process as *devaluation* (of labour power) *through dequalification* (of skills). It is this process which reduces skilled to unskilled labour and thus (at least as far as the value of labour power is concerned) alters the exchange relations between the commodities of which those different types of labour power are an input. It is this real process which justifies the theoretical reduction of skilled to unskilled labour, or the expression of the former as a multiple of the latter...
>
> The process of devaluation through dequalification is a constant tendency in capitalist production, due to the constant need

Understanding the System: Marx and Beyond

capitalists have to reduce the level of wages. On the other hand, the same techniques create new and qualified positions (the counter-tendency) which, in their turn, are soon subjected to dequalification... At any moment in time we can observe both the tendency (the dequalification of certain positions and thus the devaluation of the agents' labour power) and the counter-tendency (the creation of new, qualified positions for which agents with a high value of labour power are needed).[31]

Labour may not be reducible to socially necessary labour time instantaneously. But it is so reduced over time through the blind interaction of different capitals with each other. Again the law of value has to be understood as pressurising the individual components to operate in a certain way, not as a formula establishing fixed, fast frozen relations between them.

Marx's basic concepts survive all the criticisms once they are not interpreted through the static framework, ignoring the process of change through time that characterises the neoclassical system.

CHAPTER THREE

The Dynamics
of the System

Illusions and reality

The history of capitalism in Marx's time and that of his immediate successors was punctuated by economic crises that occurred
about once every ten years—there were 15 in the US in the 110
years between 1810 and 1920. For a few years firms would invest
on a large scale, taking on new workers; building new factories
and buying new machines would create a demand for the products
of industries like construction, steel and coal, which in turn would
take on new workers; the new workers would receive wages which
in turn enabled them to buy goods. Very fast rates of economic
growth led firms to do everything they could to lure people from
the countryside—and increasingly from other, poorer countries—
into selling their labour power in the towns. Unemployment
would fall to around 2 percent. Then something always seemed to
go wrong. Giant firms would suddenly go bust, cancelling the
demand for the products of other industries, where firms would
also go bust; right across the economy workers—many only recently drawn into industry—would be sacked; their loss of buying
power then ensured that the crisis ricocheted from industry to industry; panic would sweep through the capitalist class, while
unemployment shot up virtually overnight to 10 percent or higher,
where it would stay for months or even years until a new period of
rapid growth took off.

The mainstream economics of the time denied that such "crises
of overproduction" were endemic to the system, basing their arguments on a populariser and vulgariser of Adam Smith's ideas,
Jean-Baptiste Say. His "law" argued that supply and demand
must always coincide, since every time someone sold something

someone else must have bought it: supply, it was claimed, created its own demand. So John Stuart Mill argued:

> Each person's means for paying for the production of other people consists in those [commodities] that he himself possesses. All sellers are inevitably by the meaning of the word buyers... A general over-supply...of all commodities above the demand is...[an] impossibility... People must spend their... savings...productively; that is, in employing labour.[1]

The founders of the neoclassical school had to accept that in practice the economy experienced a "trade cycle" or "business cycle" of booms and recessions, in which for some reason supply and demand did not always balance as their theory claimed. Their reaction was to blame these things on external factors that somehow led to temporary distortions in an otherwise fundamentally healthy system. So Jevons wrote that the business cycle was a result of sun spots which, he claimed, affected the climate and therefore the productivity of agriculture and the profitability of trade, while Walras saw crises as disturbances caused by the failure of prices to respond to supply and demand, comparable in effect to passing storms on a shallow lake.[2]

Some later neoclassical economists did try to develop theories of the business cycle. Anwar Shaikh has summed up their approach:

> the system is still viewed as being self-regulating; only now the adjustment is seen as being cyclical rather than smooth... In orthodox theory a cycle is not a crisis... Cycles must be viewed as "small fluctuations"... which at first approximation one may justifiably neglect... Violent or prolonged expansions and contractions arise from external factors... Crises, therefore, remain outside the normal process of capitalist reproduction.[3]

This view still persists in what is known as "real business cycle theories". These hold that:

> business cycles are the aggregate result of the optimum response of individuals to changes in the economic environment... The economic cycle is assumed to have a stochastic [irregular—CH] oscillation around a trend.[4]

Understanding the System: Marx and Beyond

They still do not allow what they see as short-term aberrations to undermine their faith in an unchallengeable system of laws which lay down how any efficient economy must operate.

The possibility of crisis

Karl Marx, by contrast, argued that the possibility of general crises of overproduction was built into the very nature of capitalism. He destroyed the arguments based upon Say's law in a couple of paragraphs in the first volume of *Capital*. Of course, he acknowledged, every time someone sells an article someone else buys it. But, argued Marx, once money is used to exchange goods through the market, it does not follow that the seller has then immediately to buy something else. Money acts not only as a measure of value in directly exchanging goods, but also as a means of storing value. If someone chooses to save the money they get from selling a good rather than spending it immediately, then there will not be enough money being spent in the system as a whole to buy all the goods that have been produced:

> Nothing can be more childish than the dogma that because every sale is a purchase and every purchase a sale, therefore the circulation of commodities necessarily implies equilibrium of sales and purchases. If this means that the number of actual sales is equal to the number of purchases, it is mere tautology. But its real purport is to prove that every seller brings his buyer to market with him. Nothing of the kind. The sale and the purchase constitute...an exchange between a commodity-owner and an owner of money, between two persons as opposed to each other as the two poles of a magnet...
> No one can sell unless some one else purchases. But no one is forthwith bound to purchase, because he has just sold. Circulation bursts through all restrictions as to time, place, and individuals, imposed by direct barter, and this it effects by splitting up, into the antithesis of a sale and a purchase, the direct identity that in barter does exist between the alienation of one's own and the acquisition of some other man's product. If the interval in time between the two complementary phases of the complete metamorphosis of a commodity become too great, if the split between the sale and the purchase become

too pronounced, the intimate connexion between them, their oneness, asserts itself by producing—a crisis.[5]

The inevitability of crisis

These arguments used by Marx in Volume One of *Capital* "imply the possibility, and no more than the possibility, of crises".[6] But in Volume Three he went further, to argue for the inevitability of crises. He did so by moving beyond the most abstract considerations about the buying and selling of commodities with money to look at the concrete process involved in capitalist production and exchange. As is often remarked, Marx did not provide a single, integrated account of the crisis. Rather he refers to different aspects of the crisis in writings that are scattered in different parts of the text.[7] But it is not that difficult to construct a coherent account from these.

The starting point is that competitive accumulation means that capitalists are simultaneously trying to increase the output of their goods as much as possible at the same time as trying to maximise profits by holding down wages. But wages constitute a major part of the money available to buy goods. Production tends to move in one direction, the consumption of the masses in the other:

> The conditions of direct exploitation, and those of realising it, are not identical. They diverge not only in place and time, but also logically. The first are only limited by the productive power of society, the latter by the proportional relation of the various branches of production and the consumer power of society. But this last-named is based on antagonistic conditions of distribution, which reduce the consumption of the bulk of society to a minimum varying within more or less narrow limits. It is furthermore restricted by the tendency to accumulate, the drive to expand capital and produce surplus value on an extended scale... The more productiveness develops, the more it finds itself at variance with the narrow basis on which the conditions of consumption rest...[8]

Some people have interpreted this passage as meaning that the mere fact that workers are exploited limits the scale of the market and creates crises.[9] Such "underconsumptionist" versions of Marxism share some features in common with the form of the mainstream economics that developed in the 1930s under the influence of Keynes. The conclusion seems to be that capitalism can escape crisis if the state intervenes to raise consumption the moment a recession seems likely to develop.

But Marx's own argument does not stop with pointing to the possibility of consumption falling below production. He goes on to insist that the double nature of one set of commodities, those that make up the means of production, as both values and use values, makes that inevitable. A Russian Marxist economist of the late 1920s, Pavel V Maksakovsky, spelt out how this double nature works itself out.[10] As we have seen, the exchange value of goods is determined by the amount of labour required to produce them using the average level of techniques and skill operating in the system as a whole (what Marx refers to as "abstract labour"). But their production involves concrete human labour bringing objects ("use values") into physical interaction with each other. The correct relations between different exchange values and different use values must exist for production to take place.

The more industry develops, the more complicated these relations become. Textile machines cannot be produced without steel; steel without iron ore and coal; coal without cutting machinery, winding gear and so on. But the chains of physical interaction depend on chains of buying and selling, in which coal firms sell to steel firms, steel firms to textile firms and textile firms to consumers—that is, to people who get wages or profits to spend from other firms so long as these can sell their goods.

Such long, intertwined chains linking production to final consumption only function if two completely different conditions are fulfilled. The correct physical relations between things that go to produce other things has to exist determined by the law of physics, chemistry and biology. But, at the same time, each act of production has to expand the amount of value (ie the amount of average abstract labour) in the hands of the owners of each particular firm. The physical organisation of the production of use values has somehow to correspond with the capitalist determination of prices by values.

Discrepancies between the two requirements mean that the expansion of production inevitably leads to bottlenecks in the supply of raw materials, causing their prices to rise, cutting into the profits of those capitalists who buy them, and so redistributing surplus value from the capitalists producing finished goods and components to those producing raw materials. It also means that the demand for one vital commodity, labour power, can begin to exceed the supply, leading to upward pressure on wages (at least in money terms, although workers may not see it like this if rising raw material prices cut into the buying power of the expanded wage).

That is not all. If it were, the problem would simply be a tendency towards disproportionality between the different parts of the economy.[11] But there are further problems. Production will not take place at all unless capitalists think they can sustain themselves in competition with other capitalists, by getting a rate of profit at least equal to the average in the system as a whole. To guarantee this they have repeatedly to reorganise production, using more advanced techniques to increase productivity per worker. But as all the capitalists try to do this, they continually reduce the average amount of labour needed to produce goods—and therefore the value of the goods. The physical quantity of goods produced by the system will tend to rise, but the value of each individual good will tend to fall. The two things necessary for the system to function, the physical organisation of production and the flow of value through the system, both change repeatedly—but without there being any automatic compatibility between the changes taking place.

Firms undertake production by buying physical equipment (machines, buildings, computers and so on) at prices dependent on the average amount of labour needed to produce them at a particular moment in time. But even as production is taking place, increases in productivity elsewhere in the system are reducing the value of that equipment and of the goods the firm is producing with it. The firm's calculations of profitability were based on the amount it had to spend on this equipment in the past, not on what its present value is—but it is on its initial investment that the firm has to make a profit. So the rapid rate of accumulation that characterises the boom has the effect of cutting the prices of each unit of output, and this hits the profits to be made on investments made earlier in the boom.

Not only do the values of goods keep changing, but, Maksakovsky shows, the reaction of capitalists to these changes leads prices to diverge from values. As profits fall, some firms stop new investments for a period. This reduces the demand for the goods of the other firms that previously supplied them. These then

Understanding the System: Marx and Beyond

try to maintain their sales by cutting their prices below the levels determined by value while they sack workers in order to try to protect their profits on the goods they are selling at reduced prices and at that same time cancel their own investments for fear they will not be profitable. A wave of contraction goes through the economy and with it a general reduction of prices below values.

The contraction does not last forever. Some firms go bankrupt, allowing other firms to buy plant and equipment on the cheap and to cut the wages which workers are prepared to accept. Eventually, a point is reached where they can expect to get higher than average profits it they embark on a new round of investment and a new wave of expansion takes off as capitalists rush to take advantage of the better business conditions. Competition leads firms to undertake a level of investment which temporarily exceeds the existing output of new machinery, components and raw materials. The "overproduction" of the downturn is replaced by "underproduction" in the upturn, and just as prices before were below values in the slump, now they rise above values in the boom. But this only lasts until all the new plant and machinery pass into production, increasing output at the same time as reducing the value of individual goods, making some investment unprofitable and giving rise in time to yet another downturn.

The central point is that the cycle is not a result of mistaken decisions by individual capitalists or their governments, but of the very way value expresses itself in prices. This takes place through a continual oscillation with prices arising above and falling below values, not through some continuous equilibrium.

This cannot be grasped without starting with the objective contradictions expressed in the notion of value. Only by dialectically drawing out these contradictions was Marx able to provide an overview of the system's dynamic.

Credit and financial capital

The spells of expansion and contraction are modified and intensified by the role played by credit—and those who play a special part in the development of this, the bankers.

Capital passes through different forms in the course of capitalist production.[12] It begins as money. This is used to buy instruments and materials of production and labour power as commodities, which in turn are combined in the production process to produce other commodities. These are sold to get more money, which is then used to buy more means of production and labour power. In this way one cycle of production follows another endlessly, so that "every element" in it "appears as a point of departure, transit and return".[13]

So capital takes the form of money, of commodities, of means of production and labour power, then of commodities again and finally of money. For the system to operate, all these forms have to exist simultaneously. If production is to keep going without a stop, there has to be a supply of money to buy commodities, a supply of commodities to be bought as productive capital and a supply of labour power. The cycle of capitalist production, then, is made up of three interconnected circuits—of money, of productive capital and of commodities. Each circuit fulfils a function for capital accumulation—and does so to some extent according to a dynamic of its own.

In the early stages of capitalism, when the units of production were small, the productive capitalist could operate to some degree independently. He had the possibility of financing the buying of plant and machinery and paying his workers from his own pocket. He also had the possibility of selling his output directly to those who consumed it.

But as the individual enterprises grew bigger, the capitalist often found his own resources were not enough to pay in advance for all the plant, machinery and materials he needed. He had to borrow from others. He came to rely on credit, and on special institutions, banks, ready to lend to people in return for interest on these loans.

At the same time, as the scale of the market grew, he could only sell his goods by relying upon specialists in the wholesale and retail trades, who would not be able to pay him for all those goods until they had, in turn, sold them to the final consumers. The productive capitalist borrowed on the one hand and lent on the other. Credit became an indispensable part of capitalist production. And the greater the extent of capitalist production within a particular economy, the longer and more complex became the chains of credit, of borrowing and lending.

The productive capitalist could also become a large scale lender. His fixed capital—his factory building and machinery—was only renewed every few years. But production provided a more or less constant flow of profits. He could lend these profits to others in the interim before renewing his own fixed capital—and would do so in return for the payment of interest.

Once capitalism is fully developed as the dominant way of producing in a particular economy, the lending of past profits by those productive capitalists who do not wish to immediately reinvest becomes the chief source of the funds for those capitalists who do wish to invest but lack sufficient past profits to do so. The financial system emerges as a network of institutions that mediate between different productive capitalists (and the state, insofar as discrepancies that exist between its immediate tax income and its immediate expenditure lead it to also borrow and lend).

Those who run the financial institutions are out to make profits just as much as the productive capitalists are. They have funds of their own (their banking capitals) which pay for the expense of their operations and bridge any gap that might open up between their lending and borrowing (or, at least, are meant to bridge the gap—all too often in the history of the system they have not), and they expect to earn a profit on them, just as the productive capitalists do on their capitals. There is a difference, however. The financial capitalists' profits do not come directly from production, but from a share they get of the productive capitalists' profits in return for lending to them—that is, interest payments.

The rate of interest has often been confused in mainstream economic writings with the rate of profit. But in fact the level and direction of movement of the two are quite different. The rate of profit, as we have seen, is determined by the ratio of surplus value to investment in the production process. By contrast, the rate of interest depends solely upon the supply and demand for loanable funds. If there is more money available for lending in an economy, then the rate of interest will tend to fall; if there is an increased demand for borrowing it will tend to rise.

Since the profits of productive capitalists are the major source of the funds for lending, a high rate of profit will encourage a lower rate of interest. On the other hand, if profits are low, more productive capitalists will themselves want to borrow and this will exert a pressure for interest rates to rise. How these contradictory pressures on interest rates work themselves out depends on other factors, particularly borrowing and lending by the state and the movement of funds in and out of a national economy. But these other factors cannot do away with the pressures of real production on the financial sector.

Other complications arise out of this state of affairs. The lending that financial institutions make is not necessarily restricted to the amount they actually have at their disposal as a result of their own investment and borrowing. The financial institutions can assume that what they have borrowed will not have to be paid back immediately. Therefore they can extend their lending beyond their immediate means, trusting that enough of it will be paid back for them to meet their own debts as they become due.

This makes sense so long as the productive sector of the system is expanding its output; increased lending today can be paid back out of increased output and surplus value in the not too distant future.

Such prophecies about increased lending being recoverable are self-fulfilling up to a degree, since the increased lending to productive capital encourages it in turn to increase its own levels of investment, and to produce more profits from which to repay the bankers. But invariably a point is eventually reached when the drive for financial profits leads to levels of lending above what can be paid back out of the expansion of real output, producing financial crises on the one hand and attempts to escape their impact through fraud on the other. As Marx puts it, "The credit system accelerates the material development of the productive forces and the world market", but does this through developing "the incentive to capitalist production, enrichment through exploitation of the labour of others, to the most pure form of gambling and swindling".[14] Finance drives "the process [of production] beyond its capitalist limits" resulting in "overtrade, overproduction and excessive credit"[15] in ways that rebound on production itself.

Marx's view of this process foreshadowed by a century the currently fashionable account of Hyman Minsky,[16] according to which financial operations invariably move on from a stage of normal profitable business ("hedging") to one of speculation which culminates at a point (a "Minsky moment") when all of what is lent cannot be recovered—and encourages Ponzi[17] or pyramid schemes whereby money from new investors is simply used to pay high interest rates to old investors.

The final complication is that financial institutions do not only use their funds to lend to productive capital. They also lend to individuals for their own requirements (notably for buying property), or to buy shares in already existing companies through the stock exchange. Such use of funds is expected to earn the going rate of interest, just as lending to productive concerns does, and

Understanding the System: Marx and Beyond

for this reason is regarded by the financial institutions as an "investment" of "capital". Yet it in no way contributes to the process of capital accumulation, and the interest earned is parasitic on what is taking place in the productive sector of the economy. For this reason Marx calls it "fictitious capital", describing it as "the most fetish like form of the relations of capital",[18] since "capital appears as a mysterious and self-creating source of interest" and "it becomes the property of money to generate value and yield interest, much as it is an attribute of pear trees to bear pears".[19]

Finance, speculation and the crisis

We have seen that the profits of productive capital are the main source of the funds that the banks have at their disposal for lending, and that the productive capitalists' need for funds for accumulation is a major source of borrowing from the banks. This means that the cycle of expansion and contraction of new investment is accompanied by a cycle of expansion and contraction of lending. But the two cycles are not fully in phase with each other.

Credit expands as the boom begins to take off, with some capitalists keen to lend rising profits and other capitalists keen to borrow, all convinced that there will be no problems of repayment with interest. But eventually a point is reached where the frenzy of investment begins to exceed the funds coming from pools of previous profits. Firms outbid one another as they try to get access to these pools, raising the level of interest they are prepared to pay to get credit. Rising interest rates cut into profits just as rising raw material prices and money wages do so as well. They add to the pressures tipping the system from expansion into crisis. The contraction that follows makes firms and banks much less willing to lend—they fear they may need every penny themselves as their revenue from sales threatens to decline. But contraction also increases the need for many firms to borrow if they are going to make up the shortfall in their sales incomes and not be forced into bankruptcy by unpaid bills. Interest rates continue to rise for a time, despite the shortage of profits to pay them, and add to the downward forces in the system.

Fluctuations are intensified because of something else that happens at the height of the boom. Firms and banks see that lending is a quick way to boost their profits. They offer credit through "financial paper" (in effect promises to pay) of various sorts far in excess of their cash reserves on the assumption that other people and institutions will trust in such "paper" and accept it as payment for commodities without trying immediately to turn it into cash. In effect, credit created by the banks comes to be treated as a form of money—and as "credit money" is counted in certain measures of the money supply.

Such easy credit encourages each firm to undertake massive productive investments as it competes to get a bigger slice of the expanding market than its rivals, even though this causes their combined output to far exceed the capacity of the market to absorb it. Easy credit also enables those on friendly terms with the banks to embark on an orgy of luxury spending, and all sorts of crooks and fraudsters to join in the very profitable business of borrowing in order to lend and lending in order to borrow. The real, underlying processes of production, exploitation and creation of surplus value get completely hidden from view—until the economy suddenly starts turning down and all the bits of paper which represent credit have to be repaid from profits which are too small to do so. At this point firms and banks come to distrust the ability of each other to pay back what has been borrowed, and lending can grind to a virtual stop in what is today called a "credit crunch":

> The chain of payment obligations due at specific dates is broken in a hundred places. The confusion is augmented by the attendant collapse of the credit system...and leads to violent and acute crises, to sudden and forcible depreciations, to the actual stagnation and disruption of the process of reproduction, and thus to a real falling off in reproduction.[20]

The behaviour of "fictitious capital" serves further to intensify the general boom-recession cycle of capitalism. Despite its nonproductive nature, the monetary value of fictitious capital at any point in time represents a claim on real resources that can be converted into cash and from cash into commodities. When, say, share prices are rising during a boom, they add to the capacity of their owners to buy goods and tend to intensify the boom; when they fall with a recession, this adds to the pressure, reducing expenditure through the economy as a whole. The inevitably unstable, suddenly fluctuating, prices of the various sorts of fictitious capital add to the general instability of the system as a

Understanding the System: Marx and Beyond

whole. They intensify the swings from boom to recession and back, and they also play havoc with the capacity of money to provide a fixed measuring rod for value.

Major economic crises almost invariably involve crashes of banks and other financial institutions as well as the bankruptcy of productive firms and rising unemployment for workers. It is easy then for people to misunderstand what is happening and to blame finance, the banks or money for the crisis, rather than the capitalist basis of production.

The modernity of Marx

Marx's picture of crisis was far ahead of his contemporary mainstream economists. It was not until the 1930s that study of crises began to be taken seriously by the mainstream. Even the archpriest of free market economics, Friedrich August von Hayek, could admit in one passage that Marx was responsible for introducing, in Germany at least, ideas that could explain the trade cycle, while "the only satisfactory theory of capital we yet possess, that of Böhm-Bawerk", had "not helped us much further with the problems of the trade cycle".[21]

Recurrent economic crises are as much a part of our world as of Marx's. Some at least of the ideological heirs of John Stuart Mill, Jevons and Böhm-Bawerk do not try to conceal the fact—at least when they are writing for an elite upper class audience in the *Financial Times* or the *Economist*, rather than propagandising to the masses. So the long-time Conservative chancellor of the exchequer in Britain, Nigel Lawson, who once embraced the "monetarist" doctrine that crises were an accidental result of central bankers allowing the money supply to go wrong,[22] was eventually arguing that he was not responsible for the slump which followed the implementation of his policies because the "business cycle" is inevitable. They see the crisis as "creative destruction" without making clear that the creative element consists of wealth for one class, while the destruction is of the livelihoods of others.

I will return to the question of crises in the 21st century later in this book. All that needs to be said for the moment is that there is no problem accounting for them by starting with Marx. Indeed, the only serious question confronting Marx's crisis theory does not arise from the occurrence of crises today, but rather from the fact that for three and a half decades, from 1939 to 1974, a major capitalist country like Britain did not experience a recession in which economic output fell, while the biggest economy, the US, only experienced one very brief such recession (that of 1948-9). The absence of such crises became a major element in economic discussion in the decades of the 1950s, 1960s and early 1970s. And without coming to terms with it, one cannot grasp the intractability of the boom-recession cycle today.

However, if crises were an inevitable feature of capitalism for Marx, they were not in themselves the central point in his analysis of its long-term dynamic. They were a cyclical feature of the system which it had managed to cope with several times by the time *Capital* was published, however great the hardship they had caused to the mass of the population, the distress to those capitalists who went bust, or the occasional outburst of popular discontent. They were not in themselves going to bring the system to an end. As the Russian revolutionary Leon Trotsky put it nearly 40 years after Marx's death, "capitalism does live by crises and booms, just as a human being lives by inhaling and exhaling".[23] The long-term dynamic came from elsewhere than the crisis—from two long-term processes at work in the system, processes that were a product of its ageing as it went through each repetition of the cycle of expansion and contraction.

The tendency of the rate of profit to fall

The theory
The first of these processes is what Marx called "the law of the tendency of the rate of profit to fall" (sometimes called, for short, by Marxists since, "the falling rate of profit"—the phrase I will often use here).

This is one of the most difficult parts of Marx's theory for newcomers to his ideas to understand, and also one of the most contentious. Non-Marxist economists reject it. So the often perceptive *Observer* economic columnist William Keegan has denounced Marx's account as "an obsolete economic textbook which was itself written during the early, faltering phase of unreformed capitalism" quoting the French economist Marjolin to the effect that, "A modicum of experience and some knowledge of history was enough to cast doubt on the [Marxist] theory of an inevitable decline of capitalism owing to a falling rate of profit".[24] Many Marxists who accept the theory of value and the main contours of Marx's account of the crisis are just as dismissive of it.[25] Others hedge round their support for it with so many provisos as to effectively cut it out of any account of the system's long-term development.

Yet Marx himself regarded it as absolutely central. It enabled him to assert that capitalism is doomed by the very forces of production which it itself unleashes:

The rate of self-expansion of capitalism, or the rate of profit, being the goal of capitalist production, its fall…appears as a threat to the capitalist production process.[26]

This "testifies to the merely historical, transitory character of the capitalist mode of production" and to the way that "at a certain stage it conflicts with its own further development".[27] It showed that "the real barrier of capitalist production was capital itself".[28]

Marx did not pick the idea that profit rates fall out of thin air. It was common among economists who preceded him.[29] As Eric Hobsbawm has said, "Two things worried the early 19th century businessmen and economists: the rate of their profits and the rate of expansion of their industries." Adam Smith had believed profit rates must fall as a result of increased competition and Ricardo because of supposed "diminishing returns" in agriculture.[30] Marx provided an explanation which did not depend on such questionable assumptions,[31] but upon grasping that the dynamic of capitalist accumulation contains within it an irresolvable contradiction.

Each individual capitalist can increase his own competitiveness through increasing the productivity of his workers. The way to do this is for each worker to use more and more "means of production"—tools, machinery and so on—in his or her work. That involves the means of production expanding more rapidly than the workforce. There is a growth in the ratio of the *physical* extent of the means of production to the amount of labour power working on them—a ratio that Marx calls the "technical composition of capital".[32] But other things being equal, a growth in the physical extent of the means of production will also be a growth in the level of investment needed to buy them. So there will also be an expansion in the ratio of investment to the work-force, in the value of the means of production compared with wages (or, to use Marx's terminology, of "constant capital" to "variable capital"). This ratio is Marx's "organic composition of capital" (as explained in Chapter One).[33] Its growth, for Marx, is a logical corollary of capital accumulation.

Yet the only source of value and surplus value for the system as a whole is labour. So if investment grows more rapidly than the labour force, it must also grow more rapidly than the creation of new value, and profit comes from this. In short, capital investment grows more rapidly than the source of profit. As a consequence, there will be a downward pressure for the ratio of profit to invest-ment—on the rate of profit.

The reason for the growth of investment is competition—the need of each capitalist to push for greater productivity in order to stay ahead of competitors. But however much competition may compel the individual capitalist to take part in this process, from the point of view of the capitalist class as a whole it is disastrous. For, as we saw in the previous chapter, capitalists measure the suc-cess or failure of their undertakings not in terms of the total profit they bring in but in terms of the rate of profit.

Two objections are often raised to this picture of Marx's. The first is that technological advance does not always involve increas-ing the ratio of means of production to workers—that it can be "capital saving" rather than "capital intensive". If scientific knowledge is progressing and being applied as new technologies, then some of these technologies may employ less machinery and raw materials per worker than old technologies. At any one time there will be *some* new technologies that are capital-saving.

This is true. But it does not refute Marx. For there are likely to be a greater number of "capital intensive" rather than "capital saving" innovations. At any given level of scientific and technical knowledge some innovations may indeed be capital-saving. But when all these have been employed, there will still be other inno-vations (or at least capitalists will suspect there are other innovations) to be obtained only by increasing the level of invest-ment in means of production. The fact that some technical progress can take place without any rise in the ratio of capital to labour does not mean that *all* the advantages of technical progress can be gained without such a rise. If an individual capitalist can in-crease the ratio of capital to workers he will be able to invest in

Understanding the System: Marx and Beyond

and take advantage of innovations that need more capital as well as those that do not. If he cannot increase this ratio then he will benefit only from those innovations that do not—and he will lose out in competition with those who can. Since, in theory at least, there is no limit to the possible increase in the ratio of means of production to workers, there is no theoretical limit to possible innovation based on this method of competition.

In the real world, every operating capitalist takes it for granted that the way to gain access to the most advanced technical change is to increase the level of investment in means of production or "dead labour" (including the dead labour accumulated in the results of past research and development). It is only in the pages of the most esoteric journals of political economy that anyone imagines that the way for the Ford Motor Company to meet competition from General Motors or Toyota is to *cut* the level of physical investment per worker. The capitalist usually recognises that you cannot get the benefits of innovation without paying for it.

For these reasons the average amount of means of production per worker, Marx's "technical composition of capital", will rise—and with it the "organic composition of capital". Only one thing could stop the pressure for this rise: if for some reason there was a shortage of profit-seeking investment. In such a case the capitalists would be forced to forego hopes of achieving the innovations possible through greater investment and settle for those they might stumble upon by accident.

The second argument against Marx's account claims that changes in technique alone *cannot* produce a fall in the rate of profit. For, it is said, capitalists will only introduce a new technique if it raises their profits. But if it raises the profit of one capitalist, then it must raise the average profit of the whole capitalist class. So, for instance, Ian Steedman states, "The forces of competition will lead to that selection of production methods industry by industry which generates the highest possible uniform rate of profit through the economy".[34] The same point has been accepted by various Marxists economists over the last 40 years, for instance by Andrew Glyn,[35] Susan Himmelweit,[36] Robert Brenner[37] and Gérard Duménil and Dominique Lévy[38]—and has been elaborated mathematically by Nobuo Okishio.[39] They conclude that capitalists will only adopt capital intensive techniques that seem to reduce their rate of profit if that rate is already being squeezed either by a rise in real wages or by external competition. These things, not the organic composition of capital, hit the rate of profit.

Marx's own writings provide a simple answer to any such argument: that the first capitalist to invest in a new technology gets a competitive advantage over his fellow capitalists which enables him to gain a surplus profit, but that this surplus will not last once the new techniques are generalised.

What the capitalist gets in money terms when he sells his goods depends upon the average amount of socially necessary labour contained in them. If he introduces a new, more productive, technique, but no other capitalists do so, he is producing goods worth the same amount of socially necessary labour as before, but with less expenditure on real concrete labour power. His profits rise.[40] But once all capitalists have introduced these techniques, the value of the goods falls until it corresponds to the average amount of labour needed to produce them under the new techniques. The additional profit disappears—and if more means of production are used to get access to the new techniques, the rate of profit falls.[41]

The implications of Marx's argument are far reaching. The very success of capitalism at accumulating leads to problems for further accumulation. Eventually the competitive drive of capitalists to keep ahead of other capitalists results in a massive scale of new investment which cannot be sustained by the rate of profit. If some capitalists are to make an adequate profit it can only be at the expense of other capitalists who are driven out of business. The drive to accumulate leads inevitably to crises. And the greater the scale of past accumulation, the deeper the crises will be.

The countervailing tendencies

Marx's theory, it should be stressed, is an abstract account of the most general trends in the capitalist system. You cannot draw from it immediate conclusions about the concrete behaviour of the economy at any individual point in space and time. You have first to look at how the general trends interact with a range of other factors. Marx himself was fully aware of this, and built into his account what he called "countervailing tendencies". Two are of central importance.

First, there is increasing the rate of exploitation. If each worker contributes more surplus value this will counteract the fact that there are fewer workers per unit of investment. The increased exploitation could result from increasing the length of the working day (Marx's "absolute surplus value"), cutting real wages, increasing the physical intensity of labour or a fall in the cost of providing workers with a livelihood as a result of increased productivity. In this case the capitalist could increase the proportion of each individual worker's labour that went into surplus value, even if the worker's living standard was not reduced. Such an increase in the *rate of exploitation* could counteract some of the downward pressures on the rate of profit: the total number of workers might not grow as fast as total investment, but each worker would produce more surplus value even if he or she did not suffer a wage cut or have to work any harder.

There is, however, a limit to the capacity of this method to counter the downward pressure on profit rates—the number of hours in the working day. The number of hours per day that go into providing for the upkeep of the worker can fall from four to three, or from three to two, but it cannot fall below zero! By contrast investment in means of production can increase without limit.[42]

Take the example of a firm which employs a static workforce of 30,000. Even if it worked them as long as was physically possible each day (say, 16 hours) and paid them no wages, its daily profit could not exceed the value embodied in 30,000 x 16 hours labour. This is a limit beyond which profit cannot grow. But there is no such limit on the degree to which investment can grow (and with such a high level of exploitation there would be an enormous quantity of old surplus value to be turned into new enlarged investment). So a point will be reached where profits stop growing, even though competition forces the level of investment to continue rising. The ratio of profits to investment—the rate of profit—*will* tend to fall.

The second "countervailing factor" is that the increase in the productivity of labour means there is a continual fall in the amount of labour time—and therefore of value—needed to produce each unit of plant, equipment or raw materials. The "technical composition of capital"—the physical ratio of factories, machines, etc to workers—grows. But the factories, machines and so on get cheaper to buy. And so the expansion of investment in value terms would be rather slower than the expansion in material terms. This would counteract to some extent the tendency for the value of investment to outstrip the growth in surplus value.

There have been claims that this is more than just a "countervailing tendency" to Marx's law and in fact completely destroys it. Critics argue, using mathematical equations provided by Okishio, that technical progress means that goods are always being produced more cheaply than in the past.[43] If a rise in the ratio of dead to living labour in a certain industry increases productivity, the price of its output will fall compared to the output of other industries. But that in turn will reduce the costs of investment in these industries and its ratio to labour. Lower investment costs will lower the organic composition of capital and *raise* the rate of profit.

At first glance the argument looks convincing. It is, however, false. It rests upon a sequence of logical steps which you cannot take in the real world. Investment is a process of production that takes place at one point in time. The cheapening of further investment as a result of improved production techniques occurs at a later point in time. The two things are *not* simultaneous.[44]

There is an old saying, "You cannot build the house of today with the bricks of tomorrow." The fact that the increase in productivity will reduce the cost of getting a machine in a year's time does not reduce the amount a capitalist has to spend on getting it today. And if some other capitalist buys the cheaper machine, it immediately reduces the value of the machine owned by the first capitalist. While the new capitalist might be able to turn out goods in a more profitable way, the first capitalist has to deduct from his profits the loss in the value of his machine.[45]

When capitalists measure their rates of profit they are comparing the surplus value they get from running plant and machinery with what they spent on acquiring it at some point in the past—not what it would cost to replace it today. The point has added importance when it is remembered that the real process of capitalist investment takes place in such a way that the same fixed constant capital (machines and buildings) is used for several cycles of production. The fact that the cost of the investment would be less if it took place after the second, third or fourth round of production does not alter the cost before the first round of production.

The alleged disproof of Marx arises, as does the so-called transformation problem, from applying simultaneous equations to processes taking place through time. Simultaneous equations, by definition, assume simultaneity, with no passage of time.

The decline in the value of their invested capital certainly does not make life any easier for the capitalists. To survive in business they have to recoup, with a profit, the full cost of their past investments, and if technological advance means these investments are now worth, say, half what they were previously, they have to pay out of their gross profits for writing off that sum. What they have gained on the swings they have lost on the roundabouts, with "depreciation" of capital causing them as big a headache as a straightforward fall in the rate of profit.[46]

Capitalism is based not just on value but upon the *self-expansion* of the values embodied in capital. This necessarily implies a comparison of current surplus value with the prior capitalist investment from which it flows. The very notion of "self-expanding values" is incoherent without it. And the loss of value of the equipment and materials of production that have already been paid for is detrimental to the self-expansion of value.

The fall in the cost of investment might help the new capitalist. But he in turn is under pressure from still other capitalists who invest after him in still cheaper equipment. And all the time the existence of surplus value made in previous rounds of production and available for investment in still newer techniques serves to push up the ratio of investment to the labour force.

There is continual growth in the mass of surplus value seeking an outlet for investment. The more of this surplus value an individual capitalist can get hold of, the bigger the investments he can make and the more productivity-increasing innovations he will be able to introduce compared to his competitors. A capitalist may be able to buy today a machine which is twice as productive as one he paid the same price for a year ago. But that is no help to him if a rival is using greater accumulated surplus value to buy a machine four times as productive. The individual capitalist can stay in business only if he spends as much surplus value as possible on new means of production. If the means of production become cheaper, that only results in his having to buy more of them in order to achieve competitive success. So long as there is more surplus value available for investment than there was previously, the organic composition of capital will tend to rise, other things being equal.[47] It makes no difference if the physical means and materials of production are cheaper—that just causes more of them to be employed.

Crisis and the falling rate

But if the depreciation of capital through increased productivity cannot by itself save the rate of profit, it can if it is combined with something else—the crisis. For the crisis involves some capitals being made bankrupt. They are then forced to dispose of their capital not just at its depreciated value, but for anything they can get, however little. The beneficiaries are those capitalists who survive the crisis. They can pick up means of production—accumulations of value—on the cheap, enabling them to restore their own rates of profit.

In this way depreciation can ease the pressure on the capitalist system as a whole, with the burden of paying for it falling on those capitalists who were driven out of business, but not on those who remained. Those capitalists who die bear many of the costs of depreciation for the system as whole, making it possible for those who live on to do so with lower capital costs and eventually higher rates of profit than would otherwise be the case. "The crises are always but momentary and forcible solutions of the existing contradictions. They are violent eruptions which for a time restore the disturbed equilibrium".[48]

There is a continual double interaction between the long-term tendency for the rate of profit to fall and cyclical crises. The rise in the ratio of investment to labour employed as new investment takes place during periods of expansion exerts a downward pressure on the rate of profit, just as it is under pressure from rising raw material prices and wages. This can have a direct effect, with the fall in the rate of profit causing firms to stop investing, so causing recession in the capital goods industries which then spreads elsewhere. Or it can happen indirectly if firms are successful in protecting the rate of profit temporarily by forcing down real wages. In that case, firms in the consumer goods industries cannot sell all their goods—or, as Marx puts it, they cannot "realise the surplus value" that they have exploited—and their profits fall, again producing recession.[49]

But the crisis in turn leads to some firms going bust and provides opportunities for other firms to buy up their equipment and raw material and take on workers at lower wages. If enough firms go bust, the crisis itself can work to completely counteract the long-term downward tendency of the rate of profit. In short, the decline in the rate of profit helps produce the cyclical crisis, but the cyclical crisis helps resolve the long-term decline in the rate of profit.

Marx's account of the falling rate of profit was not published until 11 years after his death and did not have a big impact on the analyses of his followers in the next two decades. It barely featured

Understanding the System: Marx and Beyond

in the most important works of Marxist analysis by Rosa Luxemburg, Vladimir Lenin and Nicolai Bukharin. It was accepted by Rudolf Hilferding but was not central to his analysis.[50] It was not until the 1920s that a concerted attempt was made to use it to analyse the long term trajectory of the system by the Polish-Austrian Marxist Henryk Grossman. He was reacting to the propensity of many Marxists to deny that capitalism was inevitably heading to a great crash, a "breakdown". He took up the argument in the form in which it had been put by the Austrian social democrat Otto Bauer, who claimed to show that capitalism could expand indefinitely, using schema from Marx in Volume Two of *Capital* depicting the interrelation between different sectors of capitalist production.[51]

Grossman claimed to prove, as against Bauer, that if these schema were applied over a sufficiently large number of cycles of production a point would be reached at which the rate of profit would be too low to allow production to continue without cutting into workers' real wages and the consumption of the capitalist class itself. This would happen because "the scope of accumulation expands...in proportion to the weight of the already accumulated capital" even as the rate of profit tends to decline. Eventually a point would be reached where sustaining accumulation absorbed all existing surplus value, leaving none for the luxury consumption of the capitalist class, and then beginning to eat into the value needed to sustain the working class.[52]

Alternatively, if surplus value was used on an increasing scale to maintain the rate of profit on existing investment, there would be a collapse in the mass of surplus value available for new investment. The industries catering for investment would not be able to function. There would be "absolute over-accumulation" and "a state of capital saturation in which the over-accumulated capital faces a shortage of investment opportunities and finds it more difficult to surmount this saturation".[53] In either case the system would no longer be able to reproduce itself.

There have been many objections to Grossman's arguments.[54] It is not clear from his argument why the rate of expansion of investment has to remain constant from one cycle to another, rather than slowly decline in response to the decline in the rate of profit and in doing so reduce the tendency of the organic composition of capital to rise. In that case the "breakdown", it might seem, could be postponed for a very long time. Further, Grossman's book is ambiguous about whether his theory proves the inevitability of crisis or the inevitability of a complete breakdown of the system. He recognises that the crisis can counteract the tendency of the rate of profit to fall, but still concludes that:

> the mechanism as a whole tends relentlessly towards its final end with the general process of accumulation... Once these counter-tendencies are themselves defused or simply cease to operate, the breakdown tendency gains the upper hand and asserts itself in the absolute form of the final crisis.[55]

Yet it is possible to see hypothetical circumstances in which Grossman's arguments would apply. Intense competition between capitals—itself intensified by falling profit rates—could compel each to invest in ever more expensive means of production so as to obtain the advanced technology that is a precondition for survival. In this way the technical prerequisites of successful competition would contradict the possibility of maintaining profitability; the embodiment of capital in certain use values would contradict the possibility of expanding its value. Resistance from the working class could prevent restoration of profit rates through the method of paying for labour power at below its reproduction costs. And something might prevent the usual boom-recession cycles from driving some firms out of business and easing the long-term problems of others. Grossman's theory can then show how the falling rate of profit can produce deep problems for the system, without being treated as definitive proof that capitalism has to collapse of its own accord.

The concentration and centralisation of capital

The second long-term process recognised by Marx was what he called the "concentration and centralisation" of capital.[56] It is not difficult to grasp what is involved. Concentration refers to the way in which exploitation enables individual capitals to accumulate and so grow larger. The small firm becomes a big firm and the big firm becomes a giant—providing it can survive each cyclical crisis. Centralisation refers to the way in which each crisis weeds out some capitals, leaving those that remain controlling a bigger part of the whole system.

This process has important implications—not all of which were fully drawn out by Marx himself. The bigger the individual units of capital and larger the proportion of the system as a whole they constitute, the greater will be the impact on the rest of the system every time one of them goes bust. If a small firm stops making profits and goes bust, this will destroy only a small part of the market for other, previously profitable, small firms that supply it. There will be a very limited domino effect. If, however, one of the giants of the system goes bust, it can have a devastating impact on other previously profitable big firms that depended on it for their own markets, and on any banks or other firms that have lent it money. The domino effect becomes an avalanche effect.

At the same time, however, the very size of firms can provide them with protection from market forces up to a certain point. The individual acts of labour within a great capitalist enterprise are not directly in competition with individual acts outside it. Instead managerial decisions determine how they relate to each other. As Marx puts it:

> In manufacture...the collective working organism is a form of existence of capital. The mechanism that is made up of numerous individual detail labourers belongs to the capitalist... Manufacture proper not only subjects the previously independent workman to the discipline and command of capital, but, in addition, creates a hierarchic gradation of the workmen themselves... Not only is the detail work distributed to the different individuals, but the individual himself is made the automatic motor of a fractional operation...[57]

The great enterprises are like islands within the system where the relation between the work done by individuals is organised by a plan, not by the interrelation of their products through the market:

> What...characterises division of labour in manufactures? The fact that the detail labourer produces no commodities. It is only the common product of all the detail labourers that becomes a commodity. Division of labour in society is brought about by the purchase and sale of the products of different branches of industry, while the connexion between the detail operations in a workshop is due to the sale of the labour power of several workmen to one capitalist, who applies it as combined labour

power... While within the workshop, the iron law of proportionality subjects definite numbers of workmen to definite functions; in the society outside the workshop, chance and caprice have full play in distributing the producers and their means of production among the various branches of industry.[58]

The islands of planning within the enterprises do not exist apart from the sea of commodity production around them. The internal regime is a response to the external pressure to extract and accumulate surplus value in order to compete: "Anarchy in the social division of labour and despotism in that of the workshop are mutual conditions the one of the other".[59] The despotism arises from the pressure on the capitalist to relate the productivity of labour within the enterprise to the ever changing productivity of labour in the system as a whole. But this cannot be done without using compulsion, pressing down on each worker, to achieve what is brought about in the wider society by the blind interplay of commodities.

The law of value operates between enterprises through the market. Within the enterprise it has to be imposed by conscious regulation on the part of the capitalist. Planning within capitalism is not the opposite of the market; it is the way in which the capitalist tries to impose the demands of the market on the workforce.[60]

The capitalist can often still have a certain leeway within which to operate. The enterprise can make profits if the market for its output is growing rapidly despite costs of production internally departing markedly from those currently prevailing in the system as a whole. Things are similar when it has gained a major share of the market in a sector of production that requires very large amounts of fixed capital. The production methods associated with the physical structure of its fixed capital (its use value) can be much more costly than those available in the system as whole (eg when old machines using many workers are used), but the enterprise is protected from serious competition for a long period of time by the sheer cost to new firms of entering the industry to compete with it. The existence of a certain capital as a fixed, physically constituted use value as well as a potentially fluid exchange value means that the law of value does not apply to it directly and instantaneously.

This is not a state of affairs that can last indefinitely. Eventually the development of new, more advanced production methods in the wider system will lead to it facing sudden serious competition.

It is then, through the impact of crisis on it, that the enterprise is forced to restructure so as to produce according to the law of value or to go under. The more enterprises there are that have been relatively protected in the past—that is, the higher the concentration and centralisation of capital—the greater will be the crisis when it eventually breaks.

But in the interim the giant firm can evade the crisis—and sometimes the interim can be a very long time. If many giant firms are able to do this for a period, the impression can arise that that system—or part of it—has become crisis free. What is not noticed is that the price it pays for avoiding crises is that it is there is no restructuring to offset the long-term downward pressure on profitability. Capitals avoid small crises, only to be hit, eventually, by a much greater one.

The other limit of capitalism?

There is a final point that has often been lost in expositions of Marx's ideas: his stress on the expansion of the "forces of production" has been interpreted as identification with economic growth at all costs. Yet in both the earlier and the later writings of Marx and Engels there is a keen awareness of the contradictory character of such growth within class societies in general and within capitalism in particular. They wrote in 1845-6:

> In the development of the productive forces there comes a stage when productive forces and means of intercourse are brought into being which, under existing relations, can only cause mischief, and are no longer productive but destructive.[61]

Marx and Engels did not just view capitalism as generally destructive. They also provided the outlines of a critique of the particular ecological damage wrought by it, as writers like John Bellamy Foster have emphasised in recent years.[62]

Marx saw human beings as an integral part of the natural world. "Labour", he wrote:

> is, in the first place, a process in which both man and Nature participate, and in which man of his own accord starts, regulates, and controls the material reactions between himself and

Nature. He opposes himself to Nature as one of her own forces, setting in motion arms and legs, head and hands, the natural forces of his body, in order to appropriate Nature's productions in a form adapted to his own wants.[63]

But the drive of capital to create surplus value leads to it undermining of the vitality of nature—and the conditions for human life:

> Exploitation and squandering of the vitality of the soil takes the place of conscious rational cultivation of the soil as eternal communal property, an inalienable condition for the existence and reproduction of a chain of successive generations of the human race.[64]

There arises "an irreparable break in the coherence of social interchange prescribed by the natural laws of life".[65] "Capitalist production develops technology, and the combining together of various processes into a social whole, only by sapping the original sources of all wealth—the soil and the labourer..."[66] Just as "large-scale industry...lays waste and destroys...labour-power", "large-scale mechanised agriculture...directly exhausts the natural vitality of the soil..."[67] Capitalist production, Marx recognised, was slowly destroying the very basis on which it, like all human production, rested—the metabolic interaction between humanity and the rest of the natural world.

Marx's remarks were mainly concerned with the immediate effects of capitalist agriculture on soil fertility, which in his time could only be overcome by the use of guano—nitrous mineral deposits resulting from thousands of years of bird droppings to be found mainly on the coast of northern Chile. Marx's insights were taken up and developed in this sense by Karl Kautsky in the 1890s as implying a crisis of food production in the short term. But they seemed to lose their relevance with the discovery of how nitrous fertilisers could be made artificially (through the Haber-Bosch process) during World War One and world food production was able to expand without difficulty throughout the 20th century. But analyses of the relation between humanity and nature had wider implications than a simple concern with food output, as was spelt out by Engels in his manuscript *The Dialectics of Nature*, which was not published until 30 years after his death, in the mid-1920s.

Understanding the System: Marx and Beyond

Here Engels noted that, although humans differ from other animals in being able to "master" nature, this historically has often had unforeseen negative consequences which cancelled out initial gains. He took as an example the way in which deforestation had wreaked havoc on Greece, Mesopotamia and Asia Minor:

Thus with every step we are reminded that we by no means rule over nature as over a foreign people, like someone standing outside nature—but that we, with flesh and blood and brain, belong to nature and exist in its midst.[68]

Scientific progress was slowly providing the means to avoid causing ecological calamities by controlling and regulating "production activity". But "this regulation" required "something more than mere knowledge". It required "a complete revolution in our hitherto existing mode of production, and simultaneously a revolution in our whole contemporary social order".[69] This was necessary because:

The individual capitalists, who dominate production and exchange, are able to concern themselves only with the most immediate useful effect of their actions... In relation to nature, as to society, the present mode of production is predominantly concerned only about the immediate, the most tangible result; and then surprise is expressed that the more remote effects of actions directed to this end turn out to be quite different, are mostly quite the opposite in character.[70]

The implication is that capitalism contained another inbuilt limit besides that of its inbuilt tendency to economic crises. It is that left to itself it could eventually destroy the very environmental conditions for any form of human existence, including its own. Neither Marx nor Engels developed this implication. But it would become very important a century later.

A dynamic and contradictory system

The recognition that capitalism is an ever expanding system of alienated labour runs through the pages of Marx's economic writings. It is a system in which people's living force is taken from them and turned into a system of things that dominate them. Capital is labour that is transformed into a monstrous product whose only aim is to expand itself: "Capital is dead labour, that, vampire-like, only lives by sucking living labour, and lives the more, the more labour it sucks".[71] It is this which gives capitalism a dynamic of growth unparalleled in previous societies.

The endless drive to pump out surplus value in order to further pump out yet more surplus value, of accumulation in order to further accumulate, knows no bounds. As capitalism emerged in parts of north west Europe, it was compelled to stretch out its tentacles to encompass the whole earth, subjecting ever more living labour to it:

> The need of a constantly expanding market for its products chases the bourgeoisie over the entire surface of the globe. It must nestle everywhere, settle everywhere, establish connections everywhere. The bourgeoisie has through its exploitation of the world market given a cosmopolitan character to production and consumption in every country. To the great chagrin of reactionists, it has drawn from under the feet of industry the national ground on which it stood. All old-established national industries have been destroyed or are daily being destroyed. They are dislodged by new industries, whose introduction becomes a life and death question for all civilised nations, by industries that no longer work up indigenous raw material, but raw material drawn from the remotest zones; industries whose products are consumed, not only at home, but in every quarter of the globe. In place of the old wants, satisfied by the production of the country, we find new wants, requiring for their satisfaction the products of distant lands and climes. In place of the old local and national seclusion and self-sufficiency, we have intercourse in every direction, universal interdependence of nations.[72]

What stands out from Marx's analysis is precisely what has been missing from mainstream economics since his time—a sense of the mass forward rush of capitalism.[73] His model provides, as no other has, an account of a system that had expanded to fill most of Western Europe and North America by the time of his death in 1883—and expanded further to fill the whole globe in the 20th century. But that is not all. His model was not only of a self-expanding system, but of one whose expansion is based upon the interplay of

Understanding the System: Marx and Beyond

contradictory forces that finds expression in the crisis and the downward pressure on the rate of profit. The expansion of the system simultaneously leads to a massive growth in the productive forces—the capacity of humanity to produce its livelihood—and of the transformation of these into destructive forces through the crippling of people's lives.

Capitalism has been a totalising—I am tempted to write "totalitarian"—system, in a way in which no previous mode of production had been, compelling the whole world to dance to its frenzied rhythms of competiton and accumulation. As it has done so, the system as a whole has continually reacted back upon the individual processes on which it depends. It forces each capital to force down the price of labour power to the minimum that will keep its workers able and willing to work.[74] The clash of capitals compels each to accumulate in a way that will produce downward pressure on profit rates for all of them. It stops any of them standing still, even if they occasionally become aware of the devastation they are causing. It is a system that creates periodic havoc for all those who live within it, a horrific hybrid of Frankenstein's monster and of Dracula, a human creation that has escaped control and lives by devouring the lifeblood of its creators.

It is this understanding which above all distinguishes Marx's approach from every school of mainstream economics, orthodox and heterodox alike, and which means it alone provides a guide for analysing capitalism in our century. But doing so means using Marx's concepts to go beyond Marx.

CHAPTER FOUR

Beyond Marx: Monopoly, War and the State

New developments

Marx depicted a system that was very dynamic, but also plagued with seemingly insuperable contradictions. Its very dynamism continually led capital to try to expand at a greater rate than could be sustained by the living labour power on which it ultimately depended. The barrier to capitalist production, Marx wrote, lay in capital itself. The implication was that as capitalism engulfed the whole world, it would be subject to longer and deeper slumps, interspersed with shorter and shallower periods of boom. At the same time, the concentration and centralisation of capital would produce an ever greater polarisation between a capitalist class which was diminishing in size and a working class that absorbed into itself the rest of society.

The model was by design an abstraction. Marx consciously ignored much of the day to day functioning of markets and many of the features of particular capitalist societies in his attempt to grasp the underlying tendencies built into the mode of production as such—its "general laws". The way each of the three volumes of *Capital* operated at a different level of abstraction meant that the third volume, by integrating production and circulation, was closer to the actual operating detail of any really existing capitalist society than the first volume, even though its analysis depended on the basic concepts developed there. It dealt not only with the equalisation of profit rates, the deviation of prices from values, crises and the tendency of the rate of profit to fall, but also with credit and the banking system, commercial profits, interest payments to money lenders and rents to land owners. But even the third volume deliberately paid little attention to many important things: foreign trade, the impact on the capitalist system of absorbing the still enormous pre-capitalist parts of the world or the role of the state. Marx had intended in the original plan for *Capital* he drew up in the early manuscripts of the work further volumes dealing with such things. But he never had time to do so, immersed as he was in day to day revolutionary political activity, compelled to make a livelihood for himself through journalistic articles and, in the last years of his life, plagued by illness, although the three volumes he did fully or partially complete were themselves an incredible achievement.

The gap between the model and the reality left many questions unanswered about the course capitalism would take. These questions did not necessarily seem to matter that much either to Marx and Engels or to the activists in the new workers' movements of the 1870s and 1880s. These were the years of a long period of crises known as the Great Depression. The US steel magnate Andrew Carnegie expressed the mood even in capitalist circles in 1889:

> Manufacturers...see savings of many years...becoming less and less, with no hope of a change in the situation. It is in a soil thus prepared that anything promising of relief is gladly welcomed. The manufacturers are in the position of patients that have tried in vain every doctor of the regular school for years, and are now liable to become the victim of any quack that appears...[1]

A quarter century of falling profit rates[2] led to massive pools of poverty in London and other cities and to mass unemployment in the mid-1880s.[3] It was not surprising that Frederick Engels could feel that the logic of Marx's model was working itself out right in front of his eyes in England as "the decennial cycle of stagnation, prosperity, overproduction and crisis" seemed to give way to "a permanent and chronic depression".[4]

The trajectory of capitalism soon, however, proved to be more complicated than the experience of the 1880s suggested. Profit rates recovered in Britain in the 1890s, and the US and Germany went through a new wave of economic expansion.[5] There were certain positive reforms for workers that seemed to contradict Marx's picture: Otto von Bismarck granted pensions to Germany's workers in 1889 and a British Liberal government produced a similar scheme in Britain 20 years later, along with free school meals; real wages rose in the last two decades of the 19th century, even if they tended to stagnate after that;[6] working hours everywhere

Understanding the System: Marx and Beyond

tended to fall from 12 or 14 hours a day to eight, and the working week to fall from six days to five and a half.[7]

The apparent refutation of the predictions drawn from Marx's model led to a crisis within Marxist ranks, known as the revisionist controversy. Out of it emerged two very different trends in the analysis of capitalism which were to confront each other again and again over the next century.

Edward Bernstein, only a few years previously a close collaborator of Engels, produced a root and branch critique of Marx's methods and conclusions. "Signs of an economic worldwide crash of unheard of violence have not been established", he wrote. "Overproduction in single industries does not mean general crises".[8] "Workingmen", he concluded, are not "universally pauperised as was set out in the *Communist Manifesto*".[9] These changes, he argued, had arisen because of "the enormous extension of the world market" and the regulation of production with "the rise of the industrial cartels" so that "general commercial crises" were "improbable".

Bernstein's "revision" of Marx was rejected by Engels' other collaborator, Karl Kautsky. But this did not prevent many socialist activists coming to accept in practice that capitalism had stabilised itself for the indefinite future. Challenging such views meant going further than Kautsky and adding to Marx's analysis. It is this which, each in their own way, Rudolf Hilferding, Vladimir Lenin, Nicolai Bukharin and Rosa Luxemburg tried to do.

Soon it was not only the purely economic functioning of the system that required something more than the basic account provided by Marx. So too did a new period of immense political convulsions as 44 years of peace in western Europe gave way to the most horrific war humanity had yet known.

Hilferding: finance capitalism and imperialism

The first Marxist economist to publish a detailed analysis of the changes was the Austrian Rudolf Hilferding in his work *Finance Capital*, in 1910. Basing himself on developments in Germany, he argued that banking capital and industrial capital were merging to produce a synthesis of the two, which he labelled "finance capital". On this basis giant trusts and cartels were emerging that could dominate whole sectors of industry:

There is a continual tendency for cartelisation to be extended. The individual industries become increasingly dependent upon the cartelised industries until they are finally annexed by them. The ultimate outcome of this process would be the formation of a general cartel. The whole of capitalist production would then be consciously regulated by a single body which would determine the volume of production in all the branches of industry.[10]

Hilferding did not see competition as disappearing completely. He emphasised the importance of international competition, pointing to the way the merger of finance and industry inside a country led to pressure on its state to use protectionist tax duties to aid its capitalists in their struggle against rivals in the world market. "It is not free trade England, but the protectionist countries, Germany and the United States, which become the models of capitalist development", wrote Hilferding.[11] Far from continuing with the traditional liberal notion of a minimal "night-watchman state" the great trusts wanted it to have the power to widen its boundaries so as to enlarge the market in which they could gain monopoly profits: "While free trade was indifferent to colonies, protectionism leads directly to a more active colonial policy, and to conflicts of interest between different states",[12] Hilferding argued. "The policy of finance capital is bound to lead towards war".[13]

This analysis went beyond anything in Marx. He had witnessed the wars of his lifetime and written about them: the opium wars of Britain against China, the Crimean War, the American Civil War and the Franco-Prussian War. But these were wars, as he saw it, resulting from the drive of capitalism to impose itself on the remnants of the pre-capitalist world around it. Capitalism had come into the world "mired in blood", but Marx's model contained no more than a few hints as to why fully established capitalist countries would be driven to war with each other. Hilferding had taken a first step towards a Marxism for the 20th century that explained what had changed since Marx's time in this all-important respect.

There were, however, ambiguities in Hilferding's approach. The main trend in his book was to argue that the growth of monopolies did not do away with the tendency of capitalism to crisis, and their growing reliance on the state would lead to intensified international competition, imperialism and the drive to war. But at points there were suggestions that pointed to a very different conclusion—that

Understanding the System: Marx and Beyond

the monopolies and the state could work together to dampen the tendency towards crisis: "The specific character of capital is obliterated in finance capital" which was able to resolve "more successfully the problems of the organisation of the social economy", even though it was still a class society, with "property concentrated in the hands of a few giant capitalist groups".[14] This meant the mitigation of the old style economic crisis:

> As capitalist production develops, there is therefore an increase...in the part of production that can be carried on under all circumstances. Hence the disruption of credit need not be as complete as in crises in the earlier period of capitalism. Furthermore, the development of the credit crisis into a banking crisis on the one side and a monetary crisis on the other is made more difficult...[15]
>
> The mass psychoses which speculation generated at the beginning of the capitalist era...seem gone for ever.[16]

Hilferding did not carry his argument through to its logical conclusion in *Finance Capital*, and still wrote that the system could not do away with "the cyclical alternation of prosperity and depression".[17] But by the 1920s, when he served as a minister in two Weimar Republic governments, he veered towards Bernstein's approach with a theory of "organised capitalism" in which the anarchy of the market and the trend towards crisis disappear.[18] One corollary was to deny that there was anything in capitalism inevitably leading to war, since the "organised capitalisms" in different countries would want to cooperate with each other.

A similar conclusion had already been reached in 1914 by Karl Kautsky, leading him too to a position that barely differed in practice from Bernstein's. But where Hilferding pointed to the merger of finance and productive capitalism, Kautsky's argument rested on seeing a fundamental distinction and antagonism of interests between them:

> The finance capitalists...had a direct interest in transforming each national state into an apparatus of support for their own expansion. Imperialism was therefore directly linked to finance capitalism. But the interests of finance capital were not identical to those of industrial capital, which could expand only by broadening its markets through free trade. It was from the industrial

sector that impulses towards international concord arose in the bourgeois camp... Imperialism, the expression of one phase of capitalist development and the cause of armed conflicts, was not the only possible form of development of capitalism.[19]

Kautsky stressed the role of arms firms in particular as having an interest in imperialism and war. But he maintained that the economic costs of rearmament, while they favoured the development of some sectors of industry, were detrimental to others. Capital in the industrial countries needed to dominate the "agricultural" countries in order to get raw materials. But there was no reason why capitalists should not be able to cooperate to do this through a "sort of super-imperialism".[20]

In holding that the drive to war was something that happened despite the interests of most capitalists, Hilferding and Kautsky were articulating a view very similar to that of some liberals. One was the influential economist Hobson, who had produced his own theory of imperialism some eight years before Hilferding. He saw imperialism as the product of one interest group, those connected with certain financial institutions.[21] These opted for guaranteed returns of interest on overseas loans rather than taking the risks involved in industrial investment at home, and welcomed colonial expansion as a way of making sure their state guaranteed the safety of their investments. So for Hobson the root of imperialism lay not with capitalism as such but with finance capital and those he saw as benefitting directly from it—the bond-holding *rentiers* who received their dividends regularly without ever having to worry themselves with productive or commercial activity of any sort.

Another British liberal, Norman Angell, argued a similar position, identifying an essentially peaceful dynamic in capitalism, although ascribing a more benign role to finance—no doubt influenced by the unhesitating way the central banks of France and Germany had sent gold to help Britain, and Russia had then sent gold to help Germany, during the major financial crisis of 1907.[22] "In no department of human activity", he wrote, "is internationalisation so complete as in finance. The capitalist has no country, and he knows, if he be of the modern type, that arms and conquests and jugglery with frontiers serve no ends of his..."[23]

Such arguments have percolated down through the years to the present day. So the former revolutionary Marxist Nigel Harris argues that "business has in general no more power over

Understanding the System: Marx and Beyond

governments than populations" and the threat to the world comes not from untrammelled capitalism but from the states which guard their own interests.[24] Ellen Wood is still a militant Marxist, but her arguments are not that different. She has criticised what she calls "classical-Marxist theories of imperialism" of the First World War years for failing to see that the "'political' form of imperialism, in which exploitation of colonial peoples and resources depends on political domination and control of territory", is "the essence of *pre*-capitalist empires".[25] "Capitalist class exploitation", she insists, is a "purely economic process which, like capitalist class relations, concerns the commodity market".[26] From this it follows that, while capitalism needs a state to exert control over society, it does not need states that enter into conflict with each other. Much the same argument is put by Michael Hardt and Toni Negri in their book *Empire*. Hardt wrote shortly before the US invasion of Iraq that the "elites" behind the decision to go to war "are incapable of understanding their own interests".[27]

The classical theory of imperialism

Writing in the middle of the First World War, Nicolai Bukharin[28] and Vladimir Lenin[29] drew very different conclusions. They began with Hilferding's description of the integration of banking capital, industrial capital and the state, but removed from it any sense of the result being harmonious by stressing the way in which the role of the state in international economic competition led to war.

This was the overriding theme of Lenin's pamphlet *Imperialism*. Its aim was to be a "popular outline", showing how the resort to war was a product of the "latest stage of capitalism"—the original subtitle to the work:

Half a century ago, when Marx was writing *Capital*, free competition appeared to the overwhelming majority of economists to be a "natural law"... Marx had proved that free competition gives rise to the concentration of production, which, in turn, at a certain stage of development, leads to monopoly...

This is something quite different from the old free competition between manufacturers...producing for an unknown market. Concentration has reached the point at which it is possible to make an approximate estimate of all sources of raw materials (for example, the iron ore deposits) of a country and even...of the whole world... These sources are captured by gigantic monopolist associations... The associations "divide" them up amongst themselves by agreement.[30]

Once this stage is reached, competition between the giant corporations is no longer based simply—or even mainly—on the old purely market methods. Taking control of raw materials so that rivals cannot get them, blocking rivals' access to transport facilities, selling goods at a loss so as to drive rivals out of business denying them access to credit, are all methods used. "Monopolies bring with them everywhere monopolist principles: the utilisation of 'connections' for profitable deals takes the place of competition in the open market".[31]

The capitalist powers had partitioned the world between them, building rival colonial empires, on the basis of "a calculation of the strength of the participants, their general economic, financial, military and other strength." But "the relative strength of these participants is not changing uniformly, for under capitalism there cannot be an equal development of different undertakings, trusts, branches of industry or countries". A partition of the world that corresponded to the relative strength of the great powers at one point no longer did so a couple of decades later. The partitioning of the world gives way to struggles over the repartitioning of the world:

Peaceful alliances prepared the ground for wars and in their turn grow out of wars. One is the condition for the other, giving rise to alternating forms of peaceful and non-peaceful struggle on one and the same basis, that of imperialist connections and interrelations of world economics and world politics.[32]

The epoch of the latest stage of capitalism shows us that certain relations between capitalist associations grow up, based on the economic division of the world; while parallel to and in connection with it, certain relations grow up between political alliances, between states, on the basis of the territorial division of the world, of the struggle for colonies, of the "struggle for spheres of influence".[33]

Britain and France had been able to build great empires, dividing Africa and much of Asia between them. The Netherlands and

Understanding the System: Marx and Beyond

Belgium controlled smaller but still enormous empires in Indonesia and the Congo. By contrast, Germany had only a few relatively small colonies, despite its economy beginning to overtake that of Britain. It was this discrepancy that lay behind the repeated clashes between the rival alliances of great power that culminated in the First World War.

Finally, where Kautsky focused simply on the control of the "agrarian" parts of the world (what today would be called the Third World or the Global South), Lenin was insistent that the imperialist division of the world was increasingly centred on industrial areas. "The characteristic feature of imperialism is precisely that it strives to annex *not only* agrarian territories, but even most highly industrialised regions (German appetite for Belgium; French appetite for Lorraine)".[34]

Bukharin's *Imperialism and World Economy*, written shortly before Lenin's work, but appearing afterwards with an introduction by Lenin, made the argument just as forcefully as he draws of the consequences of the tendencies that Hilferding had described:

> Combines...in industry and banking...unite the entire "national" production, which assumes the form of a company of companies, thus becoming a state capitalist trust. Competition...is now competition of the state capitalist trusts on the world market... Competition is reduced to a minimum within the boundaries of the "national" economies, only to flare up in colossal proportions, such as would not have been possible in any of the preceding historical epochs... The centre of gravity is shifted in the competition of gigantic, consolidated and organised economic bodies possessed of a colossal fighting capacity in the world tournament of "nations"...[35]

Writing three years after the end of the war, he drew out the implications even more sharply:

> The state organisation of the bourgeoisie concentrates within itself the entire power of this class. Consequently, all remaining organisations...must be subordinated to the state. All are "militarised"... Thus there arises a new model of state power, the classical model of the imperialist state, which relies on state capitalist relations of production. Here "economics" is organisationally fused with "politics"; the economic power of the

bourgeoisie unites itself directly with the political power; the state ceases to be a simple protector of the process of exploitation and becomes a direct, capitalist collective exploiter...[36]

War now becomes central to the system, arising from the competition between the "state capitalist trusts", and also feeding back into and determining their internal organisation:

> With the formation of state capitalist trusts, competition is being almost entirely shifted to foreign countries. The organs of the struggle waged abroad, primarily state power, must therefore grow tremendously... In "peaceful" times the military state apparatus is hidden behind the scenes where it never stops functioning; in war times it appears on the scene most directly... The struggle between state capitalist trusts is decided in the first place by the relation between their military forces, for the military power of the country is the last resort of the struggling "national" groups of capitalists... Every improvement in military technique entails a reorganisation and reconstruction of the military mechanism; every innovation, every expansion of the military power of one state, stimulates all the others.[37]

The logic of the argument presented by Lenin and Bukharin was that the period of peace that followed the First World War would, sooner rather than later, give way to a new world war unless capitalism was overthrown. "The possibility of a 'second round' of imperialist war is...quite obvious", wrote Bukharin.[38] As we shall see later, the reaction of the great capitalist powers to the economic crisis that began in 1929 confirmed this prediction. That has not, however, stilled the argument against the Lenin-Bukharin account.

The economics of empire

This argument assumed—and still assumes[39]—that peaceful free trade rather than a militaristic struggle to control chunks of territory would have been the most profitable course for the majority of capitalists to pursue. This claim is easy to deal with. The great period of growth of the Western empires was the last quarter of the 19th century. In 1876 no more than 10 percent of Africa was under European rule. By 1900 more than 90 percent was colonised. In the same period Britain, France, Russia and Germany each established colonial enclaves and wide spheres of influence in China; Japan took over Korea and Taiwan; France conquered all of Indochina; the US seized Puerto Rico and the Philippines from Spain; and Britain and Russia agreed to an informal partitioning of Iran.

At the same time there was a massive growth in the export of capital from Britain, still the biggest capitalist economy and the centre of the world financial system, even if the US and Germany were rapidly catching up in industrial output. Total British investment in foreign bonds rose from £95 million in 1883 to £393 million in 1889. It soon equalled 8 percent of Britain's gross national product and absorbed 50 percent of savings.[40] Not all exports of capital, let alone of goods, went to the colonies. Much went to the US and quite a lot went to Latin American countries like Argentina. But the colonies were important. Britain's biggest colony, India, alone accounted for 12 percent of exported goods and 11 percent of capital exports; it also provided a surplus to Britain's balance of payments that could help pay for investments elsewhere in the world; and it provided Britain, free of charge, with an army for conquering other places.[41] The raw materials required for the most technologically advanced industries of the time came from colonial areas (vegetable oils for margarine and soap manufacture, copper for the electrical industry, rubber and oil for the fledgling automobile industry, nitrates for fertilisers and explosives). On top of this, there was the strategic importance of the colonies. What mattered for both politicians and industrial interests was that "Britain ruled the waves" and could use its bases in the colonies to punish states that threatened those interests.

It hardly seemed a coincidence to the theorists of imperialism that the decades which witnessed this massive expansion of colonisation, of exports of capital and of extraction of raw materials also saw the recovery of profitability and markets from the gloom of the Great Depression. They may not always have managed to theorise this clearly, but the coincidence of empire and capitalist boom was real enough.

The Lenin-Bukharin theory therefore stands up as an account of the pre-World War One decades—and of the drive to war. Nevertheless, there was a weakness in Lenin's version of the theory. It generalised from the experience of British imperialism at the end of the 19th century to the whole of imperialism, and tended to make the entire theory rest upon the key role of the banks in exporting financial capital. But this did not fit with the picture even when Lenin was writing, let alone in the decades afterwards. The export of finance had indeed been a central feature of *British* imperialism, but the situation was rather different with its new competitors. In the German case it was the industrial combines, especially those in heavy industry, rather than finance as such, that sought to expand beyond national frontiers by the establishment of colonies and spheres of influence. And the characteristic feature of the US and Russian economies in the pre-First World War decades was not the export of capital but the inflow of funds from other capitalist countries (although there was some re-export of capital). The focus on finance became even more problematic in the quarter of a century *after* Lenin wrote. The quantity of capital invested abroad never rose above the level of 1914 and then declined.[42] Yet the great capitalist powers remained intent on imperialist expansion during the interwar years, with Britain and France grabbing most of the Middle East and the former German colonies, Japan expanding into China, and German heavy industry looking to carve out a new empire in Europe.

The phraseology of certain parts of Lenin's pamphlet has led to some interpretations of it that see financial interests, rather as Hobson and Kautsky did, as mainly responsible for imperialism. This was especially so when, basing himself on Hobson, Lenin insisted on the "parasitic" character of finance capital, writing of:

> the extraordinary growth of…a social stratum of *rentiers*, ie people who live by "clipping coupons", who take no part in any enterprise whatever, whose profession is idleness.[43]

This stress on the "parasitism" of finance capital has even led to some on the left embracing strategies based on anti-imperialist alliances with sections of industrial capital against finance capital—precisely the Kautsky policy that Lenin attacked so bitterly.

Bukharin's account of imperialism by and large avoids these faults. He uses the category of "finance capital" repeatedly. But he explicitly warns against seeing it as something distinct from industrial capital. "Finance capital… must not be confused with money capital, for finance capital is characterised by being simultaneously banking *and* industrial capital".[44] It is inseparable, for Bukharin, from the trend towards domination of the whole national economy by "state capitalist trusts" struggling globally against other "state capitalist trusts".

Such a struggle did not have to concentrate on investing in foreign countries. It could turn into something else: the effort to wrest from other countries already industrialised areas or sources of important raw materials by force. As Bukharin put it, "The further it [imperialism] develops the more it will become a struggle for the capitalist centres as well".[45]

It was necessary, in other words, to turn vast amounts of value into means of destruction—not only in order to try to obtain more value but to hold onto that already possessed. This was the logic of the capitalist market applied to the relations between states. Each had to invest in preparations for war in order not to lose out as the other invested more, just as each capital had to invest in new means of production so as to hold its own in market competition. "Imperialist policies" were "nothing but the reproduction of the competitive struggle on a worldwide scale," with "state capitalist trusts", not individual firms, "the subjects of competition". The "explosions of war" were a result of "the contradiction between the productive forces of the *world economy* and the 'nationally' limited methods of appropriation of the bourgeoisie separated by states".[46] In other words, just as competition between capitals (and with it the free operation of the law of value) was reduced within states, it operated on an ever more ferocious scale between them.

Rosa Luxemburg: imperialism and the collapse of capitalism

Lenin and Bukharin were not the only Marxist opponents of imperialism to attempt to prove that it was an essential stage of capitalism. Rosa Luxemburg also did so with a rather different theoretical analysis in her *The Accumulation of Capital*, published in 1913.[47] It rested on what she believed to be a central contradiction within capitalism that had escaped Marx's notice.

Marx had produced tables in Volume Two of *Capital* showing the interrelation between accumulation and consumption. Each round of production involved using the products of the previous round, either as material inputs (machinery, raw materials, etc) or as means of consumption for the workforce. This required that the material products in one round corresponded to what was needed for production to proceed at the next round. It was not merely a question of the right amounts of value passing from one round to the next, but also of the right sorts of use values—such and such quantities of raw materials, new machinery, factory building, etc, and such and such quantities of food, clothing, etc, for the workforce (plus luxury goods for the capitalists themselves). Rosa Luxemburg, in examining Marx's tables, came to the conclusion that discrepancies were bound to arise between the distribution of value from one round to another and the distribution of the use values needed to expand production. More consumer goods would be produced than could be bought with the wages paid out to workers or more investment goods than could be paid for out of profits. In other words, the system inevitably produced an excess of goods for which there was no market within it. Overproduction was not just a phase in the boom-slump cycle, but endemic. Conceived of as a closed system, in which all the outputs of one round of production had to be absorbed as inputs in later rounds, capitalism was doomed to tend towards a complete breakdown.

In the early stages of capitalism this was not a problem. It was not a closed system. Precisely because it grew up within a pre-capitalist world it was surrounded by people who were not part of it—artisans, the remnants of feudal ruling classes and vast numbers of subsistence peasants. They could absorb the surplus goods, providing raw materials in return. But the more capitalism came to dominate in a particular country, the more it would be faced with this contradiction—unless it expanded outwards to seize control of other, pre-capitalist, societies. Colonisation was in this way essential for the continued functioning of the system. Without it capitalism would collapse.

Luxemburg did not simply produce this argument in an analytical form. She supplemented it with chapter after chapter showing in horrifying detail how the historical development of capitalism in Europe and North America had been accompanied by the subjugation and exploitation of the rest of the world. Her conclusion, like Lenin and Bukharin's, was that socialist revolution was the only alternative to imperialism and war.

Her analysis was, however, subject to trenchant and devastating critiques, most notably by the Austrian reformist Marxist Otto Bauer and by Bukharin. Bauer produced his own versions of the reproduction tables, claiming that there was no problem getting the inputs and outputs to balance properly over several rounds of production. Bukharin concentrated on refuting points Luxemburg

Understanding the System: Marx and Beyond

made in her "anti-critique" reply to Bauer. She had argued that there had to be something outside capitalism to provide an incentive to the capitalists to keep investing. It was not good enough for ever increasing amounts of investment to absorb the growing output of society, since, she argued, this would provide no gain to the capitalists to justify such investment:

> Production to an ever greater extent for production's sake is, from the capitalist point of view, absurd because in this way it is impossible for the entire capitalist class to realise a profit and therefore to accumulate.[48]

Bukharin's reply, in essence, amounted to pointing out that it was precisely such apparently absurd accumulation for the sake of accumulation that characterised capitalism for Marx.[49] Capitalism did not need a goal outside itself. It could be added that it is precisely this which epitomises the extreme alienation of human activity in the system: it is driven forward not by the satisfaction of human need, not even by the human need of the capitalist, but by its own dynamic.

Bukharin did not deny that discrepancies arise in the course of capitalist development between production and consumption. He insisted in his comments on Luxemburg that they are inevitable— but it is precisely the capitalist crisis that overcomes them. Over-accumulation and overproduction occur, but not all the time. They arise in the course of the crisis and are liquidated by its further development. And Bukharin quoted Marx: "There is no permanent crisis".[50] For him imperialism was not to be explained by the problems of overproduction, but by the way in which it aids the capitalist pursuit of higher profits.

Bukharin's argument against Luxemburg cannot be faulted. But he and Lenin do leave something unexplained: why the export of capital during the high tide of imperialist expansion was able to lead capitalism out of the Great Depression. For all its problems, Rosa Luxemburg's theory did attempt to find a link between imperialism and the temporary mitigation of crisis, which Lenin and Bukharin failed to.

Writing in the 1920s, Henryk Grossman, critical both of Rosa Luxemburg and her detractors,[51] did point to a way of making the link. The flow of capital from existing centres of accumulation to new ones overseas could ease the pressure leading to a rising organic composition of capital and a falling rate of profit, even if such a solution would "only have a short time effect".[52]

This insight can make sense of the actual pattern of economic development during the high tide of imperialism at the end of the 19th century. Had the half of British investment that went overseas been invested domestically it would have raised the ratio of investment to labour (the organic composition of capital) and so lowered the rate of profit. As it was, estimates suggest that the capital-output ratio actually fell from 2.16 in 1875-83 (the years of the first "Great Depression") to 1.82 in 1891-1901,[53] and that the early 1890s were a period of rising profit rates (following a fall from the 1860s to the 1880s).[54] And in these years what happened in Britain still had a major impact on the rest of the system.

This points to a wider and very important insight into the dynamic of capitalism in the 20th and 21st centuries to which we will return in later chapters. For the moment it is sufficient to recognise that imperialism arose out of the competitive drive of capitals to expand beyond national frontiers—and led, as a temporary side-effect, to a lessening of the pressures otherwise driving up the organic composition of capital and so lowering the rate of profit. But it could only be a temporary effect because eventually investments made in the new centres of accumulation would produce new surplus value seeking investment and exerting a downward pressure on profit rates. As that happened the old contradictions in the system would return with a vengeance, opening up a new period of economic instability which would lead to intensified competition, not only of an economic but also of a military sort. This is effectively what happened in the first decades of the 20th century, with an international tendency towards falling profit rates and increased tensions between states. Amended in this way, the insistence by Lenin, Bukharin and Luxemburg on the connection between capitalism and war could be made theoretically watertight.

A problem Marx left behind

The classic theory of imperialism has one important implication. It raises the question of the relation between states and the capitals within them. Marx left the question unresolved. He took up some of its aspects in his non-economic writings,[55] but did not get

Understanding the System: Marx and Beyond

as far as integrating them into his analysis of the capitalist system as a whole. But the question is not one that any serious analysis of capitalism in the century after his death can avoid. A quick glance at the growth of state expenditure shows why (see the graph below for the United States). From its share of national output being more or less static through the 19th century, except at times of all-out war, it started growing in the second third of the 20th century and has never stopped doing so.

US Government Spending as Proportion of Gross Domestic Product[56]

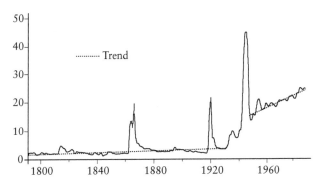

The most common view of the state, among Marxists and non-Marxists alike, has been to see it as something external to the capitalist economic system. This approach has long been accepted by the mainstream "Realist" school in the academic discipline of international relations. It sees states as self-contained entities clashing internationally according to a logic which has nothing to do with the economic form of organisation existing within them.[57] A somewhat similar approach is to be found in some Marxist writings.

Capitalism, in this view, consists of the pursuit of profits by firms (or, more accurately speaking, the self-expansion of capitals) without regard to where they are based geographically. The state, by contrast, is a geographically based political entity, whose boundaries cut across the operations of individual capitals. The state may be a structure that developed historically to provide the political prerequisites for capitalist production—to protect capitalist property, to police the dealings of different members of the ruling class with each other, to provide certain services which are essential for the reproduction of the system, and to carry through such reforms as are necessary to make other sections of society accept capitalist rule—but it is not to be identified with the capitals that operate within it.

Those who view the state as simply external to capitalism tend to refer to the "state" in the singular—and often to "capital" in the singular as well. This way of putting it may make sense when providing an account of capitalism at the most abstract level, with the state providing a level playing field on which different capitals compete on equal terms. But the actually existing capitalist system is made up of many states[58] and many capitals.[59]

But even those who see states as existing in the plural, as does Ellen Wood, often conclude that they serve the interests of capital in general, not of particular capitalists based within them. "The essential role of the state in capitalism", she argues:

> is not to serve as an instrument of appropriation, or a form of "politically constituted property", but rather as a means of creating and sustaining the conditions of accumulation at arms length, maintaining the social, legal and administrative order necessary for accumulation.[60]

As against these views, there are those whose analyses start from the classic theories of imperialism, with their language about the state "merging" with capital, of "state monopoly capitalism", or simply of "state capitalism", and their view of the clashes between states as an expression of international competition of the capitals operating within them.

A bowdlerised version of this view became part of the orthodoxy of Stalinised Marxism in the years from the 1930s to the 1970s, known for short as "stamocap". A more serious attempt to describe the world system as composed of state capitals in the decades after the Second World War was made by Mike Kidron.[61] In his account individual states and individual capitals became completely congruent with each other: every state acted at the behest of a set of nationally based capitals, and every significant capital was incorporated in a particular state. Any exceptions, for Kidron, were a hangover from the past, relics which would disappear with the further development of the system.

A parallel attempt to see the world in terms of states representing capitals was developed in the early 1970s in debates between German Marxists.[62] Claudia von Braunmuhl, for instance, wrote:

it is not the state in general that must be analysed but *"the spe-cific political organisation of the world market in many states"*... the role of the state in question in its specific relation-ship with the world market and with other states must always be included in the analysis from the outset.[63]

Few people have followed through such attempts to develop such insights into a rigorous interpretation of the world system. But some of their presuppositions are taken for granted in everyday ways of talking and writing about the world. People habitually speak of "the economic interests" of this or that state, of how one is doing compared with another, of the "profits" of one or other country. So the recent very useful account of capitalism since the Second World War by Robert Brenner emphasises the interactions of "US capitalism", "Japanese capitalism" and "German capital-ism", with negotiation by states playing a central role.[64] There is the implication of a tight alignment of interest between a particu-lar national state and a particular sector of the international capitalist system.

The view of national states as wholly congruent with "na-tional" capitals is a big oversimplification, especially in today's world, with multinational corporations operating in scores of countries, as we shall see later. But this does not mean that states simply stand at "arms length" from particular capitals, or that states do not act at the behest of particular nationally based group-ings of capital. They remain tied to them in complex ways.

The genesis of the capitalist state

A starting point for understanding this can be found in the relation-ship between the development of modern states and capitalism. This was not dealt with explicitly by Marx, and it was Engels who first did so in a manuscript written after Marx's death and not published until 1935. His studies led him to conclude that as merchants and tradespeople of the towns (the "burghers") grew in importance at the end of the Middle Ages they allied themselves with the monar-chy against the rest of the feudal ruling class: "Out of the confusions of the people that characterised the early Middle Ages, there gradu-ally developed the new nationalisms"—and the beginnings of national states very different to the earlier political structures.[65]

Lenin further theoretically elaborated similar insights as the revolutionary movement in Russia tried to come to terms with the demand for independent states arising among the Tsarist empire's minority nationalities on its borders in south eastern Europe and in the colonial possessions of the West European powers.

He spelt out the deep connections between the struggle to establish national states and the emergence of groups in the pre-capitalist world who wanted to base themselves on capitalist forms of economic organisation:

> Throughout the world, the period of the final victory of capitalism over feudalism has been linked up with national movements. For the complete victory of commodity production, the bourgeoisie must capture the home market, and there must be politically united territories whose population speak a single language, with all obstacles to the development of that language and to its consolidation in literature eliminated... Therefore, the tendency of every national movement is towards the formation of *national states*, under which these requirements of modern capitalism are best satisfied... The national state is *typical* and normal for the capitalist period.[66]

Modern states have not developed, according to this conception, as external to the capitals (or at least, to most of the capitals) based within them. They have been shaped historically by the process by which capitalist methods of accumulating wealth began to take root, first in parts of Europe and then in the rest of the world. Those groups identifying with such methods needed to protect themselves against the various social forces associated with the pre-capitalist society in which they developed—and very soon against other capitalist groups located elsewhere. This meant seeking to shape political structures to defend their common interests, by force if necessary, in what could be a hostile world. Where old pre-capitalist state forms existed, they had to get control of them and reorganise them to fit their own interests (as in England or France) or break apart from them to form new states (as with the Dutch Republic, the United States and the ex-colonial countries of the second half of the 20th century). By the late 19th century it was not only existing capitalist interests which sought to build such states. So too did elements from old exploiting classes in places like Germany, Tsarist Russia and Japan who wanted to survive in a world increasingly dominated by capitalist powers on the one hand, and the middle class intelligentsia who came to play a leading role in many of the national movements in the colonial world on the other.

This picture has been rejected by some Marxists on the grounds that states existed before the rise of capitalism. The "system of states" is then seen as something completely distinct from the system of capitalism, and there is a "logic of states" that differs from the "logic of capital". But the old states were not left as they were with the rise of capitalism. They were reshaped fundamentally, with a redrawing of old territorial boundaries and the establishment for the first time of centralised structures that reached down into the lives of every inhabitant (for the first time they were all "citizens").[67] The fact that the new structures functioned through the deployment of force, not the production of commodities for sale, did not stop them being shaped by the changing relations of production and exploitation created by the rise of capitalism. And they were from the beginning—and remain today—structures that feed back into the organisation of production by capitals, influencing the tempo and direction of their accumulation. The logic of states was a product of the wider logic of capitalism, even if it frequently came into contradiction with other elements in the system.[68]

Capital exists in three forms—as productive capital, as commodity (or merchants') capital and as money capital.[69] Every process of capital accumulation under fully developed capitalism involves repeated changes from one form to another: money capital is used to buy means of production, raw materials and labour power; these are put together in the production process to turn out commodities; these commodities are then exchanged for money; this money is then used to buy more means of production, raw materials and labour power, and so on. The forms of capital are continually interacting as one changes into the other. But there can also be a partial separation of these three different forms. The organisation of direct production, the selling of commodities and the supply of finance can devolve upon different groups of capitalists.

Money capital and commodity capital can be continually mobile, moving from place to place and across national boundaries, unless obstructed by the state or other bodies exercising force. Things are rather different with productive capitals. Regarded simply as accumulations of value, they differ from each other only in their size. But each individual capital, like each individual commodity, has a twofold character. As well as being measurable in terms of exchange value, it is also a concrete use value—a concrete set of relations between people and things in the process of production. Each particular capital has its concrete ways of bringing together labour power, raw materials and means of production, of raising finance and getting credit, and of maintaining networks for distributing and selling its output. These all involve interaction with other people and with nature, interactions of a physical sort, which take place on a day to day basis in fixed geographical locations.

No productive capital can function without, on the one hand, a guarantee of its control of its own means of production (a guarantee which, in the last resort, relies upon "armed bodies of men"), and, on the other, a labour force that is doubly "free"—free from coercion by non-capitalist exploiters on the one hand and free from any way of making a livelihood than by selling its labour power on the other. The productive capitalists in any particular locality necessarily act together to try to shape its social and political conditions, that is to exercise influence over the state. As sociologist Neil Brenner puts it:

> In its drive to accumulate surplus value, capital strives to…overcome all geographical barriers to its circulation process. Yet to pursue this continual dynamic…capital necessarily depends upon relatively fixed and immobile territorial infrastructures, such as urban regional agglomerations and territorial states… Capital's endemic drive … is intrinsically premised upon the production, reproduction, and reconfiguration of relatively fixed and immobile configurations of territorial organisation, including urban regional agglomerations, transportation networks, communication systems, and state regulatory institutions.[70]

Most capitalist enterprises operate not simply on market calculations, but also on the long-term relations they establish with other enterprises that sell to them and buy from them. Otherwise they would live in continual fear that any change in market conditions would cause their suppliers to sell elsewhere and those who transport and retail their goods suddenly to lose interest in them. They seek to "lock in" these other firms by a combination of financial incentives, business favours and personal contact. To this extent production does not take place in individual firms, but in "industrial complexes", which have grown up over time.[71]

The market models of classical and neo-classical economics portray capitals as isolated atoms which engage in blind competition with other capitals. In the real world capitalists have always tried to boost their competitive positions by establishing alliances with each other and with ambitious political figures—alliances cemented by money but also by intermarriage, old boy networks and mutual socialising.[72]

Even the fluidity of money capital does not diminish the importance of the particular national states for particular financial institutions. As Costas Lapavitsas has noted in his analysis of money under capitalism, "Trade credit depends on trust among individual capitalist enterprises that is subjective and private, since such trust draws on knowledge that enterprises have accumulated about each other in the course of their commercial relations".[73] And the networks that provide such knowledge have to a very high degree been organised on a national basis, with the state, through the central bank, playing a key role. "The institutions and markets of the credit system, regulated and managed by the central bank, place social power and trust at the service of capitalist accumulation".[74]

The relationship between states and capitals are relationships between people, between those engaged in exploiting the mass of the population and those who control bodies of armed men. Personal contact with the leading personnel of the state is something every capitalist aims at—just as every capitalist seeks to cultivate ties of trust and mutual support with certain other capitalists. The "connections" Lenin referred to[75] are immensely important.

Such interactions inevitably leave an imprint on the internal make up of each capital, so that any particular capital would find it very difficult to cope if it were suddenly to be torn apart from the other capitals and the state with which it has co-existed in the past. The national state and different nationally based capitals grow up together, like children in a single family. The development of one inevitably shapes the development of the others.

The groups of capitals and the state with which they are associated form a system in which each affects the others. The specific character of each capital is influenced by its interaction with the other capitals and the state. It reflects not only the general drive to expand value, to accumulate, but also the specific environment in which it has grown up. The state and the individual capitals are intertwined, with each feeding off the other.

Neither the state nor the particular capitals can easily escape this *structural interdependence*. The particular capitals find it easier to operate within one state rather than another, because they may have to profoundly restructure both their internal organisation and their relations with other capitals if they move their operations. The state has to adjust to the needs of particular capitals because it depends on them for the resources—particularly the revenues from taxation—it needs to keep going: if it goes against their interests, they can move their liquid assets abroad. The pressures which different states apply on each other are indispensable for the capitals based within each to ensure that their interests are taken into account when they are operating globally. The existence of rival states is not something produced from outside capitalism nor is it optional for capitalists. It is integral to the system and to its dynamic. Failure to grasp this, as, say, Nigel Harris does, leaves a great hole in any attempt to understand capitalism over the last century.

The "autonomy" of the state and the class nature of its bureaucracy

The mutual dependence of states and capitals does not, however, mean that states can simply be reduced to the economic entities that operate within them. Those who do the actual running of the state take on functions which competition between firms prevents firms themselves undertaking. They have to mediate between rival capitals, providing judicial systems and overseeing, through central banks, the financial system and the national currency. As Claus Offe put it, "Since 'capital as a whole' exists only in the ideal sense...it requires special guidance and supervision by a fully differentiated political-administrative system".[76]

The state also has to provide mechanisms for integrating the mass of people into the system: on the one hand the coercive institutions that beat people into submission (police, secret police, prisons); on the other hand the integrative mechanisms that divert grievance into channels compatible with the system (parliamentary structures, frameworks for collective bargaining, reformist, conservative or fascist parties). The proportions in which these two sets of mechanisms operate vary from situation to situation, but everywhere they exist to complement each other. The coercive mechanisms persuade people to take the easier path of integration into the system; the integrative mechanisms provide the velvet glove which conceals the iron hand of state coercive power, so legitimising it. The Italian revolutionary Marxist Antonio Gramsci rightly used Machiavelli's metaphor of the "centaur", half animal, half human, to capture the way in which force and consent are combined in the state.[77]

The coercive and the integrative mechanisms depend on organisation and leadership from outside the sphere of capitalist exploitation and accumulation as such—from military and police specialists on the one hand, from political leaders able to mobilise some degree of social support on the other. An effective state requires the building of coalitions that obtain the support—or at least the compliance—of such elements while allowing them a certain leeway to pursue their own interests.[78] It then, inevitably, reflects not just the interests of capital in general, but the concessions it makes to integrate other social groups and classes into its rule. It necessarily displays an important degree of autonomy.

Marx commented in 1871 that "the complicated state machinery...with its ubiquitous and complicated military, bureaucratic, clerical and judiciary organs, encoils the living society like a boa constrictor..." The state bureaucracy arises to assure the domination of the existing ruling class, but in the process becomes a "parasite" which is capable of "humbling under its sway even the interests of the ruling classes..."[79]

This autonomy reaches its highest points when governmental power lies with reformist, populist or fascist parties with a powerful base among workers, peasants or the petty bourgeoisie. There are cases when those who exercise such autonomy are able to break with and even expropriate important capitalist interests within their territory. This was to be true on numerous occasions in the course of the 20th century—German Nazism, Argentine Peronism, Nasserism in Egypt, Ba'athism in Syria and Iraq, are all examples. There are also innumerable cases in which individual capitals behave in ways detrimental to the interests of "their" state—moving funds and investment abroad, doing deals with foreign capitalists that undercut other local capitals, even selling weapons to states fighting their own.

Yet there are limits to the extent to which a state can break free from its capitals, and capitals from their state. A state may override the interests of particular capitalists; it cannot forget that its own revenues and its own ability to defend itself against other states depend on the continuation of capital accumulation. Conversely, the individual capital can, with considerable difficulty, uproot itself from one national state terrain and plant itself in another; but it cannot operate for any length of time in a "Wild West" situation with no effective state to protect it both against those forces below which might disrupt its normal rhythms of exploitation and against other capitals and their states.

A break between either a state with its capitals or by capitals with their state is a difficult and risky business. If a state turns on private capital, it can create a situation in which people begin to challenge not merely private capital but capital accumulation as such and, with it, the hierarchies of the state. If a private capital breaks with "its" state it risks being left to fend alone in a hostile and dangerous world.

This mutual interdependence between states and capitals has implications for an issue which many analysts never even touch on—the class character of the state bureaucracy itself. The assumption is usually either that it is simply a passive creature of a private capitalist class or that it is a separate political formation with interests quite different to those of any form of capital. Class is seen as depending on individual ownership (or non-ownership) of property, and the conclusion drawn is that the state bureaucracy cannot be an exploiting class or part of an exploiting class. This is implicit in the view of, say, Ellen Wood and David Harvey, who see state run economic activities as lying "outside" the system of capitalist production.[80]

Such an approach leaves a huge hole when it comes to analysing capitalism in the century and a quarter since Marx's death. The total income of society passing through the hands of the state has reached levels much greater than income going directly to private capital as profits, interest and rent. Investment directly undertaken by the state is often more than half of total investment,[81] and the state bureaucracy directly disposes of a very big portion of the fruits of exploitation.

An analysis of class in such a situation cannot restrict itself to looking at things as they appear in the official "common sense" of a society as expressed in its juridical definitions of property. Classes, for Marx, depend not on such formal definitions, but on the real social relations of production in which people find

Understanding the System: Marx and Beyond

themselves. They are aggregates of people whose relationship to material production and exploitation forces them to act together collectively against other such aggregates. In an unfinished final chapter to Volume Three of *Capital* Marx insists that classes cannot be identified simply by the "sources of revenues" since this would lead to an infinite division of classes, paralleling "the infinite fragmentation of interests and rank into which the division of social labour splits labourers as well as capitalists and landlords".[82] What makes such diverse groups come together into the great classes of modern society, he argues elsewhere, is the way in which the revenues of one set of groups arise out of the exploitation of those who make up other groups. As he put it in his notebooks for *Capital*, "Capital and wage labour only express two factors of the same relation".[83] The capitalist is only a capitalist insofar as he embodies the self-expansion of value, insofar as he is the personification of accumulation; workers are workers only insofar as "the objective conditions of labour" confront them as capital.

Since the directing layer in the state bureaucracy is compelled to act as an agent of capital accumulation, whether it likes it or not, it comes to identify its own interests as national capitalist interests in opposition to both foreign capital and the working class. Just as the individual capitalist can choose to enter one line of business rather than another, but cannot avoid the compulsion to exploit and accumulate in whatever line he goes into, so the state bureaucracy can move in one direction or another, but cannot ignore the needs of national capital accumulation without risking its own longer term future. Its "autonomy" consists in a limited degree of freedom as to how it enforces the needs of national capital accumulation, not in any choice as to whether to enforce these or not.

The dependence of the state bureaucracy on capitalist exploitation is often concealed by the way in which it raises its revenues—by taxation of incomes and expenditure, by government borrowing or by "printing money". All of these activities seem, on the surface, to be quite different from capitalist exploitation at the point of production. The state therefore seems like an independent entity which can raise the resources it needs by levying funds from any class in society. But this semblance of independence disappears when the state's activities are seen in a wider context. State revenues are raised by taxing individuals. But individuals will attempt to recoup their loss of purchasing power by struggles at the point of production—the capitalists by trying to enforce a higher rate of exploitation, the workers by attempting to get wage increases. The balance of class forces determines the leeway which exists for the state to increase its revenues. These are part of the total social surplus value—part of the total amount by which the value of workers' output exceeds the cost of reproducing their labour power.

In this sense, state revenues are comparable to the other revenues that accrue to different sections of capital—to the rents accruing to landowners, the interest going to money capital, the returns from trade going to commodity capital and the profits of productive capital. Just as there is continual conflict between the different sections of capital over the sizes of these different revenues, so there is continual conflict between the state bureaucracy and the rest of the capitalist class over the size of its cut from the total surplus value. The state bureaucracy will, on occasions, use its own special position, with its monopoly of armed force, to make gains for itself at the expense of others. In response to this, the other sections of capital will use their own special position— industrial capital its ability to postpone investment, money capital its ability to move overseas—to fight back.

Yet in all this, the different sections of capital cannot escape their mutual interdependence more than temporarily. It eventually asserts itself in the most dramatic fashion, through crises—the sudden collapse of the system of credit, the sudden inability to sell commodities, sudden balance of payment crises or even the threat of state bankruptcy. Those who direct the bureaucracies of the state may not own individual chunks of capital, but they are forced to behave as agents of capital accumulation, to become, according to Marx's definition, part of the capitalist class.

Marx points out in *Capital* that with the advance of capitalist production there takes place a division of function within the capitalist class. The owners of capital tend to play a less direct part in the actual organisation of production and exploitation, leaving this to highly paid managers. But, insofar as these managers continue to be agents of capital accumulation, they remain capitalists. Hilferding developed the argument further, pointing to the divisions within a single capitalist class between the mass of *rentier* capitalists, who rely on a more or less fixed rate of return on their shares, and "promoter" capitalists who gain extra surplus value by gathering together the capital needed by the giant

Understanding the System: Marx and Beyond

corporations.[84] We can add a further distinction, between those who manage the accumulation of individual capitals and those who, through the state, seek to promote the development of the sibling capitals operating within an individual state—what may be called "political capitalists".

State capitalism and state capitalists

One of the most significant developments of the 20th century was the emergence of big state-owned economic sectors. The state came to plan the whole of internal production in Germany in the latter part of the First World War, in the US and Britain as well as Germany throughout most of the Second World War— and, of course, in the USSR from Stalin to Gorbachev and in China under Mao.

Just as many analysts accept the "common sense" view that the state is something outside of capitalism, so they also refuse to accept that state-run industries and economies can be capitalist.[85] The classical Marxists, however, saw things rather differently. Marx in Volume Two of *Capital* was already "including" among "the sum of individual capitals", "...the state capital, so far as governments employ productive wage labour in mines, railways etc, perform the function of industrial capitalists".[86] Engels spelt this out much more fully in reacting to Bismarck's nationalisation of the German railway system:

> The modern state, no matter what its form, is essentially a capitalist machine, the state of the capitalists, the ideal personification of the total national capital. The more it proceeds to the taking over of productive forces, the more it actually becomes the national capitalist, the more citizens it exploits. The workers remain wage workers—proletarians. The capitalist relation is not done away with. It is rather brought to a head.[87]

Kautsky could argue in the 1890s that the original economic liberalism (from which present day neoliberalism gets its name) of the "Manchester school" "no longer influences the capitalist class" because "economic and political development urged the necessity of the extension of the functions of the state", forcing it "to take into its own hands more and more functions or industries".[88]

Trotsky could write a quarter of a century later, in *The Manifesto of the Communist International to the Workers of the World*:

> The statisation of economic life, against which the capitalist liberalism used to protest so much, has become an accomplished fact... It is impossible to return not only to free competition but even to the domination of trusts, syndicates and other economic octopuses. Today the one and only issue is: Who shall herefort be the bearer of statised production—the imperialist state or the victorious proletariat.[89]

What all of them recognised was that state rather than private ownership of the means of production did not alter the fundamental relations of production or the dynamic of capitalist accumulation. For the state, the purpose of nationalised industry was to enable domestic accumulation to match that undertaken by foreign rivals so as to be able to survive successfully in economic and/or military competition. To this end, the labour employed remained wage labour, and the attempt was made to hold its remuneration down to the minimal level required to sustain and reproduce labour power. The state might plan production within the enterprises it owned, but its planning was subordinated to external competition, just as the planning within any privately owned firm was. The self-expansion of capital remained the goal, and this meant that the law of value operated and made itself felt on the internal operations of the enterprises.

In behaving like this, state appointees behave as much like capitalists—as living embodiments of capital accumulation at the expense of workers—as do private entrepreneurs or shareholders.

It was a failure to recognise this that led Hilferding in the 1920s to come to the conclusion that "organised" capitalism was overcoming the contradictions analysed by Marx. By the late 1930s state planning in Nazi Germany led him to conclude that what existed was no longer capitalism at all, but a new form of class society, in which "organisation" had superseded "capitalism", and where the driving force had ceased to be profit making to feed the competitive accumulation of rival capitals.

What Hilferding failed to grasp—as do all those today who still identify capitalism with the private ownership of firms competing in free markets—is that the system remained based on competitive accumulation between different capitals, even if these were now military state capitalisms. It was driven forward by the same dynamic and subject to the same contradictions analysed by Marx. This was true during the period of total war, in which the rival states did not trade directly with each other and naval blockades greatly limited their competition in foreign markets. Every success in accumulating military hardware by a state forced efforts to accumulate similar levels of military hardware in its rivals. Just as the efforts of rival car producers to outsell each other bring the concrete forms of labour in different car plants into an unplanned inter-relationship with each other, transforming them into different amounts of a homogenous abstract labour, so too the efforts of rival tank-producing states to outshoot one another have the same result.

Marx described how under the market capitalism of his time:

the labour of the individual asserts itself as a part of the labour of society only by the relations which the act of exchange establishes directly between the products, and indirectly through them, between the producers.[90]

In the world system as it developed after Marx's death, military competition came to play the same role in bringing individual acts of labour performed in different, apparently closed, state entities, into a relationship with each other.

Acquisition of the means of destruction on the necessary scale to assure success in war depended upon the same drive to accumulate means of production as did the struggle for markets—and with that went the holding down of wages to the cost of reproduction of labour power, the forcing up of productivity to the level prevailing on a world scale, and the drive to use the surplus for accumulation.

As Tony Cliff pointed out more than 60 years ago, the only difference, in this respect, between military and economic competition was the form the accumulation took—whether it was terms of an accumulation of use values that could be used to produce new goods or of use values that could be used to wage war. In either case the importance of these use values to those controlling them was determined by comparison with use values elsewhere in the system, a comparison which transmuted them into exchange values.

This also meant the rate of profit continued to play a central role. It no longer determined the distribution of investment between different sectors of the internal economy. The requirements of the military did this. But it operated as a constraint on the economy as a whole. If the ratio of total national surplus value to total investment in the military-industrial machine fell, this weakened the ability of the national state capitalism to sustain itself in warfare with its rivals. The decline in the rate of profit could not lead to economic slump, since the war machine would go on growing as long as there was any remaining mass of surplus value to be used up, however small. But it could contribute to military defeat.

The same capitalist logic could be seen as operating in the states where new bureaucracies emerged to take control of the means of production (the USSR from the late 1920s onwards,[91] Eastern Europe and China after World War Two, various former colonial states in the late 1950s and 1960s). Although they called themselves "socialist" their economic dynamic was dependent on their inter-relations with the wider capitalist world. If they traded with the capitalist countries beyond their borders, they were drawn into the logic of commodity production—and the requirement to remain competitive in markets by undertaking accumulation in an essentially capitalist way. But even if they tried to adopt an autarchic policy of cutting themselves off economically, they could not avoid having to defend themselves against predatory foreign imperialisms. In either case, they were subject to the logic of capitalism as a world system in the 20th century in the way Bukharin had described in the early 1920s. And those who ruled these societies were as much "personifications" of accumulation as were the private capitalists of Marx's time, driven into historic opposition to the wage labourers who toiled on the means of production. They were, in other words, members of a capitalist class, even if it was a class which collectively rather than individually carried through exploitation and accumulation.

The state seemed, on the face of it, a great island of planning—at one time even half a continent of planning—within a world of market relations. But so long as states competed to expand the forces of production within them more rapidly than each other, the planning was, like the islands of planning within the individual capitalist enterprise of Marx's time, simply planning to keep labour productivity abreast with the labour productivity prevailing on a world scale. The law of value imposed itself through such competition on all the units in the world system. Those running whole states, particular state sectors or individual enterprises were

Understanding the System: Marx and Beyond

alike subject to pressure to reduce the price paid for every exertion of labour power to its value within the system as whole.

The individual capitalist managers and individual state managers could rely for a time on the sheer size of the resources at their disposal to try to ignore these pressures. But they could not do so indefinitely. At some point they had to face hard choices if they were not to risk collapse: they could try to impose the law of value on those who laboured for them through what could be a painful and hazardous process of internal restructuring; or they could take desperate gambles in order to try to shift the global balance of forces in their favour. For the civilian corporation this might mean pouring resources into one last, possibly fraudulent, marketing ploy; for those running the state, to try to use its military force to compensate for its economic weakness. Hence the way in which the real history of capitalism in the 20th century was very different to the picture of peaceful and honest competition presented in economic textbooks—and accepted by some Marxists who have not understood the need to look at the real social relations which lie beneath surface appearances.

CHAPTER FIVE

State Spending and the System

An important distinction

If the enormous growth of the economic importance of the state was one feature which distinguished 20th century capitalism from the capitalism of Marx's time, another was the growth of all sorts of expenditures that were not directly productive.

Marx had taken over from Adam Smith a distinction between "productive" and "unproductive" labour. Smith had been writing at a time when the capitalist mode of production was still in its infancy and he sought to work out what was needed for it to overcome obstacles to its further advance. He therefore distinguished between the uses of hired labour that enabled the capitalist to make profits so as to further advance production and those which simply absorbed existing resources. Employing someone to make things to sell was productive; employing someone to tend to one's individual desires was not. Or, as it was sometimes put, employing someone in a factory created wealth; employing someone as a personal servant simply used wealth up. But it was not only servants who Smith regarded as unproductive and wasteful in this sense: he had the same attitude to the hoards of placemen and women who lived off the revenues of a state which had not been reformed fully to suit the needs of capitalist production.[1]

Marx took up this distinction as he prepared various drafts for *Capital* and developed his own understanding of it. He, like Smith, was interested in what made capitalism function—even if out of opposition to, not support for, the system. And so his concern was with what was "productive" in capitalist terms.[2] It was, he argued, that which was productive of surplus value. Labour which produced surplus value enabled capitalists to accumulate;

labour which did not produce surplus value was of no use in this respect—it was "unproductive".

In all this, he was careful to make it clear that the "productiveness" of labour did not depend on the physical form or how socially useful the product was. What mattered was its ability to create surplus value—nothing else. "This distinction between productive and unproductive labour", he wrote in one of his notebooks, "has nothing to do with either the particular speciality of the labour or with the particular use value in which...[it]...is incorporated".[3]

Marx's distinction was not between material production and what today are categorised as "services". Some "services" have a use value that is bought and sold as a commodity on the market—or make a useful addition to some other commodity. These have an exchange value which is determined by the socially necessary labour time needed to produce them and so can provide capitalists with new surplus value. They are therefore productive. Acting in a film, for instance, is productive insofar as it creates a use value (adding to people's enjoyment and so improving their living standard) that is sold profitably as a commodity by the capitalist who employs the actor. Similarly, moving things from where they are made to where they can be consumed, as is done by some transport workers, is productive, since it is in effect part of the process of completing their production. By contrast, actors who appear on television to urge people to buy a particular good are not productive, since their labour does not create new use or exchange values. It merely aids in the selling of goods that have already been produced.

Guglielmo Carchedi has rightly argued:

The category "services" only confuses matters and should be dropped. "A service is nothing more than the useful effect of a use value, be it of a commodity, or be it of labour" [according to Marx].[4] Therefore, "services" encompass productive labour (hotels, entertainment) and unproductive labour (advertising, market research)...[5]

In his first discussions on the issue in the early 1860s Marx assumed, like Smith, that unproductive labour is concerned with services provided by individuals for the upper classes.[6] These included providing "entertainments", dealing with "physical infirmities" (doctors) and "spiritual weakness" (parsons), and resolving "the conflict between private interests and national interests" (eg statesmen, lawyers, police and soldiers). The last sort were regarded "by the industrial capitalists themselves" as incidental expenses of production to be kept down to the most indispensable minimum and provided as cheaply as possible.[7]

Marx recognised that sometimes personal services for the ruling class were provided not by individuals working on their own account, but by capitalists employing paid labour to provide them to others. In these cases, he argued, the labour was productive because it created surplus value. The capitalists who employed it, after all, sold the produce of the labour at more than they paid for the labour power and pocketed a profit as a result. So a teacher employed personally in someone's home to teach their children was providing a service from which no profit was made and was unproductive; by contrast, a teacher employed by a company which made a profit by running a school was productive. One did not in any way help capitalists to accumulate value; the other did. The distinction was between labour that was integral to capitalist production and accumulation, and that which was not.

But in *Capital* Marx also found himself having to revisit the distinction between productive and unproductive labour in a different context—a context which was integral to, not external to, capitalist production in its totality. For as capitalism developed, it became increasingly dependent on many forms of labour that produced nothing.

There was the labour involved in maintaining discipline inside the capitalist enterprise—the "work" of managers, supervisors, foremen. There was the commercial labour involved in the exchange of already produced commodities as they went through the various chains of buying and selling before reaching the final consumer. There was the financial labour involved in reckoning up profit and loss, advancing credit, and dividing up surplus value between the various sections of the capitalist class. Marx recognised that these sorts of labour would grow in quantity as capitalism expanded:

It is clear that as the scale of production is extended, commercial operations required constantly for the recirculation of industrial capital…multiply accordingly… The more developed the scale of production, the greater…the commercial operations of industrial capital.[8]

Such labour could not be regarded as productive if the capitalist employed it in these ways, any more than the labour of the servant could be. Maintaining discipline, selling goods or getting the accounts done were necessary functions that had to be paid for by deductions from surplus value, not creative labour that added to surplus value. They did not produce something new, but were merely concerned with controlling the production of value by others, with transforming it from one form (commodities) into another (money), or with dividing it up between people. The activities of a supervisor, a bank clerk or a shop assistant could no more create value (and therefore surplus value) than could the valet.

But what happened if the productive capitalist used other capitalists to carry out some of these functions on his behalf? The labour employed by these other capitalists should be counted as productive according to Marx's established definition since it enabled them to make a profit. But seeing things like this presented a problem. The profit did not arise from increasing the total amount of output any more than it did when productive capitalists directly employed people to perform the tasks. It simply amounted to the second capitalist getting a slice of the surplus value originally in the hands of the first capitalist. Marx concluded that from the point of view of capitalist production such labour was unproductive, even though this seemed to be based on a different definition of productive labour to that he used elsewhere. For this reason Jacques Bidet, for instance, has argued that Marx was inconsistent.[9] Yet it made sense in terms of the thing both Adam Smith and Karl Marx were interested in—the distinction between what advanced capitalist development and what retarded it.

So long as capitalists were operating in an economic environment in which capitalist production was not yet dominant, those who employed workers to provide personal services were providing them mainly to those whose wealth came from outside the capitalist system. The payments received, for instance, by the owners of a school constituted a transfer of resources into the capitalist sector from the pockets of pre-capitalist exploiters—resources that could then be used for productive accumulation. By contrast, the merchants or shopkeepers who handled the goods of the productive capitalists got their profit from the already created surplus value of the productive capitalist. They were not adding to total surplus value and with it the further accumulation of capital.

As Marx put it at one point:

To industrial capital the costs of circulation appear as unproductive expenses, and so they are. To the merchant they appear as a source of profit, proportional, given the general rate of profit, to their size. The outlay to be made on these circulation costs is therefore productive investment for mercantile capital… And the commercial labour which it buys is likewise immediately productive for it.[10]

The competition between commercial capitalists with each other meant that each was subject to the same pressures as the capitalists involved in production to keep wages down to the value of labour power. For this reason their workers were exploited in the same way as workers for capital involved in production. The more a commercial capitalist held down the wages and increased the workload of his employees, the greater was the share he could keep for himself of the payment he got from the productive capitalists for providing services to them. If it took eight hours of socially necessary labour time to perform, say, a certain sales task, but only four hours to cover a sales worker's wage, then the shopkeeping capitalist could pocket four hours worth of the surplus value supplied from elsewhere in the system.

But this did not mean that commercial labour could be equated with productive labour when it came to understanding the dynamics of the system as a whole. One created resources that could be used for further accumulation, and the other did not. That is why Marx is insistent:

Costs which enhance the price of a commodity without adding to its use value, which are therefore to be classed as unproductive expenses so far as society is concerned, may be a source of enrichment to the individual capitalist. On the other hand, as this addition to the price of the commodity merely distributes the costs of circulation equally, they do not cease to be unproductive in character. For instance, insurance companies divide the losses of individual capitalists among the capitalist class. But this does not stop these equalised losses from being losses so far as the aggregate social capital is concerned.[11]

The distinction between productive and unproductive labour is often seen as a merely scholastic question. But once seen in terms of what contributes to accumulation and what does not, it has enormous implications—including some that Marx himself never developed. What is "productive of surplus value" for the individual capitalist (the definition of productive labour Marx used in his notebooks) is not necessarily what is productive in terms of adding to the surplus value available to capital in general for accumulation. And it is this that is central for the dynamic of the system.

The scale of unproductive labour

The level of unproductive expenditures involved in sales and finance grew throughout the 20th century. Anwar Shaikh and Ertugrul Ahmet Tonak calculate that the number of workers employed in trade in the US grew from 10,690,000 in 1948 to 24,375,000 in 1989, and of those in finance and insurance from 1,251,000 to 7,123,000. Meanwhile, the number of productive workers only grew from 32,994,000 to 41,148,000.[12] Fred Moseley estimates the numbers in commerce as growing from 8.9 to 21 million between 1950 and 1980, and the number in finance from 1.9 to 5.2 million, while the productive workforce only grew from 28 to 40.3 million.[13]

The figures do not include the large number of managerial employees who Marx regarded as non-productive because they are involved in policing those who actually produce value. Simon Mohun has calculated that the growth in their numbers and remuneration caused the share of "unproductive" wages and salaries in the "material value added" in the US to rise from 35 percent in 1964 to over 50 percent in 2000.[14] These figures also understate the total growth of unproductive labour because they do not include employees involved in non-productive state functions like the military and the legal system.

Unproductive expenditures and waste production

There is another sort of labour that also has to be taken into consideration when examining 20th and 21st century capitalism. This is the labour that goes into producing commodities that are sold like other commodities but which do not then re-enter later rounds of production, whether as means of production or as wage goods. The labour producing luxury goods for the capitalist class falls into this category. So too does labour that goes into military weaponry. Although such labour has usually been regarded as "productive" by Marxists, it shares with non-productive labour the fact that it does not add to capitalist accumulation. For these reasons it was argued by Mike Kidron in the early 1970s that it should also be regarded as non-productive:

> The ageing of capitalism...opened a gulf between the two criteria of productiveness that he [Marx—CH] used interchangeably—employment by capital and augmenting capital... Now that capital is king...the two criteria are no longer congruous. Millions of workers are employed directly by capital to produce goods and services which it cannot use for further expansion under any conceivable circumstances. They are productive by one criterion and unproductive by the other... Given the need to choose, productive labour today must be defined as labour whose final output is or can be an input into further production. Only such labour can work for capital's self-expansion... To spell it out, in late capitalism only part of the surplus can be used for the expansion of capital. The rest is waste product.[15]

More recently Alan Freeman has also suggested that the notion of unproductive labour has to be extended to involve the use of labour to produce things that are then used in an unproductive manner. "The workers who decked the European Bank for Reconstruction and Development in marble are just as unproductive as the clerks who now walk across it".[16] Guglielmo Carchedi, by contrast, argues there is labour that is productive if it has created new value, even if this does not then contribute anything to the next round of accumulation.[17] Regardless of how it is categorised, the proportion of labour that is waste from the point of view of capital accumulation has become enormous. Kidron calculated that "three fifths of the work actually undertaken in the US in the 1970s was wasted from capital's own point of view".[18]

The state sector and non-productive labour

Expenditures by individual capitals that are neither going to capital investment nor to the wages of productive workers can be broken down into different categories:

(a) Those concerned with the disciplining of the workforce and ensuring it works flat out—expenditures on internal security, supervisory labour and time and motion measurement, checking on work speeds.

(b) Those concerned with keeping the allegiance of the workforce, eg expenditures on internal public relations, works bulletins, management-run works committees, subsidies to works sports teams.

(c) Those devoted to financial transactions, obtaining credit, bank charges, etc.

(d) Those devoted to sales, advertising, etc.

(e) Those concerned with keeping the workforce fit and able to work—company medical facilities, factory canteens, etc, in some cases the provision of housing for the workforce.

(f) Those concerned with training the workforce—what mainstream economists often call "human capital".

(g) Expenditures on research and development.

Expenditures (a) and (b) are unambiguously unproductive. They create nothing and are only concerned with getting the maximum of already created value from the workers. Expenditures (c) and (d) are unproductive from the point of view of capital in general. They do not in any way add to the capacity of the system as whole to accumulate. But the individual firm can regard them as productive in the same way as Marx wrote that the individual merchant capitalist did—they serve to get control of surplus value which would otherwise go to rival firms. So advertising expenditure, for example, may be seen by the firm, like expenditure on new equipment, as a way of expanding its position in the market, of forestalling attempts to enter the market by other capitalists, and so on. Similar expenditure on patents and patent protection may be seen as a way of getting a stranglehold on the market (I will return to the other types of expenditures (e) to (g) below).

The growth of state expenditures in the course of the last century has involved states taking over partial responsibility for many of these outlays from the hands of the private capitals based in their national territory. So state expenditures can be broken down into categories playing the same or analogous functions to the expenditures of firms.

There are those expenditures which are clearly unproductive in terms of accumulation throughout the system as a whole.

Among these are those concerned with protecting property, maintaining social discipline and ensuring the smooth reproduction of class relations; maintaining state-run or financed forms of maintaining popular allegiance to the system, such as state produced propaganda and subsidies to religious institutions; the perpetuation of the ruling ideology through sections of the educational system; maintaining the financial infrastructure of the system through the printing of national currencies and running central banks.

Alongside these there are expenditures beneficial to nationally based capitals in competition with foreign capitals, but which, like the individual capitalists' expenditure on marketing or advertising, do not add to accumulation as a whole. This includes military expenditure, spending on export promotion schemes, negotiations with other governments over international trade and investment regulations, etc.

It was these unproductive expenditures that Marx referred to when he wrote:

> Political economy in its classical period, like the bourgeoisie itself in its parvenu phase, adopted a severely critical attitude to the machinery of the state etc. At a later stage it realised and learnt from experience that the necessity for classes which were totally unproductive arose from its own organisation.[19]

Such growth in unproductive expenditures came to have a big impact on the dynamic of the system after Marx's death.

Waste output and the system's dynamic

Marx hinted at one important point about non-productive labour in his first attempt at a draft for Capital, the *Grundrisse*. He includes among the "moments" that can delay the rise in the organic composition of capital and the fall in the rate of profit:

> the transformation of a great part of capital into fixed capital which does not serve as agency of direct production; unproductive waste of a great portion of capital etc (productively employed capital is always replaced doubly, in that the posing of a productive capital presupposes a countervalue). The un-

productive consumption of capital replaces it on one side, anni-
hilates it on the other...[20]

Marx is saying that if for some reason part of the surplus value
available for investment is diverted into some other use, there is
less new capital available for firms seeking innovations that will
cut their costs, and the trend towards capital-intensive investment
will be reduced. The same point was made much more explicitly
in the 1960s by Mike Kidron—apparently without knowing that
Marx had spelt the argument out.[21] He pointed out that Marx's argument about the falling rate of profit:

> rested on two assumptions, both realistic: all output flows
> back into the system as productive inputs through either
> workers' or capitalists' productive consumption—ideally
> there are no leakages in the system and no choice other than to
> allocate total output between what would now be called in-
> vestment and working class consumption; secondly in a closed
> system like this the allocation would swing progressively in
> favour of investment.
>
> If the first assumption, that all outputs flow back into the
> system, was dropped—in other words, if some of these outputs
> are lost to the production cycle—then there would be no need
> for investment to grow more rapidly than the labour employed.
> The law of the falling rate of profit would not operate. "Leaks"
> of surplus value from the closed cycle of production/invest-
> ment/production would offset the tendency of the rate of profit
> to fall.[22]

As Kidron put it in a later work:

> In Marx the model assumes a closed system in which all
> output flows back as inputs in the form of investment goods
> or wage goods. There are no leaks. Yet in principle a leak
> could insulate the compulsion to grow from its most impor-
> tant consequences... In such a case there would be no decline
> in the average rate of profit, no reason to expect increasingly
> severe slumps and so on.[23]

The argument is impeccable, and Kidron goes on to suggest the
form these leaks have taken:

Capitalism has never formed a closed system in practice. Wars and slumps have destroyed immense quantities of output, incorporating huge accumulations of value, and prevented the production of more. Capital exports have diverted and frozen other accumulations for long stretches of time.[24]

As we saw in Chapter Four, Henryk Grossman had recognised that imperialism in diverting surplus value overseas had temporarily reduced the upward pressures on the organic composition of capital in the domestic economy and the therefore tendency to crisis. He also at least partially anticipated Kidron's point about the effect of military expenditure. He noted that, while wars were enormously destructive of use values, they had the effect of easing the purely economic contradictions of capitalism since they "pulverise values" and "slow down accumulation". By reducing the tendency for accumulation to rise faster than the employed labour force they countered the fall in the rate of profit:

> The destructions and devaluations of war are a means of warding off the immanent collapse [of capitalism], of creating a breathing space for the accumulation of capital... War and the destruction of capital values bound up with it weaken the breakdown [of capitalism] and necessarily provide a new impetus to the accumulation of capital... Militarism is a sphere of unproductive consumption. Instead of being saved, values are pulverised.[25]

Military expenditure is a particular form of waste that can appeal to capitalists connected to a particular state. For it enhances their capacity to struggle for control of worldwide surplus value with rival capitalists. It is functional for nationally based complexes of capital in the same way that advertising is for individual firms, even while wasting resources for the system as a whole. It was therefore a characteristic phenomenon of the classical form of imperialism that led to the First World War—and it survives today in the massive arms spending of the United States in particular.

The logic of arms-based economic expansion has escaped many Marxist economists. It is absurd, they argue, to see a deduction by the state from the total surplus value as somehow countering the tendency for surplus value to grow more slowly than total investment costs, and so overcoming the fall in the rate of profit. What they have failed to understand is that this "absurdity" is just part of the greater absurdity of the capitalist system as a whole, of its contradictory nature. They have not seen that engaging in military competition can be just as much a "legitimate" capitalist goal as engaging in economic competition for markets.

As we saw in the last chapter, one of the greatest followers of Marx, Rosa Luxemburg, could not understand how capitalism could continually expand the value embodied in means of production without producing more goods for consumption. Similarly, these Marxists have not been able to understand how capitalism could possibly benefit from continually expanding the means of destruction. They have been so bemused by the irrationality of what capitalists are doing as to try to deny that this is how the system works.

But such expenditures had enormous implications for capitalism in the latter part of the 20th century. Waste expenditures played a contradictory role. They reduced the amount of surplus value available for productive investment, so counteracting the tendency towards over-rapid accumulation and crisis. But the eventual effect in slowing down accumulation was to create a whole new series of problems for the system, as we will see in Chapter Nine.

Welfare and the supply of labour power

Not all the state expenditures listed earlier fall into the unproductive category as narrowly defined or into the wider category of waste. State-financed research and development (corresponding to category (g) in the list above) that feeds through into aiding accumulation in the wider economy clearly plays a role for those capitals that benefit from it, similar to that of dead labour embodied in means of production. But what of expenditures on health, education and welfare services (equivalent to the expenditures (e) and (f) of individual capitalists)? Here it is necessary to examine something Marx only discusses in passing—the reproduction of the working class that capitalism needs for exploitation.

The first industrial capitalists of the late 18th and early 19th centuries in Britain did not have to worry over much about the supply of labour power. It was available in abundance once "primitive accumulation" had driven sufficient peasants from the land.

They assumed they could bend former peasants and their children to the discipline of unskilled machine minding,[26] while relying on drawing men trained as artisans into the factories for more skilled work. For these reasons, Marx, who dealt at length with primitive accumulation and the treatment of workers in the factories, virtually ignored the problem for capitalists of getting a labour force with the right physiques and skills. Yet by the time of his death, the spread of capitalist industry to ever newer new sectors of production was making the supply and management of labour power—outside as well as inside the factory—something of increasing concern to those promoting capitalist accumulation.

The individual capitalist aimed to pay the individual worker just enough by the hour, day or week to keep him or her fit and motivated to work. But this did not cater for a number of important things if labour power of the right quantity and quality was going to be available for the capitalist class as a whole over time. It did not take into account the need for workers to learn necessary skills nor did it sustain them through periods of unemployment so as to be able to supply their labour power when the crisis ended. It did not deal with the problem of workers temporarily losing their capacity to be productively exploited through illness or injury. And it did not provide for the upbringing of working class children who would be the next generation of labour power.[27]

There were various ad hoc attempts to deal with each of these problems through the 19th century. Religious and other charitable funds provided some relief for the unemployed or the sick. Pressure was put on working class women to bear the burden of child rearing through the propagation of ideologies that treated men as the wage earner and men's wages as a "family wage" (even though working class women always worked to some extent and a man's wage was rarely adequate to keep a family).[28] Some firms would provide housing under their own control—and sometimes minimal health facilities as well—for their workforces. Groups of skilled workers would run funds to provide for periods of unemployment or sickness. Firms would incorporate into the factory system a version of the apprenticeship system of pre-capitalist artisanship, with youngsters learning a trade by working under skilled workers for five or seven years on minimal wages.

But over time it became clear that the ad hoc methods were inadequate and that the state had to take over many of the tasks from private capitalists and charitable concerns. In Britain it intervened as early as the 1834 Poor Law to ensure that the conditions under which the unemployed or the infirm could get poverty relief were so arduous that those who could work would, however low the pay. In 1848 it established a Board of Health to act against the spread of diseases in working class areas—which was affecting richer areas too. Over the decades it was cajoled into limiting the working hours of children and barring women from occupations that might damage their capacity to bear and bring up the next generation. In the 1870s it moved to set up a state system of elementary education and to encourage the building of homes for skilled workers. Then in the first decade of the 20th century it made the first moves to coordinate the various ad hoc measures of the previous 70 years into national structures to provide minimal social insurance benefits for unemployment, old age and sickness.[29] The impetus to do so came from the shock of discovering in the course of recruitment for the Boer War how few of the working class were healthy enough to undertake military service. Ann Rogers has summarised the reaction of the upper and middle class:

> The belief that change was necessary if Britain was to compete successfully with Germany and the United States remained central. Whether the argument was formulated by the Fabians or by Liberal imperialists the concentration was on the damage that poverty was doing to society rather than the misery it caused individual workers... The underlying reason for the desire to improve the health of the working class was the need for a healthier labour force in the factories and the army.[30]

These measures were not simply a result of capitalists getting together and deciding what was rational for their system. They came into being only after recurrent campaigns involving upper class philanthropists with a conservative disdain for the money-grabbing grubbiness of capitalism, middle class moralisers about working class behaviour, political opportunists out to get working class votes, factory inspectors and doctors with professional concerns about people's safety and well-being—and, alongside them and often independently of them, trade union and socialist activists. But such coalitions framed the projects they pursued in terms of what they saw as rational for capitalism. And that meant what was necessary to supply it with pools of sufficiently healthy and skilled labour power. This was shown clearly by one feature that characterised the reforms of the early 20th century just as much as it had the charitable efforts of the early 19th century. Any benefits were always to be provided in such a way as to coerce into seeking work all those who were fit and able. The principle of "less eligibility" had to apply: getting the benefit must still leave the recipients worse off than the worst paid work. What is more, the benefits were not meant to come from a diversion of value from capital to labour, but by a redistribution of income within the working class through the "the insurance principle". Weekly payments from those able to work were to sustain those unable to do so because of sickness or unemployment.

The role of the state in the supply, training and reproduction of labour power grew through the 20th century, reaching a peak in the long boom from the mid-1940s through to the mid-1970s, and continuing into the new period of crises which followed. All through this the "welfare state" continued to be tailored to the interests of nationally based capitals, even when the impetus for extending its role came from below, as during the Second World War, when the British Tory politician Quintin Hogg famously declared, "if you do not give the people social reform, they are going to give you social revolution".[31] The British Labour minister of the 1940s Aneurin Bevan argued that public health measures had become part of the system, "but they do not flow from it. In claiming them capitalism proudly displays medals won in battles it has lost".[32] The fact, however, is that those who formulated them—including Bevan—did so in ways that could fit in with the needs of the system.

This has important implications for the labour power that goes into such services—and for the people who supply it. There is a widespread tendency for Marxists—as well as some non-Marxists[33]—to insist that such labour cannot be productive since it does not produce commodities directly. But that also applies to much labour inside any capitalist enterprise, which is merely a precondition for other labour that produces the final products. It is productive as part of the labour of the "collective worker"[34] in the enterprise. A fully trained carpenter or bricklayer can be many times more productive than an unskilled one; a fully trained toolmaker can do jobs an unskilled labourer is incapable of. The labour of those who train them is adding to the capacity of the collective worker to produce value. And they are exploited, since they are paid the value of their labour power, not of the training they provide. There can be a debate over exactly how the skills added by their labour fit into Marx's categories: are they to be equated with plant and equipment as a form of constant capital or as simply enhanced labour power, as variable capital?[35] There are also debates between individual firms over the merits of undertaking training programmes. They may gain in the short term, but what is to prevent other firms "poaching" their skilled labour without ever having paid for its training.[36] Finally, there are arguments about how to characterise the labour used to train other workers: is it "productive" or "indirectly productive"? But there should be no doubt about its role in increasing overall potential output and productivity: it is part of the total productive labour of the firm and of the system as a whole.[37]

A big portion of the labour that goes into the educational system plays an identical role in providing the skills capital needs, although in this case the skills are not available simply for individual capitalists, but for all the capitalists operating from within the state that provides it. The training in skills which future workers get from a teacher in an educational institution adds to the amount of socially necessary labour they can produce in an hour in exactly the same way as the training they might get inside an enterprise. And the cost of the training is part of the cost of providing labour power, just as much as the wage that goes into buying the food, clothing and shelter the workers require. Enterprises under modern capitalism require labour power with at least minimal levels of literacy and numeracy. The teachers who provide this have to be considered as part of the collective worker, ultimately working for the complex of nationally based capitals that the state services. Apologists for capitalism recognise this inadvertently when they refer to the provision of education as "adding to social capital" and demand "value added" in schools.

The same general principle applies to health services that cater for actual, potential or future workers. Spending on keeping the workforce fit and able to work is in reality a part of the wage even when it is paid in kind rather than in cash and goes to the workers collectively rather than individually. In Marx's terminology, it is part of "variable capital". This is absolutely clear in countries like the US where healthcare is provided for most workers through insurance schemes provided by their employers. It should be just as clear in countries like Britain where the state provides them on behalf of the nationally based capitals. The popularly used term "social wage" is an accurate description. It is just as accurate when applied to unemployment benefits available only to those who show they are able and willing to work, and to pension schemes dependent on a lifetime of labour. The capitalist wants contented workers to exploit in the same way that a farmer wants contented cows. Workers cannot be expected to labour with any commitment to their work unless there is some sort of promise that they will not starve to death once they reach retirement age. As Marx put it, there is a historically and socially determined element to the cost of reproducing labour power as well as a physiological one.

But labour power is not an object like other commodities, which are passive as they are bought and sold. It is the living expression of human beings. What from a capitalist point of view is "recuperation of labour power" is for the worker the chance for relaxation, enjoyment and creativity. There is a struggle over the social wage just as over the normal wage, even if both are, to a certain degree, necessary for capital.

The problem is compounded from capital's point of view by the fact that not all welfare provision is in any sense productive. A good portion of it is concerned solely with maintaining the existing relations of exploitation. Studies of the schooling of working class children in the 19th century emphasise the degree to which what was involved was not education in skills so much as inculcating into them discipline and respect for authority.[38] Not until late in the 19th century did a concern with basic skills for the workforce begin to become a central preoccupation for British capitalism facing foreign competition.[39] Today disciplines like economics and sociology are about trying to reproduce bourgeois ideology, while others like accountancy are concerned with the unproductive redistribution of surplus value among members of the capitalist class.

If capital has no choice but to tolerate these unproductive "expenses of production", there are other elements in welfare expenditure it would love to be able to do without and does its utmost to minimise. These go to those who are not needed as labour power (the long-term unemployed without needed skills) or are incapable of providing it (the chronic sick and disabled). It has a similar attitude to provision for the mass of the elderly, but is restrained to some degree by its need to give the impression to currently employed workers that their future is assured. Marx pointed out that there exists, alongside the "reserve army of labour", able to enter the active labour force when the system undergoes periodic expansion (and in the meantime exercising a downward pressure on wages), a surplus population in whose survival it has no real interest apart from that of warding off rebellion and preventing a demoralising impact on the employed working class.

The history of welfare legislation over the last 180 years has been a history of attempts to separate that provision which is necessary for capital in the same way that wage payments are and that which is unnecessary but forced on it by its need to contain popular discontent. This finds expression in repeated debates among those who would manage national capitalisms over how welfare policy interacts with labour market policy, among mainstream economists about the "natural" or "non-inflationary" level of unemployment, and among sociologists and social work theorists about the "underclass".

The division between social expenditures that are in some way productive for capital and those that are non-productive cuts across some of the normal ways of dividing up national budgets. So education is both training for productive labour and also training for unproductive forms of labour (eg in sales promotion or finance) and the inculcation of bourgeois ideological values. Health services and unemployment benefits *both* keep the workforce fit and ready to provide labour power *and* are mechanisms for maintaining social cohesion by providing at least minimal provision for the old, the infirm and the long-term unemployed. These ambiguities become important whenever capital finds the costs of state provision begin to cut into profit rates.

At such points states come under the same pressure as do big capitals when faced with sudden competition—the pressure to restructure and reorganise their operations so as to accord with the law of value. On the one side this means trying to impose work measurement and payment schemes on welfare sector employees similar to those within the most competitive industrial firms. On the other side it means cuts in welfare provision so as to restrict it as much as possible to servicing labour power that is necessary for capital accumulation—and doing so in such a way that those who provide this labour power are prepared to do so at the wages they are offered.

These pressures grow as managing labour power becomes more important for the state. In the process, employees working

Understanding the System: Marx and Beyond

in the welfare, health and educational sectors who could at one stage of capitalist development regard themselves as part of the professional middle class—with salaries and conditions comparable to lawyers or accountants—find themselves subject to a traumatic process of proletarianisation. This, as we shall see, adds to the problems that beset national capitalist states as they attempt to cope with sudden crises. Public expenditures become a central focus for class struggle in a way in which they were not in Marx's time.

Part Two

CAPITALISM
IN THE
20th CENTURY

CHAPTER SIX

The Great Slump

An unprecedented crisis

The deepest slump capitalism had ever known followed by the most sustained boom, interspersed with the bloodiest war in human history. Such was the course of capitalism in the middle 50 years of the twentieth century.

The epicentre of the slump was the United States, which had emerged from the First World War as the greatest economic power, with 50 percent of global industrial production, overtaking both victorious Britain and defeated Germany. The onset is often identified with the Wall Street Crash of 29 October 1929, when the New York stock exchange fell by almost a third. But "business was already in trouble before the crash", with auto output down by a third in September compared with March 1929.[1] Over the next three years US industrial production fell by about half, and the slump spread across the Atlantic to Europe, where there were already incipient signs of crisis. German industrial production also fell about half and, with a slight delay, French fell by nearly 30 percent. Only Britain saw a smaller fall— of about 20 percent—but that was because its heavy industries were already in a depressed condition.

By 1932 a third of the workforce in the US and Germany were unemployed and a fifth in Britain. Those hit were not only manual workers as in previous crises, but white collar employees who thought of themselves as belonging to the middle class. Hundreds of local banks went bust in the US and some giant banks in Europe collapsed spectacularly, destroying people's savings and aggravating the general sense of disaster. Hitting all industrial countries at once, the crisis destroyed the demand for the output of agricultural countries, driving down the prices farmers received and creating vast pools of misery. No region of the globe avoided at least some decline in output,[2] and world trade fell to a third of its 1929 level.[3] By comparison, both world output and world trade had grown during the previous "Great Depression" of the 1870s and 1880s.[4]

The 1920s boom

The ideological shock of the crisis was increased by the way capitalism had seemed to have recovered in the preceding years from the destruction of the First World War. Industrial output in the US had doubled from 1914 to 1929, with the emergence of a host of new industries that began to revolutionise patterns of consumption—radio, rayon, chemicals, aviation, refrigeration, and the replacement of horse-borne by motorised transport. The boom in the US had a beneficial impact in Europe. Germany, racked by civil war in 1919-20 and then unparalleled inflation in 1923, had then seen industrial output grow 40 percent above its 1914 level. In France industrial production had doubled. The press had displayed an unbounded optimism about capitalism, proclaiming a "new era" of endless prosperity. Mainstream economists had been just as confident. Alvin Hansen wrote that the "childhood diseases" of capitalism's youth were "being mitigated", while America's most eminent neoclassical economist, Irving Fisher, had stated on the eve of the Wall Street Crash that "stock prices have reached what looks like a permanently high plateau", *and* continued to exude optimism for some months after, while in Britain John Maynard Keynes had assured his students, "There will be no further crash in our lifetime".[5] Social democrat Marxists joined in the chorus, with Hilferding's theory of "organised capitalism", as a system in which the anarchy of the market and the trend towards crisis had disappeared.[6] Suddenly they were all proved wrong.

The initial reaction of mainstream politicians and their fellow travellers in the economics profession was to assume that they only had to wait a short time and the slump would begin to correct itself. "Recovery is just around the corner," as US president Herbert Hoover assured people. But recovery did not come in 1930, 1931 or 1932. And the economic orthodoxy which had been so confident in its praise of the wonders of capitalism so recently could not explain why—and it still cannot explain why today.

There have been attempts at explanation. The most common among the most orthodox at the time was that articulated by the

English economist Arthur Cecil Pigou. Workers, according to his argument, had priced themselves out of their jobs by not accepting cuts in their money wages. Had they done so, the magic of supply and demand would have solved all the problems. Irving Fisher belatedly put forward a monetarist interpretation, arguing that the money supply was too low, leading to falling prices and so cumulatively increasing debt levels. More recent monetarist theorists put the blame on the behaviour of the central bankers. If only, the argument went, the US Federal Reserve Bank had acted to stop the money supply contracting in 1930 and 1931, then everything would have been all right—the arch monetarist of the post-war decades, Milton Friedman, traced its mistakes and the depth of the slump back to the death of New York Reserve Bank president Benjamin Strong in October 1928.[7] By contrast Friedrich von Hayek and the "Austrian" school argued that excessive credit in the 1920s had led to "an imbalance in the structure of production",[8] which would be made worse by increasing the money supply. Still other economists blamed the dislocation of the world economy in the aftermath of the First World War, while John Maynard Keynes stressed an excess of saving over investment that led to a lack of "effective demand" for the economy's output. Finally, there was the claim, still perpetuated in much media commentary today, that the raising of US tariffs by the Smoot-Hawley Act in the summer of 1930 unleashed a wave of protectionism preventing a recovery that would otherwise have occurred if free trade had been allowed untrammelled sway.

Ever since then the proponents of each view have found it easy to tear holes in the arguments of those holding the other views, with none being able to survive serious criticism. That is why the current Federal Reserve head, Ben Bernanke, sees explaining the slump as the ever illusive Holy Grail of his profession. Yet if the slump of the 1930s cannot be understood, neither can the chances of it recurring in the 21st century be seriously assessed.

Disentangling the real causes of the slump from this mishmash of contradictory argument involves, first of all, looking at what really happened during the 1920s.

Rapid economic growth and the proliferation of new consumer goods had encouraged people to see this as a decade of continual rises in living standards and enormous productive investment—a story that is still frequently accepted today. But in fact wages rose by a total of only 6.1 percent between 1922 and 1929[9] (with no increase after 1925) and the manufacturing workforce remained static while industrial production expanded by about a third. Michael Bernstein notes that "the lower 93 percent of the non-farm population saw their per capita disposable income fall during the boom of the late 1920s".[10] The fall in labour's share of total income meant that the proportion of national output that could be bought with wages fell. The economy could only keep expanding because something else filled the resulting gap in demand.

Many analyses have argued that investment fulfilled this role. Gordon Brown tells how much recent literature sees "that the most notable aspect of the 1920s was overinvestment".[11] A chastened Hansen noted in his analysis of the slump that, although a "vast sum of $138,000,000,000" of "investment" had "led consumption" during the 1920s, only half of that was business investment, and of that only a third was new investment, ie a mere $3 billion a year.[12] In other words, beneath the appearance of rapidly expanding investment, the reality was a relatively low level of productive accumulation despite the impetus provided by the new industries. Other analyses, by Simon Kusznets,[13] Steindl,[14] and Gillman,[15] bear this out.

Only one, stark, conclusion can be drawn from such figures. The boom could not have taken place if it had only depended on the demand for goods created by productive investment and wages. A third element had to be present to prevent the piling up of unsold goods and recession in the mid-1920s. As Hansen recognised, "Stimulating and sustaining forces outside business investment and consumption were present…with these stimuli removed, business expenditures would have been made on a more restrictive scale, leaving the economy stagnant if not depressed".[16]

Hansen, as a mainstream economist, even if by now a critical one, saw these forces as being "non-business capital expenditures (residential building and public construction)" and " the growing importance of durable consumer goods financed in large part by a billion dollar per year growth of instalment credit" and "rather feckless foreign lending".[17]

A classic Marxist analysis of the slump by Lewis Corey puts the stress on the growth of luxury consumption, unproductive expenditures and credit. The 1920s were a decade in which incomes from dividends and managerial salaries rose several times faster than real wages,[18] until "the bourgeoisie" (including the non-farm petty bourgeoisie) were responsible for over 40 percent of consumption,

Capitalism in the 20th Century

according to him.[19] Then there was growing expenditure on advertising and sales drives as firms sought markets for the growing number of goods they were turning out—this expenditure, in the form of incomes for sales personnel in these same industries, could then create a market for some of the goods businesses were trying to sell. A doubling of consumer credit[20] enabled the middle class and some layers of workers to buy "on the never never" some of the new range of consumer goods, with car sales at a level in 1929 they were not to reach again until 1953. And finally there were upsurges of non-productive speculative investment in real estate and the stock market. Such things could not create fresh new surplus value to solve the problem of profitability (they merely involved funds passing from one capitalist pocket to another). But their by-product was unproductive expenditure in new building, new managerial salaries and conspicuous consumption, all of which absorbed some of the goods being poured out by industry, encouraging further speculation:

> Superabundant capital became more and more aggressive and adventurous in its search for investment and profit, overflowing into risky enterprises and speculation. Speculation seized upon technical changes and new industries which were introduced regardless of the requirements of industry as a whole...[21]

Spending on new non-residential construction rose by more than half over the decade, and was "most intense in the central business districts of cities". This was most notable in New York, where work on the world's tallest building, the Empire State Building, began in 1929—only for it to be known by 1931 as "the Empty State Building".[22]

While the US boomed, there was also a boost to economic expansion in Europe with an inflow of American funds that could make up for some of the destruction caused by the war—the impact of the US Dawes plan of 1924 was particularly important in encouraging loans to Germany.

These factors were already losing their capacity to sustain the boom in industry before the Wall Street Crash. There was the beginning of a recession in 1927, but a brief upsurge of investment in heavy industry and autos in 1928-9 pulled the rest of the economy forward.[23] Then, in the late spring and early summer of 1929, this came to a sudden end, with a sharp fall in fixed investment[24] and auto production.[25] The expansion of credit and the scale of speculation that sustained unproductive expenditures had hidden the underlying problems right up to the last minute. But once there was a single tiny break in the chain of borrowing and lending that held it up, the whole edifice was bound to come tumbling down. Marx's comment on crises could not have been more apposite:

> The semblance of a very solvent business with a smooth flow of returns can easily persist even long after returns actually come in only at the expense partly of swindled money-lenders and partly of swindled producers. Thus business always appears almost excessively sound right on the eve of a crash. Business is always thoroughly sound until suddenly the debacle takes place.[26]

The recession precipitated a sudden contraction of speculative ventures and unproductive expenditures, so reducing still further the market for industrial output. Faced with declining sales, industrialists were already beginning to borrow from the banks, rather than lend to them. Those who had engaged in the speculative boom (including both industrialists and banks) now tried to borrow more in order to cover their losses after the crash, but borrowing was now very difficult. Those who could not borrow went bust, creating further losses for those who had lent to them. The slump spread from one sector of the economy to another.

Once the decline started there seemed no end to it. Industrial decline led to pressure on the banks, which in turn deepened industrial decline and put more pressure on the banks. But that only further exacerbated the disproportion between productive capacity and consumer demand, further worsening the crisis in industry. As firms tried to sustain sales by competitive price cutting, profits everywhere fell and with them the willingness even of firms that survived to invest. The non-productive expenditures that helped to fuel the boom were cut right back as companies tried to conserve their funds and the slump grew deeper.

The position in Europe was no better, with recession also already under way when Wall Street crashed. Conditions were worst in Germany, the world's second biggest industrial economy, which began experiencing an economic downturn in 1928:[27] "By the summer of 1929 the existence of depression was unmistakable",[28] as unemployment reached 1.9 million and the

Capitalism in the 20th Century

spectacular failure of the Frankfurt Insurance Company began a series of bankruptcies.

Problems in each country impacted on those in others. There had already been an outflow from Germany of some of the American funds associated with the Dawes plan before the Crash. It now became a torrent as hard-hit American institutions recalled their short-term loans from Germany, creating difficulties for German industrialists who had been relying on them to finance their own industrial overcapacity. Austria's biggest bank, the Creditanstalt, went bust in May 1931. Britain was hit by the withdrawal of foreign funds from its banks, and broke with the world financial system based on the gold standard. This in turn created vastly exaggerated fears in the US where the Federal Reserve Bank raised interest rates, and there was "a spectacular increase in bank failures" [29] and industrial production slumped even more.

The proliferating impact of the crisis made it easy for people to confuse effects with causes. Hence the contradictory interpretations from mainstream economists, with some blaming too much money, some too little; some central bank interventions, some lack of intervention; some excessive consumption, some too little consumption; some the gold standard, some the turn of states to protectionism and competitive currency devaluation; some the rapidity of the growth of investment, some its tardiness; some the forcing down of wages, some their "stickiness" in falling; some the scale of indebtedness, some the refusal of the banks to lend. [30]

Yet amidst the contradictory interpretations there was an occasional partial glimpse that something fundamental was causing havoc to the system to which all the mainstream economists and politicians were committed. The two economists usually thought as representing polar opposite attitudes, Keynes and Hayek, both stumbled on the same factor but in such a way that neither they nor their apostles took it seriously.

The main theme running through Keynes's *General Theory of Employment, Interest and Money* was that saving can exceed investment, opening up a gap that reduced the effective demand for goods, and therefore output, until the reduced level of economic activity had cut saving down to the level of investment. This could be overcome, he argued, by cutting the rate of interest ("monetary measures") and putting more money in people's pockets by tax cuts and increased government spending ("fiscal measures"). But he recognised that these measures might not work, since people and firms might still decide to save rather than spend. In particular he was "somewhat sceptical of the success of a merely monetary policy directed towards influencing the rate of interest".[31] He is best known for explaining the weakness of investment on the crowd psychology of speculators—"when the capital development of a country becomes a by-product of the activities of a casino, the job is likely to be ill done"[32]—and the flagging "animal spirits" of entrepreneurs.[33] But at points in the text he threw in another factor. He argued that the very process of expanding capital investment led to a decline in the return on it—in "the marginal efficiency"—and therefore to a blunting of the spur to further investment.[34]

He believed the declining "marginal efficiency of capital" to be an empirical fact which could be found, for instance, in the inter-war "experience of Great Britain and the United States". The result was that the return on capital was not sufficiently above the cost to the entrepreneurs of borrowing as to encourage new investment, so tending "to interfere...with a reasonable level of employment and with the standard of life which the technical conditions of production are capable of furnishing".[35]

This he sees as both a long-term trend and a short-term effect turning the boom into a slump in each cycle:

the essence of the situation is to be found in the collapse of the marginal efficiency of capital, particularly...of those types of capital which have been contributing most to the previous phase of heavy new investment.[36]

Keynes's explanation for this was grounded in his overall "marginalist" approach, with its acceptance that value depended on supply and demand. As the supply of capital increased it would grow less scarce, and the value to the user of each extra unit would fall until, eventually, it reached zero.[37] This theoretical reasoning seems to have been too obscure for most of Keynes's followers. The "declining marginal efficiency of capital" hardly appears in most accounts of his ideas. Yet it is the most radical single notion in his writings. It implies that the obstacles to full employment lie with an inbuilt tendency of the existing system and not just with the psychology of capitalists. If that is so, there would seem to be no point in governments simply seeking to "restore confidence", since there is nothing to restore confidence in.

Hayek expressed in passing the same view of what was happening to profits, although from a different reasoning. He claimed that cyclical crises resulted from disproportions between different sectors of production—with "excessive credit" causing the output of producer goods to grow too rapidly in the relationship to the output of consumer goods.[38] In this way, he believed, he could explain the cycle as an inevitable means by which the different sectors adjusted to each other, much as Marx saw the crises as able partially to resolve internal contradictions in capitalism—but what Marx viewed negatively Hayek viewed positively. His theory still, however, had a big hole in it. Why should the lag between the sectors cause so much greater problems than in previous decades? Why, in particular, should the production goods sector not keep growing fast enough to pull the rest of the economy behind it? The answer he put forward in passing in 1935 (and which never made it into the Hayekian orthodoxy) was that profitability fell with the expansion of what he called "roundabout processes of production"—that is processes with a high ratio of means of production to workers, or as Marx would have put it, a high organic composition of capital:

That [profit] margins must exist is obvious...if it were not so, there would exist no inducement to risk money by investing it in production rather than to let it remain idle... These margins must grow smaller as the roundabout processes of production increase in length...[39]

In other words, both Keynes and Hayek recognised, though they could not clearly explain, the feature which is central to Marx's theory of capitalist crisis—the downward pressures on the rate of profit.

In fact, Marxist theory can provide an explanation of the slump which avoids the contradictions of all the mainstream theories. Profit rates in the US had fallen about 40 percent between the 1880s and the early 1920s,[40] those in Britain were already in decline before 1914[41] and those in Germany had failed "to return to their pre-war 'normal' level".[42] Such declines could be traced back to long-term rises in the ratio of investment to the employed workforce (the "organic composition of capital"), about 20 percent in the case of the US.[43] American profitability was able to make a small recovery through the 1920s on the basis of a rise in the rate of exploitation. But the rise was not sufficient to induce productive investment on the scale necessary to absorb the surplus value accumulated from previous rounds of production and exploitation. Firms were torn between the competitive pressures to undertake investment in massive new complexes of plant and equipment (the Ford River Rouge plant, completed in 1928, was the largest in the world), and the fear that any new equipment would not be profitable. Some would take the risk, but many did not. This meant that the big new plants that came into operation towards the end of the boom necessarily produced on too big a scale for the market, flooding it with products which undercut the prices and profits of old plants. New investment came to a halt, leading to a fall in employment and consumption that worsened the crisis.

The blind self-expansion of capital had led to an ever greater accumulation of constant capital compared with living labour. This expressed itself on the one side by a rate of profit considerably lower than a quarter of a century before and on the other by employers holding back wages and so diminishing the share of output that could be absorbed by workers' buying power. "Overproduction" and the low rate of profit were aspects of the same process that would eventually lead to the slump. An upsurge of unproductive expenditures and credit could postpone this, but do no more. The stage was set for a deep crisis—and it only required scares in the stock exchange and the financial sectors for it to occur.

The crisis in these respects was very similar to those described by Marx in passages where he analysed the crises of 1846 and 1857 in Britain.[44] It also fits with Grossman's interpretation of Marx's account, with its stress on the way in which firms are pushed to undertake new investments that threaten to make the already low rate of profit drop to such an extent that much of the new investment becomes unprofitable so as to cause all investment to freeze up.[45]

But there remains something else that has to be explained—why the automatic market mechanisms which had always in the past been capable, ultimately, of lifting the economy out of crisis no longer seemed to be working. Three years after the crisis started, industrial production in the US, Germany, Britain and France was still declining. To explain this it is not enough just to look at the tendency of the rate of profit to fall. The other long-term trend in Marx's account—the concentration and centralisation of capital as the system aged—also played a role, as was suggested in Chapter Three.

At first it delayed the outbreak of the crisis. The Bolshevik economist Preobrazhensky, attempting to analyse the crisis in 1931, argued that there had been a big change since Marx's time. Then recessions had led to the elimination of inefficient firms and allowed the rest to enter into new rounds of accumulation. But now the system was dominated by big near-monopolies which were able to prevent the liquidation of their inefficient plants. They would do their utmost to keep their operations intact, even if it meant their plants operating at only a fraction of their usual capacity and cutting investment to the minimum. This produces a "thrombosis in the transition from crisis to recession" and prevents—or at least delays—the restructuring necessary for an emergence from the crisis: "Monopoly emerges as a factor of decay in the entire economy. Its effects delay the transition to expanded reproduction".[46]

Once the crisis erupted, the sheer size of individual industrial or financial capitals was such that the collapse of any one of them threatened to drag others down with it. The banks would lose the money they had lent it, and so cut off credit to other firms. Its suppliers would be driven out of business and so damage other firms dependent on them. And the end to its spending on investment and wage bills would reduce demand in the economy as a whole. The delayed crisis was now a much magnified one, which could not automatically resolve itself. The response of the big capitals was to turn to the state for "bail-outs" to keep the system going.

The turn to state capitalism

At first governments continued to place their hopes in the untrammelled operation of the market mechanism, with only limited actions to protect some banks. But the crisis continued to get worse, particularly in the US and Germany. Enormous damage was being done to capital itself as it tried to operate with little more than half its previous production levels. At the same time desperation was leading the mass of people to look to remedies that might turn the whole of society over. Major sections of capital began to look for an approach that might solve their problems, however much it broke with old ideological shibboleths. By the summer of 1932 the head of General Electric in the US was campaigning for state intervention. The shift which eventually took place was from forms of monopoly capitalism in which the state kept in the background, providing services to big capital but keeping away from attempting to direct it, to forms in which it attempted to ensure the international competitiveness of nationally based capital. That came to involve consciously restructuring industry by shifting surplus value from one section of the economy to another.

The shift had been foreshadowed in the later stages of the First World War, when the state had taken draconian powers to force individual capitals to concentrate their efforts on the military struggle. But in the aftermath of the war, the state had given up the power it had acquired. Now the sheer scale of the crisis forced a rethink. Political crises in the US and Germany brought governments to power early in 1933 prepared to implement radical change in order to save capitalism from itself.

In the US this took the form of Roosevelt's New Deal. It extended already existing public works schemes to mop up some of the unemployment, guaranteed the funds of the banks which had not gone bust, encouraged the self-regulation of industry through cartels, destroyed crops so as to raise agricultural prices and incomes, carried through very limited experiments in direct state production and also made it a little easier for unions to raise wages (and therefore the demand for consumer goods). Federal expenditure, only around 2.5 percent of GDP in 1929 reached a peacetime peak of just over 9 percent in 1936. It was a recognition that capitalism in its monopoly stage could no longer solve its problems without limited state intervention. But it was still limited intervention: federal expenditure fell back in 1937.

Such timidity could have only a limited impact on the crisis. All the efforts of the New Deal could not push the upturn that began in the spring of 1933 beyond a certain point. The number of unemployed fell by 1.7 million—but that still left 12 million jobless. It was not until 1937—eight years after the start of the crisis—that production reached the 1929 figure. But even then fixed investment in industry remained low[47] and there was 14.3 percent unemployment. Yet this "miniboom" gave way in August 1937 to "the steepest economic decline since the history of the US" which "lost half the ground gained by many indexes since 1932".[48]

Capitalism in the 20th Century

The 1920s had shown that the non-productive expenditures associated with monopoly capital (marketing expenditures, advertising, speculative ventures, luxury consumption) could postpone crisis but not stop its eventual impact being greater than previously. The 1930s showed that "pump priming" by governments might produce a shortlived and limited revival of production, but could not give a new lease of life to the system either. A more profound change in the direction of state capitalism was needed.

From slump to war

It was here that the German and Japanese examples were significant. The major sections of their ruling classes accepted political options that subordinated individual capitalists to programmes of national capitalist accumulation imposed by the state while repressing the working class movement. The major capitalist groups remained intact. But from now on they were subordinated to the needs of an arms drive which they themselves supported. Armaments and the expansion of heavy industry drove the whole economy forward, providing markets and outlets for investment, as wages lagged behind rising output and profit rates were partially restored.

In Germany such methods pulled the economy right out of the slump (after two years of less effective "pump priming") and kept it booming while the American economy was slumping again in 1937. By 1939 output had climbed 30 percent above the 1929 level and unemployment had fallen from six million to 70,000, with the creation of eight million new jobs.[49] Most of the new production went into arms and the heavy industries that provided military preparedness, but a tenth of increased output did go into raising private consumption.[50] And the economic expansion itself paid for a large percentage of the cost of fuelling the boom, with only about a fifth of government spending being covered by a budgetary deficit. In effect, the Nazi dictatorship was able to ensure that new investment took place, even though initial profit rates were low.

However, there were major problems with any such policy. Germany was not a self-contained economic unit. The forces of production internationally had long since developed to the point where they cut across national boundaries, and there was a growing need for certain strategic imports as the armaments boom took off. The only way to overcome this while keeping the German economy self-contained, and therefore immune to international recessionary pressures, was to expand the boundaries of the German Reich so as to incorporate neighbouring economies, and to subordinate their industries to the German military drive.

The logic of state-directed monopoly capitalism led to a form of imperialism Lenin had referred to in 1916—the seizure of "highly industrialised regions".[51] Beyond a certain point such expansion led to inevitable clashes with other great powers which feared threats to their own empires and spheres of influence. As they reacted by building up their own armed forces, the German and Japanese regimes in turn had to direct even more of the economy towards arms—and to reach out to grab new territory—in order to "defend" the lands they had already grabbed. This provided their capitalists with new sources of surplus value to counter any downward pressure on profit rates. But at the same time it increased the hostility of the existing empires—leading to the need for a greater arms potential and further military adventures. The breaking points were the German seizure of western Poland and the Japanese onslaught on Pearl Harbor.[52]

Just as deepening slump in each major capitalist country had fed into the slumps developing elsewhere, so now did the path out of the slump through military state capitalism.

British and American imperialism could only defend their own positions in the world after the fall of France in 1940 and Pearl Harbor in 1941 by moving on from the half baked state-directed capitalism of the mid-1930s to fully militarised economies of their own. The British state took charge of all major economic decisions, directing which industries should get raw materials and rationing food and consumer goods, with the civilian economy reduced to a mere adjunct of the centrally organised war economy. The US government "not only controlled the armaments sector of the economy, which represented about half the total production of goods. The state decided what consumer goods should be produced and what consumer goods should not be produced".[53] It spent huge sums building armaments factories which it handed over to private corporations to run. Government capital expenditure in 1941 was 50 percent higher than the country's entire manufacturing investment in

1939, and in 1943 the state was responsible for 90 percent of all investment.[54] Again a militarised state-dominated economy seemed to provide answers to the problems that had faced the economy before the war. Nine million unemployed became less than one million within three years, and there was a growth in the civilian economy despite the vast expenditure on non-productive output. Total output doubled between 1940 and 1943, and consumer expenditure in 1943—even when measured in 1940 prices—exceeded those of earlier years.[55] The war economy could achieve what eight years of the New Deal could not—full employment of the productive capacity of the largest of the ageing capitalisms. As John Kenneth Galbraith has noted, "The Great Depression of the 30s never came to an end. It merely disappeared in the great mobilisation of the 40s".[56]

The Russian variant

There was one other major economy where state direction seemed to provide an alternative to being torn apart in the maelstrom of the world system. This was the USSR. In the 1930s nearly all commentators saw it as based on radically different principles to those of Western capitalism—and this view persisted among many right up until its implosion in 1989-91. The right defined it simply as "totalitarian", as if there was no dynamic to its economy, and many on the left adopted a mirror image view, speaking of it as "communist" or "socialist", or those who were more critical as "post-capitalist"[57] or a "degenerated workers' state"[58]. All these different approaches assumed a high degree of continuity between the Soviet system as it operated in the 1930s and the revolutionary state established in 1917.

But the central mechanisms directing the Soviet economy were not established during the revolution, but in 1928-9 under the impact of a profound economic and political crisis. By that time little remained of the revolutionary democracy that had characterised the country in the immediate aftermath of the October Revolution of 1917. A new bureaucratic layer had increasingly concentrated power in its own hands amidst the devastation of an already economically backward country suffering from three years of world war followed by three years of civil war. Nevertheless, the driving force behind the economy through to the mid-1920s remained the production of goods to satisfy the needs of the population, and living standards rose from the abysmal levels of the war and civil war years, even if bureaucrats' living standards rose disproportionately more than those of workers and peasants.

Then in late 1928 a wave of panic hit the bureaucracy in the face of warlike threats from Britain and a domestic crisis as peasants held back supplies of food, creating hunger in the cities.[59] Afraid of losing their control over the country through a combination of rebellion at home and armed pressure from abroad, the bureaucracy, led by Joseph Stalin, turned pragmatically to a series of measures that involved super-exploitation of the peasantry and the working class in order to build the industry the country lacked. The cumulative effect was to push the whole economy towards a new dynamic other than that of fulfilling people's needs—a dynamic ultimately determined by military competition with the various Western states.

As the Czech historian Michael Reiman has said:

> There were not enough resources to guarantee the proposed rate of industrial growth. The planning agencies therefore decided...to balance the plan by means of resources the economy did not yet have at its disposal... The fulfilment of the plan depended on a very brutal attack on the living and working conditions of industrial workers and the rural population... This was a plan of organised poverty and famine.[60]

Stalin, justifying the subordination of everything else to accumulation, insisted, "We are fifty or a hundred years behind the advanced countries. We must make good this lag in ten years. Either we do it or they crush us".[61] "The environment in which we are placed...at home and abroad...compels us to adopt a rapid rate of growth of our industry".[62]

In undertaking the task of accumulation, the bureaucracy substituted itself for a capitalist class that no longer existed. But the methods it used were essentially those of capitalist industrialisation elsewhere in the world. "Collectivisation"—in reality the state takeover of the land—increased the proportion of agricultural output available for industrial accumulation while driving a very high proportion of the peasantry from the land, just as enclosures had for England's early capitalists. The growing industries were

Capitalism in the 20th Century

mainly manned by wage labour—but some subordinate tasks were carried out by some millions of slave labourers. The rights workers had held onto through the 1920s were abolished.

Control of the economy by a single centralised state bureaucracy with a monopoly of foreign trade meant accumulation could proceed without interruption, as in the militarised state monopoly capitalisms of the West. But the economy could not be isolated completely from the wider world system, any more than those of Germany and Japan could in the late 1930s. Importing machinery for industrialisation from the West depended on export earnings from grain at a time of falling world prices—and that depended on the state seizing the grain from starving peasants, some millions of whom died. Preobrazhensky noted, "As exporters we [the USSR] are suffering severely from the world crisis".[63]

There was, however, a relative isolation from the world economy, and this meant the accumulation could proceed as long as there was some surplus value, regardless of the rate of profit at any particular time. This did not, however, overcome economic contradictions. Fulfilling the production plans for heavy industry and armaments invariably involved diverting resources to them from consumer goods industries, whose output fell even as the economy as a whole expanded at great speed. Such an outcome was the opposite of "planning" in any real sense of the word. If two of us plan to go from London to Manchester but one of us ends up in Glasgow and the other in Brighton, then our "plan" did not guide our action. The same was true of Soviet planning. As in the West competitive accumulation produced a dynamic of growth on the one hand and of chaos, inefficiency and poverty on the other. It also produced a tendency to imperialist expansion beyond national borders, as was shown in 1939 when Stalin divided Eastern Europe with Hitler, taking half of Poland, Estonia, Lithuania and Latvia—only to find in 1941 that Hitler had set his eyes on seizing and pillaging the USSR for German capitalism.

Balance sheet of a decade

In the 1930s there had been a widespread feeling among the supporters of capitalism that it was in deep trouble; among its opponents that it was finished. Lewis Corey had written of the "decline and decay of capitalism",[64] John Strachey that "there can only exist for the capitalist areas of the world an ever more rapid decay" with "the permanent contraction of production",[65] Preobrazhensky of "the terminal crisis of the entire capitalist system",[66] Leon Trotsky of "the death agony of capitalism".[67] Their prophesies did not seem absurd at a time when the supporters of capitalism were tormented by worries as to what had gone wrong with their supposedly infallible system. Yet the desperate turn to state capitalism and massive arms production allowed the system to enter into a new phase of expansion. The question remained: for how long?

Capitalism in the 20th Century

CHAPTER SEVEN

The Long Boom

The "Golden Age" of Western capitalism

Many economic forecasters expected the world economy to slip
into crisis again after the war, after a brief period of boom as in
1919. It did not happen. What followed was the longest boom that
capitalism had ever known—what is often now called "the golden
age of capitalism", or in France, "the glorious thirty years". By the
1970s American economic output was three times the 1940 level;
German economic output was five times the (depressed) level of
1947; French output up fourfold. A thirteen-fold increase in industrial output turned Japan, still thought of as a poor country in
the 1940s, into the second largest Western[1] economy after the US.
And along with economic growth went rising real wages, virtually
full employment and welfare provision on a scale people had only
been able to dream of previously.

Conditions were very different in Asia, Africa and Latin
America—what became known as the "Third World" after the
Bandung conference of 1955. There massive poverty remained the
lot of the vast mass of people. But the European powers were
forced to relinquish their colonies, and increased per capita economic growth[2] created the expectation that eventually the
economically "less developed" countries would begin to catch up
with the most advanced.

It became the orthodoxy on both the right and much of the
left to proclaim that the contradictions in the system perceived
by Marx had been overcome. The key change, it was argued,
was that governments had learnt to intervene in the economy to
counteract tendencies to crisis along the lines urged in the 1930s
by John Maynard Keynes. All that was needed for the system to
work was for the existing state to disregard old free market orthodoxies and to intervene in economic life to raise the level of

161

spending on investment and consumption. This could be done either by changes in interest rates ("monetary measures") to encourage private investment, or through increasing government expenditure above its tax revenues ("fiscal measures"). "Deficit financing" of the latter sort would increase the demand for goods and so the level of employment. It would also pay for itself eventually through a "multiplier effect" (discovered by Keynes's Cambridge colleague Richard Kahn). The extra workers who got jobs because of government expenditures would spend their wages, so providing a market for the output of other workers, who in turn would spend their wages and provide still bigger markets. And as the economy expanded closer to its full employment level, the government's revenue from taxes on incomes and spending would rise, until it was enough to pay for the previous increase in expenditure.

These two measures were soon seen as the archetypal "Keynesian" tools[3] for getting full employment and accepted as essential for economic management by both Conservative and social democratic politicians in the 1940s, 1950s, 1960s and early 1970s. Keynes had, as we saw in the last chapter, expressed more radical notions at points, notably the contention that the very process of expanding capital investment led to a decline in the return on it—"the marginal efficiency of capital".[4] He had even gone so far as to urge the gradual "euthanasia" of the "rentier" who lives off dividends[5] and to argue that "a somewhat comprehensive socialisation of investment will prove the only means of securing an approximation to full employment".[6] But Keynes himself shied away from these more radical insights—"in practice he was very cautious indeed",[7] writes his ultra-moderate biographer Robert Skidelsky, and the version of Keynesianism[8] that hegemonised mainstream economics for the 30 years after the Second World War purged Keynes's theory of its radical elements. For this reason, the radical Keynesian Joan Robinson denounced it as "bastard Keynesianism".[9]

Mainstream economics believed in those years that it had the capacity to enable governments to do away with the crises that had plagued capitalism since the early 19th century. The capitalist system could now, the orthodoxy preached, deliver endless prosperity, rising living standards and a decline in the level of class struggle—providing governments accepted its diktats and avoided the "mistakes" of 1929-32.

John Strachey had been by far the best known Marxist writer on economics in Britain in the 1930s. His books, *The Nature of Capitalist Crisis*, *The Coming Struggle for Power* and *The Theory and Practice of Socialism* had taught Marxist economics to a whole generation of worker activists and young intellectuals, with the message that capitalism could not escape from recurring and ever deeper crises. Yet by 1956 he was arguing, in his book *Contemporary Capitalism*, that Keynes had been right and Marx wrong on the crucial question of whether the capitalist crisis could be reformed away.[10] Keynes's only mistake, Strachey held, was that he failed to see that the capitalists would have to be pressurised into accepting his remedies: "The Keynesian remedies...will be opposed by the capitalists certainly: but experience shows they can be imposed by the electorate".[11]

The belief that Keynes's ideas were responsible for the long boom persists today, with a widespread view on the left that the abandonment of those ideas is responsible for the crises of recent years. This is essentially the position put forward by the journalists Dan Atkinson and Larry Elliot in a series of books,[12] the *Observer* columnist Will Hutton[13] and the radical economic consultant Graham Turner.[14] A version of it is accepted by some Marxists. Gérard Duménil and Dominique Lévy ascribe the post-war growth to a "Keynesian" approach by industrial capital, in which accumulation was based on a "compromise" with working class organisations on the terrain of the welfare state.[15] David Harvey presents a picture of capitalism expanding on the basis of "a class compromise between capital and labour" in which "the state could focus on full employment, economic growth and the welfare of its citizens", while "fiscal or monetary policies usually dubbed 'Keynesian' were widely deployed to dampen business cycles and to ensure reasonably full employment".[16]

Yet the most amazing fact about the period in which Keynesianism reigned supreme as the official economic ideology was that the measures it proposed for warding off crises were not used. The economy expanded despite their absence until the 1960s in the US and the 1970s in Western Europe and Japan.

As R C O Matthews long ago pointed out, the economic expansion of the post-war years in Britain did not depend on the specific Keynesian "remedies" to recurrent crises of budget deficits or a higher level of government investment than in the pre-war years.[17] Meghnad Desai has noted, "In the USA Keynesian policies were slow to be officially adopted... They finally triumphed with the Kennedy-Johnson tax cut of 1964".[18] That was after the Great Boom had already lasted 15 years (25 years if you exclude the shortlived recession of the late 1940s). The same point is made for Germany by Ton Notermans: "Countercyclical demand management policies were only pursued in Germany... during the 1970s".[19] In so far as government intervention was used to determine the speed of the economy, it was to slow down booms, not to avert recessions, as with the "stop go" policies of British governments faced with balance of payments problems in the 1950s and 1960s. Michael Bleaney, re-analysing the figures used by Matthews and others, concludes that Keynesianism played little role in the West European long boom, and only a limited one in the US. And he notes that it was the big increase in US levels of military expenditure compared with the pre-war years that provided most of the "fiscal stimulus": "Largely because of much higher defence spending, total government spending on goods and services increased by nearly 9 percent of potential GNP".[20]

The explanation of the boom as a result of Keynesian policies is often combined with references to a "Fordist" period in which the great capitalist corporations accepted a compromise with workers based on wages high enough to buy a continually increasing amount of output. The French economist Michel Aglietta, for instance, has argued that "Fordism" regulated "private working class consumption" by "generalising the wage relation" to guarantee "the maintenance cycle of labour power".[21] So, for him and his "Regulation School" version of Marxism, Keynes is the prophet of Fordism, with Keynes's criticism of neoclassical economics and his notion of "effective demand" a partial recognition of the need for production and consumption to be integrated at a certain stage of capitalist development.

Certainly, one element in the dominant state interventionist ideology of the post-war decades was the contention that welfare provision could counterbalance cyclical ups and downs in the demand for consumer goods. The "supply side" need of capital to ensure the reproduction of labour power for it to exploit (which we have looked at in Chapter Five) seemed to coincide with "demand side" worries about keeping markets expanding. Promises to expand welfare provision also suited social democrat and Christian Democrat parties in Europe as a way of winning votes and luring workers away from the Communist parties to their left. Yet none of this is adequate to explain why the global economy should boom in the post-war years after slumping pre-war.

What is more, there was no conscious policy by the "Fordist" managers of mass production industries to opt for such a supposed "Keynesian" policy of raising real wages and welfare provision. As Robert Brenner and Mark Glick say, US capital never:

> resigned itself to the principle of maintaining labour's share or failed to fight tooth and nail to limit the degree to which wages kept up with the cost of living or with productivity. There was never anything resembling a generalised "social contract" on how revenue was to be divided between investment and consumption or between profits and wages.[22]

The reality was that as capitalism expanded in the post-war decades, the full employment that resulted forced employers and the state to pay much more attention than previously to reproducing labour power and deflecting working class discontent. Both the conventional Keynesian account and "Regulation" theory confuse causes with effects. In the process they fail to account for the most significant feature of the post-war decades: the rate of profit in the US was between 50 and 100 percent higher than in the four decades before the Second World War. And it more or less sustained that higher level until the late 1960s.[23] It was this which explained why capitalists kept investing on a scale sufficient to keep the economy booming without most states needing even to try using the "counter-cyclical measures" suggested by Keynes. But how were such high profit rates achieved and sustained alongside rapidly rising real wages?

Part of the answer lies in the impact of the slump and the war. Some firms had gone bankrupt in the slump. Much capital had been written off. Restructuring through crisis had begun to perform some of its old role of allowing capital to undertake renewed accumulation with a lower rate of profit. The destruction of the war provided further assistance. Vast amounts of investment which would otherwise have raised the ratio of investment to labour (and therefore profits) were instead used for military purposes. Shane Mage, for instance, estimated the combined effect of the crisis of the 1930s and the Second World War on the US economy: "Between 1930 and 1945 the capital stock of the US fell from 145 billion dollars to 120 billion dollars, a net disinvestment of some 20 percent".[24] Written off was an amount equal to a fifth of the pre-existing accumulated surplus value plus all the additional surplus value produced over those 15 years. Meanwhile, capitalists in the defeated states, Germany and Japan, emerged from the war with much of their capital destroyed. They had no choice but to write off much of the value of old investments as they began accumulation afresh, with a skilled labour force forced to accept low wages by the massive unemployment resulting from military devastation.

But these factors are not, in themselves, a sufficient explanation for the length and continuity of the boom. They do not explain why profit rates did not resume their downward slope once new productive investment came into effect. Had capitalism continued on its pre-war trajectory there would have been crises at least every ten years or so. Yet, although there were periodic dips in growth rates, sometimes described as "growth recessions", there was only one brief spell of falling output in the US (in 1949) and none in the other major industrial countries for more than a quarter of a century.

Attempts have been made to explain the boom as a result of rapid technological innovation, the waves of immigration of young workers in the 1950s and 1960s, or the cheapening of raw materials from the non-industrial countries. But such things had not been able to prevent cyclical crises previously. Technological innovation might have reduced the cost of each unit of new investment, but it would also have reduced the life span of old investments, so increasing deductions from profits due to depreciation costs; massive immigration to Britain from Ireland and to the US from Europe had characterised the 19th century without stopping pressures on profit rates; the cheapening of raw materials was in part caused by the way the boom itself encouraged capitalists to produce synthetic substitutes within the industrial economies (artificial fibres, plastics, etc).

There was, however, one new factor that could explain what was happening. There was an unprecedented level of peacetime arms spending. It had been only a little over 1 percent of GNP in the United States before the war. Yet post-war "disarmament" left it at 4 percent in 1948, and it then shot up with the onset of the Cold War to over 13 percent in 1950-53, remaining between five and seven times the level of the inter-war years throughout the 1950s and 1960s.

Capitalism in the 20th Century

The military consumed an enormous quantity of investible surplus value that would otherwise have gone into the productive economy—according to a calculation by Michael Kidron, an amount equal to 60 percent of US gross fixed capital formation. The immediate impact of such spending was to provide a market for the output of major industries:

> More than nine-tenths of the final demand for aircraft and parts was on government account, most of it military; as was nearly three-fifths of the demand for non-ferrous metals; over half the demand for chemicals and electronic goods; over one-third the demand for communication equipment and scientific instruments; and so on down the list of eighteen major industries one-tenth or more of whose final demand stemmed from governmental procurement.[25]

The role of military expenditure has been ignored by most mainstream Keynesian accounts of the post-war boom and by many Marxists. On both sides there has been a tendency to identify capitalism with the pure "free market" form it took for a brief period in Britain in the 19th century and to see the state and the military as extraneous to it. Missing has been any sense of the changes that had already begun to be analysed by Hilferding, Bukharin and Lenin, let alone the further transformations brought about through slump, war and the Cold War.

Some Marxists and a few Keynesians did, however, grasp one important impact of arms spending. It provided a market for the rest of the economy that was not affected by the ups and downs of the wider economy—a buffer that limited the downward movement of the economic cycle. So the American Marxists Paul Baran and Paul Sweezy could see arms spending as an important mechanism for absorbing an ever growing "surplus" and overcoming overproduction.[26] They could not, however, explain why taxation to pay for it did not have the effect of reducing demand elsewhere in the economy. And, as Michael Bleaney has pointed out, the military purchases of the US government could not have played a major direct role in boosting the European economies.[27]

The account of the impact of waste expenditure (see Chapter Five) on the dynamic of the wider economy provided by Kidron was able to deal with such problems, since its starting point was not "underconsumptionism" but the rate of profit. Arms expenditure, like "unproductive" expenditures, might be a deduction from profits in the short term, but in the long term it had the impact of reducing the funds available for further accumulation and so slowed the rise in the ratio of investment to the employed labour force (the "organic composition of capital").

Kidron's logic found empirical confirmation in what actually happened to the organic composition of capital. Its rise in the post-war decades in the US was much slower than in the pre-slump decades.[28] It was also much lower than that which occurred in post-war Europe, where the proportion of national output going into arms spending was considerably lower than in the US.[29]

Arms, accumulation and planning

The arms economies were not a result of a conscious strategy aimed at warding off slumps. They followed from the logic of imperialist competition in the Cold War era. But sections of capital certainly appreciated their effects in keeping the boom going. "Military-industrial complexes" emerged, drawing together the military and those in charge of the arms industries, which had a direct interest in pushing forward the inter-imperialist conflicts. They were able to unite the ruling class as a whole behind their policies not only because of fear of the rival power, but also because of the effect of arms budgets in sustaining accumulation.

John Kenneth Galbraith described in the 1960s the inter-relation between government expenditure and what he termed the "planning system" by which each large corporation planned its investments many years in advance:

> Although there is a widespread supposition to the contrary, this increase [in state expenditures]…has the strong approval of the businessmen of the planning system. The executive of the great corporation routinely opposes prodigality in government expenditure. But from his pleas for public economy defence expenditures are meticulously excluded.[30]

One effect of such expenditures was to allow the great corporations to undertake long-term planning of their own investments with the assurance that they would be able to make a profit on them and turn it into cash by selling their goods ("realising their

Capitalism in the 20th Century

surplus value", to use Marx's terminology). This changed their internal operations in ways which seemed to contradict the usual assumption about capitalist behaviour being motivated by short-term profit requirement and price competition for markets. Galbraith painted a picture of how the situation appeared:

> The market is superseded by vertical integration. The planning unit takes over the source of supply or the outlet; a transaction that is subject to bargaining over prices and amounts is thus replaced with a transfer within the planning unit... As viewed by the firm, elimination of a market converts an external negotiation and hence a partially or wholly uncontrollable decision to a matter for purely internal decision. Nothing, we shall see, better explains modern industrial policy—capital supply is the extreme case—than the desire to make highly strategic cost factors subject to wholly internal decisions. Markets can also be controlled. This consists in reducing or eliminating the independence of action of those to whom the planning unit sells or from whom it buys... At the same time the outward form of the market, including the process of buying and selling, remains formally intact.[31]

At a time when "the largest 200 manufacturing enterprises had two thirds of all assets used in manufacturing and more than three fifths of all sales, employment and net income",[32] this represented a huge section of the US economy in which most economic operations were not subject to the immediate vagaries of the market. There was competition between the giants, but it was to a large extent undertaken by means different to the old competition to sell goods more cheaply than one another. The giant firms learnt that they could ward off potential competitors by resorting to non-productive methods—the use of their wealth to get a tight grip over distribution outlets; the use of advertising to hype up their own products, regardless of their intrinsic merits; the systematic cultivation of well greased contacts with buyers from governmental bodies.

Galbraith thought this represented a fundamental change in the nature of capitalism itself. And Marxists who defined capitalism simply in terms of the "free market" competition between rival private capitalists could easily come to the same conclusion, since the huge area of production internal to the great corporations was not directly subject to the law of value. Extreme variations in the degree of "x-efficiency"—the internal efficiency of companies—showed how far many differed from the capitalist ideal. And capital did not automatically move under the impact of market forces out of sectors with big fixed investments, a high organic composition of capital and a low rate of profit, as a simplistic reading of *Capital* might suggest. Whether it did so or not depended on the decisions of managers who might decide to sacrifice short-term profitability for long-term growth within markets over which they already had a stranglehold. If the law of value continued to operate it was in the long term, since eventually corporations would not be able to grow and to keep rivals and newcomers to the industry at bay unless they continued to get enough surplus value to make massive new investments. But often they would only discover whether they had done so once the long boom itself came to an abrupt end.

The other advanced capitalisms

The picture so far has been of the US economy in the post-war boom. It was responsible for approaching half of total world output at the end of the war, and its dynamic determined to a great extent what happened elsewhere. But the big European economies, with substantial but lower levels of arms spending, showed many of the same features. In Britain and to a lesser extent France, great investments in arms industries had the effect of drawing the rest of the economy forward, counteracting some of the pressures for the organic composition to rise and the rate of profit to fall, and permitting continual economic expansion—all without resort to Keynesian measures.

In Germany armaments were less important. But the role of the government remained important. One Marxist account tells how:

> far more than in any other capitalist country the bourgeoisie in the Federal Republic made use of the state apparatuses and the monetary and fiscal system to force capital accumulation by means of favourable depreciation rates, credits for reconstruction at favourable rates of interest and finance for investment. All this took place in contradiction to the official neoliberal economic theory...[33]

In Japan state capitalism advanced further in its influence over civilian industry than almost anywhere else in the Western world—despite a low level of direct state ownership. The state and the largest private firms worked together to ensure that that portion of the national income that had gone into arms before 1945 now went into productive investment:

> The motive force for rapid growth was fixed investment in plant and equipment. Private fixed investment grew from 7.8 percent of GNP in 1946 to 21.9 percent in 1961.[34]

When imported raw materials were in short supply in the late 1940s and the 1950s the government took charge of their allocation to industries it thought would best contribute to the growth of the economy, to the building up of key industries like coal mining, iron and steel and the expansion of exports.

The Ministry of International Trade and Industry (MITI) issued "guidelines" to industry which it ignored at its peril. The giant firms that had accepted the dictates of the war economy before August 1945 as essential to military expansion now accepted the dictates of MITI as essential to peaceful economic expansion:

> Japanese entrepreneurs are vigorous in investing. They will not confine their fixed investment within the limit of gross profits or internal accumulation, unlike the case of entrepreneurs in other advanced countries. Even if the fixed investment is over and above their gross profits, the enterprise will undertake investment so long as bank finance is available.[35]

In other words, the heads of big business and the state worked together to ensure the growth of Japanese national capitalism by mobilising the whole mass of surplus value and directing it towards "strategic" sectors, regardless of considerations of short-term profitability. What other state capitals did with military considerations uppermost, Japanese state capitalism did in the interests of overseas market competition. Exports played a very important role in driving the economy forwards. And that meant that Japanese growth was ultimately dependent on the US arms economy. As Robert Brenner shows in a highly empirical study:

> German and Japanese manufacturers derived much of their dynamism by means of appropriating large segments of the fast-growing world market from the US and UK, while beginning

to invade the US domestic market. This redistribution of market share—the filling of orders (demand) by German and Japanese manufacturers that had formerly been supplied by US producers—gave a powerful boost to their investment and output.[36]

It was not "social compromise" and the "welfare state" that produced the long boom and the "golden age". Rather they were all by-products of militarised state capitalism. Prosperity rested on the cone of the H-bomb.[37]

Labour power in the Great Boom

Throughout the first post-war decades unemployment was at levels known previously only during brief boom periods. In the US unemployment was less than 3 percent in the early 1950s; in Britain it hovered between 1.5 and 2 percent; in West Germany a high level of unemployment caused by the economic dislocation of the early post-war years fell to 4 percent in 1957 and a mere 1 percent in 1960.

So the problem for industrialised capitalist states was not coping with unemployment, but its opposite—ensuring that employment grew at sufficient speed to feed capital's seemingly insatiable appetite for labour power. The US employed workforce rose by 60 percent between 1940 and 1970. Such expansion demanded completely new supplies of labour power. Whether politicians and government administrators liked it or not, the state could not leave supplying the key raw material for economic or military competition, labour, to the vagaries of a "free" labour market. The state had to supplement—and even partially *supplant*—the wages system with services and subsidies provided by itself on a much greater scale than previously.

One answer to the shortage of labour power lay in reducing the agricultural workforce still more, with state-sponsored amalgamations of small farms—an approach followed in much of Western Europe. Another lay in encouraging massive emigration of people from less developed countries to the cities of the industrial countries (from Turkey, Eastern and Southern Europe to Germany; from Yugoslavia, Portugal, Spain and Algeria to France; from the West Indies and the Indian subcontinent to Britain; from Puerto Rico to the US). A third solution—again adopted almost everywhere—was the drawing of married women into paid employment. Yet each of the ways of enlarging the labour force created new problems for capital and the state.

Squeezing labour from agriculture could work only if resources were put into agriculture in order to increase its productivity. This could be very expensive. But the alternative was that the provision of food for the growing urban population and raw materials for industry would suffer, creating working class discontent and bottlenecks in accumulation. And eventually there was little in the way of spare labour power left in the countryside to provide for the needs of industry as the peasantry shrank in numbers.

Migration from the Third World was a very cheap way of getting labour power. The advanced country had to bear none of the costs of rearing and educating this part of its labour force—effectively, it was getting a subsidy from the immigrant workers' country of origin.[38] The new workforce was usually younger than the "native" workforce, and demanded less in the way of health care, old age pensions and so on. And its members were usually more prepared to tolerate low wages, harsh working conditions, rigid discipline and so on—in short, to be super-exploited. The pool from which this new labour came was potentially limitless.

Yet there were practical limits. As migrant workers became accustomed to living and working in their new home, they demanded conditions closer to those of established workers; they wanted decent accommodation and welfare benefits. The state had either to increase its expenditure on these things—or to see growing social tensions that could lead to either intensified class struggles (to a considerable extent the revolt in France in 1968 was a revolt of such new workers) or to "racial" clashes between old established and newer workers. Unable to afford the social expenditure needed to head off such sources of social instability—and eager to deflect discontent away from itself—the state usually reacted by imposing controls on further immigration.

The wholesale entry of married women into the workforce also demanded a certain level of investment by the state. Means had to be found to ensure that it did not lead to the neglect of child rearing—the socialisation of the next generation of workers—or a breakdown in the provision of food, shelter and clothing for the male workforce. Many of these means could be provided, at relatively low cost, with the application of new technology. The refrigerator, washing machine and vacuum cleaner, the replacement of the coal fire by electricity, gas or oil heating, the popularisation of frozen foods, the spread of fast food outlets, even the television set—all had the effect of reducing the amount of effort needed to ensure the reproduction of both present and future labour power. And they usually cost not a penny to the state or capital, being paid for by the family out of the enlarged income it received as the wife took up paid employment. Caring for young children while both their parents worked created greater difficulties, since the provision of nursery facilities could be costly for the state—even if these costs too could often be recouped from the wage of the working wife.

So all the methods of expanding the labour force could work, up to a certain point—but beyond that they tended to imply quite considerable overhead costs. Welfare costs could be borne while the system was expanding rapidly. The "insurance" principle ensured, as we saw in Chapter Five, that some sections of the working class paid for welfare provision to other sections. The extra cost amounted to only 2 or 3 percent of GNP in Western Europe, while in the US the state made a small surplus.[39] But the costs would become a burden once the Great Boom collapsed.

There was another solution available to the labour shortage. But it was even more expensive. It was to increase state expenditure on the reproduction of the labour force, so as to increase the average level of skill. In all the advanced countries there was a considerable increase in educational expenditures during the Great Boom—particularly in the upper grades of secondary education and in higher education.[40]

Finally, there was a third area of expansion of state expenditures designed to increase productivity—expenditures designed to provide a feeling of security for employed workers. Into this category fell old age pensions and unemployment benefits. As James O'Connor noted, "The primary purpose is to create a sense of economic security within the ranks of employed workers and thereby raise morale and reinforce discipline".[41] Hence in many countries in the late 1960s wage-related unemployment benefits and redundancy payments were introduced. They were the other side of the "shake-out" of labour from older industries.

This "socialisation" of labour costs had some important consequences for the system as a whole. Under conditions of acute labour shortage, the national capitalist state had to tend and care for labour power as well as exploit it if productivity was to match international levels. But this meant that workers had some

Capitalism in the 20th Century

possibilities of being able to sustain themselves without selling their labour power. There was a partial negation of the character of free labour—but only a *partial* negation, since the state applied all sorts of pressures to keep people in the labour market.

Yet even this limited "negation" of the free labour market was a burden that put up the overheads of each national capital. As such they exerted a downward pressure on the rate of return on the total national investment. For a long period this did not seem to matter. Other factors were at work protecting the rate of profit. But once the upward dynamic of the boom began to weaken, the costs of welfare became a crucial problem. The two functions—of increasing productivity *and* buying consent—were no longer complementary. Capital had to try to reduce the cost of maintaining and increasing productivity, even if doing so upset its old mechanisms for keeping control over the working class. This was to be an important factor shaping class struggle once the long boom faltered.

The Eastern bloc

The Western economies and Japan were not the only ones to achieve rapid growth rates during the post-war decades. So too did the USSR and the countries it dominated in Eastern Europe. Soviet electricity output grew by 500 percent between 1950 and 1966, steel output by just under 250 percent, oil output by 600 percent, tractor output by 200 percent, fabric output by 100 percent, shoe output by 100 percent, the housing stock by 100 percent.[42] By the mid-1970s the same consumer goods which had transformed people's lives in Western Europe and North America—the television set, the refrigerator, the washing machine—were also making their appearance in Soviet and East European homes, even if more slowly.[43] Since the collapse of the Eastern bloc in 1989-91 it has usually been forgotten that in the 1950s and 1960s even by many Western opponents of the USSR took it for granted that its growth rate was higher than regimes elsewhere in the world had achieved. A trenchant critic of the system, Alec Nove could write, "The success of the Soviet Union... in making itself the world's second industrial and military power is indisputable".[44]

But simply growing fast did not overcome the external pressures for more growth, since even after decades of industrialisation the

Soviet economy was still less than half the size of its then main military competitor, the US. Indeed, in some ways the pressures grew greater. At the beginning of industrialisation, there were enormous reserves of labour that could be released for industry from agriculture. That meant it was not of any great concern to those at the top of the bureaucracy if much of this labour was used wastefully. It started to matter as the countryside began to empty of young men—leaving much of the agricultural production needed to feed the cities to be done by diminishing numbers of ageing people. The slave labour camps were run down soon after Stalin's death in 1953, in part for political reasons but also to release inefficient slave labour for efficient exploitation as wage labour. It was an indication that the phase of "primitive accumulation" was at an end. There was recurrent talk within official circles from that time onwards about economic "reform". During one such phase, in 1970, the leader Leonid Brezhnev spelt out the rationale:

> Comrade Brezhnev dwelt on the question of the economic competition between the two world systems. "This competition takes different forms," he said. "In many cases we are coping successfully with the task of overtaking and outdistancing the capitalist countries in the production of certain types of output…but the fundamental question is not only how much you produce but also at what cost, with what outlays of labour… It is in this field that the centre of gravity between the two systems lies in our time".[45]

This was the same logic of competitive accumulation that operated on the sometimes huge state sector of the Western industrial capitalisms—or, for that matter, on the giant corporations described by Galbraith. The organisation of production inside the USSR might involve the putting together of different use values (so much labour, so many physically distinct raw materials, such and such a particular sort of machine) to produce further use values. But what mattered to the ruling bureaucracy was how these use values measured up to the similar conglomerations of use values produced inside the great corporations of the West. And that meant comparing the amounts of labour used in the USSR to the labour used in the Western corporations. Or, to put it in Marx's terms, production within the USSR was subject to the law of value operating on the global scale.[46]

Capitalism in the 20th Century

One of the illusions created by the rapid non-stop growth of the USSR was that it proceeded smoothly and rationally according to the various Five Year Plans, in contrast with the ups and downs in the West. But the relentless drive to accumulate had as a necessary by-product disorganisation, chaos and waste in whole areas of production. At the beginning of every "plan" vast new industrial projects would begin to be constructed. But after a while it would become clear that they could not all be finished. Some (usually catering for people's consumption needs) would be "frozen", while the resources for them were diverted elsewhere (to the production of means of production). This meant a continual chopping and changing of the goods resources were expected to produce; sudden pressure on people to produce more of one product and less of another; concealment by people at every level in the production process of the resources at their disposal in case they were suddenly pressed to produce more; massive amounts of waste as some of the things contained in the plans were produced, but not other things necessary for their use (such as the case in the 1980s when vast amounts of fertiliser were wasted because one of the frozen projects was the building of the factory to provide the bags for packing the fertiliser).[47]

Since the collapse of the Soviet Union it has become habitual on both the left and the right to blame all this simply on bureaucratic irrationality, without acknowledging its similarity to the irrationality of the managerial despotism within Western enterprises—and the common roots of both in the subordination of human labour to competitive accumulation, that is, to the self-expansion of capital. Yet it was possible to trace each of the forms of irrationality within the Soviet economy back to overinvestment—just as it is with managerial irrationality within Western corporations.

There was not only waste in the Soviet-type economies. There was also unevenness in growth over time, as in the West. Studies in the 1960s, mainly by Eastern European economists, revealed the presence of cyclical ups and downs in economies modelled on the USSR. The Czechoslovaks Josef Goldman and Karel Korba told in 1968 how:

Analysis of the dynamics of industrial production in Czechoslovakia, the German Democratic Republic and Hungary supplies an interesting picture. The rate of growth shows relatively regular fluctuations... These fluctuations are even more pronounced if analysis is confined to producer goods.[48]

The Yugoslav Branko Horvat was able to publish a book called *Business Cycles in Yugoslavia*[49] which pointed out that even before the market reforms of 1968 the Yugoslav economy was "significantly more unstable" than ten other economies that were cited, "including the United States". A Western academic showed that such unevenness was already visible in the Soviet Union from the time of the first Five Year plan onwards.[50]

The pattern of unevenness showed great similarities with the Western capitalist states during the long boom. Its origin lay in the dynamics of competitive accumulation. As we saw in Chapter Three, at a certain point in any boom the competitive drive of capitalists to invest leads to a drying up of existing supplies of raw materials, labour and loanable capital (ie non-invested surplus value). The prices of all these things—commodity prices, money wages and interest rates—begin to rise until the least profitable firms suddenly find they are operating at a loss. Some go out of business. Others survive, but only by abandoning planned investments and closing down factories. Their actions in turn destroy markets for other capitals, forcing them to abandon investments and close down factories. The "excess demand" of the boom gives rise to the overproduction of the slump. The secret of the Western long boom of the 1940s, 1950s and 1960s lay in the way the national state could reduce the pressures leading to over-accumulation (by diverting a portion of capital into non-productive military channels); take direct action to try to maintain a high rate of exploitation (through wage controls); intervene to slow down the boom before it led key firms to become unprofitable; and maintain a minimum guaranteed level of demand through military orders. The state monopoly capitalist arms economy was not able to do away with the cyclical pattern of capitalist accumulation. Specifically, it could not stop competitive pressures causing capitalists to tend to expand production during upturns in the economy on a scale which exceeded the available resources. But it was able to prevent such spells of "over-accumulation" leading to slumps of the pre-Second World War sort.

Something of the same pattern existed in the Soviet-type economies. Bottlenecks arose throughout the economy, threatening the closure of vast sectors of production through shortages of inputs. Output never rose nearly as rapidly as planned. The monetary funds paid out by enterprises for materials and labour exceeded the output of the economy, giving rise to inflationary pressures which found direct expression as price rises or "hidden" expression as acute shortages of goods in the shops.

Left to itself, over-rapid accumulation by certain key enterprises would soon have absorbed the resources many enterprises depended on to keep operating at existing levels, leading to the wholesale closure of their plants and the destruction of the markets for the output of other enterprises. It would have become a crisis of overproduction of commodities. But as in the West in the long boom, the state stepped in to try and pre-empt this by "cooling down" the economy. It ordered enterprises to "freeze" certain investments and to divert resources to others. This involved factories suddenly switching from one sort of output to another. The myth of the pre-planning of production gave way to the reality of after the event, "a posteriori", allocation, with a repeated shifting of inputs and outputs. One plan target which always suffered in the process was that for consumer goods production. The result was to increase still further the discrepancy between the funds laid out by enterprises on wages and the goods available for these wages to buy—to increase open or hidden inflation.

Deep social and political crises in 1953 (East Germany), 1956 (Poland and Hungary), 1968 (Czechoslovakia) and 1970-71 (Poland again) showed how the tensions this produced could find sudden expression. But so long as it was possible to restore growth rates, the tensions could be reduced, usually by a combination of repression on the one hand and concessions over living standards on the other. Such remedies hid temporarily the underlying pressures towards crisis

Those who failed to analyse the system in terms of competitive accumulation failed to see this. This was true of the Western pro-capitalist theorists of "totalitarianism". One can search their writings of the 1950s and 1960s in vain for some hints that Russian type systems contained inbuilt economic contradictions. It was also true of most of those who saw them as some sort of socialist or workers' states. They were continually over-optimistic about the economic prospects—in their own way mirroring the illusions of the Western Keynesians.

Arms, profits and of the Cold War

The arms budgets of the great powers were central to their economic development. But their roots were not narrowly economic. They flowed from a new struggle to divide and redivide the world between the main victors of the Second World War, the US and the USSR—the Cold War.

The US had aspirations for its industries, the most advanced and productive in the world, to penetrate the whole world economy through "free trade". The Western European powers, exhausted by the war, were in no position to challenge it directly (although British politicians often expressed a private desire to do so). Russia's rulers were in a different situation. The war's end left them dominating virtually the whole of northern Eurasia, from the borders of Western Europe right through to the Pacific. With levels of industrial productivity less than half those of the US, they were in no position to sustain themselves in economic competition through free trade. But they could contest the US attempt at global hegemony by blocking its access to the economies under their control—not just the territory of the old Russian Empire, but also the countries of Eastern Europe which they subordinated to their military-industrial goals. The US, for its part, rushed to cement its hegemony over Western Europe through financing pro-American Christian Democrat and Social Democrat political parties, the Marshall Plan for reviving European industry within parameters favourable to US interests, and the creation of the NATO military alliance and setting up US bases in Western Europe.

The pattern was laid for the next 40 years, of each of the two great powers reaching out to draw as much of the world as possible into its sphere of influence so as to gain a strategic advantage over the other. They fought a bloody war over control of the Korean peninsula, not because of the little wealth it then possessed, but because of the strategic implications for the whole of the East Asian and Pacific region. Each tried over the following decades to extend its sphere of influence by giving aid and arms to states which fell out with its rival.

The Cold War conflict could not be explained by economics as often understood, in terms simply of profit and loss accounting. The armaments bills of both great powers soon exceeded anything their rulers could hope to gain from the increased exploitation of the lesser powers under their control. At no stage in the 1940s or 1950s did total US overseas investment (let alone the much smaller return on that investment) exceed US spending on arms. Even in the period of "disarmament" prior to the outbreak of the Korean War "military expenditure totalled something like $15 billion a year. Thus it was 25 times as high as the sum of private capital exports".[51] By 1980 total expenditure on "defence" had risen to around $200 billion—less now than total overseas investment of $500 billion, but still substantially more than the profits that could possibly accrue from that investment.

The picture for the USSR was somewhat similar. In the years 1945-50 it pillaged Eastern Europe, removing plant and equipment wholesale from East Germany and Romania, and forced the region as a whole to accept prices below world market levels for goods going to the USSR proper.[52] But even in that period the economic gains from this must have been substantially less than the escalation of the USSR's arms budget once the Cold War had well and truly begun. And from 1955 onwards fear of rebellion in Eastern Europe led the Soviet government to relax the direct economic pressure on its satellites.

The imperialism which necessitated arms spending was not that of a single empire in which a few "finance capitalists" at the centre made huge super-profits by holding billions of people down. Rather it was the imperialism of rival empires, in which the combined capitalists of each ruling class had to divert funds from productive investments to military expenditure in order to ensure that they hung on to what they already possessed.

The calculation in both Washington and Moscow was simple. To relax the level of military spending was to risk losing strategic superiority to the rival imperialism, enabling it to extend its sphere of dominance. So the Russians lived in fear of an attempted US "rollback" of Eastern Europe, which would have broken these economies from the USSR's grasp, leading in turn to the possibility of an unravelling of the ties which bound the other constituent parts of the USSR to its Russian centre (something that did in fact happen eventually with the great economic and political crisis that shook the whole Eastern bloc in the years 1989 to 1991). At the same time, the US feared for its hegemony. As one US spokesman put it at the time of the Korean War, "Were either of the two critical areas on the borders of the

Communist world to be overrun—Western Europe or Asia—the rest of the free world would be immensely weakened...in economic and military strength..."[53]

It was necessary, in other words, to turn vast amounts of value into means of destruction—not in order to obtain more value but to hold onto that already possessed. Such was the logic of capitalist competition applied to the relations between states. So the Cold War amounted to a new inter-imperialist conflict of the sort described by Bukharin, and it soon overshadowed the old imperialist conflicts between the West European powers.

Decolonisation and developmentalism in the Global South

Eighty five percent of humanity lived outside the advanced industrial countries. Their experience of the "golden age" was very far from golden. The great majority still lived in the countryside, and there was little change in the poverty that plagued their daily lives.

One important political change did, however, take place. The West European powers were forced, bit by bit, to abandon direct colonial rule, a process starting with a weakened Britain ending its 190 year old empire in India in 1947 and ending with Portugal handing over power to liberation movements in Africa in 1975. The US replaced Western European influence in some regions. It took control of South Vietnam when the French withdrew in 1954—until it too was forced to withdraw after the most bitter of wars in the mid-1970s. It became the dominant influence in most of the Middle East and parts of Africa. But, like the European powers, it retreated from formal colonisation, granting independence to the Philippines and keeping direct control only over Puerto Rico.

This retreat from direct colonisation had as a direct corollary the end of the old clashes between the Western powers over the partitioning of the rest of the world. The drive to war between them seemed to have gone once and for all. It was also accompanied, as we have seen, by something else unexpected by the classic theories of imperialism—losing their colonies did not stop Western economies participating in the long boom and conceding regular rises in living standards to their workers. And the advanced countries without any colonies—West Germany, Japan and Italy—had the economies which expanded fastest of all. Meanwhile, for the first two post-war decades, exports of capital stayed down at the very low levels they had sunk to in the great slump of the 1930s. As Mike Kidron pointed out in 1962:

> Even in Britain...the significance of capital exports has declined tremendously: latterly they have run at about 2 percent of gross national product compared with 8 percent in the period before World War One; they now absorb less than 10 percent of savings compared with some 50 percent before; and returns on foreign investment have been running at slightly over 2 percent of national income compared with...10 percent in 1914.[54]

The foreign investment that did take place was decreasingly directed towards the less industrialised parts of the world: "The concentration of activity is increasingly within the developed world, leaving all but a few developing countries outside the reach of the new dynamism".[55]

There was also a shift in the demand for Third World products. Raw materials from agricultural countries had been indispensable for industrial production in the West before the First World War, and colonial control was an important way for industrialised countries to ensure their own supplies and block access to their rivals. But now there were synthetic substitutes for most raw materials—artificial fertilisers, synthetic rubber, rayon, nylon, plastics. A parallel transformation of agriculture in Western Europe and North America reduced food imports from the rest of the world. By the late 1950s withdrawal from colonies in Africa and Asia was no longer the threat it would once have been to the industrialists of the European countries. Companies which had made their fortunes from plantations and mines of the Global South began to diversify their investments into new lines of business.

There was one great exception to this picture—oil. Here was the raw material of raw materials, the ingredient for manufacturing plastics, synthetic rubber and artificial fibres, as well as providing for massively expanding energy needs and propelling the ever greater proliferation of motor vehicles, tanks and aircraft. And the supplies of it were increasingly to be found outside Europe and North America. By the mid-1970s Saudi Arabia, Iraq, Iran, Kuwait, and the petty sheikhdoms around the Arabian Peninsula were the countries that mattered—as was shown by the temporary interruption of supplies during the Arab-Israeli war of 1973. It was not an accident that the one version of old style colonialism that continued to get untrammelled support from all the Western states was the settler state of Israel—fostered in its early years as a "Jewish homeland" by British imperialism, armed for its seizure of 78 percent of Palestine in 1948 by the US and the USSR, allied with Britain and France in their attack on Egypt in 1956, and backed wholeheartedly by the US in the aggression that gave it control of the rest of Palestine in June 1967.[56]

Indigenous governments and capitalist development

The dismantling of the European colonial empires was a fact of immense importance for something like half the world's people who had lived under their thumb. It also raised very important questions for those who had, in one way or another, fought against the hold of those empires. What happened to imperialism—and the fight against it—if empires no longer existed?

The reaction of many social democrats and liberals in the West was to say that imperialism no longer existed. This was, for instance, the conclusion drawn by John Strachey. In *End of Empire* (1959) he argued that rising living standards meant businesses no longer needed colonies to absorb the surplus and prevent overproduction. In effect, he was saying that Hobson's alternative to imperialism, a reflation of the domestic economy, had prevailed and solved the system's problems.

An important section of the left rejected such reasoning. They could see that the former colonial countries were still plagued by poverty and hunger—and that the Western firms that had benefited from empire remained entrenched in them. What is more, the end of the European empires was not the end to the violence inflicted on the peoples of Third World, as the US state picked up the cudgel of the departing Europeans.

Yet rejection of facile talk about an end to imperialism was often accompanied by quotes, parrot fashion, from Lenin's 1916 analysis without recognising the changes that had occurred since it was written. His insistence that the great Western powers were driven to divide and redivide the world between them through direct colonial rule hardly fitted a situation in which colonies had gained independence. The response of most of the left was quietly to redefine imperialism to mean simply the exploitation of the Third World by Western capitalist classes, dropping the drive towards war between imperialist powers so central to Lenin's theory for what was in reality a version of Kautsky's ultra-imperialism. At the same time they simply replaced talk of colonialism with talk of "neo-colonies" or "semi-colonies".

Lenin had written of "semi-colonies". For him these were places like China at the time of the First World War, where "independence" concealed continued political subordination to foreign armed forces in partial occupation of the country. There were some places where things did seem like this after the end of direct colonial control in the 1950s and 1960s. In many cases the departing colonial administrations were able to ensure that their place was taken by their own creatures, with enormous continuity in the personnel of the state, especially when it came to key positions in the armed forces. So, for instance, France had granted "independence" to huge areas of West and Central Africa by handing power to people who continued, as in the past, to work with French companies, use the French currency—and periodically invite French troops in to maintain "order".

But in some of the most important cases independence did mean independence. Governments proceeded not only to take seats in the United Nations and set up embassies all over the world. They also intervened in the economy, nationalising colonial companies, implementing land reforms, embarking on schemes of industrialisation inspired by the preaching of theorists of economic development or often by Stalin's Russia. Such things were undertaken with varying degrees of success or failure in India, Egypt, Syria, Iraq, Algeria, Indonesia, Ghana, Equatorial Guinea, Angola and South Korea, as well as by the more radical regimes of China, Cuba and Vietnam. Over time even some of the "docile" ex-colonial regimes began to follow the same path. This was true, for instance, of the Malaysian regime,[57] of the Shah's regime in Iran in the 1960s and early 1970s, and of the Taiwanese regime. Even the dictator Mobutu, brought to power with the help of the CIA in Congo-Zaire in 1965, nationalised the mighty Union Miniere de Haut Katanga mining corporation along with 70 percent of export earnings three years later.

To call regimes like Abdul Nasser's Egypt or Jawaharlal Nehru's India "neo-colonial" or "semi-colonial" was a travesty—as it was with "populist" regimes in Latin America or the Fianna Fail governments in Ireland. Attempts were made in each case to establish not only independent political entities, but also independent centres of capital accumulation. These still operated within a world dominated by the much stronger capitalisms of the advanced countries, but they were by no means mere playthings of them.

A new "developmentalist" orthodoxy pointed the means by which such economies were meant to close the gap with the advanced industrial nations. It held that capitalist market mechanisms could not achieve that goal. As the staff of the World Bank later recalled of "the dominant paradigm at that time":

> It was assumed that in the early stages of development markets could not be relied upon, and that the state would be able to direct the development process… The success of state planning in achieving industrialisation in the Soviet Union (for so it was perceived) greatly influenced policy makers. The major development institutions (including the World Bank) supported these views with various degrees of enthusiasm.[58]

Just as Keynesianism was dominant within bourgeois economics in the advanced countries at the time, so statist, "import substitutionist", doctrines were hegemonic when it came to the Third World. The main proponent of these in the 1940s and 1950s was the very influential United Nations Economic Commission for Latin America, directed by the Argentinian economist Raoul Prebisch. It argued that development could only take place if the state intervened to block imports to foster the growth of new local industries,[59] since otherwise "dependence" on the advanced capitalist economies would prevent industrialisation."[60]

More radical versions of such "dependency theory" dominated much of the left worldwide in the 1960s. The writings of Paul Baran (especially *The Political Economy of Growth*) and Andre Gunder Frank (who talked of the "the development of underdevelopment")[61] dominated most Marxist thinking on the subject (even though Gunder Frank did not see himself as Marxist).[62] Baran wrote that:

> Far from serving as an engine of economic expansion, of technological progress and social change, the capitalist order in these countries has represented a framework for economic stagnation, for archaic technology and for social backwardness.[63]

Capitalism in the 20th Century

Adding:

> The establishment of a socialist planned economy is the essential, indeed indispensable, condition for the attainment of economic and social progress in underdeveloped countries.[64]

Gunder Frank was just as adamant:

> No country which has been tied to the metropolis as a satellite through incorporation in the world capitalist system has achieved the rank of an economically developed country except by finally abandoning the capitalist system.[65]

"Socialism" for Baran and "breaking with capitalism" for Gunder Frank meant following the model of Stalinist Russia.[66]

The "dependency" argument, whether in its mainstream or radical form, was a weak one. It assumed that capitalists from the advanced countries who invested in the Third World would deliberately choose not to build up industry even when it would have been profitable. This did not fit the facts. There was considerable foreign finance of industrial development in Tsarist Russia, Argentina and the British dominions before the First World War. Nor did Western states at all times use their power to prevent industrialisation. Sometimes they did and sometimes they did not. Finally, a ruling class of one country which depends on bigger capitalist countries for much of its trade and investment does not completely lose its ability to forge an independent path of capital accumulation. The European economies, for instance, have long been to a high degree dependent on what happens in the US economy without the European ruling classes simply becoming American puppets.

So pervasive was the view that "capitalism means underdevelopment" that people read it back into some of the Marxist classics. Baran quoted Lenin to back up his case, while even someone as perceptive as Nigel Harris could ascribe such views to "the Bolsheviks in 1917".[67]

Lenin's writings on imperialism had in fact put forward a completely different view, as did Leon Trotsky's writings of the late 1920s. Lenin wrote that the export of capital "accelerates the development of capitalism in the countries to which it is exported",[68] while Trotsky wrote that capitalism "equalises the cultural and economic development of the most advanced and most backward countries",[69] even if as it did so "developing some parts of the world economy while hampering and throwing back the development of others".[70]

What mainstream dependency theory did do for a period was provide an ideological justification for methods which enabled the rulers of some politically independent states to achieve impressive levels of accumulation, even if only for a period. Argentina's rate of economic growth through the 1950s and 1960s was comparable with that of Italy[71] and by the early 1970s a third of its workforce was in industry, with only 13 percent on the land.[72] Brazil's 9 percent growth rate was one of the highest in the world[73] and by the mid-1980s the *Economist* could refer to Sao Paulo as "a Detroit in the making".[74] South Korea experienced rapid economic growth of about 8 percent a year after a general, Park Chung Hee, seized power in 1961 and forced the big firms (or *chaebols*) to work within a framework established by the state and embarked on state capitalist industrialisation.

China, where state control of the economy came closest to the Russian model endorsed by the radical dependency theorists, had an economic growth rate no higher than these figures once it had completed the first short stage of economic recovery from 20 years of civil war and Japanese invasion. The imposition of plans which diverted resources towards new heavy industries—steel, cement, electricity—in a very poor, overwhelmingly agricultural country like the China of the early 1950s meant squeezing the living standards of the mass of the population. What the peasants had gained through land reform in the previous decade, they now lost through rigorously enforced taxation of their output. Then came the ultimately disastrous attempt at collectivisation through so-called People's Communes, in an attempt to bring about a "Great Leap Forward" in economic development. The leap cut total agricultural output, led to famine in vast areas of the countryside and had to be abandoned. Much of the new industry was far from efficient. The growth of heavy industry out of all proportion to what was happening in the rest of the economy led to acute shortages of inputs needed to keep plants running, and to the production of other goods which had no immediate use. There were massive swings between spells of fast industrial expansion and spells of near stagnation, and many of the grandiose new giant plants were only able to work at a fraction of their capacity.

There was usually growth even in countries that were not as successful as Brazil and South Korea. The manufacturing output

Capitalism in the 20th Century

in India grew by 5.3 percent a year from 1950 to 1981, and agricultural output by 2.3 percent, even if there was continual disappointment at the economy's inability to exceed a "Hindu" growth rate of 4 percent. Sub-Saharan Africa had "per capita growth rates of around 2 percent in the early 1960s" which "rose to nearly 5 percent by the end of that decade".[75] Egypt, whose leader Abdul Nasser nationalised almost all of industry, grew about 6 percent per year through the first half of the 1960s. Such outcomes in terms of levels of economic growth were enough to convince one "revisionist" Marxist, Bill Warren, to come to the conclusion in the early 1970s that most of the rest of the left were wrong. Countries in the Third World could catch up with the West without breaking with capitalism:

> The prospects for successful capitalist economic development (implying industrialisation) of a significant number of major underdeveloped countries are quite good... Substantial progress in capitalist industrialisation has already been achieved... In so far as there are obstacles to this development, they originate not in current imperialist-Third World relationships, but almost entirely from the internal contradictions of the Third World itself... The imperialist countries' policies and their overall impact on the Third World actually favour its industrialisation...[76]

He provided figures showing the real per capita economic growth that was in fact happening. In challenging the assumption of the radical version of dependency theory he was on strong ground. So too was he when he made the point that if the left saw its main priority as supporting industrialising regimes as "anti-imperialist" it could "find itself directly supporting bourgeois regimes which, as in Peru and Egypt, exploit and oppress workers and peasants while employing anti-imperialist rhetoric".[77]

But lacking from his analysis was any real accounting for the enormous unevenness between Third World countries, even though his own figures showed that per capita annual growth in two of the most populous countries, India and Indonesia, was only 1.2 percent and 1 percent (compared to 6.8 percent for South Korea, 4.9 percent for Thailand and 7.1 percent for Zambia). He also failed to see that rapid capitalist development was not necessarily smooth and uninterrupted through time:

Private investment in the Third World is increasingly creating the conditions for the disappearance of imperialism as a system of economic inequality between nations of the capitalist world system, and...there are no limits, in principle, to this process.[78]

This led him to make a prediction that would soon be put to the test—and proved dramatically wrong:

As for future prospects, the World Bank's view is that the majority of countries in the 1970s will, as in the 1960s, remain free of debt servicing problems... The first three years of the 1970s strongly suggest that this will be the case.[79]

Warren had taken the crude account by Gunder Frank and Baran that had maintained development was an impossibility of and simply turned it upside down. Lacking was any sense of the chaotic, unpredictable character of economic growth for the weaker sections of the world system that Trotsky insisted on when recognising that capitalism does not always lead to stagnation:

By drawing countries economically closer to one another and levelling out their stages of development, capitalism operates by methods of its own, that is to say, by anarchistic methods which constantly undermine its own work, set one country against another, one branch of industry against another, developing some parts of the world economy while hampering and throwing back the development of others... Imperialism...attains this "goal" by such antagonistic methods, such tiger leaps and such raids upon backward countries and areas that the unification and levelling of world economy which it has effected is upset by it even more violently and convulsively than in the preceding epoch.[80]

It was a truth that would affect the lives of many hundreds of millions of people over the next four decades.

In the Global South, as in the West, Japan and the Eastern bloc, variants of what Lenin and Bukharin had called "state capitalism" did permit a long period of economic growth. But those who extrapolated from that to see a smooth, crisis-free future were soon to be proved wrong.

CHAPTER EIGHT

The End of the Golden Age

The crisis of Keynesianism

"The National Bureau of Economic Research has worked itself out of one of its first jobs, namely business cycles." So proclaimed Paul Samuelson in 1970. Less than three years later the crisis which was supposed now to be impossible broke upon the world—or at least upon the advanced capitalist countries and a big part of the Third World. The "golden age" had come to a sudden end.

The reaction of governments everywhere was to try to keep it going by resorting to the Keynesian methods they had come to believe infallible. Government budget deficits, rare in the previous three decades, now became the norm. They failed to restore the system to its previous health. Not only was there the first lapse into negative growth—a real recession as opposed to the "growth recessions" sometimes known previously—with soaring levels of unemployment, but it was accompanied by rising levels of inflation, which in a country like Britain could approach 25 percent.

There were attempts to explain what happened as a result of the impact of the sudden very big increase in the price of oil in October 1973 due to the brief "Yom Kippur" war between Israel and the Arab states and the accompanying embargo on oil exports by Saudi Arabia. But the effect of the price increase was only to reduce the national incomes of the advanced countries by about one percent—and most of the money that accrued to the oil producers ended up being recycled back to the advanced countries via the international banking system. It was hardly enough in itself to explain the scale of the impact on most of the world system—an impact which Keynesian methods should have been sufficient to deal with according to the then conventional economic wisdom. What is more, the oil price increase did not take place in isolation from other developments. Already three years earlier a "growth recession" had hit all the major economies simultaneously in a way which had not happened in the previous quarter century, and had been followed by a very sharp economic upturn and accelerating inflation even before the oil price rise.[1] In short, the recession that began at the end of 1973 was the culmination of precisely the sort of economic cycle that Keynesian-style state interventions had supposedly consigned to the history books.

Mainstream Keynesians were at a loss. They found that their theory no longer did any of the things they had claimed for it. As one Keynesian, Francis Cripps of the *Cambridge Economic Policy Review*, later put it, they suddenly realised that:

> Nobody really understands how the modern economy works. Nobody really knows why we had so much growth in the postwar world…how the various mechanisms slotted together.[2]

Many Keynesians dropped their former ideas overnight and endorsed the "monetarist" theories propagated by Milton Friedman and the Chicago School of economists. These held that the attempts by governments to control economic behaviour had been misconceived. There was, they argued, a "natural non-inflationary rate" of unemployment, and attempts to reduce it by government spending were bound to fail and to merely cause inflation. All states should do, they insisted, was to control the supply of money so that it grew at the same speed as "the real economy"—and take such action as was necessary to break down "unnatural monopolies" by trade unions or nationalised industries, while holding down unemployment benefits so that workers would then be persuaded to accept jobs at lower wages.

The reply of apologists for capitalism to its critics for 30 years had been that it could be made to work with state intervention. Now it was that it could only be made to work if state intervention was scrapped. As the dissident radical Keynesian Joan Robinson summed up the mainstream shift:

> The spokesmen of capitalism were saying: Sorry chaps, we made a mistake, we were not offering full employment, but the natural level of unemployment. Of course, they suggested that a little unemployment would be enough to keep prices stable. But now we know that even a lot will not do so.[3]

Capitalism in the 20th Century

Labour's prime minister James Callaghan virtually admitted this when he told his party's conference in September 1976:

> We used to think you could just spend your way out of recession by cutting taxes and boosting government borrowing. I tell you in all candour that that option no longer exists; and insofar as it ever did exist, it worked by injecting inflation into the economy. And each time that has happened, the average level of unemployment has risen.

The point was repeated 20 years later by the future Labour prime minister, Gordon Brown:

> Countries which attempt to run national go it alone macro-economic policies based on tax, spend, borrow policies to boost demand, without looking to the ability of the supply side of the economy, are bound these days to be punished by the markets in the form of stiflingly high interest rates and collapsing currencies.[4]

Politicians and academics who had been brought up on Keynesianism came to accept the same parameters for deciding economic policy as their old opponents, with no alternative to high levels of unemployment, welfare cuts, "flexibility" to make workers "more competitive" and laws to restrain "trade union power". Keynesians who did not drop their old beliefs were pushed to the margins of the economic establishment. By 2007 a study showed that "72 percent of economic students" were at educational institutions without a single "heterodox economist" who challenged "the neoclassical and neoliberal assumptions".[5]

But the rush towards monetarism by supporters of the system was not any more able to come to terms with the crisis than Keynesianism. Monetarism was, after all, little more than a regurgitation of the neoclassical school which had dominated bourgeois economics until the 1930s. Just as it had been incapable of explaining the unprecedented severity of the inter-war slump, it was incapable of explaining the crisis of the 1970s and 1980s, still less of dealing with it. In Britain the monetarist Howe budget of 1979 was followed by a doubling of both inflation[6] and unemployment, and left industrial output in 1984 15 percent below its level of 11 years before.[7] The monetarist measures did not even manage to control the money supply; its broadest measures (what economists call M3) grew in 1982 by 14.5 percent instead of the intended 6 to 10 percent.[8] The policy merely served to destroy much of local industry, exacerbate the crisis of the early 1980s and lay the ground for another crisis in 1990.

Some economists who had abandoned Keynesianism for monetarism in the mid-1970s could be seen deserting monetarism in its turn in the early 1980s. *Financial Times* columnist Samuel Brittan, who had done much to popularise monetarist ideas in Britain, was by 1982 criticising many monetarist policies and calling himself a "new-style Keynesian". In the United States, Reagan's economic advisers, faced with the failure of monetarist policies to end a severe slump, quietly ditched monetarism[9] and abandoned one of monetarism's central principles—the balanced budget.

But much mainstream economic theory moved in a different direction. A "new classical" school gained influence that contended, very much along the lines of Hayek in the 1930s, that what was wrong with monetarism was that it left a role for the state—intervening in money markets. Friedman, they claimed, had fallen into the same trap as Keynes by urging government moves to shift the money supply: he was, in a certain sense, "a Keynesian".[10] Such moves, they insisted, could not alter business behaviour in the hoped for way, since the "rational expectations" of entrepreneurs would always lead them to discount government intervention in advance. Fiddling with the money supply, like government deficit spending, stopped supply and demand interacting with each other properly. "Booms and slumps", it was claimed, "are the outcome of fraudulent Central Reserve banking".[11] It is an amazing commentary on the remoteness of most academic economics from any contact with reality that the new classicals could maintain intellectual credibility when they denied the instability and irrationality of the laissez faire economy in a period which saw three major international recessions.

The high point of these ideas was with a shortlived boom in the mid to late 1980s. It seemed to vindicate their optimism about the benefits to economic growth of deregulation, privatisation and the removal of all restraints on the greed of the rich. But they lost some of their lustre with the renewed deep recession of the early 1990s. A different school of free market economists gained some support within the mainstream. This was the variant of the "Austrian school" influenced by the ideas of Joseph Schumpeter, which saw the slump-boom cycle as inevitable—and a good thing. The system, it argued, was capable of non-stop expansion, but only on the basis of "creative destruction" which destroyed old forms of production to clear the way for new ones.[12] But it was no more able than the mainstream Keynesians, the monetarists and the new classicals to answer a central question: Why was the system plagued once again by recurrent crises and by a long term decline in average growth rates after three decades of unprecedented, almost crisis-free growth?[13]

It was the failure of the anti-Keynesians to come to terms with such problems that led some Keynesians—and some on the far left influenced by Keynesianism—to blame them for the demise of the "golden age". It was not the system as such, they argue, that was behind the recurrent crises. But, as Notermans has pointed out:

> If neither the recovery from the Great Depression or post-war growth can be attributed to Keynesian policies…[it] cannot serve as an explanation for the termination of full employment.[14]

So where does the explanation lie?

Where the crises came from

Missing from all the most influential mainstream explanations for the end of the "golden age" was what was happening to the rate of profit. Yet various efforts at measuring it have come to a single conclusion: it fell sharply between the late 1960s and the early 1980s.

The results are not always fully compatible with each other, since there are different ways of measuring investment in fixed capital, and the information on profits provided by companies and governments are subject to enormous distortions.[15] Nevertheless, economists Fred Moseley, Thomas Michl,[16] Anwar Shaikh and Ertugrul Ahmet Tonak,[17] Gérard Duménil and Dominique Lévy, Ufuk Tutan and Al Campbell,[18] Robert Brenner, Edwin N Wolff,[19] and Piruz Alemi and Duncan K Foley[20] have all come to very similar conclusions. A certain pattern emerges, which is shown in graphs given by Duménil and Lévy (Figure 1) for the whole business sector in the US and by Brenner (Figure 2) for manufacturing in the US, Germany and Japan.

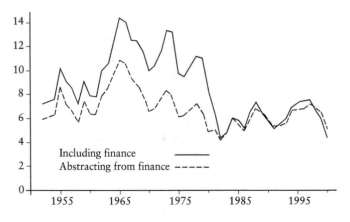

Figure 1: US profit rates accounting for (—) and abstracting from (--) the impact of financial relations[21]

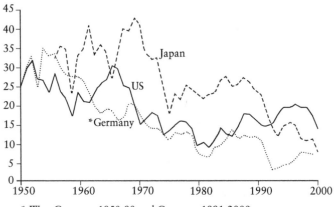

Figure 2: US, German and Japanese manufacturing net profits rates[22]

* West Germany 1950-90 and Germany 1991-2000

There is general agreement that profit rates fell from the late 1960s until the early 1980s. There is also agreement that they partially recovered from about 1982 on, but with interruptions at the end of the 1980s and the end of the 1990s, and never making up more than about half the decline since the long boom. According to Wolff, the rate of profit fell by 5.4 percent from 1966 to 1979 and then "rebounded" by 3.6 percent from 1979 to 1997; Fred Moseley calculates that it "recovered...only about 40 percent of the earlier decline";[23] Duménil and Lévy that "the profit rate in

Capitalism in the 20th Century

1997" was "still only half of its value of 1948, and between 60 and 75 percent of its average value for the decade 1956-65".[24]

There were attempts to explain the decline in profitability in the 1970s as resulting from a wave of workers' struggle internationally which had supposedly forced up the workers' share of total income and cut into the share going to capital. That argument was put forward by Andrew Glyn and Bob Sutcliffe,[25] by Bob Rowthorne[26] and accepted in part by Ernest Mandel.[27] Glyn's analysis has been given a favourable mention much more recently by Martin Wolf.[28] But statistical analysis at the time suggested there had been no increase in the share of wages when tax, capital depreciation and various other factors were taken into account.[29] The argument also failed to explain why all the Western economies moved into crisis at the same point in the mid-1970s. In Italy, Britain, Spain and France there were important improvements in the level of working class organisation in the late 1960s and early 1970s. But there was no similar improvement in Japan and West Germany, while in the US "there was a sharp decline in real wages of non-agricultural workers from late 1972 to spring 1975, while productivity on the whole increased".[30]

What did seem to make sense—and still does—was Marx's argument about the organic composition of capital. A mainstream study of the US economy showed a rapid growth in the ratio of capital investment to workers employed in manufacturing by over 40 percent between 1957-68 and 1968-73.[31] One study of the UK showed a rise in the capital-output ratio of 50 percent between 1960 and the mid-1970s.[32] Samuel Brittan noted with bewilderment:

There has been an underlying long term decline in the amount of output per unit of capital in manufacturing... This is a fairly general experience in the industrial countries... One can construct a fairly plausible story for any one country, but not for the industrial world as a whole.[33]

The more recent calculations of Michl,[34] Moseley, Shaikh and Tonak and Wolff[35] have all concluded that the rising ratio of capital to labour was an element in reducing profit rates. It is a conclusion that validates Marx's position that a rising ratio of capital to labour can cut into profits—and is an empirical refutation of the position held by Okishio and others that this is impossible. But it still leaves open why this happened then and not earlier.

It is an issue that can be resolved by looking at contradictions within the long boom already being highlighted in the early 1960s by those who explained the boom in terms of the massive level of arms expenditures.

Arms spending was very unevenly distributed among the most important economies. They consumed a very high proportion of the national output of the US and the USSR in the 1950s (up to 13 percent in the first case, probably 20 percent or more in the second case), a lower proportion in Britain and France, and a much smaller proportion for Germany and Japan. This did not matter unduly in the first years after the Second World War, when there was a relatively low level of foreign trade and most firms were subject to low levels of international economic competition. The taxation to pay for the US arms budget cut into the profits of American firms, for instance, but this did not greatly disadvantage any one such firm in its domestic competition with another. And there was little for capitalists to complain about so long as the overall rate of profit did not decline much from its high level in the immediate post war period. The positive effects of arms spending more than compensated for the negative effects.

But over time the unevenness did come to matter. The US, as part of its programme to use its dominant economic position to cement its hegemony outside the Russian bloc, allowed access to its markets to the West European states and Japan. But economies with low levels of arms expenditure could invest proportionately more and achieve faster growth rates than the US could. Over time they began to catch up with its levels of productivity and to increase their relative importance in the world economy.

Capital growth in Japan over the period 1961-1971 was 11.8 percent per year, while in West Germany over 1950-62 it was 9.5 percent; these compared with figures for the US for 1948-69 of only 3.5 percent.[36] Japan accounted for 17.7 percent of the combined advanced countries' GNP in 1977 and West Germany 13.2 percent; in 1953 the figures had only been 3.6 and 6.5 percent respectively. Meanwhile, the US share had fallen to 48 from 69 percent.[37] The shift was explained by the benefits Japan and Germany gained from the high level of worldwide arms expenditure, especially by the United States, without having to sacrifice their own productive investment to pay for it. Had all countries had comparable levels of productive investment to that of the West Germans and Japanese there would have been a very rapidly rising

Capitalism in the 20th Century

global organic composition of capital and a downward trend in the rate of profit. As it was, capital had grown in Japan "much more rapidly than the labour force—at more than 9 percent a year, or more than twice the average rate for the Western industrialised countries..."[38] Non-military state capitalisms could only expand without crises because they operated within a world system containing a very large military state capitalism.

So the Japanese and German experiences did not contradict the thesis of arms expenditure as an explanation of *world* growth and stability. But they were a contradictory factor in this growth. Their very success meant that a growing chunk of the world economy was not wasting investible output on arms. Nor was that the end of the matter. The very success of the low arms spending economies began to put pressure on the high arms spenders to switch resources away from arms and towards productive investment. For only then could they begin to meet the challenge they faced in market competition from Japan and West Germany.

This was most clearly the case for Britain. Its economy was highly dependent on foreign trade and it ran into balance of payments crises with every spell of rapid economic growth between the late 1940s and the late 1970s. Successive British governments were forced, reluctantly, to abandon their notions of imperial grandeur and to reduce the proportion of the national product going on defence—from 7.7 percent of GDP in 1955 to 4.9 percent in 1970.

In the case of the US, the pressure was less obvious at first, since even in 1965 foreign trade only amounted to about 10 percent of GNP and the country enjoyed a trade surplus throughout the 1950s and 1960s. Nevertheless, arms spending declined from around 13 percent of GNP during the Korean War to between 7 and 9 percent in the early 1960s. The pressure of arms spending on its international competitiveness was suddenly revealed when it shot up by a third with the Vietnam War. The new level was not anything like that of the Korean War. But it was too much for a US industry facing vigorous competition for markets. There was an upsurge of inflation at home and Wall Street turned against the war.[39] Then, in 1971 for the first time since the Second World War, US imports exceeded US exports. President Nixon was forced into two measures which further undermined the stability of the world economy: he cut US arms spending[40] and he devalued the US dollar, in the process destroying the "Bretton Woods" system of fixed international currency exchange rates that had acted as a framework for the expansion of world trade throughout the post-war period.

The dynamic of market competition was relentlessly undercut-ting the dynamic of military competition. What some people called the "crisis of hegemony"[41] of the system in the 1970s was, in fact, the offspring of something else—the inherent instability of a world of state capitalisms engaged in two quite different dimensions of competition, economic and military, with each other.

One of the paradoxes of capitalism, we saw in Chapter Three, is that, although a rising organic composition of capital reduces av-erage profit rates, it raises the profits of the first capitalist to introduce new machinery. So the Japanese and West Germans, by engaging in capital intensive forms of investment, cut world profit rates, while raising their own national share of world profits.[42] Their increased competitiveness in export markets forced other capitalisms to pay, with falling rates of profit, for the increased Japanese and German organic compositions of capital. But this, in turn, put pressure on these other capitalists to increase their com-petitiveness by raising their own organic compositions. The falling profit rates of the 1970s were the result. By 1973 the rates were so low that the upsurge in raw material and food prices caused by the boom of the previous two years was sufficient to push the ad-vanced Western economies into recession.

Suddenly there was no guarantee for the major capitalist con-cerns that new investments on the scale they needed to keep up with international competition would be profitable. Investment began to fall sharply and firms tried to protect their profits by cut-ting back on employment and labour costs. Declining markets then led to further falls in profits and investment.

The old pattern of boom turning into slump had returned after its 30-year break. When governments reacted by trying to boost demand with budgetary deficits, firms did not immediately re-spond, as the mainstream Keynesians held that they should, by increasing investment and output. Instead they increased prices to try to recoup their profits, to which workers who still had a degree of confidence from long years of full employment responded by fighting for wage increases. Governments and central banks were then faced with a choice. They could allow the money supply to expand so as to allow firms to further raise prices and protect prof-its. Or they could try to restrict the money supply with high short-term interest rates, relying on firms then being forced to resist workers' demands. Typically they turned from the first approach in the mid-1970s to the second in the late 1970s. But the success in restoring investment and creating a new period of growth did not last long even when governments had succeeded in subduing working class resistance. The rate of profit could not be raised above the pre-crisis level of 1973, and in 1980-82 a second "oil shock" was sufficient to push the world into a second serious recession, proving that monetarism could no more restore conditions to those of the long boom than could Keynesianism.

The limits of state directed capitalism

Capitalism was coming up against the limits of the state capitalist strategy for maintaining accumulation. That strategy had worked so long as states were able to ignore the immediate effects on the rate of profit of directing some of the mass of investible surplus value into areas that were not immediately particularly profitable (the Japanese prioritising growth over profitability) or into waste production (the arms economy). But this depended, firstly, on the rate of profit not dropping too sharply, and, secondly, on being able to ignore how the competitiveness of the production of particular goods within the national economy compared to that taking place elsewhere in the world system (or, in Marx's language, to ignore the law of value on a world scale compared with production within the individual units of the national economy). By the mid-1970s both preconditions had been undermined by the contradictory development of the long boom itself.

The rate of profit had now fallen to a degree which made unproductive expenditures or not particularly profitable areas of investment an increasing burden on further accumulation. And the very dynamism of the long boom had produced a growing interconnectedness between national economies. By 1979 US foreign trade amounted to 31 percent of output, as against 10 percent in 1965.[43] A much larger proportion of industry than before had to worry about the international comparisons of its costs. Whole industries suddenly found that the value of their output had to be recalculated on the basis of what it would cost to produce it with the more advanced techniques and lower labour costs of other countries—and that meant it was not high enough to provide "adequate" profits.

This seems to explain the well known stagnation of labour productivity in the US in the 1970s—the value of the machinery on which labour worked was originally reckoned in terms of how much it cost to produce or replace inside the US, but with rising international trade, what mattered was the lower figure that would have been obtained if world comparisons were used.[44]

In any case, the feature described by Galbraith, of firms being able to downplay the importance of profit in the interests of growth, was undermined. And this was not only a very significant change for the state monopoly capitalism of the US. It was to have devastating consequences for those countries which had gone much further in the direction of full blooded state capitalism in the Eastern bloc and the Third World. They too were to enter into a new period of crises.

The end of the Stalinist model

The assumption of conventional thinking on the right as well as the left was that the Soviet-type economies displayed a very different dynamic to that of the West. It was assumed, with very little dissent[45] until the 1970s and sometimes the 1980s, that they could sustain high levels of growth indefinitely, even if they were also marked by major inefficiencies and tended to produce low quality goods. Typical of the attitude on the left, even from people who were scathing about the denial of workers' rights in such societies, was the position Ernest Mandel held. He wrote in 1956:

> The Soviet Union maintains a more or less even rhythm of economic growth, plan after plan, decade after decade, without the progress of the past weighing on the possibilities of the future... All the laws of development of the capitalist economy which provoke a slowdown in the speed of economic growth are eliminated...[46]

Mandel still argued in the mid-70s, that "while the recession is hitting all the capitalist economies, the countries with non-capitalist economies are escaping the overall effects of the recession".[47]

Such attitudes received a rude shock in the late 1980s when Mikhail Gorbachev, recently appointed as general secretary of the Communist Party of the USSR, revealed that the economy had been suffering from "stagnation" for some years.[48] His economic advisor, Abel Aganbegyan, said:

In the period 1981-85 there was practically no economic growth. Unprecedented stagnation and crisis occurred during the period 1979-82, when production of 40 percent of all industrial goods actually fell.[49]

The official figures for the Soviet-type economies had already in the late 1960s shown a long-term tendency for their growth rates to decline, by between a third and two thirds.[50] The long-term decline in growth rates was paralleled by—and dependent on—something else. The output/capital ratio kept falling—from 2.4 in 1951-5, to 1.6 in 1956-60 and 1.3 in 1961-65. Or, to put it another way, the amount of constant capital required to produce a certain amount of new output kept rising.

The problem was made worse because growing gross output in material terms was not good enough for the ruling bureaucracies. Their concern was with how this material output compared with that produced by their international rivals—that is with the value of the output in international terms. This led to recurrent attempts by sections of the bureaucracy to implement economic reforms, amid complaints about productivity and the quality of what was produced: in the early 1950s after Stalin's death, in the early 1960s under Nikita Khrushchev and then in the late 1960s under Leonid Brezhnev and his prime minister, Alexei Kosygin.

The reforms had only limited effects. A rise in workers' living standards, in contrast to the very sharp fall in the 1930s, encouraged greater commitment by the workforce and a rise in productivity. But the pressures of competitive international accumulation (military in the case of the USSR, market as well as military in the case of the East European states) led to a repeated tendency of increased consumer goods and food output to be sacrificed to the needs of industrial investment. As Soviet statisticians explained in 1969, "Owing to the international situation it has not been possible to allocate as many resources as intended to agricultural investment".[51] Such a switching of resources from one sort of production to another necessarily led to increasing waste, undermined the morale of the workforce, and led people at every level of managerial hierarchies to hide the resources at their disposal so as to enable them to cope if inputs were suddenly curtailed.[52]

It is necessary to note in passing that such a phenomenon was not unique to the Soviet-style economies. Exactly the same pressures apply to those below the top managerial ranks in Western corporations as they are expected to be able to respond to sudden changes in the pressures on them from above in response to changing competition. Under such conditions, the firms' costs of production can depart very widely from those which ought to be achieved. The result can be what one economist has called "x-inefficiency"—a level of inefficiency in the company amounting to 30 or 40 percent of production costs.[53] Production costs and the prices which would prevail in a "perfect market" depart massively from each other—to use Marxist terminology, there are massive short-term infringements of the law of value.

Such things are rarely studied by mainstream economists because both their micro- and macro-economics deal with what happens between firms, not within them. But there are repeated references to such problems in managerial studies. Interestingly, some Western studies concluded when it came to relationships between enterprises in the USSR "allocative efficiency" (that is, for Marxists, the law of value) did apply: "Inter-firm trade in factors of production may be as efficient as in market economies".[54]

What produced crisis and waste inside Western enterprises and Soviet-style economies alike was the drive to accumulate at all costs. It meant, as we saw in Chapter Seven, investment expanding repeatedly at the expense of consumption, increased imbalances in the economy, a continual cyclical pattern to growth and increased alienation of the workforce. Figures given by the Russian economic journalist Vasily Selyunin in 1987 showed the increasing subordination of consumption to accumulation over nearly six decades, with only 25 percent of output going to consumption in 1985 as compared to 39 percent in 1940 and 60.5 percent in 1928. He concluded, "The economy is working more and more for itself, rather than for man".[55]

His words echoed (probably unintentionally) those of Marx describing the logic of capitalism as "accumulation for accumulation's sake, production for production's sake".[56] But the drive to such accumulation was not only an expression of the alienation of the capitalist system for Marx. It was also the force ultimately behind the outbreak of crises. For it meant that accumulation reached a point at which it attempted to proceed faster than the extraction of the extra surplus value necessary to make

Capitalism in the 20th Century

it possible. At such a point new accumulation could only proceed at the expense of existing accumulation, as Grossman spelt out in his theory of "capitalist breakdown". There was "over-accumulation of capital". The only response open to capitalists in this situation was to shut down the plant, sack some workers and try to restore profits at the expense of the wages of the others. Each of these moves had the effect of making it impossible for some of the already produced commodities to be sold (or, in Marx's words, for the "realisation of surplus value" to take place), creating a general overproduction of goods in relation to the market.

The Soviet Union had always experienced cyclical downturns as a result of attempts to accumulate too rapidly, as we saw in the previous chapter. But as with the major Western capitalisms in the long boom, the downturns had not turned into economic contraction, a "real recession." Now these became more difficult to avoid as the slowdown in growth had its impact.

Poland and the foretaste of a dire future

Two young Polish Marxists, Jacek Kuron and Karol Modzelewski, produced a pathbreaking study of the economic contradictions in an Eastern bloc country in 1964. They pointed to the findings of certain East European economists about the way over-accumulation affected the rest of the economy. Accumulation came up against three "barriers". The "inflation barrier" signified that too rapid expansion of investment had led either to normal inflation (as the state printed money to pay for it, so raising prices and cutting living standards) or to "hidden inflation" (as cutbacks in the supply of goods to the shops led to shortages, queues and a growing black market.) The "raw material barrier" signified that there were just not enough inputs for production to reach the projected level. The "export barrier" meant that attempts to make up for the shortages of inputs by importing from abroad led to foreign exchange crises. Kuron and Modzelewksi concluded that a point was soon going to be reached in which the internal reserves would no longer exist for accumulation to continue without creating an immense social crisis. They argued against those who looked to reform:

What we have here is not a contradiction between the objectives of the plan and the anti-stimuli resulting from faulty directives, but a contradiction between the class goal of the ruling bureaucracy (production for production) and the interests of basic groups who achieve the production (maximum consumption). In other words, it is a contradiction between the class goal of production and consumption, and it results from existing conditions, not from mismanagement.[57]

Their analysis was partially vindicated in 1970 when attempts to resolve a crisis caused by over-investment at the expense of living standards led to workers occupying the country's Baltic shipyards, attacks on them by the police and the enforced resignation of the country's leader, Gomulka. But at first it seemed that the new leadership had found a way out of the crisis, with a new boom based on massively expanding trade with the West and borrowing from Western banks which permitted imports to rise by 50 percent in 1972 and 89 percent in 1973.

Polish state capitalism was overcoming the limits to accumulation created by the narrowness of its national economy by integration into the world economy through market competition. The other side of this, however, was that the Polish economy was bound to suffer whenever the world economy went into recession. And dependency on the rest of the world system for inputs to production and for export earnings prevented the state shifting resources from one sector of the economy to another so as to ward off any incipient internal recession turning into an actual one. From 1980 to 1982 there developed "a crisis unprecedented in the history of Europe since the second world war".[58] The "national net material product" fell by nearly a third; prices increased by 24 percent in 1981 and 100 percent in 1982; and real wages fell by about a fifth.[59]

The regime attempted to place the burden of the crisis on the mass of workers—and produced a sudden upsurge of resistance through the Solidarnosc workers' movement. The events served as a warning to the whole of the Russian bloc. Soviet-style state capitalism was not immune to a crisis similar in important ways to that then hitting Western state monopoly capitalism. Both had their roots in the system of competitive accumulation as a whole.[60] Catastrophic crisis was inevitable at some point in the not too distant future throughout the Soviet bloc—including in the USSR itself:

By 1981, the choice between maintaining the closed economy and opening up to the rest of the world was indeed the choice between the frying pan and the fire. The first option meant deepening stagnation, growing waste, an inability to satisfy the demands of the mass of the population, and the continual danger of working class rebellion. The second option meant binding oneself into the rhythm of a world economy increasingly prone to stagnation and recession—and giving up the administrative means to stop recession involving contraction of the domestic economy. That is why the Polish crisis of 1980-81 was so traumatic for all the rulers of Eastern Europe. It proved there was no easy solution to the problems besetting every state.[61]

The Soviet crash

The Soviet bureaucracy was not long in discovering this the hard way. Its levels of accumulation were reaching the limits of what could be sustained. It depended more on foreign trade than previously, using oil revenues to buy wheat abroad to feed the population in the 1970s and early 1980s (adding to worldwide inflationary pressures). A fall in the world price of oil in the course of the mid-1980s then threw its domestic economic calculations into some disarray. And the decision of the Reagan administration to reassert US hegemony by raising arms spending put pressure on the USSR to do likewise. The external factors added to the internal problems caused by trying to sustain accumulation in the face of declining growth rates.

Gorbachev's promotion to head of the ruling Communist Party was a sign that influential people had recognised the urgency of the situation—his rise owed much to Yuri Andropov, who had witnessed what crisis could lead to as ambassador to Hungary in 1956 and as general secretary of CPSU during the Polish events of 1980-81. Gorbachev has been blamed since as a "counter-revolutionary" by some people on the left nostalgic for the Soviet style set-up. But his intention was to try to save that set-up through top-down reforms before economic, social and political crisis on Polish lines could arise. His misfortune was that the crisis had reached a point where it could not be overcome by reform.

Reports from ministerial meetings in the winter of 1988-9 provide a picture of increasing economic chaos, with the regime not seeing any way to deal with it. There were bitter clashes over "the balance (or rather the imbalance) between different sectors of the economy", the "number of enterprises" which were "significantly refusing to supply planned output" or were "significantly reducing deliveries" and the way "the volume of new investment continued to grow".[62] "The supply of goods to the consumer market" had "suddenly begun to deteriorate sharply and noticeably before our eyes in the second half of 1987 and especially in 1988".[63] There was an:

> increasingly strained situation as regards satisfying the public money-backed demand for goods and services... The problem of supplying the population with food has worsened... The money supply has reached critical dimensions... Everything in the economy is in short supply.[64]

By October 1989 there was open talk of "the crisis in many parts of the economy, the shortages, the unbalanced market, the collapse of old relations before new ones are put in place, an atmosphere of uncertain prospects and scarcities".[65] Prices were rising, since factories and shops found they could reduce production and simply raise prices, disrupting supplies for the rest of the economy.

The economic crisis, as in Poland, turned into a political and social crisis. Gorbachev had intended to permit a limited opening ("glasnost") of discussion in the ruling party and the media to isolate those in the bureaucracy opposed to his reforms. But people increasingly took advantage of this to give expression to old grievances and their discontent with the deteriorating economic situation. An unprecedented series of mass demonstrations and riots took place in the non-Russian national Soviet republics of Armenia, Kazakhstan, the Baltic states, Georgia, the Ukraine, Byelorussia and Azerbaijan, fusing struggles for national rights with grievances at the social conditions people experienced. So the protests by the Armenian minority in the Karabakh region of Azerbaijan "began as protests against catastrophic mismanagement and miserable economic conditions".[66] The newspaper *Pravda* said that in 1986 (even before the crisis deepened) there was 27.6 percent unemployment in Azerbaijan and 18 percent in Armenia.[67] In Kazakhstan "only half the young people had a chance to find a job in 1981-85".[68] The head of the state-run unions said that across the USSR as a whole 43 million people were living below the poverty line.[69] Estimates of the total number of unemployed varied from 3 percent to 6.2 percent (8.4 million people). Then miners right across the USSR struck in

Capitalism in the 20th Century

the early summer of 1989 and soon after Abalkin complained, "A wave of strikes has engulfed the economy".[70] This was happening as huge mass movements in Eastern Europe—partly in response to their economic crises—were breaking Soviet control on the region and deepening the general sense of political crisis, encouraging further protests in the USSR's non-Russian republics and weakening the capacity of the central state to impose its will.

Those running the enterprises did not know how to cope with the wave of protests from below apart from making concessions which raised money wages, and they had even less of an idea about what do about the shortages of inputs needed to maintain the level of production. Stagnation gave way to economic contraction—the beginnings of a slump—in the second half of 1989.

There were calls from economists who claimed that only greater competition between enterprises, and eventually direct competition between firms inside Russia and those elsewhere in the world economy could force managers to be efficient and to produce the things that were needed. But they had no more idea than the ministries at the centre as how to find the resources to complete the investments that were meant to provide the outputs that would restore balance to the economy. The economic collapse continued regardless of what the government did, leading to ever greater discontent and political upheaval. An attempt by Gorbachev to take a hard line to restore central control in the spring of 1991 produced a new wave of discontent which forced him to retreat. A coup against him by those who hankered after a return to the past in August 1991 fell apart, lacking support from the most important generals. There was no popular constituency for trying to return to the old order. But those who preached reform did not have a way forward either, despite the brief popularity for "100-day" or "300-day" programmes promising miraculous economic recovery.

Such programmes were utopian in the extreme. The collapse of central control left the giant Soviet enterprises in a monopolistic or semi-monopolistic position. They were able to dictate to the market and to produce what they wanted rather than what was needed by the economy as a whole; they were in a position to raise prices and to simply ignore contractual obligations to other enterprises. There was no stopping the combination of deepening recession, inflation and acute shortages of consumer goods and food. Economists, planners and frightened bureaucrats began to look for any scheme to get them out of the mess, until finally they gave up attempting to control what was happening. When Yeltsin and the Communist leaders of the other national republics announced the dissolution of the USSR into its component republics at the end of 1991 they were only giving political expression to the economic fragmentation that was already under way, with the heads of each industrial sector trying to protect themselves from the general economic crisis by relying on their own resources. This was turned into a supposed economic strategy through "shock therapy" policies of Yeltsin's "liberal" ministers and Western advisers like Jeffrey Sachs. The assumption was that, left to compete with each other without restraints from the state, enterprises would soon be pricing goods rationally in a way that would lead the efficient ones to establish links with each other, and that this would restore stability. In fact, all it did was to provide governmental blessing to a slump already under way whose only precedent anywhere in the 20th century was that of 1929-33 in the US and Germany.

The failure of economic reform was not just a failure of implementation. There was a flaw in the very notion of reform itself. The aim was to restructure the Soviet economy so that those sections of it capable of adjusting to the current international level of the forces of production would expand while others closed down. But this was bound to be an enormously painful undertaking, not just for those workers who suffered in the process but for the mass of the individual members of the bureaucracy as well. Restructuring the British economy between the mid-1970s and the mid-1980s had involved shutting down about one factory in three and destroying capital on such a scale that gross industrial investment in 1990 was still no higher than in 1972. It is very doubtful that it could have proceeded smoothly if British capitalism had not had the lucky bonus of enormous North Sea oil revenues. The USSR's economy was much larger than Britain, and its enterprises had been much more insulated from the rest of the world for 60 years. The proportion that was to be destroyed by an immediate opening to international competition was correspondingly greater. This, in turn, did considerable damage to the remaining competitive enterprises as they lost suppliers of materials and components on the one hand and buyers for their output on the other.

The roots of the crisis lay in the pressure to accumulate for the sake of accumulation that arose from the bureaucracy's position as part of a competitive world system. The Soviet economy had reached the point at which the precondition for a further wave of

Capitalism in the 20th Century

self-expansion of capital was a crisis involving the destruction of at least some past accumulation. The only difference between Russia and, say, France or Britain, was that the destruction was to be on a considerably greater scale. And this was because the Soviet Union had undergone six decades of accumulation without restructuring through crises and bankruptcies, while for the British and French economies it was only four and three decades respectively.

Few people were prepared to see things in these terms at the time. The vast majority of those who had struggled for democratic reform in Russia believed that the turn to market capitalism would open up a glorious future. What they got instead was a devastating slump, the corruption of the Yeltsin years and the domination of the economy and society by former members of the ruling bureaucracy and mafiosi reborn as private capitalist oligarchs. Meanwhile, in the rest of the world the great majority of politicians and theorists in the social democratic and former Stalinist left drew the conclusion that it was socialism that had failed and that the future lay with Western style markets, failing to perceive the depths of the crises brewing there too.

Japan: the sun that stopped rising

The world's second economic power at the beginning of the 1980s was the USSR. Japan took its place as the Soviet crisis of the late 1980s turned into collapse.[71] Japan's average growth rate throughout the 1980s was 4.2 percent as against 2.7 percent for the US and 1.9 percent for West Germany. Its annual investment in manufacturing equipment was more than twice that of the US.[72] That the future lay with Japan was the near universal conclusion of media commentators. A committee of the US Congress warned in 1992 that Japan could overtake the US by the end of the decade. "After Japan" became the slogan of European and North American industrialists trying to motivate their workforces to greater feats of productivity. The "threat" from the "rising sun" became the excuse for the job losses experienced by American auto workers. Keynesian commentators like Will Hutton and William Keegan wrote books extolling the Japanese model of capitalism.

Then in 1992-3 a financial crisis pushed Japan into its own "period of stagnation", with a growth rate averaging just 0.9 percent a year between 1990 and 2001.[73] By 2007 its economy was only a third of the size of the US's (and the European Union's)[74] as against estimates as high as 60 percent in 1992.[75]

The blame for what happened is usually ascribed to faults in the running of its financial system—either due to financial markets not being "free" enough in the 1980s, or to inappropriate action by the central banks once the crisis had started. The conclusion from such reasoning is that the Japan crisis was unique and has little to tell us about the direction in which the global system is going. The sudden inability of the world's second biggest economy to grow then becomes the result of accidents.

Yet all the elements of the Marxist account of the crisis of the inter-war years are to be found in the Japanese case. Japan had a rapidly rising ratio of capital to workers from the 1950s to the late 1980s. This grew in the 1980s by 4.9 percent a year—more than four times as fast as in the US and 70 percent faster than in Germany.[76] The result, as Marx would have predicted, was down-ward pressure on the rate of profit. It fell by about three quarters between the end of the 1960s and the end of the 1980s.

Japanese profit rate[77]

	Manufacturing	Non-financial corporate
1960-69	36.2	25.4
1970-79	24.5	20.5
1980-90	24.9	16.7
1991-2000	14.5	10.8

Return on gross non-residential stock[78]

1960	28.3
1970	18.0
1980	7.8
1990	3.9

The decline seemed manageable until the end of the 1980s. The state and the banks worked with private industry to sustain growth without much attention to profit rates. So long as there was a mass of profit available for further investment, the Japanese system en-sured that it was used. Japan had been hit hard by the global recession of the mid-1970s, but was able not only to recover from it before most other countries but also to restructure industry in such a way as to keep expanding throughout the early 1980s when the US and Europe were in recession:

Capitalism in the 20th Century

The crisis [of 1973-5] indicated that future growth on the basis of heavy and chemical industrialisation was untenable. The role of the state in changing the strategic direction of Japanese capitalism was fundamental. Administrative guidance by MITI [Ministry of International Trade and Industry—CH] began to nudge Japanese capital in the direction of electronics, automobiles, capital equipment and semiconductors...[79]

This required high levels of investment. The United States, for example, invested just 21 percent of its GDP during the 1980s compared with a Japanese figure of 31 percent. According to one estimate, the ratio of capital stock to GNP in Japan was nearly 50 percent higher than in the US.[80] The concentration of investment into certain industries in this way raised their productivity, even though it remained fairly low in the rest of the Japanese economy.[81] But such high investment could only be sustained by holding down the consumption of the mass of people. Partly this was done by keeping down real wages; partly it was done through providing minimal state provision for sickness and pensions, forcing people to save. As Rod Stevens pointed out when the boom was at its height:

Real wages in Japan are still at most only about 60 percent of real wages in the US, and Japanese workers have to save massively to cope with the huge proportion of their lifetime earnings which is absorbed by such things as housing, education, old age and health care.[82]

But this level of real wages restricted the domestic market for the new goods Japanese industry was turning out at an ever increasing speed. The only way to sell them was to rely on exports. As Stevens also pointed out:

Because of capital's increasingly strict wage control and authority in the workplace, growing labour productivity in the consumer goods branches of the machinery industries (eg motor cars and audio-visual equipment) had to find outlets in export markets if the Japanese working class's limited buying power was not to interrupt accumulation.[83]

High productivity in the select range of prioritised industry made the required level of exports possible, with Japanese cars and electronics increasingly penetrating the US market. But it brought complications in its wake. Japanese economic success was very dependent on US good will. When the US demanded that Japan accept an upward revaluation of its currency to make its goods less competitive against American goods, Japanese capitalism had little choice but to comply and the volume of exports suffered (even though revaluation meant their value in dollar terms did not).

The reaction of the state to this was to provide cheap funds to keep industrial investment and expansion going. As Karel van Wolferen has said, "To compensate the corporate sector for the squeeze of the exchange rate, the Ministry [of Finance] encouraged the banks vastly to increase their lending".[84] But there had been a weakening of the old mechanisms which directed bank lending into industrial development—caused in part by the growing integration of Japanese capitalism into the world system.[85] The expanded bank lending found its way into speculation on a massive scale:

> The explosion of liquidity helped set off an upward spiral of real-estate values, long used as collateral by the big companies, which then justified inflated stock values.[86]

In what was later called the "bubble economy", property values soared and the stock exchange doubled in value—until the net worth of Japanese companies was said to be greater than that of the US companies, although by any real measure the US economy was about twice the size of the Japanese one. But while the bubble lasted the Japanese economy continued to grow—and even after the bubble had started deflating, bank lending enabled the economy to keep expanding throughout 1991-2 as recession hit the US and Western Europe. Then it became clear that the banks themselves were in trouble. They had made loans for land and share purchases that could not be repaid now these things had collapsed in price. The banking system was hit by recurrent crises right through the 1990s, writing off a total of around 71 trillion yen (over $500 billion) in bad loans. The total sum owed by businesses in trouble or actually bankrupt were set at 80 to 100 trillion yen ($600 to $750 billion) by the US government, and at 111 trillion yen (nearly $840 billion) by the IMF.[87]

The role of the financial system in producing the bubble and then the long drawn out banking crisis has led most commentators to locate the origin of the Japanese crisis in faults within that system.

The problem, neoliberal commentators claim, was that the close ties between those running the state, the banking system and industry meant that there was not the scrutiny about what the banks were up to which a truly competitive economy would have provided.[88] It was this which enabled such a massive amount of dodgy lending to take place. As an explanation, it fails because very similar bubbles have happened in economies like the US which supposedly fulfil all the norms of "competitiveness". It is difficult to see any fundamental difference between the Japanese bubble of the late 1980s and the US housing bubble of the mid-2000s.

The neoliberal reasoning that blames the crisis on the state believes there was a solution—the state should simply have walked away and allowed some of the big banks to go out of business. But this assumes that some banks going bust would not bring down other banks to which they owed money, leading to a cumulative collapse of the whole banking sector. No advanced industrial state dare even contemplate that happening. Whenever it has seemed possible, other states have behaved in general as the Japanese have.

In any case, there is no reason to believe that the banking crisis was the ultimate cause of Japanese stagnation. The neoclassical economists Fumio Hayashi and Edward C Prescott have argued that firms that wanted to invest could still do so, since "other sources of funds replaced bank loans to finance the robust investment by nonfinancial corporations in the 1990s".[89] But they have had to recognise that "those projects that are funded are on average receiving a low rate of return".[90] In fact, there was a fall in productive investment, although not anything like a complete collapse. In such a situation, restructuring the banking system, whether through allowing the crisis to deepen, as the neoliberals wanted, or gradually as those of a more Keynesian persuasion suggested, would not solve the crisis. On this American economist Paul Krugman rightly made the point:

> The striking thing about discussion of structural reform, however, is that when one poses the question, "How will this increase demand?" the answers are actually quite vague. I at least am far from sure that the kinds of structural reform being urged on Japan will increase demand at all, and see no reason to believe that even radical reform would be enough to jolt the economy out of its current trap.[91]

The reason was that the trap lay outside the banking system, in the capitalist system as a whole. The rate of profit had fallen to a point in the late 1980s which precluded further substantial increases in workers' living standards. But that in turn prevented the domestic economy from being able to absorb all of the increased output. A new massive round of accumulation could have absorbed it, but for that profitability would have had to have been much higher than it was. Richard Koo's study of the crisis, *The Holy Grail of Macroeconomics*, by stressing the hidden debts of major corporations, hints at what had really gone wrong, but fails to ground the problem of insolvency in the long-term decline of profitability.[92]

The Japanese state did turn to some Keynesian type solutions, with a big programme of public works construction (bridges, airports, roads, etc). Gavan McCormack writes, "With the onset of chronic recession after the bubble burst at the beginning of the 1990s, the government turned to ever larger—and decreasingly effective—Keynesian deficits", and that "Japan's public works sector has grown to be three times the size of that of Britain, the US or Germany, employing 7 million people, or 10 percent of the workforce, and spending between 40 and 50 trillion yen a year— around $350 billion, 8 percent of GDP or two to three times that of other industrial countries".[93] According to one estimate the state's share of output increased from an average of 13.7 percent in the 1984-1990 period to 15.2 percent in the 1994-2000 period.[94]

But it was not enough to fill the gap created by the limited stimulus to investment from the rate of profit, as the graph below shows.

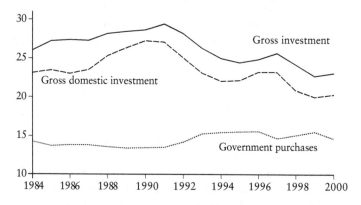

(Source: Fumio Hayashi and Edward C. Prescott, "The 1990s in Japan: A Lost Decade")

Capitalism in the 20th Century

The economy did not collapse in the 1990s in the way that the US and German economies did in the early 1930s. The state still seemed able to stop that. But it could not lift the economy back to its old growth path. Sections of Japanese capital believed they could escape from this trap by investing abroad—as the gap between Gross Investment and Gross Domestic Investment shows. But it was not an answer for the great bulk of Japanese capital which did its utmost to try to raise the rate of profit through raising the rate of exploitation, even though it could only reduce domestic demand still further and deepen its problems. Nor was it an answer for the Japanese working class, which whether it liked it or not would be compelled to struggle if it was to avoid life getting worse. Economic growth did not rise from the doldrums until the mid-2000s, when Chinese imports of machinery gave a boost to Japanese industry—but this was to prove to be very shortlived.

Japan's crisis was not as devastating to the lives of its people as that which broke out a couple of years earlier in the USSR. Yet, unnoticed by nearly all economists, mainstream and Marxist alike, there was a similarity between them. Capital accumulation had reached the point where it could no longer extract a surplus from those it exploited on a sufficiently rising scale to keep abreast of the internationally competitive level of accumulation it looked to. The barrier to capital accumulation had indeed become capital itself. Those who presided over accumulation had two choices. They could allow their bit of the system to restructure itself through blind competition, taking on trust ideological claims that it would produce new miracles. Or they could play safe, knowing they might never get out of long-term stagnation. The rulers of Russia chose the first path and saw their economy, already halved with the loss of the rest of the USSR, halve in size again. Japan's rulers took the other path, and their economy went through a decade and a half of debilitating stagnation without seeming any closer to a solution to its problems at the end than it was at the beginning. The big question both raised was, how would other countries, particularly the US, react if they fell into the same stagnation trap?

The impact on the Global South

The collapse of the two state-oriented ideological models, Keynesianism and Stalinism, had a profound effect on political forces aspiring after the "development" of Third World economies into full and equal components of the world system. It pushed them to look for new models of capital accumulation in place of the state-directed import-substitutionist model, which was already displaying problems.

In Asia the tightly regulated Chinese economy and the less tightly regulated, but still centrally directed, Indian economy both began to show worrying signs of stagnation by the mid-1970s,[95] forcing governments to look for alternatives; in Latin America the import-substitutionist model was found wanting in its Argentinian homeland as economic and political crises erupted; in Africa the promises made by proponents of "African socialism" were not fulfilled as industrial growth was restricted by the narrowness of national markets and the meagre resources left after the depredations of imperialism. Adding to these problems was a decline in the price on the world market for raw materials and foodstuffs—the main source of the export earnings needed to import equipment for new industries. Particularly after the onset of recession in the advanced countries in 1974, non oil producing Third World countries were caught between increased oil costs and a decline in the terms of trade for primary commodity exports of nearly 50 percent.[96]

Those running industries which had grown up within the protective barriers of the old model began pragmatically establishing links with foreign capital. Argentina, Brazil and Mexico were typical. Their industrial bases had been established in the 1940s, 1950s and 1960s by the state intervening to direct investment in industry, often into state-owned companies. But the more farsighted industrialists—whether in the state or private sectors—saw that they could not get the resources and modern technologies needed to keep up with worldwide productivity levels unless they found ways of breaking out of the confines of the national economy. They began increasingly to turn to foreign multinationals for licensing agreements, joint production projects and funds—and they began themselves to operate as multinationals in other countries.

The trend was reinforced by the success of a number of countries which had long oriented themselves to the world market in achieving very fast growth rates. In Asia four bastions of anti-Communism— South Korea, Taiwan, Hong Kong and Singapore—registered growth rates easily as large as those in Stalin's USSR. And in Europe countries like Spain, Greece and Portugal, which Paul Baran had included as part of the underdeveloped world, grew rapidly enough to join that rich man's club, the European Community. Brazil began following a similar export-oriented path under the military regime that had seized power in 1964. Its still very large state sector and private capital alike increasingly oriented towards the rest of the world system rather than to a protected national market. The Western financial press rejoiced in this, assuring its readers that Brazil was the great rising Third World country whose industries were destined to challenge those of the West. And there certainly was growth. "For almost 15 years (1965-80) the average rate of growth was 8.5 percent, making Brazil the fourth fastest growing country".[97]

Other Latin American states began to emulate the Brazilian policy. The military coups in Chile (1973) and Argentina (1976) were followed by an opening to external capital. And again the outcome seemed encouraging at first. Under the Videla regime in Argentina "the rate of inflation was lowered, real output grew, and a current account surplus was generated",[98] while Chile's real GDP grew 8.5 percent a year between 1977 and 1980.[99]

It seemed that a way had been found to achieve national accumulation by breaking out of the confines of the national market—and, when the policies were undertaken under military regimes, of crushing popular resistance to rising levels of exploitation. There was a similar swing of the intellectual pendulum as in the West and the former Communist states, with the wholesale conversion of "dependency theory" economists to the wonders of free markets. The conversions continued even as the Latin American "miracle" came unstuck.

Growth after 1974 had come to depend on foreign borrowing (as in Poland and Hungary in the same period). Many Latin American countries gambled on ambitious growth targets by borrowing heavily in international financial markets. The external debt of Chile and Argentina almost trebled over a few years, from 1978 to 1981.[100] But this did not seem to matter at the time—either to the national governments or the international banking system:

Up to the second oil price shock (1979-80) the gamble was worth taking. Export growth was sustained in world markets at favourable prices... As a consequence the ratio of debt outstanding to export proceeds was more favourable for all non-oil developing countries in 1979 than in 1970-72.[101]

The IMF assured people in 1980, "During the 1970s...a generalised debt management problem was avoided...and the outlook for the immediate future does not give cause for alarm".[102] This was written just months before the second international recession, in the early 1980s, and caught all these states unprepared. As export markets shrank and international interest rates began to rise, the debts they had incurred in the 1970s crippled their growth, threw them into recession and blighted their economies right through the 1980s, which became known as "the lost decade" in Latin America, with a fall in GNP per person for the continent as a whole of 10 percent.[103]

The impact on local capitalists and mainstream political forces was not, however, to question the new opening to the world market. Rather it was to insist, as in Russia and Eastern Europe that the opening had not gone far enough. The new doctrine was accepted in one form or another by the late 1980s by populist politicians and even former guerrillas in Latin America, by the politburo in China, by the Congress Party leadership in India, by those who had once proclaimed their commitment to "socialism" in Africa and by the successors to Nasser in Egypt.

The conversions were not always voluntary. The International Monetary Fund and the World Bank intervened where they could, making offers, mafia style, to debt-laden countries which their rulers rarely found themselves able to refuse, since doing so would rule out any sort of accumulation strategy. The various debt programmes were more concerned with protecting the interests of Western banks than with ameliorating conditions in the indebted countries. But more was involved than just a surrender to imperialism on the part of the governments that accepted them. Those capitals, private and state alike, that had grown during the period of state-directed "development" did not see any way of continuing to expand within the confines of limited national markets. They wanted access to markets and to technological innovations outside national borders. They might allow, even encourage, national governments to haggle over the terms on which capital in the metropolitan countries allowed this to happen, but they would not reject them outright. And in the process some of them were indeed able to develop more than a national profile.

So the Argentinian steel maker TechNet took control of the Mexican steel tube maker Tamsa in 1993, acquired the Italian steel tube maker Dalmikne in 1996, and then went on to expand into

Capitalism in the 20th Century

Brazil, Venezuela, Japan and Canada, adopting the name Tenaris.[104] There is a similar pattern for some Mexican companies. In the late 1980s Alfa, the largest industrial group in Mexico, with 109 subsidiaries spanning automotive components, food, petrochemicals and steel, embarked on a growing number of joint operations with foreign firms. The glass maker Vitro, which had bought two American companies, became "the world's leading glass container manufacturer, with its market almost equally split between the US and Mexico".[105] The logical outcome of this in Mexico was for its ruling class to forget its old nationalism and to join the North American Free Trade Area and increasingly to operate as a subordinate component of US capitalism.

Occasionally the collaboration produced positive results for wider sections of local capital, provided some job opportunities for the aspirant middle classes (in Ireland, South Korea, Malaysia, Singapore, Taiwan and coastal China), and even created conditions under which workers could boost their living standards through industrial action. All too often, however, it created still further indebtedness to foreign banks which the national states had to cope with. In such cases a narrow stratum of people gained a taste of the fleshpots of multinational capital while the conditions of the mass of people deteriorated, or at best remained unchanged. A yuppie class lived in protected enclaves as if it were in the wealthiest parts of the industrialised world (and often went a step further and lived part of the year there), while much of the population festered in ever proliferating slums and shantytowns.

The assumption of the new economic ideology—most forcefully addressed in the "neoliberal" notions of the "Washington Consensus" of the IMF and World Bank—was that if some capital accumulation in some countries had been able to gain a new lease of life by reinsertion into the world system, it could do so anywhere if only the last restrictions on trade and the movement of capital were removed. But the reality proved to be rather different. A few areas attracted new productive investment, but only a few. At the end of the century only a third of worldwide foreign direct investment went to the "emerging markets" of the Global South and the former Communist countries, and of this more than half went to just four countries—China/Hong Kong, Singapore, Mexico and Brazil. Another quarter went to just seven countries (Malaysia, Thailand, South Korea, Bermuda, Venezuela, Chile and Argentina), leaving 176 countries to share out the remaining 25 percent.[106] And much of the investment was not new investment at all, but simply the buying up of already operating companies by multinationals based in the metropolitan countries.

These problems were most felt in the poorest regions of the world, especially Africa. However much they dismantled their old, protectionist, import-substitutionist policies, they still remained unattractive to the multinationals they wanted to woo: "Small, poor countries face increased barriers to entry in industries most subject to the global forces of competition".[107]

Much the same applied to exports. China and a few other countries did continue to break into world markets. But the export orientation of these countries meant that their own internal markets for foreign-produced consumer goods did not grow at a corresponding speed and that their expansion was, in part, at the expense of other countries in the Global South. So African countries which had begun to enjoy some export growth in manufactured goods found themselves losing markets to China. The "combined and uneven development" that had characterised the long boom continued into its aftermath, with the difference that many economies actually contracted even as others grew rapidly. It was as if the "Third World" itself had split in two, except that immense pools of poverty remained even in the part that was growing.

Those who ran the local states could often feel insecure even when the developmentalist strategy was successful in its own capitalist or state capitalist terms. Their success depended upon a high level of domestic accumulation—and the other side of that, a high level of exploitation that could only be achieved by holding down workers' and peasants' living standards. But even when they succeeded in getting high levels of accumulation (which was the exception rather than the rule) they remained weak in their bargaining position with the multinationals. As multinationals took over local firms, their proportion of the local capital investment could rise to 40 or even 50 percent of the total, increasing their leverage over local decision making. But states in the poorer parts of the world did not have anything like the same leverage over multinationals, since the small size of their domestic economies meant they probably accounted for no more than 1 or 2 percent of the multinationals' worldwide investments and sales.

Huge gaps usually opened up between what those who ran the state had promised the mass of people and what they could deliver.

Capitalism in the 20th Century

High levels of repression and corruption become the norm rather than the exception. When the developmentalist strategy ran into problems, something else accompanied the repression—the hollowing out of the mass organisations that used to tie sections of the middle class to the state and, via them, some of the working class and peasantry. The oppressive state became a weak state and looked to foreign backing to reinforce its hold.

All this happened as problems of profitability in the advanced countries drove their capitalists to look for any opportunity, however limited, to grab surplus value from elsewhere. There was not much to be got from the poorest of the poor anywhere in the world, but what there was they were determined to get. Imperialism meant that at the top level of the system rival capitalist powers argued vehemently with each other about how to satisfy their different interests. At a lower level, it meant constraining the local ruling classes of the Third World to act as collectors of debt repayments for the Western banks, royalty payments for the multinationals and profits for Western investors as well as for their own domestic capitalists. Debt servicing alone transferred $300 billion a year from the "developing countries" to the wealthy in the advanced world.[108] A website dedicated to defending US overseas investment boasted:

Most new overseas investments are paid for by profits made overseas. Foreign direct investment by US companies was only $86 billion in 1996... If you subtract out the reinvested earnings of foreign operations, the result was only $22 billion... US companies' overseas operations also generate income that returns to the US... In 1995, this flow of income—defined as direct investment income, royalty and license fees, and charges and services—back into the US amounted to $117 billion.[109]

There could be no end to the squeezing. The share of foreign investors in the trading on the Brazilian stock exchange rose from 6.5 percent in 1991 to 29.4 percent in 1995,[110] and the share of new Mexican government debt held by non-residents grew from 8 percent at the end of 1990 to 55 percent at the end of 1993.[111]

Under such circumstances, the instability of the world economy in the aftermath of the "golden age" found heightened expression in the countries of the Global South. Even those expanding rapidly and extolled by neoliberal media commentators could suddenly be faced with near insuperable debt problems, deepening slump and possibly accelerating inflation—as happened in Mexico in the early 1990s, Indonesia in the late 1990s and Argentina at the beginning of the 2000s. And the fate of the mass of people in countries regarded as marginal by international capital, like most of sub-Saharan Africa, was deepening poverty, repeated famines and, all too often, recurrent bouts of ethnic conflict spilling over into civil wars, often financed by foreign firms interested in control of raw materials. There may never have been a golden age for such parts of the world. But there was certainly a leaden one.

Restructuring through crises

Global capitalism in the last quarter of the 20th century was marked once again by many of the features Marx had described. There were recurrent economic crises, and the restructuring through crisis of capitals, big and small, privately owned and state owned.

Graph: Economic Growth of Industrial Countries (—) As Against IMF Predictions (--)[112]

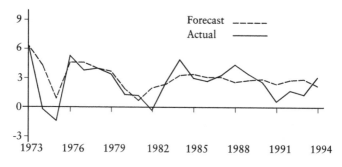

All the major industrial economies suffered at least three real recessions, except for France and Canada which each experienced one "growth recession" and two real recessions, and Japan which avoided a real recession for nearly 20 years after the crisis of the mid-1970s, only then to enter a 13-year period of near stagnation after 1992.

In the former Soviet bloc countries recessionary tendencies of the late 1980s now turned into slumps. But soon different paths emerged. The former USSR (CIS in the graph below) suffered an enormous economic contraction, and output in 2000, even after two years of recovery, was only 70 percent of the 1990s figure. The picture was similarly miserable for Romania, Bulgaria, Albania and the bulk of former Yugoslavia. By contrast, the central European economies (CSB in the graph) only contracted to a little over 80 percent of the 1990s figure and recovered to begin to surpass it in 1998—although this figure was still hardly greater than that for 1980.[113]

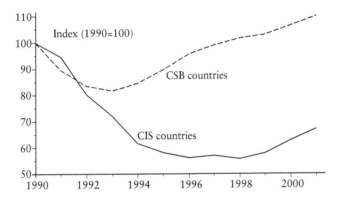

All this meant continued, recurrent pain for those who laboured for and lived within the system. The big question, however, for the system itself was whether the restructuring caused by the crises would open up a new period of expansion. This we will look at in the next section of this work.

Part Three

THE NEW AGE
OF GLOBAL
INSTABILITY

CHAPTER NINE

The Years of Delusion

The new hype

"A substantial decline in macroeconomic volatility" was "one of the most striking features of the economic landscape over the past 20 years or so", declared Ben Bernanke in 2004.[1] Such had long been the view of most mainstream economists and politicians:

New Paradigm advocates received cautious support from the US Treasury Secretary Larry Summers and chairman of the Federal Reserve, Alan Greenspan... Mr Greenspan said the recent economic performance was "not ephemeral".[2]

They spoke of the longest continuous period of American economic growth for four decades and the lowest level of unemployment for three. This was supposedly a new, unprecedented period of non-inflationary capitalist expansion, baptised "the great moderation" or "the new economic paradigm". Stagnation, unemployment and inflation had supposedly been left behind.

For Bernanke, the explanation lay in the greater capacity of the states and central banks to handle the money supply than in the 1970s. For others it lay in the new technologies associated with the microprocessor:

A new economy has emerged from a spurt of invention and innovation, led by the microprocessor...opening all sectors of the economy to productivity gains... The new economic paradigm has brought us the best of all worlds—innovative products, new jobs, high profits, soaring stocks. And low inflation.[3]

The advances of what was called "Anglo-Saxon capitalism", supposedly based on unleashing "economic freedom" and "entrepreneurship", were contrasted with the laggardly rates of growth in Europe and the stagnation in Japan. In Britain New Labour boasted it was following the US example. "No return to boom and bust" was the refrain in every budget speech of chancellor of the exchequer (and future prime minister) Gordon Brown.

The enthusiasm had received a temporary setback when the Asian crisis of 1997 spread to about 40 percent of the world. The *Financial Times* had headlines about an "economic meltdown" and "a house of cards", while the BBC ran a special *Newsnight* programme, "Is Capitalism Collapsing?" But the panic did not last for long. Within months the new paradigm was rising high again: both Patrick Minford, former economic adviser to Margaret Thatcher, and Meghnad Desai, former economic adviser to Gordon Brown, insisted in debates late in 1998 that all that had occurred was a passing storm of no significance, and all problems had been solved by quick intervention by the US Federal Reserve.[4] There was brief panic again in the summer of 2001 as the US went into recession. "The world economy is starting to look remarkably, even dangerously, vulnerable", stated the *Economist*. "Industrialists and bankers at their annual get together on banks of Lake Como did little to disguise their over-riding pessimism",[5] reported the *Financial Times*. But again amnesia soon set in and financial commentators were describing the economic panic of a few months earlier as "the recession that was over before it began"[6]—despite, or perhaps because of, the loss of one in six manufacturing jobs in the US. Renewed economic growth in the US led to even greater optimism than before. The International Monetary Fund could declare year after year that the picture for the future was of fast economic growth. So in April 2007 a typical IMF press release about its most recent world survey read, "Global economy on track for continued strong growth". There were a few mainstream doubters, but their worries were only ever discussed in order to be dismissed.

The overall message was that capitalism was going from strength to strength with supposedly record world growth figures. Even those sceptical about the claims for the advanced countries often accepted a modified version of the optimism when it came to the system as a whole. Hardly a day went past without media references to the "new giants", China and India, and soon compliments were being poured on the other countries included with them in the new "BRICS" rubric—Brazil, Russia and South Africa. Even if the old industrial states were to run into problems, these new centres of capitalist growth would maintain the stability of the world system. The faults that were recognised in the global system were regarded rather as Stalin's admirers used to speak of his "occasional errors", as "spots on the sun".

Hidden problems

For those commentators prepared to look honestly and go a little deeper than immediate appearances, there were disturbing signs. While the IMF, for instance, was exuberant about prospects, research commissioned by the World Bank painted a rather different picture. Growth for the world as a whole was well down on the levels not only of the long boom, but also of the first decade and a half after its end:

Graph three: world GDP growth rate 1961-2006[7]

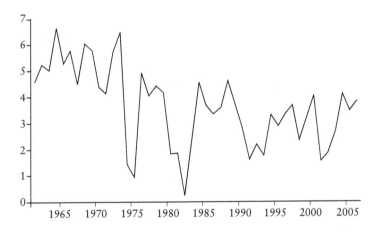

It was only possible to draw a different conclusion, as an IMF graph in the April 2007 World Review seemed to, by starting the series in 1970—with the beginning of the end of the long boom.[8] Parallel with the decline in growth rates went a long-term slowdown in global investment, as research for the IMF revealed (see graph below).

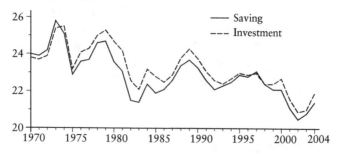

The fall in accumulation and the growth of output took place alongside a continuing low level of the rate of profit compared with the "golden age". There had been some recovery from the low point of the early 1980s, but only to reach about the level of the early 1970s—the turning point that ended the "golden age". Calculations for the US suggest that recovery of profitability from the recession of 2001-2 through the years immediately preceding the credit crunch of 2007 again failed to raise it to anything like the level of the long boom. Robert Brenner shows it moving marginally ahead of the early 1970s figure, only then to fall back. David Kotz shows the profit rate in 2005 as 4.6 percent, compared with 6.9 percent in 1997.[10] Fred Moseley shows a bigger recovery of recent profit rates, but his calculations still leave them at their high point (in 2004) as only marginally above their lowest points in the long boom.[11] The overall pattern of the 1990s and the early 2000s was a continuation of that of the 1980s—of a certain recovery of profit rates, but not sufficient to return the system to the long term dynamism of the long boom.

Marx saw restructuring through crisis as enabling capitalism to recoup the rate of profit, and the "Austrian School" of mainstream economics likewise saw crises as the only way to reinvigorate the system. Each crisis in the 1980s, 1990s and early 2000s did lead to widespread restructuring of industry. There were closures of factories, mines and docks in all the world's industrial heartlands. Industries which had characterised whole regions decamped; others saw their workforces shrink to half or a quarter of their former size, as with the heavy industries of northern China, Detroit's car plants, the Polish shipyards and the meat refrigeration plants of Greater Buenos Aires.

The New Age of Global Instability

But the restructuring through crises did not have the full effect it had had in the "free market" period of capitalism from the early 19th century until the First World War. It did not get rid of unprofitable capital on a sufficient scale to raise profit rates to the levels of the 1950s and 1960s. The neoliberal ideology may have embraced the notion of "creative destruction", with its implication that some giant firms must be allowed to go bust in the interests of the others. But the practice of states—and of the pressures which industry and finance put on states—was rather different. The fear of what the collapse of the really big corporations and banks might do to the rest of the system persisted.

Hardly any big firms had been allowed to go bust during the first two crises of the mid-1970s and early 1980s. Governments had continued to step in to keep them afloat, most notably with the US state's support for the bail-out of the car giant Chrysler at the end of the 1970s, of the Continental Illinois bank in 1984 and of the Savings & Loans corporations (the US version of building societies) in the late 1980s. Things changed to some degree from the late 1980s onwards. As the *Bankruptcy Year Book* reports:

> During the 1980s and early 1990s record numbers of bankruptcies, of all types, were filed. Many well known companies filed for bankruptcy... Included were LTV, Eastern Airlines, Texaco, Continental Airlines, Allied Stores, Federated Department Stores, Greyhound, R H Macy and Pan Am... Maxwell Communication and Olympia & York.[12]

The same story was repeated on a bigger scale during the crisis of 2001-2. The collapse of Enron was, as Joseph Stiglitz writes, "the biggest corporate bankruptcy ever—until WorldCom came along".[13]

This was not just a US phenomenon. It was a characteristic of Britain in the early 1990s, as bankruptcies like those of the Maxwell Empire and Olympia & York showed, and, although Britain avoided a full recession in 2001-2, two once dominant companies, Marconi/GEC and Rover, went down, as well as scores of recently established dotcom and hi-tech companies. The same phenomenon was beginning to be visible in continental Europe, with an added twist in Germany that most of the big enterprises of the former East Germany went bust or were sold off at bargain basement prices to West German firms,[14] and then in Asia with the crisis of 1997-8. On top of this there was the bankruptcy of whole states—notably the USSR, with a GDP that was at one stage a third or even half that of the US.

However, governments had certainly not completely given up intervening to limit the impact of crises on large capitals, nor had the most important capitalist sectors stopped demanding such intervention. This was shown by the way the US Federal Reserves stepped in to save the Long Term Capital Management hedge fund in 1998. A worldwide sample of "40 banking crisis episodes" in 2003 found that governments had spent "on average 13 percent of national GDP to clean up the financial system."[15] Governments as varied as those of Scandinavia and Japan had rushed to prop up banks whose collapse might damage the rest of the national financial system—even if this involved nationalisation as a last resort.[16] Governments took the costs of writing off losses away from particular individual capitals. But those costs had then to be covered from elsewhere in the system—either by taxation, hitting the real wages of workers or the profits of capital, or by borrowing which eventually had to be repaid somehow from the same sources. The benefits for those capitals which survived the crisis were limited as a result. The rising rate of bankruptcies only partially relieved the pressure on their profit rates.

Further relief came from a slower rise in investment compared to productive labour power (Marx's organic composition of capital). The slowdown in accumulation due to lower profitability played a role in this. So did continued waste expenditure, particularly military expenditure. This absorbed a considerably lower level of world output than in the 1950s and 1960s, let alone than during the Second World War. But it still absorbed a much higher amount than in the pre-1939 world. And there had been an increase in US military expenditure during the "Second Cold War" of the 1980s under Ronald Reagan, and again with the "war on terror" under Bush in the early and mid-2000s—and since US military expenditure was half the global total, this meant an overall increase across the system. One estimate is that by 2005 US military spending had risen to a figure equal to about 42 percent of gross non-residential private investment[17]—a big drain on resources that could otherwise have gone into accumulation. At the same time, unproductive expenditures in the financial sector soared, as we shall see later.

The effect of all of these forms of "waste" was much less beneficial to the system as a whole than half a century earlier. They could still reduce the downward pressures on the rate of profit

The New Age of Global Instability

from a rising organic composition of capital—it certainly does not rise as rapidly as it would have done if all surplus value had gone into accumulation: "The rate of growth of the capital/labour ratio fell in most countries" in the 1990s.[18] But the old industrial capitalist countries paid the price for a continued slowdown in productive accumulation and long-term growth rates.

Changes in profit rates of six decades[19]

	Manufacturing	Non-farm/ non-man	Non-financial corpns
1948-59	0.250	0.110	0.143
1959-69	0.246	0.118	0.150
1969-73	0.166	0.109	0.108
1969-79	0.135	0.107	0.103
1979-90	0.130	0.094	0.090
1990-2000	0.177	0.107	0.101
2000-2005	0.144		0.091

Evolution of capital intensity and capital stock[20]

(Average annual growth rate)

		1980-90	1990-98	1995-98
United States	Capital stock	3.0	2.6	3.3
	Capital/labour ratio	1.1	0.6	1.0
Japan	Capital stock	5.7	4.2	3.6
	Capital/labour ratio	4.9	4.7	4.4
Germany	Capital stock	2.6	2.6	2.3
	Capital/labour ratio	2.9	3.7	3.1
France	Capital stock	2.0	2.0	2.0
	Capital/labour ratio	2.3	2.3	2.3
Italy	Capital stock	2.8	2.7	2.7
	Capital/labour ratio	2.7	3.5	3.4
United Kingdom	Capital stock	1.8	1.6	1.6
	Capital/labour ratio	1.8	1.2	1.0

Two other factors can have some impact on the level of investment capitalists have to undertake to remain competitive. There is the increase in the speed at which capital produces and sells commodities (what Marx called the "turnover time" of capital) as a result of advances in transport technology and of the computerisation of warehousing and stock keeping (what are often called today "logistics"). An estimate is that "capital services" grew 2 to 3 percent faster than the capital stock in the late 1980s and 1990s for most countries.[21] This would have reduced the costs to capitals of holding stocks of raw materials on the one hand and of goods awaiting sale (their "circulating capital"). But the second factor will have worked from the opposite direction—the reduced lifetime fixed capital had before it became outdated (what is known as "moral" depreciation). Computers and software become obsolescent because of technical advances much more quickly than other capital equipment—in perhaps two or three years rather than ten, 20 or even 30—and the increased depreciation costs cut into profits.[22]

This was ignored by the argument of the late 1990s and early 2000s that the increase in productivity due to massive growth of cheap computing power was the basis of a new era of continuous growth. As we saw in Chapter Three, the more rapidly firms have to replace their fixed capital, the more it cuts into any increase in profits they got from installing it in the first place. What is more, once a new technology has spread beyond the firms that first introduce it, its effect is to reduce the value of each unit of output: the late 1990s and the early 2000s were a period in which the prices of goods produced by the new technology tumbled, leading to increased competitive pressure on all the firms in these industries. A wave of innovation could no more create an endless boom in the late 1990s and early 2000s than it could in the "new era" of the 1920s.

The most important factor in reviving profit rates was not computerisation, or the reorganisation of capital as such, but the increased pressure capital was able to put on those who worked for it as successive waves of restructuring disrupted old patterns of working class resistance. Capitals took advantage of the redundancies and dislocations caused by restructuring to put relentless pressure on workers to work harder while wages were held down.

There was a decrease in the share of national income going to labour in all of the major Western economies. In the United States, "productivity grew 46.5 percent between 1973 and 1998", while the median wage fell by about 8 percent[24] and that for production workers by 20 percent[25] (with workers only able to protect their living standards by an increase in average working hours from 1,883 hours in 1980 to 1,966 in 1997[26]). Western Europe did not see the same increase in hours (apart from in Britain, where unpaid overtime soared) or a reduction in real wages as in the US in the 1980s and 1990s, but governments and firms began to push

The New Age of Global Instability

OECD Employment Outlook, 2007, p117[23]

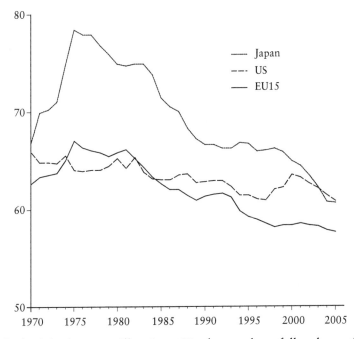

for both in the new millennium. "Real wages have fallen dramatically and working hours are nearly back to 40 a week", reported the BBC on Germany in 2005.[27]

It was not only wages and working conditions that had to be put under pressure. So too did the various services provided by the state (and in some case by private firms) that make up the "social wage": healthcare, pensions, education. During the long boom these had been, as we have seen in Chapter Seven, by and large, paid for out of the taxes on the working class, as is shown by figures by Anwar Shaikh for what he calls "the net social wage"—the difference between what workers pay in and what they get out (see Graph A below).[28] But the impact of recurrent crises, rising unemployment and an ageing population had been to push welfare expenditures upwards (Table B), until even in the US the cost could no longer always be covered by the taxation on workers and therefore tended to hit capital. The figures show enormous unevenness between the degree to which different states—and firms operating in those states—were hit by both the overall level of the "net social wage" and the rise in the welfare expenditures in the 1970s and 1980s. They responded by a series of "reforms" (in reality counter-reforms) which, under the label of "modernisation", aimed at reversing this trend.

Net social wage as percent of GNP (Graph A)

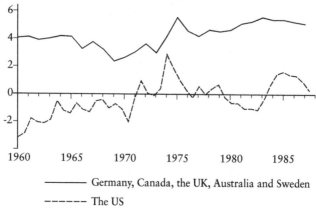

———— Germany, Canada, the UK, Australia and Sweden

- - - - - The US

Welfare expenditure as percent of GDP 1979 and 1995[29] *(Table B)*

Country	1979	1995
Australia	13.2	16.1
Canada	14.5	18.0
France	22.0	29.1
Germany	25.4	28.7
Italy	21.2	22.8
Sweden	25.1	34.0
United Kingdom	16.4	22.5
United States	13.8	15.8

Uneven competitiveness

Each success any one government had in doing this put pressure on other governments to do likewise. But real wages could not be cut, working hours prolonged, or welfare benefits curtailed without causing popular resentment with the potential to explode into all out resistance. The level of resistance varied from country to country, depending on established levels of working class organisation and the outcome of key attacks on it (like the defeat of the long 1980s strikes of air traffic controllers in the US and of miners

The New Age of Global Instability

and print workers in Britain). The most visible result was that the proportion of national output going to welfare in the mid-1990s in France and Germany was about 14 percent higher than in the US and over 6 percent higher than in Britain. The same contrast between the success of the capitalist offensive in the US and Britain and its effects in Europe was shown by the figures for working hours. In these trends lay the supposed advantage of the "Anglo-Saxon" model over the European model for the capitals based within each.

Annual hours worked per worker, 2004[30]

Koreans	2,380
Mexicans	1,848
Americans	1,824
British	1,689
French	1,441
Dutch	1,357

European capital found itself facing problems it had not faced in the years of the boom or even in the decade and a half after it collapsed. Output per head in what is now the Eurozone had grown from 40 percent of the US figure in 1950 to 75 percent in 1975, and German growth, like that of Japan, exceeded that of the US in the 1980s. In 1990 German unification was expected to provide a further massive boost. The mood by the beginning of the new millennium was very different. Overall productivity levels had long since stopped catching up with the US. Those challenging the US auto industry on its home ground were Japanese transplant plants, not Volkswagen and Fiat. Japan may have lost out to the US in computers, but at least it had a computer industry while Europe did not. And coming up on the outside in the inter-capitalist race was China. "Europe needs to wake up" was the message pumped out by scores of Euro think tanks, endorsed by centre-left and centre-right politicians alike and inscribed in the Lisbon Declaration of European leaders in 2002.

The picture for European capitalism was not as dire as that message sometimes made out. Germany, not China, was still the world's biggest exporter in 2006 and its manufacturing industry's output had grown rapidly, even if its employment had not. The EADS airbus consortium was able to compete with Boeing in a way that the Japanese aerospace industry could not. Spanish and French firms had gobbled up many of Latin America's banks, and the European Union sold and invested slightly more in the Mercosur region of that continent than did the US. And for the moment Chinese imports only amounted to 1 percent of European GDP.

There were, nevertheless, reasons for European-based capitalism to worry and to nag states to take action on its behalf. French and German based capitals faced the dilemma that although they were more productive in output per hour worked than capital based in the US[31] they lost out in terms of overall productivity because of the few hours they got from each worker in a year.

European capital therefore found itself under pressure from at least three sides in global markets—from the US and Japan in high technology products and from China in lower technology products. Its response was to push for copying the US approach of imposing "flexible labour markets" so as to get longer working hours and more intensive production (in Marx's terms absolute and relative surplus value) and to try to cut back on welfare expenditure. This was the rationale behind "neoliberal" policies, with counter-reforms of welfare and the use of marketisation and privatisation measures to get workers competing with each other.

German capital followed a policy through the Bundesbank (and then the European Central Bank) in the 1990s of sacrificing economic growth to hold down wages (which rose cumulatively 10 percent less than the European average) and so increasing exports and the share of profits. The paradoxical outcome was that Germany had a big trade surplus and good profits, but a reduced share of world investment and production. This lay behind the pressure it applied successfully in the early 2000s to getting the then Social Democrat-Green government to push through counter-reforms in the Agenda 2010 Programme. Its main planks were a drastic reduction of unemployment benefits by a third, denying any benefits at all to 800,000 people, forcing the unemployed to accept jobs with below average pay, freezing pensions and charging for visits to doctors. Meanwhile, big firms threatened to move production to low wage sites in Eastern Europe if workers did not accept increased working hours. Such "internal modernisation", said Chancellor Schroeder, was "the prerequisite for Germany's assertion into global politics."[32] The overall result was that German real wages fell for the first time in half a century. The same logic lay behind the attempts of French governments to cut back on public sector pensions, to reduce the rights of young workers and to do away with the 35 hour week.

But this was an economic strategy that raised big political problems. For half a century after the Second World War capital and the state sought to legitimise themselves through the ideology of national consensus while collaborating to various degrees with the trade union bureaucracy. This applied not only to social democracy in Germany and France, but also to the Christian Democrat and Gaullist variants of conservative politics. There had seemed no reason to disturb society by overturning this approach so long as their economies seemed to be advancing in comparison with their major competitors. Now the attempt to attack the reforms granted in the past threatened to tear apart the old ideological hegemonies, driving workers whose social democratic attitudes took for granted "partnership" with capital into an antagonistic relationship to it. Capitalists and states were caught between their economic priorities and maintaining their ideological hold on the mass of people.

Of course, there was also in operation a second option for them—that of physically moving production overseas. But this takes time with most sorts of industrial production (fully equipped factories are rarely easy to move, and even when they are there is then the question of energy supplies, transport facilities, a secure political environment, and so on). So it was that even in Britain 30 years of restructuring and factory closures, with a halving of the workforce, did not permanently cut overall manufacturing output.[33]

Even when they considered moving production in the long term, the giant European firms still depended in the interim on finding some way to increase the exploitation of their local workforces. In practice few firms envisaged, for the moment, moving all their production abroad (although the German car industry increasingly used cheap labour in Eastern Europe to solve some of its problems) and this made the need to raise the exploitation of the domestic workforce paramount.

Hope in the East?

When people like Samuel Brittan wrote of the future for capitalism lying in Asia in the early 1990s they meant the small newly industrialising countries of the region—the "tigers" of South Korea, Singapore, Hong Kong and Taiwan, and the "tiger cubs" of Malaysia, Thailand and Indonesia. These had experienced very rapid rates of economic growth, leading the OECD to write of a South Korean "economic miracle" in 1996. By this time Korean living standards approximated to those of the poorer Western European countries; some of the country's firms established themselves as global giants. Posco, the world's third largest steel producer, boasted that its Kwangyang steel complex, opened in 1992, was "the most modern in the world".[34] But much of the growth depended on each tiger holding wages down to compete with the others for Western markets. It was a classic case of blind competition between rival capitals (or in this case state monopoly capitals) and eventually led to output that was too great for the existing market to absorb. By June 1997 there was only 70 percent capacity utilisation in Korea and 72 percent in Taiwan,[35] and all the countries depended on foreign borrowing to finance trade deficits. Yet when financiers suddenly reacted by withdrawing funds from Thailand, forcing the devaluation of its currency, those enamoured of the "miracle" tried at first to think nothing serious was happening. The Thai crisis, wrote Martin Wolf in the *Financial Times*, was "nothing more than a blip on the path of rapid East Asian growth". Within weeks the crisis had spread to all the tigers and tiger cubs, causing economic contraction, reliance on IMF austerity packages, the sudden impoverishment of millions of people and growth rates in the 2000s much slower than in the 1980s and 1990s. But this did not shatter the faith in many quarters that capitalism in East Asia could see off any problems that might be encountered in the West. Communist China became the new bearer of their hopes.

Certainly the emergence of China as an economic power was one of the most important developments within the world system at the beginning of the 21st century. The scale of Chinese economic advance was awesome. Its average growth rate for the period 1978 to 2008 was about 8 percent a year; its economic output was about nine times greater at the end of the period than at the beginning; its share of world trade had risen from less than 1 percent in 1979 to over 6 percent in 2007, until it was just behind Germany, the world's biggest single exporter; by 2005 it was "the leading producer in terms of output in more than 100 kinds of manufactured goods", including 50 percent of cameras,

30 percent of air conditioners and televisions, 25 percent of washing machines and 20 percent of refrigerators.[36] Chinese cities like Beijing, Shanghai, Guangzhou or even Xian in the interior no longer bore much resemblance to Third World stereotypes. The forests of skyscrapers in Beijing or Shanghai made London's much vaunted Docklands development look like Toytown, while the vast industrial developments around Shanghai had few comparisons in Western Europe. Dramatic changes were taking place in what was previously assumed to be a "backward" country of limited economic significance to the world system.

China, like most other industrialising Third World countries, had suffered a crisis just as the long boom was coming to an end in the West. A quarter of a century of what Marx had called primitive accumulation had transformed tens of millions of peasants into wage workers and built up some of the bases of modern industry—but this industry was no match in terms of efficiency for that in many other parts of the world system. The sheer scale of exploitation of the mass of the population led to all sorts of pressures building up from below, while the inability to keep up the pace of industrialisation led to repeated crises within the ruling group. These culminated in massive political upheavals in the years 1966-75 (from the "Cultural Revolution" to the rise and fall of the "Gang of Four") which were only finally resolved after Mao Zedong's death in 1976.

The resolution of the crisis consisted of ad hoc moves to a new structure of accumulation. A series of reforms pushed through in 1978-81 began with relief for peasants through a raising of the purchasing price paid by the state for their produce. The peasants were now free to decide how to use some of the surplus left after (just about) feeding themselves. There was a huge rise in agricultural production, and the increased incomes provided a market for some of the under-utilised industrial capacity. A loosening of state controls allowed it to satisfy this demand, and overall output soared ahead.

Increasing social differentiation within the peasantry led some to accumulate a surplus and then to use the new freedoms from state control to invest in establishing locally based "village industries". Formally owned by village governments, in practice these provided a means of self-enrichment by those with connections to the local party apparatus. A new market capitalism grew up in the south east of the country alongside the old state capitalism centred

The Years of Delusion

mainly in the north, and the regime allowed the new industries to link up with overseas Chinese capitalist interests in Hong Kong and elsewhere.

The surplus passing from the peasantry into the hands of three groups of capitalists (state, "village" and overseas) was still massive despite the reforms, while low peasant incomes meant a ready supply of workers for the new industries, which did not even have to provide the guaranteed minimum living standards and social protection (the so-called "iron rice bowl") of the old state-run heavy industries. In effect, there was a new model of capitalist accumulation, combining the high level of exploitation and repression of the old state capitalism with a turn towards catering for markets—and the markets came increasingly from exporting to the rest of the world system, while providing for the increasingly conspicuous consumption of the old state bureaucracy on the one hand and its children as they took over privatised industries on the other.

The new hybrid economy had contradictions of its own, with the ups and downs of market capitalism superimposed on the ups and downs of the old state capitalist accumulation model. There were wild fluctuations in growth rates. The scale on which the new industries competed with each other for resources created shortages and forced prices up, until the state tried to impose some order on the market by curtailing funds for further investment. So the growth rate could be above 20 percent in 1984, down to around 3 percent in 1985 and back up to close to 20 percent in 1988. There then followed a major economic, social and political crisis in 1989 as growth fell right back and prices soared. This was the economic background to tumultuous student and worker demonstrations in 1989 in most of the major cities, most famously in Tiananmen Square in Beijing.

The regime found a way out of the crisis from 1992 onwards almost by accident. Unable to control things itself, it placed its hopes on unleashing a new round of accumulation based on uncontrolled competition between different industrial concerns. Those who ran village governments were able to turn the new industries into their private property and link up with foreign capital, as were the managers of the great state-owned enterprises. There was a massive rationalisation of old industries, with perhaps 30 million workers losing their jobs. These measures were acclaimed as "progressive" by pro-capitalist economists right across the world. What they meant for workers was portrayed graphically in the 2003 Chinese film *Blind Shaft*, in which the degrading conditions under which the miners work lead two of them to murder a co-worker in an attempt to blackmail corrupt managers. The closeness of reality to the fiction was shown in a mining disaster in Guangdong (supposedly China's most "advanced" province) in the summer of 2005. As more than 100 miners suffocated underground, the owner fled when it was revealed he had paid out millions of dollars in bribes to take over the previously shut down state-owned mine, and at the same time to buy himself a senior position in the local police force. In this way he had been able to ignore all safety precautions while parading himself as an exemplary "entrepreneur" for his role in supplying coal to satisfy the energy needs of a booming economy.[37]

Alongside the attack on the old working class was a renewed upping of the level of exploitation of the rural workforce, who still made up two thirds of the total. One (banned) Chinese study told of a fall of 6 percent in peasants' per capita farming incomes after 1997, and "given the rising costs of health and education, their real purchasing power has probably fallen still further".[38] But the average does not tell the whole story. Class differentiation within the peasantry involved local officials using their powers to grab money (in the form of local taxes) and land off other peasants with the aim of enriching themselves as petty agrarian capitalists—the cause of many local near-uprisings.

Enthusiasts for capitalism claimed the turn to the market had led to an unprecedented lifting of hundreds of millions of people out of poverty. And the abandoning of the crude methods of primitive accumulation in the mid-1970s had permitted much of the industry built up through its methods to be used more productively, with the result that not only the new rural capitalists but also those from peasant families who moved to work in the cities could enjoy improved living standards. But for the great majority of the population, they were still low living standards. The World Bank admitted in the early 2000s that 204 million people, or one in six of the population, still lived on less than $1 a day. Other estimates suggested that "the vast majority of the 800 million peasants" had incomes at this level.[39]

The key to China's rapid growth rates was an unparalleled level of accumulation. The proportion of national output going into investment rose to 50 percent in 2006:[40]

In recent years, no OECD or emerging market economy had a ratio greater than 30 percent (averaging over three years to smooth out cyclical effects)... Even compared to Korea and Japan during their boom years, the ratio in China today looks high.[41]

The rising investment was paid for out of total savings in the economy also rising to over 50 percent of output. Some of the saving was by workers and peasants, who needed it in order to pay for emergencies like medical care and for their old age. Effectively, they handed over a portion of their incomes to state-run banks which have then loaned it to state and privately owned enterprises. But in the early and mid-2000s an increasing proportion of saving came out of the profits made by companies, which rose by about 5 percent of GNP in the early 2000s.[42] This was possible because household consumption as a share of output fell sharply, to only about 40 percent,[43] with the share of wage income falling from 67 percent in the 1970s to around 56 percent in 2005 (see graph).[44]

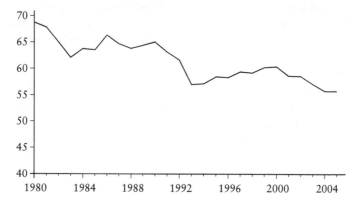

The decline in wage share did not necessarily mean a decline in real wages, since it was a declining share of rising output. What it did mean, however, was that China's economy exemplified Marx's picture of accumulation taking place for the sake of accumulation. The picture was even starker if the section of the economy devoted to exports was taken into account. By the turn of the millennium 80 percent of new growth each year was going to investment and exports as opposed to satisfying the needs of China's people, and, in a further twist, by 2007 nearly 10 percent of China's income took the form of a surplus of exports over imports that was then deposited in the United States—effectively used to finance government or private *American* consumption (graph[45]), which then provided an outlet for further Chinese exports.

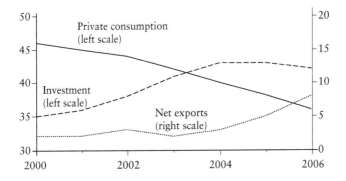

Accumulation at such a rate created three sets of problems, all of which Marx had been familiar with. First it draws in resources on a massive scale, creating shortages that push prices up. The impact of Chinese growth in the early and mid-2000s was to absorb raw materials and foodstuffs from across the world, raising their prices internationally (and in the process giving an economic boost to raw material producers in places like Latin America)—and eventually the rising prices fed back into China.

Second, it leads to a growth of output that cannot be absorbed by a national economy in which wages constitute a diminishing share of output, except by still more accumulation—or by ever greater stress by firms on exports.

But there is enormous competition in export markets—not just from enterprises abroad, but with other enterprises operating in China. The increasing pattern has been one of Chinese factories assembling components produced elsewhere in East and South East Asia, with the final output then being exported. This ties Chinese based exporting firms into competing multinational supply lines: "The percentage of exports produced by foreign-based corporations grew from 17.4 percent in 1990 to 50.8 percent in 2001".[46] By the early 2000s the result of such competition was a level of output that could not always be absorbed completely by the world market any more than by the domestic market. The National Statistics Bureau reported that "of all Chinese manufactured products, 90 percent are in oversupply",[47] despite massive price cutting: "Among Chinese companies the price war is particularly intense because competitors often chase market share rather than trying to increase short term profitability," a *Financial Times* correspondent could report: "Relentless competition among local suppliers keeps profit margins almost invisible for many firms".[48]

It was not only the output of export-directed consumer goods that tended to get out of hand. "Investment in many sectors—including property, cement, steel, cars and aluminum" was "being overdone", Chinese government officials complained.[49] In a system constructed around the goal of accumulation for the sake of accumulation and then left to run itself, top managers measured their success by the speed at which their firms grew—and the government-run banks then rewarded those that grew fastest by allowing them to accumulate debts.[50]

A third problem, which exacerbated the previous two, was that the ratio of investment to workers employed—and to output—was rising, despite the abundance of labour. While investment was increasing by about 20 percent a year, employment growth throughout the economy as a whole was only about 1 percent—and even in urban areas it was only about 3.5 percent. Total manufacturing employment fell from 98 million in 1997 to 83.1 million in 2001,[51] despite the massive rate of accumulation. The fall was due to large-scale redundancies in the old state-owned heavy industries, but it was not compensated for by the increased employment in the newer manufacturing enterprises—and employment in the "secondary sector"[52] as a whole remained more or less static at round 157 million. In other words, the organic composition of capital rose. Researchers for the IMF reported, "The increase in investment" from the mid-1990s to the mid-2000s had led to "a rise in the capital output ratio and a fall in the marginal product of capital".[53]

The effect was bound to be downward pressure on profitability. Phillip O'Hara calculates the rate for the economy as a whole as declining from 47 percent in 1978 to 32 percent in 2000.[54] Jesus Felipe, Editha Lavina and Emma Xiaoqin Fan point to the same trend, but with different absolute figures, from 13.5 percent in the 1980s to 8.5 percent in 2003. They quote results from Lardy and from Lin which show the same trend—with some of Lin's figures showing very small profit rates indeed for some industries (0.2 percent for bicycles, -0.3 percent for buses, 2.9 percent for washing machines, 2.5 percent for beer).[55] A Chinese study by Zhang Yu and Zhao Feng seems to contradict these conclusions, showing the overall rate for manufacturing as falling continually for the 20 years up to 1999, but rising considerably after that.[56] The discrepancy could be explained by the way the massive onslaught on jobs in the state enterprise sector cut into its operating costs. The great counteracting factor preventing a catastrophic fall in profit rates was the continual fall in the share of output going to wages. But this necessarily prevented domestic consumption from absorbing the growing industrial output, further increasing the dependence of accumulation on further accumulation and on exports.

At the same time, there was considerable evidence that the willingness of the banks to lend to enterprises at low rates of interest compensated for the low profit rates of many enterprises—and that parallel with this went a willingness not to push loss-making enterprises into bankruptcy, so loading the banking system with vast, probably unrepayable debts.[57]

As with any capitalist boom, there was a burgeoning of all sorts of speculation as enterprises and rich individuals sought to find quick and apparently effortless sources of profitability: "Investment in real estate grew by almost 20 percent a year over the past four years [to 2005] and reached 11 percent of GDP in 2005".[58] Everywhere in China's major cities there was apparently endless building and rebuilding of luxury apartment blocks, relatively expensive (by Chinese standards) fast food outlets, high class hotels, and shopping malls dedicated to selling designer products (even though such stores often seemed virtually empty of shoppers). And there was the lure of international speculation to add to the lure of local profiteering. In March 2008 executives of the CITIC Group in Beijing were on the verge of signing a deal to buy a one billion dollar stake in the US bank Bear Stearns when news came through that it had gone bust.[59]

This combination of contradictions meant that a smooth upward path of growth was a most unlikely scenario for Chinese capitalism. Certainly those charged with managing its economy were by no means confident that they could control the tempo of competitive accumulation in a way that could avoid unexpected catastrophes as managers of enterprises, both private and state owned, sought to outdo each other. Or, as Premier Wen Jiabao told the National People's Congress in March 2007, "the biggest problem with China's economy is that the growth is unstable, unbalanced, uncoordinated, and unsustainable".[60]

The unpredictability of the Chinese economy had important implications for the rest of the world. It had replaced the US as

Japan's biggest export market, while it was in turn the second biggest exporter to the US (just behind Canada and just ahead of Mexico).[61] Its role in importing components from elsewhere in East and South East Asia and raw material from Latin America and Africa made it central to all their economies. And, most importantly, the huge receipts from its trade—much of it with the US—were deposited in the US. Along with the similar surpluses made by Japan and the oil states, it provided the lending which enabled US consumers and the US government to keep borrowing until the "credit crunch" of the summer of 2007. Effectively it lent money to the US (and to a lesser extent to certain European states like Britain) to buy goods it itself made. This added to the appearance of stability of the world system.

Yet those who believed Chinese growth could pull the world system forward if something went wrong in the US and Europe not only forgot that the unbridled markets unleashed in China could not lead to stable as opposed to wildly fluctuating growth. They also failed to take into account the relatively small weight China still had in the world system. In terms of current exchange rates, GDP in 2006 was $2,600 billion—just behind Germany, just ahead of the UK and less than a fifth of that of either the US or the European Union. "Purchasing Power Parity" estimates (based on the buying power of incomes in the domestic currency, the yuan) seemed much higher, at about 50 percent of US or EU GNP according a revised World Bank estimate in 2007.[62] The exchange rate figures considerably underestimate the level of resources available for consumption by China's population (since domestic prices of basic foodstuffs like rice and basic services like urban transport fares cost a quarter or less of those in the West). But, it is the exchange rate measurement that is important in determining the degree to which a country can import and so provide a locomotive to pull the rest of the world economy forwards. And it was a grave mistake to believe that China, accounting for 4 or 5 percent of global buying power, could somehow compensate for the effect of a major economic crisis in much of the rest of the world system.

The Chinese economy was not yet big enough for it to be an alternative motor for the world system as a whole. But it was big enough for its rapid growth to add to the instability of the global system, as was shown by the way it added to escalating global inflation in the years up to the summer of 2008.

The New Age of Global Instability

India, the NICs and the BRICS

It became commonplace to bracket India with China as the "emerging giants" by the mid-2000s. They had more or less equal populations (around 1,300 million), both were nuclear powers and both suffered deep rural poverty. But India's real importance in the world economy was much less than China's. It was about a third of the size in exchange rate terms (considerably smaller in fact than Britain or France) and 60 percent smaller in PPP terms; its growth rates were only a little above 60 percent of that of China in the late 1990s, rising briefly to just less than 90 percent in the mid-2000s; its share of total world exports in 2003 was only 0.7 percent, putting it in 31st position.[63]

There were *some* parallels with the Chinese pattern: an early attempt at state-directed industrialisation (the period of so-called "Neruvian socialism") was followed by a few years of stagnation in the mid and late 1970s; and then the introduction of reforms aimed at a much more market based model of accumulation. But there were significant differences. Lacking the crude power of the Chinese state, India's state and private capitalists were not nearly as successful in subduing other classes (on the one side the old landowning class, on the other the workers and peasants) and so achieved less in the period of state-led primitive accumulation when the Indian growth rate was probably three quarters of China's. They were therefore less able to benefit from a turn to the world market—exporting less and remaining much less attractive to foreign capital than their Chinese competitors. "Reforms" pushed up the rate of accumulation, with investment reaching 25 to 30 percent of GNP. But this could only be sustained on the basis of a growing portion of output accruing to the capitalist class and the upper middle class, at the expense of the workers, peasants and the poor.

As a 2007 report for the IMF showed:

> In the 1990s, the top of the population enjoyed a substantially larger share of the gains from economic growth compared to the previous decade. This had significant effects on income inequality, which grew within states, across states, and between rural and urban areas.[64]

An analysis of income tax data suggests up to 40 percent of growth ended up in the hands of the top 1 percent of the population.[65]

Apologists for capitalism tend to assume rising growth must automatically lead to falling poverty and quote various official statistics showing a decline in the proportion of people living in absolute poverty by 10 percent in the 1990s. But in the same decade there was a fall in food consumption per head in the rural areas, where two thirds of Indians live. Abhijit Sen, re-analysing the official figures, concluded that the total number living in poverty probably grew in the 1990s, that the proportion below the poverty line only fell very slightly, and this was a "lost decade" in terms of fighting poverty.[66] The number below the poverty line in 2002 was 35 percent of the Indian population, some 364 million people. But even this underestimated the degree of suffering. Half of all Indian children are clinically undernourished and almost 40 percent of all Indian adults suffer chronic energy deficiency.[67] Even in the supposedly prosperous states of Gujarat, Karnataka, Kerala, Maharashtra and Tamil Nadu, "more than 70 percent of the rural population consumed less than 2,200 calories per day".[68]

India's insertion into the world system means that industrial investment, like that in China, has been overwhelmingly capital-intensive, with the capital output rising substantially in the 1990s. Employment growth was stuck at about 1 percent a year; 0.87 percent in the "organised" (ie formal) manufacturing sector,[69] even if growth was a little faster in the "unorganised" informal sector where average firm size is less than two people.[70] Most of the people flooding from the countryside to the cities have ended up trying to make a livelihood in the service sector, doing unskilled labour at very low levels of productivity in return for the 50 rupees ($1) a day needed to just about keep a family alive—sweeping and cleaning, working as domestic servants, washing clothes, pushing barrows, peddling cycle rickshaws, hawking goods, portering, waitering, guarding. The much publicised call centres employed only 400,000 people or 0.008 percent of the country's workforce in 2006.[71]

India's growth, like China's, means that by the mid-2000s it represented a much bigger portion of world capitalism than 50 or even 20 years earlier, and this had important implications for the system as a whole. But it was still quite small by the standards of the US or even Japan, Germany and China. This could change if the rates of growth of the mid-2000s were sustained for another two decades: in dollar terms the Indian economy would end up being bigger than the UK. But the most modern centres of indus-

The New Age of Global Instability

trial society in Mumbai, Hyderabad or Bangalore would still be separated by stretches of rural poverty bigger than most European countries. And long before that the whole process of rapid growth could be thrown off balance both by internal factors and by the impact of instability internationally.

We have seen what happened to the "tigers" in the late 1990s, and before that to the Brazilian "miracle" of the 1960s and 1970s. There was therefore a lot of amnesia involved when people lumped together a very disparate collection of countries, Brazil, Russia, India, China and South Africa (the "BRICS"), and claimed that somehow together they represented an alternative driver for the world system. In fact, renewed economic growth in Brazil, Russia and South Africa depended typically on an upsurge of raw material and agricultural prices in a boom which was bound to come to an end eventually—and when it did so it would hit them seriously.

The great minds that extolled the system paid no greater attention to these contradictions in their rosy picture of Asia than they did to the underlying problems in Europe and North America. Japan had problems, they usually recognised, but this was because of the lack of wisdom displayed by a government which had never really absorbed the lessons about how a free market should operate. As late as the autumn of 2007 financial journalists, government ministers and the stars of academic economics were all agreed that capitalism had found a new long-term stability—and even some Marxists spoke of a "new long upturn". They were soon to look as foolish as those who forecast endless peace in the early summer of 1914.

CHAPTER TEN

Global Capital in the New Age

Bursting through borders

The decades of the great delusion were decades in which capital burst out of national confines in trade, investment and production. By 2007 international trade flows were 30 times greater than in 1950, while output was only eight times greater.[1] Foreign direct investment shot up: flows of it rising from \$37 billion in 1982 to \$1,200 billion in 2006;[2] the cumulative stock of FDI rose from 4 percent of world gross domestic product in 1950 (less than half the 1913 figure) to 36 percent in 2007.[3] The direct organisation of production across national boundaries also took off in a way that had been very rare in the past and the multinational corporation became the generally accepted stereotype of the big capitalist enterprise.[4]

The movement of finance across national borders, which had fallen sharply since the crisis of the 1930s, now grew explosively, with governments dropping exchange controls as part of the more general process of deregulation. By the mid-1980s the trend was for "bankers to map out new strategies which, for most of them", amounted "to establishing sizeable presences in the major financial centres, London, New York and Tokyo, and some secondary ones as well".[5] There was a proliferation of banking mergers. The old-established Hong Kong and Shanghai Banking Corporation took over one of the "big five" British banks, relocated its headquarters to London and moved on to buy banks in a dozen countries. The two big Spanish banks, the Bank of Bilbao and Vizcaya, and the Bank of Santander, bought up a very large proportion of the banking systems of many Latin American countries, until they alone owned almost one third of the assets of the 20 biggest banks,[6] and then branched out into other types of business, "investment banking, insurance and in particular participation in pension fund management", acquiring "minority shares in some non-financial enterprises, basically in sectors where other Spanish investors are very active (telecommunications and energy)".[7]

There was a parallel process of concentration of industrial activities across national borders. The huge firms that had emerged in the old industrial countries in the previous period, often under the tutelage of the state, were now able to dominate not only their national market but also carve out huge chunks of the world market. Their competitors could only survive if they looked to an international mobilisation of resources, that is, if they too became multinational, not only when it came to trade but also when it came to production. The most successful firms in many key industries became those with international development, production and marketing strategies, based upon buying up, merging with or establishing strategic alliances with firms in other countries.

In motors, the Japanese car firms established production facilities in the US, turning out more vehicles than the third biggest American firm, Chrysler; the nationalised French firm Renault began a series of acquisitions in the US, beginning with the small fourth US car firm American Motors; Volvo took over General Motors' heavy truck production in the US; Ford and Volkswagen merged their car production in Brazil; Nissan built an assembly plant in North East England to produce hundreds of thousands of cars a year, while Honda bought a 20 percent stake in Rover. In tyres, the French firm Michelin made itself the world's biggest producer by taking over Uniroyal-Goodrich in the US in 1988. The pattern continued into the 1990s and the early 2000s. Mercedes Benz took over Chrysler (before selling it again in 2007); Renault formed an "alliance" with Nissan (buying 44.5 percent of it, while Nissan bought 15 percent of Renault) with a joint chief executive; General Motors bought Saab, took 20 percent stakes in Suzuki, Subaru and Fiat, and acquired 42 percent of Daewoo; the Indian group Tata took over the Anglo-Dutch steel firm Corus (formed by a previous takeover of the privatised British Steel); half of China's soaring exports were produced by corporations at least partly owned by Western multinationals; Chinese firm AVIC 1 was supplying the rudder for Boeing's 787 Dreamliner and making bids for six auctioned off Airbus plants in Europe; Russia's Aeroflot put in a bid for Alitalia. These are just a random sample of the wave of

The New Age of Global Instability

international takeovers and collaboration agreements that were reported by the *Financial Times* every day.

If the typical capitalist firm of the 1940s, 1950s or 1960s was one which played a dominant role in one national economy, at the beginning of the 21st century it was one that operated in a score or more countries—not merely selling outside its home country but producing there as well. The biggest deployed far more economic resources than many states. "29 of the world's 100 largest economic entities are transnational corporations",[8] reported UNCTAD. The process of national firms branching out into the rest of the world was not confined to the advanced industrial countries. It affected the Third World and Newly Industrialising Countries where the statification of industry had previously tended to go even further than in the West, as we saw in Chapter Seven. It intensified with the restructuring of industry that took place in each crisis of these years as firms rationalised production, shut plants and merged with others.

Myths and realities

This whole process was baptised "globalisation" by the 1990s. It was bracketed together with neoliberalism as representing a whole new phase of capitalism—for enthusiasts a phase very different to any previously. They held not only that the world should be organised according to the free flows of capital, without any intervention by governments, but that this had already come about.

We lived, it was said, in the age of multinational (or sometimes transnational) capital, of firms moving production at will to wherever it could be done most cheaply. It was, some influential voices insisted, a world of "weightless" production,[9] where computer software and the internet were much more important than "old fashioned metal-bashing" industries, and where the absolute mobility of capital had completely detached it from any dependence on states. This was an integral part of the new economic paradigm supposedly unleashing a new dynamism in the aftermath of the failures of Keynesianism, state direction and Soviet style "socialism". "Nationalities of companies" were "becoming increasingly irrelevant', declared the British Tory minister Kenneth Clark.[10] This was the age of "the stateless corporation", declared *Business Week*.[11]

Many people who rejected the politics of mainstream globalisation theory nevertheless accepted many of its assumptions. So Viviane Forrester wrote of "the brand new world dominated by cybernetics, automation and revolutionary technologies" with "no real links with 'the world of work'";[12] Naomi Klein described "a system of footloose factories employing footloose workers";[13] and John Holloway told of capital being able "to move from one side of the world to the other within seconds".[14]

The vision of a global system in which states no longer played a central part had as its corollary the argument that the wars that had plagued most of the 20th century were a thing of the past. The world was entering a "new world order", proclaimed George Bush senior after the collapse of the Eastern bloc and US victory in the first war against Iraq.[15] Francis Fukuyama gave such talk an academic gloss with his announcement of "an end to history".

Even thinkers long associated with the left came to the conclusion that capital in the new period no longer needed the state, and therefore had turned its back on war. Nigel Harris wrote of "the weakening of the drive to war", since "as capital and states become slightly dissociated, the pressures to world war are slightly weakened".[16] Lash and Urry went even further and did not include any mention of military expenditure in their account of the "postmodern" world of "disorganised capitalism".[17]

Lacking from all these varied assertions about globalisation was any real grasp of how the relations between states and capitals were really developing. For capitals were no more willing, or able, to break their relationships with states than they had been at the time of the First World War. Such relationships may have become more complex, but they retained their overwhelming importance.

This should have been most obvious in the case of productive capital. It simply could not be as mobile as globalisation theory contended. Factories and machinery, mines, docks, offices and so on still took years to build up, just as they had in the earlier period of capitalism, and could not be simply picked up and carted away. Sometimes a firm can move machinery and equipment. But this is usually an arduous process and, before it can be operated elsewhere, the firm has to recruit or train a sufficiently skilled workforce. In the interim, not only does the investment in the old buildings have to be written off, but there is no return on the investment in the machinery either. And, few productive processes are ever completely self-contained. They are rooted, as we saw in

The New Age of Global Instability

Chapter Four, in production complexes, dependent on inputs from outside and links to distribution networks. If a firm sets up a car plant, it has to ensure there are secure sources of nuts and bolts, steel of the right quality, a labour force with the right level of training, reliable electricity and water supplies, a trustworthy financial system, friendly bankers, and a road and rail network capable of shifting its finished products. It has to persuade other people, other firms or governments to provide these things, and the process of assembling them can take months or even years of bargaining, involving trial and error as well as forward planning. For this reason, when restructuring firms usually prefer the road of "gradualism"—moving piecemeal from old plant to new, keeping intact old supply and distribution networks, minimising the dislocation to the "complex" around them. So it took Ford nearly two years to implement its decision in 2000 to close down its assembly plant in Dagenham and move production elsewhere in Europe. When Cadbury Schweppes announced the "rationalisation" of its global operation including closures in June 2007, it said it expected it to take three years to implement.

Even with money capital there is no pure mobility. As Suzanne de Brunhoff noted:

Even though huge financial flows of mobile capital are daily circulating round the globe, a global single market of capital does not exist. There is no single world rate of interest and there are no single world prices for produced goods... Financial assets are denominated in different currencies which are not "perfect substitutes".[18]

Professor Dick Bryan made a similar point:

International finance provides a clear illustration of the centrality of nationality within global accumulation. The combination of satellite and computer technology has provided...all the technical preconditions for the neoclassical "perfect market" of financial flows to equalise rates of return, transcending national boundaries. Yet...finance maintains national characteristics. It does not move systematically so as to equalise savings and investment... A global financial system comprised of nationally-designated currencies signals that globalisation cannot be devoid of a national dimension.[19]

Every year UNCTAD provides a list of the top 100 multinationals and their "transnationality index"—the proportion of their sales, assets and investments which are located outside their "home" country. These figures are sometimes said to show how little multinationals depend on a national base. But in fact they can be looked at another way. In 2003 the top 50 multinationals still relied on their home base for over half their business. And the 20 with the highest ratios of foreign sales were mostly from small, open economies such as Canada, Australia and Switzerland, or are members of the EU such as Finland, France, the UK, Germany and Sweden whose sales are oriented to close neighbours. None of the US multinationals figured in the list of the most international global firms.[20]

Average Transnationality of the world's largest transnational corporations (TNCs) 2003

Top 100 TNCs	55.8
Top 50 TNCs	47.8
Those based in	
United States	45.8
United Kingdom	69.2
Japan	42.8
France	59.5
Germany	49.0
Small European countries	72.2

The proliferation of cross-border mergers did not mean that they represented the only, or even the dominant form of restructuring. They counted for only a quarter of all mergers[21]—and many were unsuccessful.[22] And only a small portion of global investment was across national borders. Tim Koechlin showed that although the stock of American FDI had "grown quite dramatically", from "$32 billion in 1960 to $2,063 billion in 2004", this represented "a relatively small share of all US investment", with the ratio of foreign direct investment outflows to all investment at only 7.3 percent".[23] For manufacturing, the ratio was higher, at 20.7 percent—"but was down on the figure of 35.4 percent in 1994".[24] He concludes, "Although the investment process has become *increasingly* 'global'...capital accumulation remains an essentially *national* phenomenon".[25] What is more, foreign direct investment figures gave an exaggerated impression of the mobility of productive capacity, rather than of the ownership of it. UNCTAD figures bore out a point Riccardo Bellofiore made at the end of the 1990s. Foreign investment mostly involved buying up existing enterprises, not new ones, so that:

> FDI flows in manufacturing are dominated by mergers and acquisitions...rather than by the creation of new capacity: and a big share of FDI is in non-productive, speculative and financial ventures.[26]

Most multinationals concentrated their investments in a particular advanced industrial country and its neighbours, and then relied on the sheer scale of investment, research and development, and production there to provide an advantage over all competitors. The foreign investment that did take place was not necessarily "global" in its character. "Sixty-six percent of the output of US foreign affiliates" was "sold locally", that is, within the boundaries of the particular country in which a particular affiliate was based.[27]

This was a trend which broke with the predominantly national basis of production without, however, turning into the global production stereotype. A multinational could seek to overcome obstacles to exporting to a particular country by establishing plants inside its borders—in a pattern which Ruigrok and van Tulder called glocalisation.[28] Even if it started off with "screwdriver plants" devoted simply to assembling components imported from the multinational's home country, it often ended up turning to local firms to provide components. The multinational gained because local firms effectively became its satellites, supplying it with resources and fighting for its interests against its local or regional competitors. It might even welcome protectionist measures by the state its subsidiary was in, since that would protect its sales there from international competitors.

Globalisation theorists failed to recognise such developments. Yet they often tried to bolster their own case by referring to investments like those of Japanese motor companies in the US and Britain which were precisely along these lines. Similarly, they stressed the "flexible production" characteristic, for instance, of part of the Italian knitwear industry, and "just in time" production methods pioneered in Japan as typical of globalisation, although, as Michael Mann quite correctly noted, both implied localised or regional, rather than global, production.[29]

The "outsourcing" overseas by advanced country firms of particular parts of their production processes became an important phenomenon, but it was still a much more limited one than was widely believed. At the beginning of the 2000s, imported "material inputs" (including raw materials) accounted for 17.3 percent of total US output.[30] Koechlin estimated that "outsourcing" accounted "for somewhat less than 4.8 percent of US gross domestic purchases and somewhat less than 9 percent of apparent consumption of manufactured goods".[31] Another study showed that the fall in "payroll employment in manufacturing" in the early 2000s had "not been caused by a flood of imports of either goods or services" but was:

> primarily the result of inadequate growth of domestic demand in the presence of strong productivity growth... To the extent that trade did cause a loss of manufacturing jobs it was the weakness of US exports after 2000 and not imports that was responsible.[32]

The different configurations of global capital

Not only did the popular globalisation accounts overstate the degree of mobility of capital, they also provided a much distorted view of what that mobility involves. Alan M Rugman pointed out that of the big multinationals:

> Very few are "global" firms, with a "global" strategy, defined as the ability to sell the same products and/or services around the world. Instead, nearly all the top 500 firms are regionally based in their home region of the "triad" of North America, the EU, or Asia...[33]

Half of most global firms were still operating mainly in their home region market at the beginning of the 2000s—including Vivendi, Pernod Ricard, Thomson Corporation, Stora Enso and Akzo Nobel, Volvo, ABB and Philips. Only six multinationals operated in anything like a balanced way across at least three continents—Nestlé, Holcim, Roche, Unilever, Diageo and British American Tobacco.[34] Most foreign-owned firms operating in European Union countries were based in other EU countries, where the predominant form of multinational ownership was "regional", not global, with "US-controlled firms responsible for

The New Age of Global Instability

only 4.5 percent of European value added".[35]

Research economists Georgios Chortareas and Theodore Pelagidis concluded in 2004:

> The increase in international trade flows is predominantly confined within the three developed trade blocs of the global economy (the USA, the EU, Asia-Japan). A large part of the world continues to be excluded from the trade boom. The emerging reality is more a process of deepening regional integration (regionalisation) of particular groups/blocs of countries rather than a global increase in cross-border trade flows and production interdependence.[36]

"Trade", they argued, "has not come to be spread over a wider range of countries, even compared with the past. It is enough to recall that developed countries' imports from developing countries are still only about 2 percent of the combined GDP of the OECD".[37] Their one exception was East Asia, which will have grown more important after their research at the turn of the century—by 2005 Chinese exports had expanded to reach to over 7 percent of the global total.

Investment flows were similarly concentrated within the "triad" of North America, Europe and Japan. In 2002-4 FDI flows into the European Union averaged about $300 billion a year. The total for the rest of the world—the "developing countries"—was only $180 billion, of which China (including Hong Kong) took two fifths, and Brazil and Mexico a fifth. Some 89 percent of the cumulative stock of FDI worldwide in 2004 was in the developed economies (roughly the same proportion as in 1990), and two thirds of that was in Europe.[38]

The pattern was not one of capital flowing effortlessly over a homogenous worldwide landscape. It was "lumpy", concentrated in some countries and regions, in a way that was not fully grasped by either the crude globalisation view, by interpretations that stressed regional blocs, or by those who still spoke solely in terms of national economies. The empirical material could be looked at in different ways—just as a bottle can be seen as half full or half empty. But the reality of capitalism was that it could not be reduced to any one of these facets.

Different firms operated at different levels. Some, the majority in simple numerical terms, still operated within national economies from which they put out tentacles to see what they could gain by buying and selling to their neighbours. Others, smaller in number but enormously powerful, increasingly operated on a regional basis and reached out to pick up what they could elsewhere in the world. And a small minority saw their future in genuinely global terms. As capitals with each perspective bought and sold, manoeuvred to expand markets, searched for cheaper inputs and for more profitable places for investment, they both influenced each other and tripped over each other. The outcome was not some new model, but an ever shifting, kaleidoscopic pattern which was upset every time it seemed about to attain some fixity. "All that is solid" did "melt into air" as Marx had put it—but not in the way the crude globalisation theory held. For capital's old companion, the state, entered into the process at every point.

States and capitals in the era of "globalisation"

All the advanced capitalist states still maintain historically very high levels of state expenditure, only surpassed historically during the time of total war. And although business often complains about the level of taxation, it never seriously suggests going back to the level of expenditure of a century ago. The reason is that capitals today, far from not needing states, require them as much as—if not more than—ever before.

They need them first because the continued concentration of capitals, in particular geographical locations, necessitates facilities that are not automatically provided by the operation of the market: police; judicial systems; a framework to limit the defrauding of some capitals by others; at least minimal regulation of the credit system; the provision of a more or less stable currency. Along with these they also need some of the functions fulfilled by the state during the period of the state-directed economy: regulation of the labour market; ensuring the reproduction of the next generation of labour power; the provision of an infrastructure for transport, communications, water and power; the supply of military contracts. Even the big multinationals, with half or more of their production and sales located abroad, still rely for much of their basic profitability on their operations in their home base, and therefore on what a state can provide for them.

Along with these functions there is continued massive support by any state for its capital's domestic accumulation—and this was true long before the most recent turn to Keynesianism. So the Pentagon played a key role in resuscitating the American microchip industry in the late 1980s by putting pressure on firms to merge, to invest and to innovate[39]—and received strong industrial support:

> "In today's global economy some central vision is required", Hackworth of Cirus Logic explained. "Somebody has to have an industrial strategy for this country", agreed LSI Logic's Corrigan.[40]

The result of that strategy was that by the end of the 1990s the world's top semiconductor company was no longer NEC (Japanese) but Intel (American), with Motorola and Texas Instruments (both American) in third and fifth position. The US state also managed to bring about a similar rationalisation of the US aerospace industry, culminating in the merger of Boeing and McDonnell Douglas into a firm that controlled 60 percent of global civil aircraft sales, and a turnover in military aircraft production twice as great as the whole of the European industry. As the *New York Times* put it, "President Bill Clinton's administration" had "largely succeeded in turning America's military contractors into instruments of making the economy more competitive globally".[41]

The internationalisation of firms' operations, far from leading to less dependence on state support, increases it in one very important respect. They need protection for their global interests. A whole range of things become more important to them than in the early post-war decades: trade negotiations for access to new markets; exchange rates between currencies; the allocation of contracts by foreign governments; protection against expropriation of foreign assets; the defence of intellectual property rights; enforcement of foreign debt repayments. There is no world state to undertake such tasks. And so the power of any national state to force others to respect the interests of capitals based within it has become more important, not less.

Floating exchange rates between major currencies mean that the capacity of a government to influence the value of its own currency can have an enormous effect on the international competitiveness of firms operating within its boundaries. This was shown, for instance, by the "Plaza Accord" of 1985, when the US persuaded the European and Japanese governments to cooperate with it in forcing up the value of the yen against the dollar. In the aftermath sales of US firms internationally "grew at their fastest rate during the post-war period, shooting up at an annual rate of 10.6 percent between 1985 and 1990".[42] It was shown again when the political decision of the government brought to office in the aftermath of the Argentinian uprising of December 2001 to devalue the currency by 75 percent gave a considerable boost to the industrial and agrarian capitals based in the country.[43]

A change in the exchange rate alters the amount of global value which a firm operating within a national economy gets in return for the labour it has used in producing commodities. As Dick Bryan has put it:

> The exchange rate is a critical determinant of the distribution of surplus value amongst capitals... Because nation-states are deemed responsible for the global commensurability of "their" currency, globalisation...is not about eradicating the national dimension of accumulation. Indeed, globalisation is not even about the national dimension "hanging on" in a process of slow dissolution. Global accumulation is actually reproducing the national dimension, albeit in ways different to past eras.[44]

Again the same centrality of states is shown in international trade negotiations conducted through the WTO. They gather as the representatives of the capitals clustered together within their borders. Different firms have different interests and will look to the individual states over which they have influence to achieve these. This is just as true of firms who look to establishing global domination through free trade as of those with protectionist inclinations. All are dependent upon "their" state to persuade other states to let them get their way. So the US state is an essential weapon for firms like Microsoft, GlaxoSmithKlein or Monsanto in getting the enormous royalty payments that accrue from world recognition of their intellectual copyrights. Likewise the financial power it exercises through the IMF and the World Bank has safeguarded the foreign loans made by American banks—and has helped US-based industrial corporations gain from the crises facing smaller states, as when Ford and General Motors gained control of two of the Korean car companies at the time of the Asian crisis.[45]

Neither do international mergers show that the importance of states is declining. Part of their rationale is for a multinational to be able to extend its influence from its home state to other states. US and Japanese firms invest in West European countries so as to be able to "jump" national boundaries and so influence the policy of these states and the European Community from within: hence the spectacle in the early 1990s of US multinationals like Ford and General Motors lobbying European governments for measures to restrict the import of Japanese cars; hence also the sight of Japanese car firms negotiating for subsidies from the British state to set up car assembly plants. The giant company does not end its link with the state, but rather multiplies the number of states—and national capitalist networks—to which it is linked.

The continued importance of such connections is shown most vividly during financial and economic crises. For states alone can marshal the resources to stop a giant firm or bank going bust—and pulling down with it whole industrial or financial complexes. The history of such crises since the early 1970s has been a history of states bailing out stricken corporations or putting pressure on some firms for "lifeboat operations" to keep others afloat. Because the period of globalisation has been one of much greater crises than the post-war decades, the reliance of corporations on governments for such rescues has been much greater. As we will see in the next chapter, the transformation of the credit crunch of 2007 into the great banking crash of 2008 showed how great that reliance had become.

The overall conclusion has to be that corporations, whether multinational or other, do not regard a state which will defend their interests as some afterthought based on nostalgia for the past, but an urgent necessity flowing from their present day competitive situation.

The successor to the state capitalism of the mid-20th century has not been some non-state capitalism but rather a system in which capitals rely on "their" state as much as ever, but try to spread out beyond it to form links with capitals tied to other states. In the process, the system as a whole has become more chaotic. It is not as if individual firms have simple demands that they merely put on individual states. As a firm operates internationally, one of its divisions can establish relations with a particular state and its associated complex of capitals, even while other divisions of the same firm can be establishing other relations with other states and their complexes of capital. And particular state apparatuses can lose a lot of cohesion as their parts try to cope with the demands of different, competing capitals. The global agenda, the regional agenda, the national agenda and, in the cases of the larger states, the sub-national agenda (of particular localised geographical complexes of capital) clash with each other, producing frictions—on occasions deep schisms—within the national political-economic structure. This was what occurred during the very long crisis inside Britain's traditional ruling class party, the Tories, through the 1990s and early 2000s: its feuds reflected a clash between those who saw British capitalism's future as tied to the US and those who saw it as dependent on integration into Europe (a clash which itself reflected British capitalism's position having the majority of its trade with Europe, but half its overseas investment in the US).

Those who see the national states as archaic hangovers from the past often speak of the emergence of an "international capitalist class" which will have as its correlate an "international capitalist state".[46] They fail to take seriously Marx's point that once "it is no longer a question of sharing profits, but of sharing losses...practical brotherhood of the capitalist class...transforms itself into a fight of hostile brothers", the outcome of which is "decided by power and craftiness".[47] And when it comes to the use of power, the national state is an instrument ready to hand. Interstate conflict, to a lesser or greater degree, is an inevitable outcome once economic competition becomes a matter of life and death for giant corporations. This is just as true today as in the time of Lenin and Bukharin, even if the interconnectedness of national, regional and global circuits of capital accumulation impacts on how the instrument is used.

Such applications of pressure by states on other states still requires the deployment of large "bodies of armed men", backed up by prodigious expenditure on military hardware—alongside such "non-violent" methods as economic aid, trade embargoes, offers of privileged trading relationships and crude bribery. Much of the time the role can be passive rather than active. The force that sustains a certain level of influence does not need to be used so long as no one dares to challenge it—as with the Mutually Assured Destruction (MAD) doctrine between the USSR and the US which prevented either moving into the other's European spheres of influence during the Cold War. Again force can play an indirect rather than a direct

The New Age of Global Instability

role as with the implicit US threat to the West European powers and Japan *not* to help them militarily during the Cold War years unless they acceded to US objectives. But the violence of the state remained a vital background factor in such cases. In this lies the continuity with the imperialism analysed by Lenin and Bukharin. Even today the rulers of Russia, China, India, Pakistan and North Korea—and for that matter Britain, France and the US—see possession of nuclear weapons as the ultimate defence against enemies.

The interaction between the great powers is not the peaceful concert of nations dreamt of by certain apostles of neoliberalism and free trade. There are contradictory interests, with military force a weapon of last resort for dealing with them. But there is still a difference with the first four decades of the 20th century. These culminated in wars which ravaged the heartlands of the great powers. Tensions since 1945 have led to massive accumulations of arms that could potentially be unleashed against the heartlands. But hot wars have been fought outside them, usually in the Third World.

One reason for this has been the "deterrent" effect, the fear that waging war on a nuclear power will lead to destruction of the whole domestic economy as well as most of its people. Another has been the very interpenetration of the advanced capitalist economies that puts pressure on states to exercise power outside their own boundaries. Few capitalists want their national state to destroy huge chunks of their property in other states—and most of it will be in other advanced capitalist countries.

This does not rule out war completely. The capitalist economy was highly internationalised in 1914, but this did not prevent all-out war. Again, in 1941, the presence of Ford factories and Coca-Cola outlets in Germany did not stop a US declaration of war after Pearl Harbor. But it does provide them with an incentive to avoid such conflicts if they can—and to settle their differences in less industrialised parts of the world. Hence the years since 1945 have been marked by war after war, but away from Western Europe, North America and Japan. And often the wars have been "proxy wars" involving local regimes to a greater or lesser extent beholden to, but not completely dependent on, particular great powers.

This was the logic which led the US in the 1980s to give tacit support to Iraq in its long war against Iran and to provide modern weaponry to the Mujahadin fighting the Russian occupation of

Afghanistan. A similar logic worked itself out in the Balkans in the 1990s, when Austria's attempt to gain from Slovenian independence from Yugoslavia led to Germany encouraging Croatian independence and then the US Bosnian independence, even though the result was bound to be bitter ethnic conflict.

The worst suffering from proxy wars has probably been in Africa. During the last decade and a half of the Cold War the US and the USSR backed rival sides in wars and civil wars as part of their attempts to gain a strategic advantage over each other. In the 1990s the US and France vied for influence in Central Africa. They backed rival sides in the war cum civil war that broke out in the border regions of Tanzania, Rwanda, Burundi and Congo-Zaire. They helped set in motion a catastrophe resulting overall in 3 or 4 million dead. In such situations freelance armies emerged whose commanders emulated the great imperial powers on a small scale by waging war in order to enrich themselves, and enriching themselves in order further to wage war. Imperialism meant encouragement to local rulers to engage in the bloodiest of wars and civil wars—and then occasionally the sending in of Western troops to enforce "peacekeeping" when the disorder reached such a scale as to threaten to damage Western interests. Contradictions which arise from the inter-imperialist antagonisms of the advanced capitalist states in this way wreak their worst havoc in the poorer parts of the world.

From the new period of crisis to the new imperialism

The pattern of the old imperialism was one of coalitions of states with comparable levels of economic and/or military capacity confronting each other. Today there is great unevenness even between the biggest states when it comes to their capacity to advance the interests of their domestically based capitals. At the top of the hierarchy is the state which has the greatest capacity for getting its way, the US. At the bottom are very weak states, hoping to be able to beg favours off those above them. The states in the middle alternatively squabble with each other over their position in the global pecking order and form ad hoc alliances in the hope of forcing concessions from those above them.

This cannot be a stable hierarchy. The unevenness in rates of economic growth (or sometimes contraction) in a period of recurrent crises means that the balance of forces between the different states is always changing, leading to rival displays of might between those who want to advance up the hierarchy and those who want to keep them in their place. Weak states get entangled in conflicts with neighbours which draw in powerful states to which they are allied, while powerful states see exemplary interventions in weak "rogue" states as a way of gaining advantage over other strong states.

The greatest source of instability has come from the attempts of the US to permanently cement its position at the front of the global pecking order. This seemed unassailable at the end of the Second World War. But in the decades that followed the US feared successive challenges from other states which were growing much more rapidly than it was. Russia was seen as an economic (as well as military) threat in the 1950s, however absurd that might seem today, Japan in the 1980s, and more recently China. The determination of the US state not to risk losing its position explains its massive levels of arms expenditure and the wars it has waged in the Global South.

The scale of the problems it faced first began to hit home in the late 1960s when the US ruling class found it could not afford the escalating cost of trying to achieve all-out victory in Vietnam. The history of US capitalism since has been very much a history of its attempts to restore its old position, amid a world marked by repeated economic crises and generally declining rates of accumulation. Its attempts have involved alternating phases of reducing arms spending as a proportion of total output in an effort to ease economic difficulties (from the late 1960s to the late 1970s, and from the late 1980s to 2000), and of increasing it in the belief that this could boost US global power and the performance of particular US corporations (in the early and mid-1980s and 2000-8). In all the phases the US state made some gains for the capitals based in it. In none of them were the gains sufficient fully to offset its long-term relative decline.

The collapse of the military challenge from the USSR and the economic challenge from Japan might have been expected to restore the confidence of the US ruling class in its global power in the 1990s. But its strategists had worries about the future. They reasoned that without the fear of the USSR to keep them in line, the European powers were more likely to resist US demands than in the past—as was shown by very hard bargaining at World Trade

Organisation sessions. And in the East, Chinese growth was replacing the older challenge from Japan. Writing in 1994, Henry Kissinger expressed his unease:

> The US is actually in no better position to dictate the global agenda unilaterally than it was at the beginning of the Cold War... The United States will face economic competition of a kind it never experienced during the Cold War... China is on the road to superpower status... China's GNP will approach that of the US by the end of the second decade of the 21st century. Long before that China's shadow will fall over Asia.[48]

What is more, a quarter of a century of growing internationalisation of finance, investment, trade and production made US capitalism vulnerable to events beyond its borders. Its great multinational corporations needed some policy which would enable the might of the US state to exercise control over such events. Already towards the end of the Clinton Administration there were moves towards a more aggressive foreign policy designed to achieve this, with the push to expand NATO into Eastern Europe, but this did not go far enough for a group of Republican politicians, businessmen and academics—the infamous neoconservative "Project for a New American Century" formed in the late 1990s. Their starting point was the insistence that the way to stop "a decline in American power" was a return to a "Reaganite" policy based on large increases in defence spending, the building of a missile defence system, and action to deal with "threats" from "dictatorships" in China, Serbia, Iraq, Iran and North Korea.[49] "Having led the West to victory in the Cold War, America faces an opportunity and a challenge. We are in danger of squandering the opportunity and failing the challenge".[50]

The Republican electoral victory of 2000 and then the national panic caused by the 9/11 destruction of the World Trade Centre gave them a chance to implement their policy.

It amounted in practice to further building up the military might of the US—and then using it to assert US global dominance against all comers. Increased arms spending and massive tax cuts for the rich were meant to pull the US out of recession, just as the "military Keynesianism" of Reagan had two decades before. Increased arms spending would lead to recovery from recession, to further military handouts to finance technical advances for computer, software or aviation corporations, and to an increased capacity to dictate policies to other ruling classes—and all paid for by even bigger investment flows into the US as it demonstrated its overriding power. The aim was for the US to more than compensate for losing its old lead in market competition by using the one thing it has that the other powers do not—overwhelming military might. It was an updated version of the logic of imperialism as described by Bukharin in the early 1920s, with the difference that the rival capitalist states were not going to be forced into subservience by wars directly against them, but by the display of the US's capacity to wield global power through wars it and its client states waged in the Global South.

Hence the attack on Afghanistan and then, 18 months later, on Iraq. The "neocons" believed they had a perfect opportunity to demonstrate the sheer level of US military power *and* to increase control over the world's number one raw material, oil. This would weaken the bargaining power of the West European states, Japan and China, since they would be at least partially dependent on the US for their supplies. The assumption was that the wars would be won by little more than a display of US airpower at very little cost. This seemed a viable way for achieving shared goals to those who ran US-based corporations, and the Democrats in Congress voted for war.

It was a gamble and by the spring of 2004 it was clear that the gamble was going seriously wrong. The US had taken control of Kabul and Baghdad easily enough. But its forces on the ground were not able to prevent the growth of resistance in Iraq—and of growing Iranian influence there. Within another two years it also faced serious resistance from a resurgent Taliban in Afghanistan.

The turn to military Keynesianism seemed at first to be successful in economic terms. There was an unexpectedly quick recovery from the recession of 2001-2: "Official military expenditures for 2001-2005 averaged 42 percent of gross non-residential private investment" and "official figures...excluded much that should be included in military spending".[51] All this provided markets, in the short term, for sections of US industry. But the high levels of military expenditure soon showed the same negative effects they had shown at the time of the Vietnam War and under the Reagan administrations. They increased economic demand without increasing overall international competitiveness and so caused ballooning trade as well as budget deficits. By 2006 the combination of escalating military costs and the risk of defeat in Iraq was worrying important sections of the ruling class. A 2006 report from the Iraq Study Group, headed by Republican Party heavyweight James Baker and Democratic Party heavyweight Lee Hamilton, bemoaned the loss of "blood and treasure" with an estimate of the costs to US capitalism of the Iraq venture of a massive £1,000 billion (equal to seven months output from the British economy).[52]

Meanwhile other states—and the capitals operating from them—were able to take advantage of the US's perceived weakness to advance their own positions. The most important West European states, France and Germany, had refused to back the 2003 Iraq War, unlike the first Iraq War of 1991. The French state in particular saw a weakening of US influence in the Middle East as an opportunity to advance the interests of French capital in regions where its interests clashed with the US's. China was able to benefit from the US entanglement in Iraq and Afghanistan to expand its own influence, particularly in Africa and Latin America. This went hand in hand with growing trade links, as it looked to mineral imports from Africa and agricultural imports from Brazil, Argentina and Chile. Soon Russia too was flexing its rather weaker muscles, as increased oil revenue allowed it to recover from the economic collapse of the previous decades and to exert pressure on some of the other former Soviet republics; Iran took advantage of the US's setbacks to increase its leverage in Iraq and Lebanon; the BRICS formed an ad hoc alliance to advance their common trade interests in opposition to both the US and the EU, so paralysing the Doha round of trade negotiations from which US corporations had hoped to get even easier access to foreign markets. The US discovered that when three of its client states launched wars for objects it supported—Israel in Lebanon in 2006, Ethiopia in Somalia in 2007, Georgia against Ossetia in 2008—it was not in a situation to stop them facing defeat.

Commentators who had not long before insisted the collapse of the USSR had created a "unipolar world" with one superpower were beginning to talk about "multipolarity", with the US only able to get its way by making concessions to other powers. Some thought this meant a more peaceable world. But the multipolarity is a world of states and their associated capitals which have different interests and are out to impose them on the others when they get the chance. It is the multipolarity in which old imperialist imperatives are strengthened just as it becomes more

The New Age of Global Instability

difficult for them to be successful. It is a world, in short, beset by a multitude of contradictory pressures and compelled, therefore, to experience one convulsive political crisis after another. This became clear when the great economic delusion gave way to a great economic crisis.

CHAPTER ELEVEN

Financialisation and the Bubbles That Burst

Credit crunched

The mood was one of "exuberant optimism", as the world business elite gathered in the Swiss resort of Davos in January 2007 to "enjoy" what the *Financial Times* called "the opportunities brought about by globalisation, new technologies and a world economy that is expanding at its fastest pace for decades".[1] The mood was rather different at their next gathering in January 2008. There was "grim determination"[2]—grim because the global financial system had begun to grind to a halt with a "credit crunch"; determination because the "real economy" was still expanding and it seemed that appropriate government action would get the banks lending again.

Governments took action in the months that followed. In January central banks slashed interest rates. In February the British government nationalised the mortgage bank Northern Rock; in March the US Federal Reserve provided $30 billion for J P Morgan Chase to take over the failing Bear Stearns bank; in April and May central banks on both sides of the Atlantic provided hundreds of billions to the banks to keep them going, and in July they provided hundreds of billions more; early in September the US government took over the giant mortgage lenders Fannie Mae and Freddy Mac in what the former government adviser Nouriel Roubini described as "the biggest nationalisation humanity has ever known".[3]

It was all to no avail. The collapse of one of the pillars of the US's financial system, the investment bank Lehman Brothers, on 15 September caused what was generally called a "financial tsunami". Bank after bank in country after country came close to collapse and had to be rescued by government bail-outs that cost further hundreds of billions and often involved partial nationalisation. The credit crunch had become the most serious financial crisis the global system had known since the slump of the 1930s. By end of the year it was clear to everyone that it was more than just a financial crisis. Tens of thousands of jobs were being lost every day in all the major economies; world trade was falling at an annualised rate of 40 percent, and the IMF was predicting "the sharpest recession since the Second World War for the rich countries".[4] But it was not only the rich countries which were affected. South Korea, Malaysia, Thailand and Singapore suffered sharp economic contraction; 20 million Chinese workers lost their jobs as its exports fell and its real estate bubble collapsed; Russian ministers began to fear a new crisis; Brazil's industrial output started falling; the economic recovery of Eastern Europe came to a sudden halt as millions of people found they could not keep up with their mortgage payments to West European banks. At Davos in January 2009 there were "ever more doom-laden prognoses".[5]

The rise of finance

The crisis followed a quarter of a century in which finance had grown on a massive scale to play an unprecedented role in the system. The stock market valuation of US financial companies was 29 percent of the value of non-financials in 2004, a fourfold increase over the previous 25 years;[6] the ratio of financial corporations' to non-financial corporations' profits had risen from about 6 percent in the early 1950s through the early 1960s to around 26 percent in 2001;[7] global financial assets were equal to 316 percent of annual world output in 2005, as against only 109 percent in 1980;[8] household debt in the US was 127 percent of total personal income in 2006 as against only 36 percent in 1952, around 60 percent in the late 1960s and 100 percent in 2000.[9]

The growing role of finance had its impact throughout the global economy. Every upturn in the recession-boom cycle after the early 1980s was accompanied by financial speculation, causing massive rises in the US and British stock markets in the mid-1980s and mid-1990s, the huge upsurge of Japanese share and real estate prices in the late 1980s, the dotcom boom of the late 1990s, and the housing booms in the US and much of Europe

The New Age of Global Instability

in the early and mid-2000s. Along with these went successive waves of takeovers and mergers of giant companies, financed by credit, from the buyouts of firms like RBS Nabisco in the late 1980s through to the wave of takeovers of old-established companies by private equity funds in the mid-2000s.

Meanwhile general levels of indebtedness tended to grow for governments, non-financial corporations and consumers alike, as bank lending rose much more rapidly in most parts of the world economy than did productive output. It doubled in the US and trebled in Japan in the 1980s; the US boom of the mid-90s was accompanied by an extraordinarily high level of borrowing by firms and consumers; the housing and property booms of the mid-2000s were similarly sustained by massive borrowing in the US, Britain, Spain and Ireland.

The impact of finance on the less industrialised countries was already very marked by the 1980s. The loans of the late 1970s had created a never ending dependence on further borrowing from financial institutions in order to keep servicing existing debt. By 2003 the total external debt of sub-Saharan Africa stood at $213.4 billion, that of Latin America and the Caribbean at $779.6 billion, and of the South as a whole at $2,500 billion.[10]

Overall the role played by finance within the system was much greater than in either the depression years of the 1930s or the boom years of the early post-war decades. In those decades the banks had certainly not played the central role Hilferding had ascribed to them at the beginning of the century with his concept of "finance capitalism" (see Chapter Four). In the US the big industrial corporations relied on their own internally generated revenues for investment funds; in Japan and Germany the banks played a greater part, but it was one of aiding the expansion of favoured sections of industrial capital. It was with the ending of the long boom that finance seemed to break the bonds that had bound and subordinated it to industrial capital. By the 1980s funds worth billions—and later hundreds of billions—of dollars were moving into and out of economic sectors and particular countries, cherry picking the most profitable outlets for investment before moving on elsewhere, often leaving economic devastation in their wake.

Finance began to impact directly on the lives of the world's workers in a way in which it had not previously. Most people until the 1980s were paid wages in cash every week; now the norm was payment into bank accounts. The spread of home purchase in countries like Britain or the US from a third to two thirds of households provided a new destination for lending—and the diversion of part of wages and salaries into interest repayments. Insurance and private pension schemes likewise spread the tentacles of finance into wider sections of the population than ever before. Credit in the form of mortgages and hire purchase agreement was already important in the 1930s, but it was only in the 1980s that indebtedness began to become central in maintaining people's regular living standards. For the majority of workers in the US or Britain, the mortgage and the credit card became part of everyday life, while governments almost everywhere preached the virtues of depositing regular savings into financial institutions as the way for the workers and middle classes to provide themselves with pensions in their old age. As Robin Blackburn has shown, pension contributions fed into the mushrooming expansion of a financial system over which the contributors had no control.[11]

This rise of finance was accompanied by a great increase in the frequency of financial crises. As Andrew Glyn said in *Capitalism Unleashed*, "Crises involving banking crises, which had almost died out in the Golden Age, reappeared in strength from 1973 onwards and became practically as frequent after 1987 as during the inter-war period".[12] Martin Wolf noted "100 significant banking crises over the past three decades".[13] Yet after each crisis the system as a whole seemed to revive again, so that on the eve of its greatest crisis there was talk of record growth rates and predictions of ever faster growth in the future. Finance, in fact, acted like a drug for the system, seeming to give it great energy and creating a sense of euphoria, with each brief hangover being followed by a further dose until the metabolism as a whole suddenly found itself being poisoned.

The debt economy and the great delusion

The growth of finance was never something separate from what was happening to the productive core of the system, but was a product on the one hand of its internationalisation, on the other of the long drawn out slowdown in accumulation.

The first big growth of international finance in the 1960s was a result of the way the growth of international trade and investment—

The New Age of Global Instability

and US overseas military expenditure associated with the Vietnam War—led to pools of finance ("Euromoney") which had escaped the control of national governments. The next big growth came with the recycling of massively expanded Middle East oil revenues through the US banking system—revenues that were a product of the increased dependence of productive capital on Middle East oil.

The restructuring of productive capital took place increasingly, as we have seen, across national borders, even if mostly it was regional, not global, in scope and did not measure up to much of the hype about globalisation. But industry could not restructure in this way without having financial connections across borders. It required international financial networks if it was to repatriate profits or establish subsidiaries elsewhere in the world. An important source of profit for some sections of financial capital lay in the fees to be gained by overseeing acquisitions and mergers of productive firms, and that meant there was a gain to be made in operating multinationally before they did. As in Marx's description of finance in his day, it led the way in encouraging productive capital to reach out beyond its established bounds.

Multinational productive capital, in turn, opened up new vistas for multinational financial transactions. The success of the Japanese car industry in penetrating US markets in the late 1970s laid the ground for the flow of Japanese finance into both productive investments (car plants) and real estate speculation in the US. And the flows of funds and commodities *within* multinational corporations provided conduits by which financial transactions could if necessary escape governmental control.

As chains of buying and selling grew longer than ever, so did the chains of borrowing and lending—and with them the opportunities grew ever greater for financial institutions to make profits through borrowing and lending that had no immediate connections with processes of production and exploitation. This took place in a wider context which made the search for profit through finance increasingly attractive to capitalists of all sorts—the fall in profit rates from their level in the long boom (as described in Chapters Eight and Nine). Capitalism internationally went through nearly four decades in which profitability was substantially lower, even in its period of recovery, than that which had enabled it to expand production and accumulate so rapidly previously.

Profitability did not collapse completely, and there was a continuous growth of a mass of past surplus value seeking opportunities for fresh profitable investment. But there were not nearly as many of these in productive sectors as previously. One consequence, as we have seen, was a general slowdown in the level of accumulation and decline in average growth rates. Fairly fast growth of productive sectors would occur in one part of the world economy or another—in Brazil and the East Asian NICs in the late 1970s, in Japan and Germany in the 1980s, in the US and the East Asian NICs again in the mid to late 1990s, in China and to a lesser extent the other BRICS in the 2000s. But profitability was not sufficient to raise productive accumulation throughout the system as a whole to its previous levels.

There were increased competitive pressures on individual firms to undertake large individual investments so as keep ahead of rival firms, but there was less certainty than before about being able to make a profit on those investments. Firms, wealthy individuals and investment funds reacted by being cautious about committing themselves to such investments lest it leave them without ready cash ("liquidity" in financial parlance) next time there was a crisis. The result was an inevitable tendency for the average level of productive investment to fall.

Growth of private sector real non-residential capital stock in industrial countries[14]

1960-69	5.0 percent
1970-79	4.2 percent
1980-89	3.1 percent
1991-2000	3.3 percent

These figures, it should be noted, understate the slowdown in productive investment, since a growing share of investment went into the non-productive financial sphere. And it was not only in the old industrial countries that a falling share of surplus value went into productive investment. The "tigers", the NICs and the BRICS drew a sharp lesson from the Asian crisis of 1997-8. They were not willing to risk being stuck again with a shortfall of ready cash the next time international instability hit their markets, and built up surpluses on foreign trade that they saved rather than invested domestically. Even China ended up with an excess of saving over investment equal to 10 percent of its national income, despite its virtually unprecedented rate of accumulation.

The New Age of Global Instability

Globally this meant there was a growing pool of growth of money capital—money in the hands of productive as well as non-productive capitals—searching for outlets that seemed to promise higher levels of profitability. Hence the pressure on firms to deliver short-term rather than long-term profits. So too the succession of speculative bubbles and the repeated "Minsky" shifts from speculation to Ponzi schemes in which financiers used the money entrusted to them by some investors to pay off other investors and line their own pockets.[15] All sorts of speculative, unproductive activities flourished, from pouring money into stock markets or real estate to buying oil paintings by old masters. In each case, the rush of speculators into buying things in the expectation of rising prices was, for a time, a self-fulfilling prophecy. As they outbid each other, prices did indeed rise. In this way the ups and downs of the productive part of the system found a magnified reflection in the ups and downs of various other assets. The financial system expanded as a consequence, since it played a key part in collecting together the funds for speculation, and could then use the assets whose value had increased because of speculation as collateral for borrowing more funds.

There developed a mass of capital wandering round the world looking for any opportunity where it seemed there might be profits to be made. Already in the economic recovery of the late 1980s:

Financial activity became frenetic, with stock and share and property values soaring upwards... Property speculation rose to new heights, and private borrowing reached record levels in the US, Britain, and Japan... There was real industrial growth, but it was dwarfed by the expansion of the property markets and by various forms of speculative activity... General business investment grew considerably faster than manufacturing investment—in sharp contrast to the 1960s and early 1970s, when manufacturing grew at the same speed. The growth of manufacturing investment was about a third lower in the US and Japan, and about two thirds lower in Europe, than in the earlier period.[16]

Robert Boyer and Michael Aglietta have accurately described what happened during the next US boom, in the mid and later 1990s:

Overall demand and supply are driven by asset price expectations, which create the possibility of a self-fulfilling virtuous circle. In the global economy, high expectations of profits trigger an increase in asset prices which foster a boost in consumer demand, which in turn validates the profit expectations... One is left with the impression that the wealth-induced growth regime rests upon the expectation of an endless asset-price appreciation...[17]

The growth of multinational finance increased the instability of the system, but did not cause it. Enhanced instability in turn encouraged productive firms to seek speculative profits in a way that further boosted the financial sector and added still more to the instability.

A prime example of this was the rise of the derivatives markets. Their original function was to provide a sort of insurance against sudden changes in interest or exchange rates. This was an extension of the long established practice of buying and selling "forward"—agreeing now on a price to be paid at some specified point in the future for some commodity. Now derivatives developed into elaborate systems of payments for options to buy and sell currencies or to lend or borrow money at various rates at different times in the future. In doing so, they provided productive firms with some protection against their calculations of future competitiveness and profitability being upset by sudden changes in various markets—and became an integral part of normal business for many companies.[18] But that was not the end of the matter. The derivatives that provided that protection could themselves be bought and sold, and it was then possible to gamble on changes that would take place in their prices if exchange or interest rates went up or down. Hedge funds, working with money provided by rich individuals putting in a few million dollars each, found they could make very large profits by borrowing in order to make such bets, assuming (as every poor gambler does) that they were bound to win.

The reliance on derivatives was not the only way in which the boundaries between productive capital and the financial sector were eroded. Many industrial concerns began to look to finance as a way of profit making. In the 1990s both Ford and General Motors turned towards financial activities such as "leasing, insurances, car rental", so that "during the boom 1995-98 a third of the [Ford] group's profit accrued from services".[19] The *Economist* has told of the US's currently biggest manufacturing firm, General Electric, that its "profits grew with the sort of predictable consistency...made possible

The New Age of Global Instability

by...making good any unexpected shortfall with last-minute sales of assets held by the firm's notoriously opaque finance arm, GE Capital," which was responsible for "40 percent of GE's revenue".[20]

As capitalism in all its forms turned to financial operations to complement productive operations from the early 1970s, governments came under pressure to abandon controls imposed on financial transactions. For a time governments still committed to the state capitalist or Keynesian notions of the previous period attempted to hold the line against the way finance could well over national borders. But one by one they gave up the attempt, partly because they saw old controls of currency and capital movements as ineffective, partly because, accustomed to adjusting their horizons to what capital said was possible, they were won over to the idea that this was the only way to achieve a new cycle of capital accumulation. The approach of those who had started off on the social democratic left was that if you could not beat them, then join them.

Usually the speculation was in non-productive spheres—repeated stock exchange and real estate bubbles. But occasionally it focused on some area where they believed there was profit to be made by productive investment. As the *Financial Times* told of the late 1990s:

> Spending on telecoms equipment and devices in Europe and the US amounted to more than $4,000 billion. Between 1996 and 2001 banks lent $890 billion in syndicated loans... Another $415 billion of debt was provided by the bond markets and $500 billion was raised from private equity and stock market issues. Still more came from profitable blue chips firms that drove themselves to the brink of bankruptcy or beyond in the belief that an explosive expansion of internet use would create almost infinite demand for telecoms capacity. The global financial system became addicted to fuelling this bonfire. Nearly half European bank lending in 1999 was to telecoms companies... about 80 percent of all the high-yield, or junk, bonds issued in the US were to telecoms operators. Five of the ten largest mergers or acquisitions in history involved telecoms companies.[21]

The fact that there was a productive element to this boom added to the great illusion that it could go on forever. But the boom was based on speculation, ascribing massive exchange value to products for which the current use value was very limited. So much "band width" had been created, the *Financial Times* said, that:

> if the world's 6 billion people were to talk solidly on the telephone for the next year, their words could be transmitted over the potential capacity within a few hours…[only] 1 or 2 percent of the fibre optic cable buried under Europe and North America has even been turned on.[22]

The telecoms boom inevitably collapsed, causing widespread disarray. By the beginning of September 2001 (before the 9/11 attack which is usually blamed for that year's recession) the "stock market value of all telecom operators and manufacturers" had "fallen by $3,800 billion since its peak in March 2000" and "probably $1,000 billion" had gone "up in smoke".[23]

Faced with the collapse of this bubble into productive investment, it is perhaps not surprising that the next bubble would be around something that seemed to be…"as safe as houses". During the recovery from the 2000-2 recessions those with money (old fashioned banks, newer financial groups such as hedge funds, and rich individuals with a few million in ready cash) found they could expand their wealth by borrowing at low interest rates in order to lend to those prepared for, or conned into, paying higher interest rates. Bits of various loans were then parcelled together into "financial instruments" to be sold at a profit to other financial institutions which in turn would sell them again. Those at one of end of the chain of lending and borrowing would not have the remotest idea where interest was coming from at the other end. In fact, many of those expected to pay it were poorer sections of the American population desperate to get somewhere to live but previously regarded as uncreditworthy. They were lured into taking out mortgages with "tickler" fixed term low rates of interest which could then suddenly be increased after two or three years. Rising house prices were supposed to make lending to them safe, since if they defaulted on their loans their homes could be repossessed and sold at a handsome profit. The fact that it was precisely the willingness of financial institutions to bid against each other to offer loans to buy houses that was raising the prices—and that prices would inevitably fall if they all began repossessing—was something that escaped the notice of the geniuses who ran these institutions.

The New Age of Global Instability

The more corporations inflated their wealth by losing touch with reality the more they were honoured. The British bank Northern Rock was "the toast of a glitzy City dinner where it was heaped with praise for its skills in financial innovation".[24] Gordon Brown praised the "contribution" of Lehman Brothers "to the prosperity of Britain".[25] Ramalinga Raju was named India's "Young Entrepreneur of the Year" and awarded the Golden Peacock award by the World Council for Corporate Governance just months before it was revealed that he had defrauded his own company of one billion dollars.

Again it has to be stressed that the speculative ventures of these years did not just involve financial capitalists. Industrial and commercial capitalists took part. More than half the supposed growth in the worth of the whole of the non-farm, non-financial corporate sector of the US in 2005 had been due to inflation in its real estate holdings.[26]

The finance-led bubbles were not, however, just important as a source of profits for the supposedly productive sector of the economy. They were also central in ensuring it had markets that neither its own investment nor what it paid its workers could provide. This was true of the bubbles of the 1980s and 1990s. The combination of reduced investment and attempts to hold down wages in the old industrial countries (and success in cutting them in the US) made consumer debt increasingly important in providing demand for output. It was even truer in the early and mid-2000s. Without the "housing" and "subprime mortgage" bubble there would have been very little recovery from the recession of 2001-2.

These were years in which the real earnings of workers in the US, Germany, France and some other countries tended to fall. They were also years in which productive investment was low in all the "old" capitalisms. "Investment rates have fallen across virtually all industrial country regions", said one IMF study.[27] Another report, for JP Morgan, told in 2005:

The real driver of this saving glut has been the corporate sector. Between 2000 and 2004, the switch from corporate dis-saving to net saving across the G6 [France, Germany, the US, Japan, Britain and Italy] economies amounted to over $1 trillion... The rise in corporate saving has been truly global, spanning the three major regions—North America, Europe, and Japan.[28]

In other words, "instead of spending their past profits", US businesses were "now accumulating them as cash".[29]

A low level of investment combined with falling real wages would, in normal circumstances, have resulted in continued recession. What prevented that was precisely the upsurge of lending via the financial system to American consumers, including the recipients of subprime mortgages. It created a demand for the construction and consumer goods industries—and via them for heavy industry and raw materials—that would not otherwise have existed. Recovery from the recession depended on the bubble, what the Italian Marxist Riccardo Bellofiore has aptly called "privatised Keynesianism".[30]

The productive capitalists who were the beneficiaries of the operation were not just to be found in the US and Europe, but also across the Pacific in East Asia. Japanese industry, still suffering from the decline in profitability in the early 1990s, staged some recovery by exporting hi-tech equipment to China which then used it (along with components from the other East Asian states and Germany) to build up ever greater exports to the US. And it was the surpluses on their trade with the United States that Japan, China and the other East Asian economies deposited in the US, which helped finance the bubble and so provided a boost to the whole world economy, including their own part of it.

As Martin Wolf rightly commented, "Surplus savings" created "a need to generate high levels of offsetting demand",[31] and lending to poor people provided it: "US households must spend more than their incomes. If they fail to do so, the economy will plunge into recession unless something changes elsewhere";[32] "The Fed could have avoided pursuing what seemed like excessively expansionary monetary policies only if it had been willing to accept a prolonged recession, possibly a slump".[33] In other words, only the financial bubble stopped recession occurring earlier. The implication is that there was an underlying crisis of the system as a whole, which could not have been resolved simply by regulating financiers.

Wolf and others who emphasised the imbalances in the global productive economy did not locate their roots in problems of profitability. To have done so would have required at least half a turn from neoclassical economics to classical political economy, and especially to Marx. But low profitability was, as we have seen, behind the slowdown in productive accumulation in North America, Europe and Japan, while the partially successful attempts to sustain profits at the expense of wages were responsible for the increasing dependence of consumption on debt. It was also the attempts to maintain profitability in the face of an ever greater piling up of fixed capital that led to the holding back of consumption in China—and, as part of doing so, efforts to stop any rise in the international value of the yuan. And the memory of the crises of the 1990s taught the other BRICS and NICs that their own economies' profitability was not high enough to protect them from global instability, leading them, too, to pile up surpluses. In general, it can be said that the different sectors of world capitalism would not have become dependent on the bubble had profit rates returned to the levels of the long boom.

Financialisation provided a substitute motor, in the form of debt, for the world economy in the decades after the US arms economy lost a good part of its effectiveness. The permanent arms economy had to be supplemented by the debt economy. But by its very nature a debt economy could not be permanent. The massive profits that banks make during any bubble represent claims on value produced in the productive sections of the economy. When there is a sudden decline in the prices of the assets they have previously bid up (in the housing, property, mortgage and share markets) they discover those claims are no longer valid and that they cannot pay their own debts unless they get cash from elsewhere. But the very process of trying to raise cash involves selling further assets; as all banks do so, asset prices decline still more and their individual balance sheets deteriorate further. The bubble bursts and the boom turns into a crash.

As Marx put it:

All this paper actually represents nothing more than accumulated claims, or legal titles, to future production whose money or capital value represents either no capital at all...or is regulated independently of the value of real capital which it represents... And by accumulation of money-capital nothing more, in the main, is connoted than an accumulation of these claims on production.[34]

What happened through the early and mid-2000s was that the banks assumed that these claims were themselves real value and entered them in the positive side of their balance sheets. A chastened Adair Turner, former head of the British employers' CBI and former vice-chairman of Merrill Lynch Europe, recognised after the event, "The system in total has become significantly more reliant on the assumption that a very wide range of assets could be counted as liquid because they would always be sellable in liquid markets".[35] Profits were measured according to "mark to market" valuations of assets—that is, according the level to which competitive bidding had raised them. But once there was a decline in the mortgage and property markets, financiers had to try to cash their assets in if they were not going to go bust—and found they could not. This is what the process which goes under the name of "deleveraging" was about.

Martin Wolf again described what was happening accurately:

> The leverage machine is operating in reverse and, as it generated fictitious profits on the way up, so it takes those profits away on the way down. As unwinding continues, highly indebted consumers cut back, corporations retrench and unemployment soars.[36]

Hence the first moment of truth of August 2007, when some of the hedge funds controlled by banks discovered they could not pay their debts and banks stopped lending to each other out of fear they would not get their money back. Hence the failure of the hundreds of billions poured into national banking systems to prevent the second moment of truth in mid-September 2008 when the collapse of Lehman Brothers was followed within days by the threatened collapse of banks in nearly all the major Western states (AIG in the US, HBOS in Britain, Fortis in Belgium and the Netherlands, Hypo Real Estate in Germany, the three major Irish banks, the Icelandic banks). Hence the way in which in the two months that followed even banks which thought they had gained from the problems of their competitors were in dire trouble—Citibank (the world's biggest) and Bank of America in the US, Lloyds in Britain.

Hence, finally, it was clear the crisis was no longer just one of finance. The vast expansion of finance had created the illusion of a new "long upturn" in productive accumulation; the crisis of finance made that illusion disappear with traumatic effects. There was "a week of living perilously" in November as "panic seized the markets".[37] In the US Chrysler lost millions by the day, General Motors said it needed $4 billion immediately to avoid bankruptcy and Ford joined in asking for a $34 billion government handout. In Britain, Woolworths and MFI went bust. The toll of sackings in every sector began to compare with the haemorrhaging of jobs in the crisis of the early 1980s. And the pain was felt not merely on both sides of the Atlantic, but on both sides of the Pacific too.

In the spring of 2008 the dominant theme in mainstream economic commentary had been that a "decoupling" of different national economies would enable Asia to keep expanding at its old speed while Europe and America suffered. By new year 2009 the recession had spread to Japan, where car output fell at a record rate, to China, where there were thousands of factory closures in the south east,[38] and to India, where a business lobby group warned that 10 million manufacturing jobs could be lost as exports collapsed.[39] The victims of the Asian crisis of 1997—Thailand, South Korea, Singapore, Malaysia, Indonesia—were battered once again. So too were the victims of the slump which swept the former Eastern bloc from the late 1980s onwards—the Baltic states, Ukraine, Hungary, Bulgaria, Romania. In Russia the collapse of the record world oil prices of only six months before led to a fall in the value of the rouble, escalating inflation and a renewed spread of poverty.

Financialisation and the debt economy had proved incapable of moving world accumulation forward at its old speed in the 1980s, 1990s and mid-2000s. It had faltered every few years and, at the end, threatened to fail completely, leading to a crisis of unpredictable depth. Governments which in words, if not in practice, had insisted that the free market could be left to cure its own faults, were now faced with the grim reality that left to itself capitalism could, as in the 1930s, threaten to fall into a catastrophic slump, with the collapse of each giant firm ricocheting through the economy and leading to the collapse of others.

Urged on by some of the giant corporations, states saw no alternative but to intervene in the economy on a scale unprecedented except under circumstances of total war. So it was the Bush administration, the most right wing in the US for 75 years, that effectively nationalised the mortgage corporations Fanny Mae and Freddy Mac early in September. There was one last attempt to rely on the market when it allowed Lehman Brothers to go bust—a decision praised by the *Financial Times* editorial as a "courageous" and a "risk that might well pay off".[40] The disastrous outcome left states with no choice not only to attempt one and half trillion dollar bail-outs, but in effect to partially, and sometimes completely, nationalise not just relatively small banks like Northern Rock and Bradford & Bingley in Britain, but some of the giants. As they did so, their advisers began to ponder whether the only solution to the crisis might be the nationalisation of whole banking systems. State capitalism, and its ideological correlate, Keynesianism, was making a massive comeback after being hidden in an ideological closet for a generation.

Finance and "financialisation"

The great crisis that erupted in 2007 led those who had rejoiced at the wonders of capitalism during the great delusion to try to pin the blame on something other than capitalism as such. The easiest way to do this was to see the "the banks" and "finance" as detached from the rest of the capitalist system. French president Nicolas Sarkozy went to a G7 meeting in January 2008 declaring that "something seems out of control" with the financial system and calling for increased controls over it.[41] All accounts of the Davos World Economic Forum in 2009 told of the deep unpopularity of the banks with the representatives of multinationals and governments: "The audience cheered in one debate when Nassim Nicholas Taleb, author of *The Black Swan*, said it was time to punish bankers by forcing them to hand back bonuses".[42]

Such arguments led to a simple conclusion: the way to prevent future financial crises was greater regulation of finance. Such was the response of many mainstream economists—former monetarists and moderate Keynesians alike, with repeated discussions in the pages of the *Financial Times* over the degree of regulation that was possible and necessary. This was also the response of some analysts on the reformist left. Robert Wade of the LSE could provide riveting accounts of the absurdities of finances that led to the crisis and then conclude that greater controls could stop them.[43] Larry Elliot and Dan Atkinson in their book *The Gods that Failed* blamed "the gods of finance", called for increased regulation and a breaking up of the gigantic financial institutions, and then saw some hope in a meeting of G7 policy makers early in 2008 that contemplated "measures to rein in the turbo charged financial interests".[44]

Rather further to the left the rise of finance had already led to the re-emergence of the old notions of Hobson, Hilferding and Kautsky

The New Age of Global Instability

of "finance" or "finance capital" as having distinct interests from productive capital. The French campaigning organisation ATTAC had started life in the late 1990s committed to opposition to financial speculation, not to capitalism as such.[45] Its central demand was for a "Tobin tax" on movement of financial funds across national borders. This, it was claimed, would counter financial crises. Such "finance is to blame" arguments found a resonance among many radical Marxists. Duménil and Lévy wrote of "neoliberalism" as "the ideological expression of the reasserted power of finance" which "dictates its forms and contents in the new stage of internationalisation.[46] James Crotty's tone was very similar, arguing that "financial interests have become much more economically and politically powerful, and...these trends have been coterminous with a deterioration in real economic performance".[47] Francois Chesnais wrote of "a globalised regime of financially dominated accumulation",[48] in which "the movement of money capital has become a fully autonomous force vis-à-vis industrial capital", forcing it either to accept a "deep interpenetration with money capital, or to submit itself to its exigencies".[49] He took up the expression of Mable, Barré and Boyer, according to which "bad capitalism" had been able to chase out "good".[50] Chesnais as a revolutionary socialist did not himself regard the old form of capitalism as "good" (hence his putting the word between quote marks). But he did argue that finance was to blame for the "mediocre or poor dynamic of investment..."[51] A similar emphasis on finance having interests strongly opposed to those of productive capital was to be found in Peter Gowan's *The Global Gamble*, a very useful account of US capitalism's attempt to maintain global hegemony. He argued that "some of the sharpest conflicts within capitalist societies have occurred...between the financial sector and the rest of society".[52]

The accounts of "financialisation" varied considerably in their detail. But they all shared a contention that the "dominance" of "finance" led to a shift in the dynamic of the system. Productive capital, it was argued, was concerned with productive accumulation. In the early post-war years this had occurred across the industrial world, even if it was organised differently in the US and Britain, where industrial corporations had used internally generated profits in order to undertake long-term investments, and in Japan and West Germany, where collaboration with the banks had provided such investment. But the rise of big investment funds and the "dominance" of finance had changed that. The situation now was that all the pressure was on firms to deliver quick returns to shareholders ("shareholder value") through high dividend payments and measures that ensured a high share price (so boosting shareholders' capital gains), and on governments and national banks to keep interest rates high. Versions of this standpoint had been presented by Keynesian writers like Will Hutton and William Keegan in the 1990s to counterpose the "short-termism" of "Anglo-Saxon" capitalism to supposedly long-term, more investment oriented approaches of Japanese and German capitalisms.[53] Now it was extended to all the advanced industrial countries—with the partial exception of Germany.[54]

Crotty, Gerald Epstein and Arjun Jayadev referred to this as a growth of rentier incomes and "rentier power". They were harking back to Keynes's application of the term rentier to idle "gentlemen" who were receiving interest or dividends payments through the post for doing nothing. But now the rentiers were "mutual funds, public and private pension funds, insurance companies and other institutional investors".[55]

Costas Lapavitsas, who provided excellent factual accounts of the development of the financial crisis of 2007-8, nevertheless put the stress in explaining it on purely financial aspects—in particular the changed behaviour of the banking system, which had shifted its lending from industry to lending to individuals and reliance on new computerised technologies. He argued that the "direct exploitation" of consumers by the banks had become a major new source of surplus value and influenced the dynamics of the system.[56] But this form of "exploitation", like that caused by supermarkets forcing up prices,[57] is only significant in so far as workers do not fight to protect the buying power of their wages at the point of production—something unions in Britain have usually tried to achieve by demanding wage increases linked to a Retail Price Index that includes mortgage interest payments. Or, as Marx would have put it, there is only increased exploitation in so far as the capitalists who employ workers get away with buying labour power at less than its value.[58] It is also worth adding that on Lapavitsas's logic it is it not only workers who are exploited by the banks but also indebted members of the capitalist class and the new middle class—the median debt of households in the US with incomes of more than $100,000 in 2003 was about four and a half times that of households with incomes in the range of $25,000-$50,000.[59]

The "shareholder value" version of the financialisation argument has often been taken for granted. But it contains big gaps. Dick Bryan and Michael Rafferty have pointed out that:

> the stock market should not be so heavily emphasised. It is, after all, a relatively minor forum for raising funds. Even in the so-called market-based systems such as the US, UK and Australia, retained earnings, loans and bond issues have been far more important...

Furthermore, pension funds etc:

> rarely if ever play an active role in the managerial decisions of firms. Institutional shareholder pressure on company boards... is the exception rather than the norm...[60]

The fact that firms hand out a bigger portion of their profits as dividends need not in itself slow down the level of investment. The "rentier" shareholders can themselves lend a portion of their incomes back for further investment—and will do so if they think it is going to be profitable enough to do so. One proponent of the "shareholder value" interpretation, Stockhammer, admits that most economists hold that:

> Financial investment is a transfer of assets, not a use of income. Buying stocks transfers liquidity from one economic agent to another, possibly from firms with bad investment opportunities to ones with good opportunities. Thus macroeconomically financial investment cannot substitute for physical investment.[61]

And Crotty suggests at one point that "financialisation", by increasing competition between firms, brings about more, "coerced", investment.[62] Certainly, big financial institutions have nothing in principle against productive investment, even if finance did come to absorb a peak figure of 25 percent of total investment in the US in 1990 as against only 12 percent in the mid-1970s[63] and rose to close to half in Britain in the same period.[64] This was shown in the late 1990s when the dotcom/new technology boom saw industrial investment in the US financed by borrowing from the institutions as it soared ahead of savings.

The supposed dominance of finance over production is often traced back to the US Federal Reserve under Paul Volcker raising interest rates sharply in 1979. Boyer, Crotty, Chesnais, Duménil and Lévy all see this "Volcker coup" as a decisive point. Duménil and Lévy regard it as the great victory of finance, and argue this was why high interest rates were "maintained through the 1980s and 1990s".[65] Implicit in such arguments is the suggestion that somehow finance in general and shareholders in particular had suffered through the decades of the long boom but were only able to express their feelings with the "coup" of the late 1970s. The argument simply does not fit the historical facts. The post-war decades were ones of enormous self-confidence among all sections of capitalism. The "golden age" for industrial capital was by no means a living hell for its shareholders and financiers. All gained as the growth of profitable productive investment translated into secure long-term capital gains.

There was some change with the crisis of the 1970s. The US's bankers and multinationals did dislike the way the "macroeconomic" "Keynesian" response to the crisis of the 1970s led to inflation and devaluation of the dollar. But, as Robert Brenner points out, had such a policy solved the problems of profitability and industrial overcapacity for the rest of US capitalism, "it is quite conceivable that even the powerful coalition of international and domestic interests arrayed against it would have failed".[66] In fact the Keynesian approach did not achieve these capitalist goals. Limited economic recovery from the recession of 1974-6 increased the level of inflation, which reached 13.3 percent. This had two negative consequences for all sections of US capital. It was likely to encourage workers to struggle over wages. And it was undermining the capacity of the US dollar to act as a measuring rod for US capitalists in their transactions with each other. Forcing up interest rates was meant to solve both problems—by reducing the level of economic activity to scare workers into accepting lower wage increases (which it did) and to reduce inflation (which it also did). This enabled some sections of finance to gain and induced a recession that damaged some sections of American productive capital. But it also served the general interests of all US capitalists.

As Marx had noted, capitalism needs money to act as a fairly stable measure of value, even if damage is done to society as a whole in order to achieve it:

The New Age of Global Instability

Raising interest rates...can be carried more or less to extremes by mistake, based upon false theories of money and enforced on the nation by the interest of money lenders... The basis, however, is given with the basis of the mode of production itself. A depreciation of credit money would unsettle all existing relations. Therefore the value of commodities is sacrificed for the purpose of safeguarding the fantastic and independent existence of this value in money... For a few million in money, many millions in commodities must be sacrificed. This is inevitable under capitalist production and constitutes one of its beauties.[67]

The suffering of many hundreds of millions as a result of the Volcker interest rate hike was a price worth paying to restore a relatively stable measure of value as far as US capitalism in its entirely was concerned—and helped cement its control elsewhere in the world. The "coup" by Volcker (and the turn to monetarism under Thatcher in Britain) consisted of turning away from one policy that was supposed to help restore the profitability of productive industry—expanding the money supply so as to allow prices and profits to rise—to another policy, that of encouraging interest rates to rise so as to squeeze out unprofitable firms and to put pressure on workers through unemployment to accept lower pay. Capital—and not just financial capital—was recognising that the Keynesian orthodoxies of the long boom could not cope with the new phase in which capital (including, not least, industrial capital) found itself.

When this manoeuvre produced only minimal results and it became clear that the high interest rates were beginning seriously to hurt US industry, Volcker cut them—not only under pressure from industrialists, but also from sections of finance.[68] The trend of real long term interest rates for the next quarter century was down, not up, although they remained above the level of the long boom until the year 2000, after which they fell to around 1 percent in 2003.

The whole claim that there are two distinct sections of capital—finance capital and industrial capital—is open to challenge. Many important financial institutions not only lend money, but also borrow it, since they are involved in "intermediation" between lenders and borrowers. What matters for them is not the absolute level of interest rates but the gaps that open up between different rates, particularly between long-term and short-term rates. And industrial concerns lend as well as borrow. Typically they accumulate surpluses between bouts of new investment, which they lend out in return for interest (see Chapter Three). They also advance credit to the wholesalers who take their produce off their hands. In short, industrial capital takes on some of the attributes of finance capital. As Makato Itoh and Costas Lapavitsas point out, "Revenue in the form of interest tends also to accrue to industrial and commercial capitalists, and cannot be the exclusive foundation for a social group".[69] Thomas Sablowski—who accepts part of the "shareholder value" position—makes the point:

> At the level of the common sense, it seems to be no problem to talk about finance and industry, like they were objects easily to distinguish. However, the definition of the concepts of industrial capital and financial capital is no easy task...[70]

But if this is true, then it is difficult to see how the recurrent crises of the last four decades—financial and industrial—could simply be blamed on finance. A coherent explanation of the crises has to look at the system as a whole, and the way in which its different components react on each other. This is what Marx tried to do in a long, if rambling and unfinished, discussion of credit and finance in Volume Three of *Capital*. It is also what Hilferding attempted to do with the earlier chapters dealing with these questions in *Finance Capital*. These insights need to be developed to take account of the extraordinary development of finance, of financial institutions and of financial crises in the late 20th and early 21st century.

Ideology and explanation

Any great crisis does not just have economic consequences. It turns capitalist against capitalist as each tries to offload the cost of the crisis on others, just as it creates deep bitterness among the mass of the population. The crisis that began in 2007 fitted this pattern, and putting the blame on the banks was an escape route for all those who had argued so vigorously that neoliberalism and capitalist globalisation promised humanity a glorious future. So Gordon "the end of boom and bust" Brown argued that this was "a completely different sort of crisis" to those of the "previous 60 years", since it was a "global financial crisis caused by

The New Age of Global Instability

irresponsible lending practices, laxity in them and problems of regulation".[71] In this way, the reality of 180 years of periodic crises was shoved aside, in a desperate attempt to continue to extol the virtues of capitalism.

Those radical economists who put the stress on financialisation in creating the crisis risk opening the door to such apologies for the system. Their characteristic argument has been to claim that profit rates had recovered in the 1980s and 1990s sufficiently to have brought about a revival of productive investment were it not for the power of financial interests. Such was the argument of the French Marxist Michel Husson, when he claimed in 1999 that there were "high levels of profitability",[72] and Stockhammer and Duménil were saying much the same thing in the summer and autumn of 2008.[73] If they were right, the crises which broke in 2001 and on a much bigger scale in 2007-8 would indeed have had causes very different to previous ones, including the inter-war slump, and greater control by the existing state over the behaviour of the financial sector would in the 21st century be sufficient to stop such crises. In accordance with such an approach, Duménil and Lévy described the "Keynesian view" as "very sensible" and looked to "social alliances" to "stop the neoliberal offensive and put to work alternative policies—a different way of managing the crisis".[74]

Yet, as we have seen from the various profit rate calculations in Chapters Eight and Nine, there seems little to justify claims that crises today have different roots to those in the past. The form of the crisis might be different each time to the last, but its impact will be just as devastating. No amount of regulation of finance alone will prevent a recurrence of crisis, and the cost to the capitalist state of trying to stop this can become almost unbearable.

It is true that "financialisation", having risen out of a situation of low rates of profit and accumulation, fed back into both. There was enormous waste as labour and skills went into moving money from one pocket to another; as potentially productive material resources were used to build and equip ever more grandiose office buildings, and as the financial "Masters of the Universe" gorged themselves in conspicuous consumption. It may also be, as Ben Fine has argued, that financialisation had the effect of driving a "wedge...between real and fictitious accumulation",[75] making it difficult for capitalists to see through the fog of the markets and recognise productive investment opportunities. But, ultimately, it was the deeper problems facing the productive sectors of capital that brought this situation about. Finance is a parasite on the back of a parasite, not a problem that can be dealt with in isolation from capitalism as a whole.

The contradictions of the new Keynesianism

The way the crisis was rooted in the economic system as a whole was shown by the sheer difficulties governments had in reacting to it. This was a crisis that hurt big capitals and not just those who laboured for them. Humpty Dumpty had indeed fallen off the wall. Yet it seemed that all the king's horses and all the king's men could not put him together again.

The response of virtually all governments to the crisis that erupted in 2007-8 was to turn away from the free market policies they had proclaimed for three decades as the only ones that would work. Overnight they ditched Hayek for Keynes and kept only that bit of Friedman that urged increasing the money supply to ward off deflation.[76]

But the conditions for applying Keynesian policies with any hope of success were worse than they had been when they had been tried and abandoned 30 years before. The known scale of the losses made by the banks dwarfed those of the mid-1970s—and no one knew, as each bank went bust, which other banks were owed money by it and might go bust too.

The promised bail-outs were massively bigger than those attempted by Roosevelt's New Deal in the 1930s. US federal expenditure then peaked at just over 9 percent of national output in 1936. This time round it was already 20 percent before the crisis began, and the Bush and then the Obama administrations raised it several percentages more. But the levels of debt in the system that somehow had to be covered were also much greater if the financial system was to begin to function again. George Soros calculated "total credit outstanding" at 160 percent of gross domestic product in 1929, rising to 260 percent in 1932; in 2008 it was 365 percent and "bound to rise to 500 percent".[77] The Bank of England estimated in the autumn of 2008 the global losses of the financial system to be as high as $2,800 billion.[78] Nouriel Roubini estimated the losses of the American banks alone at $1,800 billion early in 2009.[79] As governments poured in the money, mainstream

The New Age of Global Instability

economists offering advice debated with each other whether it would be enough to halt the transformation of recession into slump, whether governments would be able to raise the money without forcing up the interest rates they were trying to lower, whether they should turn to "quantitative easing"—that is, printing money—and whether any success with this might not risk bringing about a new inflationary spiral and an even greater slump.[80]

The problem did not just lie with the size of the banks' losses. It also lay with the massive internationalisation of the system compared with either the 1930s or even the 1970s. The Keynesian remedies which were supposed to deal with the crisis were remedies to be applied by national governments, none of which had the resources to pay for all the losses of the global system of which they were part. The biggest states might conceivably be able to salvage a good part of their national financial system. But the problems even here were vast, and many of the smaller states had very little chance of coping.

The system in a noose

The crisis had revealed one of the great fault lines running through capitalism in the 21st century. The complex interaction of states and capitals which had been simplistically referred to as globalisation makes it much more difficult for national states to fulfil their function of aiding the gigantic capitals based within them just as the need for that aid becomes greatest. As Paul Krugman puts it, there are "major policy externalities", since "my fiscal stimulus helps your economy, by increasing your exports—but you don't share in my addition to government debt" and so "the bang per buck on stimulus for any one country is less than it is for the world as a whole".[81]

It was a contradiction that inevitably led to deep political fissures within national ruling classes and to bitter divisions between the states which were supposedly cooperating to deal with the crisis. Domestically, sections of capitals complained bitterly in 2007-9 at the potential cost of bailing out other sections of capital, and internationally governments quarrelled with each other as the concentration of each on efforts to prevent the collapse of its nationally based capitals led to accusations of "financial protectionism". As one observer told the *Financial Times*:

There is a very strong law of unintended consequences taking place after all the bank bail-outs. We will see more and more activist government policies that distinguish economic activities according to the nationality of the actors. It should be a big concern to everybody.[82]

At the time of the World Economic Forum in January 2009 Gordon Brown warned against "financial protectionism", and he was then denounced in turn for that very sin as he pressurised British banks to lend domestically and not abroad;[83] the German government was criticised for not boosting its domestic economy but relying on exports to the countries that did; it in turn criticised the French and British rescue packages as a form of subsidy to their firms which would damage German interests; the new US government denounced China's government for "manipulating" its currency to aid its industries; the Chinese government retorted that US finance had caused the whole mess;[84] and "less wealthy countries fretted" that the US would "use *force majeure* to soak up capital".[85]

The ideologists of free trade warned that protectionism risked deepening the recession as the Smoot-Hawley Act in the US supposedly did in the summer of 1930 by raising tariffs on certain imports. As Peter Temin has noted, "The idea that the Smoot-Hawley tariff was a major cause of the Depression is an enduring conviction... and has found its way into popular discussion and general histories".[86] But he adds, "Despite its popularity, this argument fails on both theoretical and historical grounds." Exports only fell by 1.5 percent of US GNP between 1929 and 1931, while "real GNP fell 15 percent in the same years".[87] And the first real movement from the depths of the slump two and a half years later came after measures by Roosevelt which included putting national capitalist interests first with an effective devaluation of the dollar. Even more effective, as we have seen, were those measures taken by the Nazi state in Germany.

For those firms that produced mainly for the national market (the great majority in early 1930s), it was better to be in a protectionist state than a non-protectionist one. That was the rationale for state capitalism and its ideological correlates: Keynesianism, dependency theory and Stalinism. If the state could get control of the most important investment decisions in the national economy, it could assure that the mass of surplus value was absorbed in new

The New Age of Global Instability

accumulation even if the rate of profit continued to fall. This, however, was a policy that could only work up to the point at which the drive to accumulate collided with the restrictions imposed by the narrowness of national boundaries. This limitation showed itself in the drive of Germany and Japan to expand their national boundaries through war in the mid to late 1930s, in the declining effectiveness of the US arms economy by the early 1970s and in the crisis that tore the USSR apart in 1989-91.

Today the sheer scale of integration of national economies means that serious implementation of state capitalist solutions would cause enormous disruption to the system as a whole. Yet for national states simply to sit back and leave giant firms to go bust in the hope of crises liquidating themselves, as the Hayekians preach, would do even greater damage. The two long-term tendencies pointed to by Marx—for the rate of profit to fall on the one hand and for the concentration and centralisation of capital on the other—combine to put the whole system in a noose. The attempts of capitals and the states in which they are based to wriggle out of it can only increase the tensions between them—and the pain they inflict on those whose labour sustains them.

As states stepped in to intervene in the economy to cope with the crisis after October 2008, some sections of the left believed that the resurrection of Keynes meant the resurrection of the welfare policies of the long boom. In Britain, Ken Livingstone, former mayor of London, declared that the "economic assumptions of New Labour's thinking...have been abandoned". Polly Toynbee proclaimed, "At last, the party of social justice has woken up... The New Labour era is over." Derek Simpson, joint general secretary of the biggest UK trade union, Unite, saw the pre-budget report as "a welcome warm up exercise after 30 years of inaction and neoliberal economics". Yet reality soon proved otherwise. The government aimed to pay for a short-term economic boost with long-term cutbacks in expenditure on education, health and social services. The new Keynesianism for capital was combined with a continuation of neoliberalism for those who worked for it.

This was not a peculiarity of Britain. In every sector of the world system the attempt to deal with long-term downward pressures on profit rates continued to mean efforts to push through counter-reforms in working hours, welfare provision, wage rates and pensions. The push was intensified as global economic growth fell to zero and threatened to fall further. The turn to

Keynesianism could neither restore the system to its old vigour nor serve the interests of the workers, the peasants and the poor.

The system was only able to recover from the crisis of the inter-war years after a massive destruction of value through the worst slump capitalism had ever known followed by the worst war. The greater size and interconnectedness of capitals today means that the destruction of value would have to be proportionately greater to return the system to a new "golden age". After all, even the bankruptcy of the world's second biggest economy, that of the USSR, two decades ago had only marginal benefits for the rest of the system—a lower global price of oil than would otherwise have been the case and some cheap skilled labour power for West European firms.

It is necessary to repeat that this does not automatically mean endless slump. The limits on the degree to which some capitals can gain from the destruction of others do not mean that no gains at all are possible. The wiping out of many small and medium sized firms can provide some relief for the giant firms that states prop up. New bubbles and periods of rapid growth in one part of the world or another are not only possible but likely. But they will not involve the whole world economy moving forward uniformly and will only prepare the way for more burst bubbles and more crises. And the consequences will not only be economic.

Part Four

THE
RUNAWAY
SYSTEM

CHAPTER TWELVE

The New Limits of Capital

A system that undermines itself

Capitalism became a global system in the 20th century in a way it had not been before. Not only were there global markets and global finance but capitalist industry and capitalist structures of consumption arose in every region of the globe, although unevenly. As that happened a tendency noted in its embryonic form by only the most far sighted thinkers of the 19th century, including Marx and Engels, developed until by the end of the century it was visible to everyone who cared to look. This was the tendency for the system to undermine the very process of interaction with nature on which it, like every other form of human society, depended.

The most dramatic expression of this has been the way the accumulation of certain gases in the atmosphere are raising the global temperature and producing climate change.

Capitalist industry and its products always had devastating environmental effects. Observers of all sorts bemoaned the pollution of the water and atmosphere in the industrial areas of Britain in the mid-19th century. Charles Dickens wrote in 1854 of his fictional (but all too real) Coketown, "where Nature was as strongly bricked out as killing airs and gases were bricked in";[1] Engels told of how, "Bradford lies upon the banks of a small, coal black, foul-smelling stream. On weekdays the town is enveloped in a grey cloud of coal smoke".[2] Epidemics of cholera and typhoid would sweep through cities; tuberculosis was a curse that most working class families were acquainted with.

But the disastrous environmental effects of capitals' blind self-expansion were local effects. It was possible to escape from the smog filled cites, the rivers so polluted that fish could not survive in them, the slag heaps and the open sewers. The bigger scale of capitalist production and accumulation in the 20th century meant bigger environmental destruction—the transformation of agricultural land into a dust bowl in parts of the US in the 1930s, the horrendous escape of gases that killed thousands in Bhopal in India in 1984, the nuclear accidents at Three Mile Island in Pennsylvania and Chernobyl in Ukraine, the devastation of the lives of the people who lived around the Aerial Sea as they lost two thirds of their water to cotton production and salination set in, the collapse of cities built on earthquake fault lines. These were, however, still local disasters, despite the scale of the human toll. Supporters of capitalism—and of the state capitalism usually called "socialism"—could dismiss their relevance as passing accidents. Critics of capitalism would denounce their horrors, but not see them as having a systemic impact.

It was not until the end of the 1950s that scientists found the first evidence that man-made gases were beginning to create a global catastrophe by causing average temperatures to rise—and not until the late 1980s that definite proof emerged of how serious the situation was becoming.[3]

The scientific conclusions are well enough known for a mere summary here to suffice. The most important of these gases, as most people now know, is carbon dioxide, produced by burning carbon based substances such as oil and coal to obtain energy—although gases such as methane and nitrous oxide also have to be taken into consideration. The concentration of these gases in the atmosphere is measured in terms of parts of carbon dioxide equivalent per million, or ppm. In pre-industrial times it was 280 ppm; it now stands at 385 ppm and is rising by about 2.1 ppm a year. So far the change has been sufficient to raise the average temperature of the Earth by about 0.8 degrees celsius, and if emissions continue at their present rate, there will be further temperature rises of about 0.2 degrees a decade. This is if other things remain as at present. But there are various feedback mechanisms produced by rising temperatures that would lead to accelerated change—the melting of ice caps, the release of carbon dioxide in the sea or of methane from arctic tundra, the desertification of forests. There is no final scientific consensus as to the temperatures (the "tipping points") that would cause these feedback mechanisms to take effect, but it was widely accepted in 2007 that some would be likely to set in if the temperature rose 2 degrees above the pre-industrial level—about 1.2 degrees above that at present (that does not preclude some of these mechanisms setting in earlier, as, for instance NASA's James Hanson argued in April 2008).[4] To avoid that point being reached, carbon concentrations have to be kept down—the IPCC argues to between 445 and 490 ppm but even 400 ppm might push the temperature up to the 2 degrees threshold.[5]

Over the last two decades governments have come to accept that global warming is a threat to much of humanity. The Stern report for the British government, for instance, concluded in 2006:

All countries will be affected by climate change, but the poorest countries will suffer earliest and most. Average temperatures could rise by 5°C from pre-industrial levels if climate change goes unchecked. Warming of 3 or 4°C will result in many millions more people being flooded. By the middle of the century 200 million may be permanently displaced due to rising sea levels, heavier floods and drought. Warming of 4°C or more is likely to seriously affect global food production. Warming of 2°C could leave 15 to 40 percent of species facing extinction.[6]

There was agreement as early as 1992 at the Rio Earth Summit on the need to start negotiations on measures to reduce emissions, and the Kyoto conference five years later produced a general framework for action. By 2007 even US president George W Bush backtracked and accepted the principle of global warming.

The significant thing, however, is that such verbal agreement has not been translated into the sort of action likely to prevent the 2 percent limit—or even higher figures—being reached. It took another four years after Kyoto before a conference in The Hague agreed on its implementation. The final agreement was "weak, unenforceable and full of market loopholes".[7] It was not only that the US and Australia had refused to sign up. The European powers, who were supposedly keen on the agreement, did not keep within their targets. There was no reduction in the speed at which climate change gases continued to build up in the atmosphere. The Global Carbon Project reported a record 7.9 billion tonnes of carbon passing into the atmosphere in 2005, compared with 6.8 billion tonnes in 2000; the growth rate of CO_2 emissions from 2000 to 2005 was more than 2.5 percent a year—in the 1990s it was less than 1 percent a year.[8]

The G8 meeting in Rostock in the summer of 2007 was paraded as the occasion when more decisive action would be forthcoming.

But declaring there was a major problem, the world's leaders postponed even beginning to do anything about it for two years. And all they agreed to discuss at that date was an attempt to halve greenhouse gas emissions by 2050, whereas even an 80 percent cut in emissions would not be enough to guarantee keeping global warming below 2 degrees.[9]

Governments which have proclaimed averting climate change to be at the top of their agendas have proceeded to act as if the appearance of doing something was more important than the reality. Tony Blair spoke of climate change as the "most serious issue facing mankind".[10] His government committed to aim at a global figure of 666 ppm carbon dioxide equivalent (a fitting figure). Yet the Stern report commissioned by it estimated that with 650 ppm there was a 60 to 95 percent chance of 3°C of warming, and an Environment Department report in 2003 had found that with "with an atmospheric CO_2 stabilisation concentration of 550 ppm, temperatures are expected to rise by between 2°C and 5°C".[11]

Watching such behaviour is a bit like watching a car crash in slow motion, with the driver aware of disaster ahead but ploughing on regardless.

Competition, accumulation and climate change

What explains this behaviour? The easy answer from part of the environmental movement has been "Greenwash", that is, governments are simply pretending to care about the issue for reasons of popularity. That will be true of some politicians. But it does not explain the behaviour of all the major players in the system. Many of them, perhaps even most, have come to see that climate change will wreak havoc on the physical and biological environment that the system operates in and therefore on the system itself. They see the need to take action, yet are half paralysed when it comes to doing so.

Neither is the paralysis explained simply by the pressure on the politicians by lobbying, bribery and blackmail by particular big corporations which fear a loss of profits from any shift away from carbon-based production and transportation. These corporations are often powerfully placed and could, for instance, delay even recognition of climate change by the US government for several

　　　　　　　　　　　　The Runaway System

years. But they have faced some opposition from other capitalist interests which do have a direct financial interest in trying to avoid climate change—the insurance corporations, for instance. What has to be explained is the relative ineffectiveness of these counter-pressures.

The issues go to the heart of the system as it is currently structured. High levels of carbon-based energy are central to virtually every productive and reproductive process within the system—not just to manufacturing industry, but to food production and distribution, the heating and functioning of office blocks, getting labour power to and from workplaces, providing it with what it needs to replenish itself and reproduce. To break with the oil-coal economy means a massive transformation of these structures, a profound reshaping of the forces of production and the immediate relations of production that flow out of them.

Some people argue that such restructuring takes place all the time under capitalism, and that it is simply a question of governments encouraging it to go in one direction rather than another. This essentially was the case put by Clive Hamilton, defending the market approach of the Stern report in a polemic with George Monbiot:

> Stern is confident that once a powerful signal is sent to the market, then the market will find a way to carry out the restructuring of the energy economy. There are reasons to believe that Stern is correct. In fifty years time the world will be dramatically different: if a strong signal can be sent now, there are grounds for optimism. While we currently have the technologies to reduce the world's emissions sharply over the next decade or two, by 2050 the market—suitably guided—will present a set of possibilities we cannot foresee.[12]

What is ignored by such arguments is that even if governments do develop effective price mechanisms as signals to encourage investment and production in one direction rather than another, they are signals that have to compete with other signals—those that come from the pressure to maintain profitability from existing carbon-energy intensive investment.

An oil company may begin to establish divisions aimed at developing carbon free or low carbon energy. But it will also seek to find profitable uses for its existing massive investment in carbon intensive methods (pipelines, refineries, crackers, drilling equipment). The same goes for manufacturing and transportation companies. They will stick with their existing heavy energy using equipment and buildings at last until they have more than covered the cost of their investment in them—and will invest in more of the same, unless the counter-signals from the governments are very powerful.

The behaviour of consumers cannot be changed by a mere wave of a price wand either. Price signals alone are not going to deal with the 10 percent of carbon dioxide produced by car journeys, or the 18 percent used in heating and lighting buildings[13]—except possibly until temperatures have risen much above the 2 degree level. People are stuck with their existing, poorly insulated homes and patterns of dwelling and work that make them dependent upon car travel unless governments do much more than provide "signals".

There is an even more assertive version of the argument about the capacity of capitalism to successfully reshape itself than that put by Hamilton. It holds that the complete restructuring of industry to counter climate change would be beneficial to capitalism, since it would "create investment". The economic problem for capitalism in the 21st century is not, however, that there is some shortage of possible ways of investment. It is that such investments are not profitable enough.

The system today, as we have seen in the previous chapters, is dominated by giant firms based in particular states but operating across several states and sometimes the system as a whole. Each firm is caught between the need to undertake big and expensive investments in order to remain competitive and uncertainties about the profitability of such investments. Investing in new forms of energy or more energy efficient equipment and products is not going to overcome that contradiction. Indeed, doing so would make it worse for many firms, probably most. They can be relied on to pressurise states—and to threaten to relocate if necessary—to minimise price signals that clash with profitability. Governments themselves, identifying with nationally based accumulation, will resist anything that interferes with national competitiveness and go a fair bit of the way with the demands made by firms. This is why the "signals" are so weak, and why those who rely on influencing governments, like Stern, end up watering down targets in order to make them seem "realistic".

As George Monbiot says, "Sir Nicholas Stern spells out the dire consequences of two degrees of warming" but "then recommends a target for atmospheric concentrations of greenhouse gases of 550 parts per million" which would produce "at least a 77 percent chance—and perhaps up to a 99 percent chance, depending on the climate model used—of a global average temperature rise exceeding 2°C" and "a 24 percent chance that temperatures will exceed 4°C".[14]

Stern was unwilling to advise cuts on the scale necessitated by his own calculations because "paths requiring very rapid emissions cuts" were "unlikely to be economically viable", as was any target lower than 550 ppm.[15]

The Obama election campaign in 2008 made many promises about dealing with climate change. Mainstream economists argued the recession itself provided an opportunity for doing so through the stimulus packages. But when the packages were produced, the picture was rather different:

> The packages of tax cuts, credits and extra spending have been trumpeted for their environmental credentials by the governments proposing them, but a closer look shows that green spending accounts for only a small part of the bigger initiatives. Much of the spending will go to projects that will, in fact, increase emissions, such as new roads or fossil fuel power stations, while too little money will be devoted to low-carbon projects to make a real difference, experts believe. For instance, Barack Obama, the US president, wants $27 billion (€21 billion, £19 billion) to be spent on new roads, which will raise traffic emissions. Although some funds will be spent on developing low-carbon vehicles such as electric or hydrogen cars, the benefits gained will be outweighed by the emissions generated by the extra petrol-driven cars.[16]

Todd Stern, the US president's new chief climate negotiator, claimed that it was "not possible" for the US to aim for 25 to 40 percent cuts by 2020, despite the Intergovernmental Panel on Climate Change (IPCC) calculating that "developed nations should aim for 25 to 40 percent cuts by then to avoid dangerous climate change".[17]

In Britain "Green companies" were "in retreat, with a wave of staff layoffs and production cuts" with "Siemens, Clipper

Windpower and even BP among the big names...reacting to a slowdown in the clean energy sector". The "credit crunch" was "starving wind and solar developments of urgently needed cash" and the situation was "being exacerbated by prices crashing to record lows in the carbon trading market".[18]

None of this means that government "signals" have no effect at all. They are encouraging new areas of investment in things like wind and photoelectric power (but also in energy-absorbing biodiesel). New capitals—or innovative old capitals—are emerging that will fight for more space and more resources for their wares. Emissions will probably rise less rapidly than otherwise, although it is unlikely they will decline in the short term. But the equivocation will persist with governments and industrialists proclaiming their commitment to resist climate change one day and their determination to extract the maximum amount of oil or coal from the earth the next.

The needs of capital and the needs of capitals

The expansion of capitals in competition with each other—or as Marx put it, the self-expansion of capital—leads them to an orgy of carbon energy use just as they recognise it as self-destructive.

The phenomenon of capitalism damaging its own environmental basis is not completely new, even if it has never occurred on the scale it is today. In the early 19th century competitive accumulation in Britain led to a lack of concern about the physical health, even the physical survival, of capitalism's workers. It was a neglect that would inevitably be damaging to youthful industrial capitalism as well as to the working class, since it threatened to exhaust the supply of fit and able labour power for exploitation.

Marx summed up what was happening:

> The capitalistic mode of production (essentially the production of surplus value, the absorption of surplus-labour), produces thus, with the extension of the working-day, not only the deterioration of human labour power by robbing it of its normal, moral and physical, conditions of development and function. It produces also the premature exhaustion and death of this labour power itself. It extends the labourer's time of production during a given period by shortening his actual lifetime.

But in doing so, capitalism shortens the "duration" of the "labour power" of the individual worker, so making it necessary to replace this more quickly than otherwise, so that:

> the sum of the expenses for the reproduction of labour power will be greater; just as in a machine the part of its value to be reproduced every day is greater the more rapidly the machine is worn out. It would seem therefore that the interest [of] capital itself points in the direction of a normal working day.[19]

Did this mean that capitalists flocked to campaign for shorter working hours and more humane conditions in the factories and working class localities? A few, more farsighted about the long term needs of capital as a whole, did. Most, however, campaigned against any restrictions on hours, even for children who would one day become more productive, adult, labour power.

Again Marx summed up the capitalist logic at work:

> In every stockjobbing swindle everyone knows that some time or other the crash must come, but everyone hopes that it may fall on the head of his neighbour, after he himself has caught the shower of gold and placed it in safety. *Après moi le déluge!* [After me, the flood] is the watchword of every capitalist and of every capitalist nation. Hence Capital is reckless of the health or length of life of the labourer, unless under compulsion from society. To the outcry as to the physical and mental degradation, the premature death, the torture of overwork, it answers: Ought these to trouble us since they increase our profits?[20]

It took concerted pressure on capital from the outside, by successive acts of legislation enacted by the state—in part in response to workers' agitation—for the reproduction of labour power to be protected from the ravages of those who exploited it. It took some 80 years before anything like fully adequate protection of such reproduction was in place—and as we saw in Chapter Five it required the difficulties in military recruitment to bring home to the state the harm which capital had done to its cannon fodder by its lack of concern with supplies of labour power.

Exactly the same logic as that described by Marx is found in the attitude of capital to the pumping out of climate change gases today. Capitalist politicians make beautiful speeches about the need to do something, set up commissions and intergovernmental meetings, promise to reshape their own behaviour—and then bow down before interests which say that this or that measure to deal with climate change will be too costly for the economy to bear.

However, there is one big difference between the tendency to destroy the source of labour power in the 19th century and the devastation of the Earth's climate today. The destruction of labour power was within the industrial areas of one country. It could be repaired by the importation of workers from the countryside and Ireland. And eventually the national state could act to police the behaviour of individual capitalists in the interests of capital as a whole.

There is no global state capable of enforcing its will on all the capitalist firms and national states that make up the system. Each is afraid that taking the drastic measures needed to massively reduce gas emissions will result in other firms and states seizing the opportunity to intrude on its markets. The issue of climate change becomes inextricably linked with the other struggles within the world system—the struggles between different nationally based capitalist interests, between national states and between classes.

There will be more attempts at international agreements, perhaps with a few more teeth than in the past. It could hardly be otherwise as growing numbers of the system's capitals begin to experience the pain of climate change. But the agreements will always been riddled with weak spots because the different states will go into them with markedly different short and medium term interests.

The national structures within which accumulation takes place depend to very different degrees upon carbon energy. The US was self-sufficient in oil until the early 1970s, its structures of accumulation and consumption became very highly dependent on oil and that means that today it has 20.2 tons of carbon emission per person; the main West European states lacked domestic oil resources, developed rather different structures of accumulation and consumption (with petrol, for instance, about three times the cost it is in the US), and have so far only 8.8 tons of emissions per person; China's rapid industrialisation and urbanisation are based on massive amounts of coal and its total emissions are close to that of the US figure, even though its emissions per head in 2004 were only a little over a sixth of the US figure and 40 percent of the West European figure.[21]

The Runaway System

These enormous differences mean that measures that seriously cut back on emissions would hit firms based in different countries very differently. It is this which explains why the European Union seemed more committed to action against climate change in the early 2000s than the US: its national states stood to gain from measures that would proportionately hit US-based industries more than their own. The US figure is immensely important. "International institutions" for controlling the global system can only be effective insofar as their programmes coincide with the interests of the US-based capital, with its immense military power and financial influence. Regional powers like Russia, China, India or Western Europe might sometimes be able to block regulation in US interests, but they cannot substitute for it with regulation of their own. This applies as much to carbon gas regulation as to financial regulation through the IMF or trade regulation through the WTO. Recognition by those who run the various parts of the world system about the dangers of climate change will translate in practice to fraught international negotiations in which each major state will subordinate fighting climate change to the competitive interests of the capitals based within it. Regulation will continue to be slow, ineffective and insufficient to stop the destabilising effect of carbon gases, not only on the climate, but on the system as well.

Some of the immediate short-term effects of climate change are already with us. The most immediately visible are those that result directly from rising temperatures: for instance, evidence that glaciers are getting smaller, or that many species of birds in Britain are laying their eggs about a week earlier than in the 1950s.[22] Some of the most important effects will be less direct than these. Climate models suggest global warming causes shifts in ocean currents, in the amount of water vapour in the atmosphere and atmospheric pressures, and that these in turn lead to unexpected changes in weather patterns with, for instance, more frequent and more powerful storms on the one hand and droughts on the other. One cannot deduce from this that every short-term variation in the weather is a result of climate change, but the evidence is accumulating that both hurricanes and droughts are growing in frequency. If the global warming feedback mechanisms kick in, such local catastrophes will become much more frequent. There will be more crop failures, the flooding of rivers deltas and low lying land areas, more river inundations, more desertification of previous fertile areas, as well as shifts in patterns of cultivation.

The New Limits of Capital   317

Peak oil

One other growing ecological limit to capitalism is, paradoxically, fear that the main source of carbon gases at the moment, petroleum, may be running out. The notion of "peak oil" has been taken increasingly seriously—that the point may be at hand at which oil production cannot rise any further to meet growing demand.

The issue first came into prominence back in 1998, after an article appeared in the *Scientific American* which predicted oil production would peak within ten years. Since then there have been rebuttals and counter-rebuttals, with various economists and geologists presenting very different scenarios for what is happening to oil reserves and potential output.[23] The arguments have to a considerable extent reflected the impact of different interests. The giant oil firms tend to exaggerate the extent of the long-term supplies, since their share prices depend on these. Their figures then come under question from those worried about the long-term future of the energy needs of nationally based capitalisms as well as from muck-raking critics of the system as a whole. And there are considerable difficulties in coming to any exact conclusion as to the real picture because the big oil producing states conceal the real extent of their reserves as they bargain with each other within OPEC and with the oil companies. As one critical report points out:

> One of the big questions still waiting for an answer is the state of the oil production in the Kingdom of Saudi Arabia (KSA). Most likely, this issue will decide the timing of world peak oil... because of the secrecy surrounding the oil production in the KSA.[24]

But it is possible to draw two firm conclusions from the debate. First, peak oil is likely within the next quarter century, and may be reached within years rather than decades, forcing reliance on other energy supplies. The International Energy Agency, the OECD's energy organisation, long resistant to the peak oil argument, now accepts that there will be "an imminent 'oil crunch' in a few years time".[25] The Energy Information Administration (EIA) of the US Department of Energy concluded in July 2000 that "world conventional oil production may increase two decades or more before it begins to decline". But John Bellamy Foster points out, "The analysis itself, however...suggested that a world oil peak could be reached as early as 2021".[26]

The Runaway System

Effectively, whichever set of figures one accepts, the blind expansion of capital is close to exhausting the supply of its most important raw material, one on which almost all its production and consumption depend. Peak oil does not signify its immediate disappearance: it will continue to be available for many decades, but the cost of getting it will rise and the conflicts over who has it and who does not will get more intense.

Regardless of when the peak will be reached, states are worried in the here and now about future "energy security". So there have been repeated reports in the US expressing such concerns, going right back to the infamous National Energy Policy report in May 2001 drawn by a task force headed by vice-president Cheney. Without mentioning peak oil, it stressed concern about guaranteeing US oil supplies and urged, "Make energy security a priority of our trade and foreign policy".[27] A February 2007 US Government Accountability Office report "argued that almost all studies had shown that a world oil peak would occur sometime before 2040 and that US federal agencies had not yet begun to address the issue of the national preparedness necessary to face this impending emergency".[28]

The term "energy security", like that of "defence", has a double meaning when used by governments. It can mean protecting the energy input of domestic and industrial use. But it can also mean operating policies that allow added pressure to be applied to other states. So, for instance, control over oil outflows from the Middle East, one of the goals of the US invasion of Iraq in 2003, is more about control over oil supplies which potential regional challengers to US hegemony depend on than about the US's own supplies. Only about one eighth of these come from the region (as against three eighths from Canada, Mexico and Venezuela). Significantly, the US ensures it has bases or reliable allies at key points on international oil pipelines and oil routes—hence, for instance, the bitterness of its response to the Russian assertion of influence in the Georgia-South Ossetia war of August 2008. A world approaching "peak oil" is necessarily a world of heightened clashes between states and within states, just as the world of climate change is.

There is an inevitable interplay between the two. To some it might seem that peak oil, and the rising oil prices it will bring about, will act as a counter to climate change. There may be a limited downward pressure on oil consumption—as, for instance, happened in the case of petrol consumption when oil prices shot up in middle of 2008.[29] But there is no automatic cancelling of one effect by the other. Peak oil is compatible with a level of consumption of oil as great as at present for many years, with a corresponding build up of carbon gases. Meanwhile energy security fears are leading to an intensified search for more oil, the expansion of the other carbon gas source, coal, and the use of maize or vegetable oils to produce ethanol and biodiesel for transport fuel processes which can even increase global carbon gas emissions.[30]

Food and capitalism

The years 2006-8 provided a hint that capitalism is creating another ecological barrier to itself—that of not being able to produce enough food for those who live within it. Soaring food prices raised questions as to whether it was beginning to exhaust its capacity to keep food production rising, as commentators pointed to rapidly declining rates of global food output growth.[31]

This was not the first time there have been such concerns. Malthus had argued in the early years of industrial capitalism that there was no point in raising the living standards of the mass of the population, since this would prompt them to have more children at a faster rate than food production would rise to feed them. Marx and Engels rejected this view that a natural barrier to human welfare existed as an apology for exploitation by a defender of the system. But they did hold, as we have seen in Chapter Three, that capitalism itself created obstacles to food provision once it had developed beyond a certain point. This was because capitalist agriculture removed the nutrients necessary for fertility from the soil more rapidly than it replaced them.[32]

Marx and Engels did not put the issue at the centre of their analysis of capitalism for the simple reason that they could see that by the 1860s and 1870s the system was capable of substituting for the depredations of agriculture in its old established lands by the production of foodstuffs in North America, with the opening up of the prairies to agriculture. The issue became of marginal concern to most Marxists after their death because the use of mineral fertilisers was able to compensate for the loss of natural nutrients. Worldwide food production kept ahead of population growth right through to the end of the 20th century. There were horrific famines and persistent long-term malnutrition for hundreds of millions of people, but these were a result not of under-production but of class-induced poverty. Signs of impending absolute food shortages in South and East Asia in the 1960s were overcome by the "Green Revolution"—the introduction of new grain types dependent on big inputs of fertiliser and increased irrigation. These were normally combined with the spread of various forms of capitalist agriculture in place of the subsistent peasant farmer.

The increases in food yields were very real—it is stupid of some "organic" critics of modern agriculture to claim otherwise—with wheat yields growing between 3 and 4 percent a year between the mid-1960s and the mid-1980s, and rice yields between 2 and 3 percent. But over the last two decades the increases have fallen until they are barely ahead of (declining) population growth: "Output from the Green Revolution has reached a 'plateau'".[33] Ever greater quantities of fertiliser are required to increase output, water sufficiency becomes a growing problem, concentration on a very narrow range of crop types increases the dangers from plant diseases, and world acreage devoted to food is not growing. As a World Bank Development Report admits:

> Many agriculture-based countries still display anaemic per capita agricultural growth and little structural transformation... The same applies to vast areas within countries of all types. Rapid population growth, declining farm size, falling soil fertility, and missed opportunities for income diversification and migration create distress as the powers of agriculture for development remain low.[34]

The problem is not that somehow, after 200 years, Malthus has been vindicated. Means exist to raise food output to cope with world population, expected to grow another 50 percent and then slowly decline. The problem is the existing "structure of agricultural accumulation".[35] Global agriculture since the mid-1970s has been increasingly structured by a handful of agribusiness corporations, mainly based in the US, that control agricultural innovation, supplying the inputs (seed varieties, fertilisers, pesticides, agricultural machinery) for the world's farmers, big and small. Their interest is in keeping those inputs standardised (so keeping down their own costs of production), with as little regard for particular local growing conditions as possible. Their research has "focused on innovations that reduced costs rather than enhanced yields".[36] The result has been little in the way of innovation to suit the needs of the world's 400 million small farmers—except to preach GM crops as a magic solution, regardless of their potential side-effects on local ecologies and the inapplicability of those so far developed to conditions in very wide parts of the world. Meanwhile, individual developing countries have reduced agricultural investment to around 4 percent of GNP compared with 10 percent in 1980.[37] Yet, as Ronald Trostle of the US Department of Agriculture's economic research unit says, "it was always publicly funded research that was more likely to concentrate on innovations that would increase yields and production, particularly in parts of the world where farmers are unable to pay royalties for new varieties of seeds".[38]

The dangers to the world's food supply were brought home sharply in 2007-8 when grain prices internationally surged, creating the risk of starvation for hundreds of millions of people. Rising food prices were hurting many of those small farmers who bought as well as sold food. "Food security" suddenly joined energy security as a concern for governments. In the short term the ability of farmers in Europe and North America to cultivate land which had been left idle under "set aside" schemes raised the possibility of filling some of the gaps in the global food supply and there were limited falls in some prices by the beginning of 2009—although not to the level of two years earlier.

The crisis was more likely to be an omen for the future—the threat of immense hardship to hundreds of millions of people—than the immediate onset of global catastrophe.[39] The "real risk" remained of a "food crunch at some point in the future, which would fall particularly hard on import-dependent countries and on poor people everywhere", reported one study.[40] Indications were that the food price rises of 2006-8 had not simply just been a result of speculation during the last phase of the mid-2000s boom. Early in 2009 a report could tell how "food prices are poised to rise again" as long-term "resource scarcity trends, notably climate change, energy security and falling water availability", would put pressure on prices and production.[41]

The food shortage of 2008 showed the way in which the different elements of crisis endemic to capitalism in the 21st century can interact with each other. For the shortage was not just as a result of the exhaustion of the benefits of the Green Revolution. It was also a product of the probable effects of climate change, with crop failures in Australia due to drought and in Europe due to flooding; of the typically perverse capitalist way to offset climate change and energy security by devoting a third of the US maize crop and half the European oil seed crop to the production of bio-fuels;[42] of the rising oil price, which forced up the costs of fertilisers and fuels on which 21st century farming depends; and of the sharpness of the boom part of the capitalist cycle in the early and mid-2000s, which massively increased middle class meat consumption, especially in China.

It is the sort of interaction of the economic, the environmental and the political we should expect to see repeated again and again in the 21st century, producing recurrent, very deep social and political crises that frame the choice between global catastrophe and revolutionary change.

CHAPTER THIRTEEN

The Runaway System and the Future for Humanity

Anthony Giddens published a book with a strange title in 1999 at the high point of illusions in globalisation and the "new economic paradigm". He was (and still is) Britain's best know academic advocate of the "third way" that ditches old social democratic attempts to tame capitalism and was aptly described as "Tony Blair's court sociologist".[1] Yet the title was *The Runaway World*. It conveys the image of a bolting horse, which governments, social movements and individuals alike cannot stop but have to try to balance on precariously. The best they can do is to try to influence where it is taking them by spurring it on with investments in social capital on the one side and reining it in with cutbacks in welfare expenditures on the other. Yet the succession of crises and wars that have punctuated the last four decades show the futility of such efforts.

The runaway world is, in fact, the economic system as Marx described it, the Frankenstein's monster that has escaped from human control; the vampire that saps the lifeblood of the living bodies it feeds off. Its self-expansion has indeed led it to encompass the whole globe, drawing all of humanity into its cycles of competing in order to accumulate and accumulating in order to compete.

Its expansion has been marked, as much in the 21st century as in the mid-19th century when Marx did his research for *Capital*, by fits and starts, by frenzied forward motion suddenly interrupted by deep crises. Running through the cycles of expansion and recession has been the other feature Marx pointed to: downward pressure on profitability causing capitalists to try to cut back on wages and welfare benefits at the same time as pressuring people to work harder, even though in doing so this cuts into the market for consumer goods produced by other capitalists. We have seen how these elements came together to produce the great slump of the inter-war years, renewed crisis in the mid-1970s, and the long drawn out Japanese crisis of the 1990s. We saw also how they produced the debt economy bubble culminating in the great crash of 2007-9. We will see this happen again repeatedly, in one form or other, in the decades ahead.

In some important ways, the system is even more chaotic than in Marx's account. The very size of the units that make it up means that it has lost some of its old flexibility. The destruction of some capitals through periodic crises which once gave new life to those that remained now threatens to pull these down as well. Life support systems provided by the state may be able keep the system from complete collapse but cannot restore it to long-term vigour. At best they provide a feverish spell of brief exhilaration before yet another collapse. And the cost of providing the life support systems sooner or later stretches the resources of the state close to breaking point.

Modern states are creatures of the capitalist system, evolving to service the needs of the geographical clusters of capitals that constitute it. The more these clusters depend on their relations with the rest of the global system, the more they need the power of states to provide for their interests within it. Yet each state can only achieve this goal by pressurising other states, and in the process adding to the instability of the system as a whole. The measures national states take to aid the capitals based within them during a crisis necessarily infringe on the interests of capitals based in other states, increasing the instability still further. Their significance is not limited to a particular economic crisis. They provide a foretaste of what the rest of the 21st century is going to be like.

Capitalism is a restless system. Whether in boom or slump, in peace or war, in a great city or the remote countryside, it never stands still. Competitive accumulation remoulds everything it touches and then, when it has hardly finished, remoulds it all again. The very speed of change itself has enormous importance. It means that the relative economic weights of the different states within which the units of capital are based are continually in flux, just as the states have to try to intervene to protect their capitalists from the recurrent convulsions of the global system.

The Runaway System

The problem is acute for the US, at the top of the global hierarchy. Its position had depended on its being the policeman for the whole system, offering general protection, Mafia style, to the other ruling classes, while using that position to privilege the position of US based capitals. Crises make those capitals need that privileged position more than ever. The failures in the "war on terror" meant that already in the mid-2000s other states felt more empowered to challenge such privilege, shown by China's increased sway in Africa, Russia's in parts of the former USSR, and the BRICS in global trade negotiations. Then came the crisis that began in 2007 with widespread predictions that it would dent US global hegemony even more just as many of its great corporations looked to that hegemony to help them out.

US imperialism might be temporarily chastened as it contemplated the way in which some of its recent adventures have rebounded to its disadvantage—just as the Vietnam War did. But it can not abandon its global position, even if defending it leads to further assertions of military might in other poorer countries, with devastating and destructive consequences. Increased troop deployments were meant to ensure the retreat from Iraq did not turn into rout in Afghanistan. Significantly, Barack Obama's first budget increased, rather than decreased, military expenditure. And so did the budgets announced in the same month for Russia and China. The bloody road which led from Korea to Vietnam and from Vietnam to Iraq is not yet at an end.

But that is not all. The "new", environmental, limits of capital will react back upon its old economic limits. Climate change, peak oil and global food shortages will add to the overall economic instability of the system expressed in the boom-bust cycle, the downward pressure on the rate of profit and the flows of capital from industry to industry and country to country. We had a glimpse of this in the first half of 2008. Rising food and energy prices produced an inflationary surge which added to government difficulties in dealing with the credit crunch at the same time as causing protests, riots and strikes in a score of countries. We can expect many more clashes within and between states as problems of food security and energy security lead to shifts in surplus value from some sections of capital to others and provoke popular outrage. And all the time climate change tipping points can suddenly impact unexpectedly on hundreds of millions of people's lives, in much the same way that economic crises and wars do, but even more destructively.

The starkest recognition of the possible consequences came from the US Department of Defence, the Pentagon, at the time when the official position of the US government was still to refuse to recognise the reality of climate change. It warned of the danger of "food shortages due to decreases in net global agricultural production", "decreased availability and quality of fresh water in key regions due to shifted precipitation patterns, causing more frequent floods and droughts", and "disrupted access to energy supplies due to extensive sea ice and storminess".

The outcome, as it saw it, would be an increased occurrence of resource wars and civil wars:

> As global and local carrying capacities are reduced, tensions could mount around the world, leading to two fundamental strategies: defensive and offensive. Nations with the resources to do so may build virtual fortresses around their countries, preserving resources for themselves. Less fortunate nations, especially those with ancient enmities with their neighbours, may initiate struggles for access to food, clean water, or energy. Unlikely alliances could be formed as defence priorities shift and the goal is resources for survival rather than religion, ideology, or national honour...

There would be "an increasingly disorderly and potentially violent world".[2]

This will be disorder in a world in which eight of the biggest states possess nuclear weapons that are targeted at others, scores have "conventional weaponry" much more destructive and horrific than that of the Second World War, and proliferating civil nuclear energy can provide conventional weapons with deadly targets. The runaway system threatens more than devastating periodic slumps and horrific wars. It puts into question the very possibility of sustaining human life on Earth. The system of alienated labour is approaching its highest point of destructiveness. The question is whether those who produce that labour are capable of seizing control of its wealth and subjecting it to conscious control.

The Runaway System

CHAPTER FOURTEEN

Who Can Overcome?

The decisive question

We live in a system which is unstable, which breeds economic crises and wars, and which is eating up the very environmental basis it stands on. This is going to lead its component national sectors into repeated social and political crises in the course of the 21st century. Just as the 20th century was a century of wars, civil wars and revolutions, so too is the 21st century. But this leaves open a decisive—*the* decisive—question. What forces exist that are capable of taking on the system and transforming the world?

For classical Marxism, the answer was simple. The growth of capitalism was necessarily accompanied by the growth of the class it exploited, the working class, and this would be at the centre of the revolt against the system. It was not the first exploited and oppressed class in history. But it differed from the 200 or so generations of peasants and slaves that preceded it in very important respects. Capitalist exploitation was concentrated in huge workplaces in giant industrial conurbations, giving the working class power at decisive points in the society in which it found itself. Such exploitation tended to produce homogeneity in the conditions of its members as capital repeatedly reduced different forms of concrete labour to abstract labour. And capital required an exploited class that has a level of culture—of literacy, numeracy and knowledge of the world at large—greater not merely than preceding exploited classes, but also than most preceding ruling classes. These factors combined to create the potentiality for it to take control of society as a whole into its own hands in a way that was not true of its predecessors.

But potentiality was not actuality. The development of capitalism was not a simple smooth upward process that had its impact on the exploited class it created. There was unevenness over time, with the concentration of workers into centres of exploitation during booms and the expulsion of some from those centres during slump. There was geographic unevenness, with some centres arising in connection with national states before others, and then sometimes declining as new centres supplanted them. These forms of capitalist unevenness led to unevenness within the working class, with different levels of skill and payment arising, with competition for jobs and security of employment between different groups of workers, with sections of workers identifying with the particular state that controlled them because it seemed like a locus for achieving reforms of the system. Nevertheless, for classical Marxism, this was a class which would be driven to unite periodically by the very pressures of the system upon it. Skill differentials which had arisen at one point would be eroded at another. Competition between workers would fade as they fought together to achieve overriding common goals. National ideologies would lose their hold in the face of the horrors of imperialist wars.

This notion, that the working class provides the agency that can change society, has been challenged even more than Marx's account of the economic dynamic of the system. Marx was a brilliant economist and a pioneering sociologist, the argument goes, but fell into an apocalyptic vision of the future which ascribed a metaphysical role to the working class. The spread of modern capitalism, the argument continues, has not been accompanied by the growth of the working class, the conditions of those workers that do exist have not been homogenised, and they do not develop a consciousness in opposition to the system.

Such contentions were already very widespread during the long post-war boom. As a notable sociological study of British workers told:

> A major and recurrent theme—and most notably in liberal quarters—[was] that of the incipient *decline* and *decomposition* of the working class. As the development of industrial societies continued, it was suggested, the working class, understood as a social stratum with its own distinctive ways of life, values and goals, would become increasingly eroded by the main currents of change. The very idea of a working class had been formed in, and in fact belonged to, the infancy of industrial society: in the era to come it would steadily lose its empirical referent. Social inequalities would no doubt persist; but these would be modified

and structured in such a way that the society of the future would be an overwhelmingly "middle-class" society, within which the divisions of the past would no longer be recognisable.[1]

So pervasive were these arguments that they influenced the thinking of radicals such as the American sociologist C Wright Mills[2] and revolutionaries like Herbert Marcuse,[3] while fashionable sociologists generalised the argument about "post-industrial society" to the advanced countries as a whole. They all looked rather foolish when French workers undertook the biggest general strike in history so far in May 1968 and waves of industrial struggle swept through Italy, Britain, Argentina, Spain and Portugal in the years 1969-75. Yet the argument revived in the 1980s and 1990s as the restructuring of capitalism through crisis decimated many old established sectors of the working class and industrial defeat led to a waning of class combativity.

Ernesto Laclau and Chantal Mouffe were swimming with the tide of intellectual opinion when they asserted in an influential work in the mid-1980s, "It is impossible today to talk about the homogeneity of the working class and to trace it to a mechanism inscribed in the logic of capital accumulation".[4] So too were Michael Hardt and Antonio Negri when they claimed in 2000 that "the industrial working class" had "all but disappeared from view. It has not ceased to exist, but it has been displaced from its privileged position in the capitalist economy".[5]

Yet, not for the first time, the common sense among philosophers has departed from empirical reality. A detailed study of the world's workforce in the mid-1990s by Deon Filmer calculated that of 2,474 million people who participated in the global non-domestic labour force, 889 million worked for wages or salaries, 1,000 million people mainly for their own account on the land, and 480 million for their own account in industry and services.[6] Probably about 10 percent of those employed will have been members of the new middle class who receive more value than they create in return for helping to control the mass of workers.[7] This means there were around 700 million workers, with about a third in "industry" and the rest in "services". The total size of the working class including their dependants and those who have retired must have been between 1.5 and 2 billion. More recent figures from the United Nations Development Programme suggest a global total for those in industry substantially higher than

Filmer's.[8] Anyone who believes we have said "farewell" to this class is not living in the real world.

Marx made a distinction between a class which exists *in itself*, as an objective element in the social structure, shaped by the relations of people to the means of making a livelihood, and a class *for itself*, with a consciousness of its position and of its interests in opposition to those of another class. The key conclusion to draw from all the figures is that the working class exists as never before as a class *in itself*, with a core of perhaps 2 billion people, or a third of the global population. On top of this there are very large numbers of peasants, up to 50 percent, who do some wage labour and so are subject to much of the same logic of the system as the workers. The global proletariat and semi-proletariat combined are the majority of the population for the first time in history.

But we need to go beyond these general figures if we are to grasp the potential for the world's workers to challenge the system. It is necessary first to look how changes in the system are changing different sectors of workers.

The "advanced" countries: the effects of restructuring

The repeated restructuring of production means that the working class in the advanced countries today is different in many respects to that 40 or 50 years ago. But this does not justify the claim that the working class has disappeared as a result of "deindustrialisation", the "post-industrial society", or the "weightless economy".

Take, for instance, the world's biggest single economy, that of the US. There was much panic about "deindustrialisation" in the 1980s in the face of challenges to US industrial pre-eminence in fields like car production and computers. But in 1998 the number of workers in industry was nearly 20 percent higher than in 1971, roughly 50 percent higher than in 1950 and nearly three times the level of 1900. Baldoz, Koeber and Kraft noted at the beginning of this century, "More Americans are now employed in making cars, buses and parts of them than at any time since the Vietnam War".[9]

Even after the recession of 2001-2 had led to a massive rationalisation of industry, with the loss of about one in six manufacturing jobs, the industrial working class had far from disappeared. Industrial production in 2007 was 8 percent higher than in 2000 and 30 percent higher than in 1996,[10] and the US remained

The Runaway System

the world's biggest single centre of manufacturing, with a fifth of world output (the combined old European Union of 15 states was ahead with a quarter),[11] despite much talk of manufacturing moving to the Third World in its entirety.

The Japanese figures were even more astounding. The industrial workforce more than doubled between 1950 and 1971 and was another 13 percent higher in 1998. The fall in industrial employment in a number of countries over the last three decades does not signify deindustrialisation of the whole of the old advanced industrial world. It had 112 million industrial jobs in 1998[12]—25 million more than in 1951 and only 7.4 million less than in 1971. Toni Negri's Italy may not have been in the same league as the US or Japan, but industrial workers had certainly not disappeared. There were 6.5 million in 1998, down only one sixth since 1971.[13]

These figures for industrial employment, it should be added, underestimate the economic importance of industry in general and manufacturing in particular. As Bob Rowthorn has rightly noted:

> Almost every conceivable economic activity in modern society makes use of manufactured goods… Many of the expanding service industries make use of large amounts of equipment.[14]

The small decline in the total industrial workforce is not because industry has become less important, but because productivity per employee in industry has risen more quickly than in "services". Slightly fewer manufacturing workers are producing many more goods than three decades ago.[15] The industrial workers are as important for the capitalist economy today as in the early 1970s. Glib statements like those of Hardt and Negri about their declining significance could not be more wrong.

The usual distinction between "industry" and "services" obscures more than it reveals. "Services" is a catch-all residual category of everything that does not fit into the sectors of industry and agriculture. So some of the shift from "industry" to the "service sector" amounts to no more than a change in the name given to essentially similar jobs. Someone (usually a man) who worked a typesetting machine for a newspaper publisher 30 years ago would have been classified as a particular sort of industrial worker (a "print worker"); someone (usually a woman) working a word processing terminal for a newspaper publisher today will be classified as a "service worker". But the work performed remains essentially the same, and the final product more or less identical. Rowthorn undertook a statistical breakdown of the total "service" category for the OECD as a whole. There was a small fall in "total goods and goods-related services"—from 76 percent of all employment in 1970 to 69 percent in 1990.[16] But this was certainly not a revolutionary transformation in the world of work.

There are many other jobs characterised as "services" that are essential to accumulation in the modern world—especially, as we saw in Chapters Five and Seven, health provision and the education service. Today there are over 10 million employed in health and educational services in the US (around one in 13 of the workforce), and US capitalism could not function without them. And the long-term trend is for most of them to be forced increasingly into conditions comparable to those of industrial and routine office workers, with payment by results, assessment and appraisal systems, increased concern with timekeeping, and enhanced discipline codes.

There is the myth that the "service" sector workforce is made up of well paid people with control over their own working situation who never need to get their hands dirty. So *Guardian* columnist Polly Toynbee writes:

> We have seen the most rapid change in social class in recorded history: the 1977 mass working class, with two thirds of people in manual jobs, shrunk to one third, while the rest migrated upwards into a 70 percent home-owning, white collar middle class.[17]

If Toynbee had looked at the Office for National Statistics' *Living in Britain 2000* she would have found 51 percent of men and 38 percent of women in its various "manual" occupational categories.[18] This is because the "service industries" include refuse workers, hospital ancillary workers, dockers, lorry drivers, bus and train drivers, and postal workers. Alongside them are a huge number of women— 50 percent—in the "intermediate and junior non-manual" categories, where wages are typically lower than in most manual occupations and working conditions often at least as hard. In the US in 2001, 50 percent of the 103 million employees in service related occupations had manual or routine clerical or similar jobs.[19] Together with the 33 million workers in traditional manual industries they made up three quarters of the country's workforce.

Two related processes are taking place in all "advanced" economies (and many "non-advanced" ones). The traditional manual working class is put under more and more pressure as capital tries to squeeze its directly productive labour so as to get more profits from it. At the same time, the new "non-goods-producing service" working class is subject to proletarianisation as capital sets out to reduce the costs to it of non-productive and indirectly productive functions.

Each crisis in the last four decades has involved sudden increases in unemployment—in some cases permanent—and the wiping out of old established centres of production (factories, docks, mines, etc). Capital and its apologists have then tried to take advantage of workers' feelings of insecurity to remould their lives around its own continually changing requirements. Its slogans have become "flexibility" in labouring time, methods of work and labour markets, all justified by the claim that "lifetime employment belongs to a past age". Much academic research has accepted its message, and "Third Way" social democrats and those on the "autonomist" left have taken it for an unquestionable truth. Typical—and excessively influential—is the sociologist Manuel Castells who argues there is:

> Structural unstability [sic] in the labour markets everywhere, and the requirement for flexibility of employment, mobility of labour, and constant reskilling of the workforce. The notion of the stable, predictable, professional career is eroded, as relationships between capital and labour are individualised and contractual labour conditions escape collective bargaining.[20]

The claim about the ability of capitalism to destroy industrial jobs instantaneously is a vast exaggeration of what is happening with restructuring. As we have seen in Chapter Ten it takes time and effort for capital to liquidate industrial investment in one part of the world and shift it to another—and new investment is still predominantly within the triad of the advanced countries, although the emergence of China as a manufacturing centre is adding a new twist to that pattern. Even in the electronics industry, in which components and most final products are very light and cheap to move, there was not an unambiguous move from centralised production in the advanced countries to contracting out in the Global South in the 1990s and early 2000s:

Although the proportion of production beyond the Triad of Europe, North America and Japan was high, and was indeed associated with international rather than local markets, it was confined to a few East Asian countries. At the same time, the "domestic" production workforce in the US continued to grow.[21]

In general, capital still finds it more profitable to locate itself in the regions which had industrialised by the mid-20th century. Workers may usually be better paid there, but a combination of established skill levels and existing investments in plant and infrastructure means they are also more productive, providing much more surplus value for the system than most of their poorer brothers and sisters in the Third World. This explains why the picture for most of Latin America in the 1990s was one of very slow average growth or stagnation, and for most of Africa of absolute decline.

The most important impact of offshoring and rising imports has not been their role in destroying jobs, but in helping employers to destroy workers' confidence in their capacity to defend conditions, wages and working hours.

A study by Kate Bronfenbrenner found that during the economic upturn of the 1990s American workers felt more insecure about their economic future than during the depths of the 1990-1 recession. "More than half of all employers made threats to close all or part of the plant" during union organising drives. But afterwards "employers followed through on the threat and shut down all or part of their facilities in fewer than 3 percent" of cases.[22] In other words, it is in the interests of employers to overemphasise how precarious jobs are in order to demoralise workers and lower the level of resistance. Those voices on the left who exaggerate that insecurity can add to that demoralisation, rather than countering it with a recognition of the counter-factors that provide workers with continued strength if they have the confidence to deploy it.

The evidence does not justify a picture of a uniform, relentless spread of precarious jobs. The crisis of the early 1990s did cause a substantial increase in "precarious" jobs in Western Europe. But that still left 82 percent in permanent jobs, as against only 18 percent in non-permanent jobs—a proportion that remained almost unchanged between 1995 and 2000. There has been a huge variation between countries,[23] but a 2001 ILO study of Western Europe as a whole concluded that:

The Runaway System

The evidence simply does not sustain the view that we are witnessing the emergence of a "new" kind of employment relations, seen in the "end of the career" and the "death of the permanent job for life".[24]

One survey in 2000 showed only 5 percent of British employees on temporary contracts,[25] while the number of people who had worked at the same workplace for more than ten years had risen from 29 to 31 percent.[26] Even in Spain, which has the highest level of "precariety" in Europe, 65 percent of workers have permanent jobs.

Capital cannot manage without workers who have certain skills and it prefers workers who have some sense of responsibility for the job. It takes employers time to train people and they are rarely keen to lose them if they can avoid it. They therefore do not always treat workers as "disposable", even when it comes to semi-skilled and unskilled labour. They can benefit from a generalised insecurity making the majority of workers with relatively secure jobs fear that they may lose them. But that does not mean that capital can really dispense with such workers. And that means they have the potential to put up resistance to its demands, even if they are often not aware of it.

The new working classes of the "Third World"

Around 60 percent of the world's industrial workers are outside the "advanced" countries of the OECD, with perhaps 25 percent in China, about 7 percent in India and around 7 percent in Latin America.[27] Such statistics do no more than provide a snapshot of the enormous change brought about by the sweep of capitalism's self-expansion across the world.

Sixty years ago 80 percent of the world's population lived in the countryside; and 30, 40, or even 50 percent worked on the land even in countries thought of as "advanced" like France, Italy or Japan. Today close to half the world's population live in towns and cities, and the urban population is a majority even in countries people often think of as rural—84 percent in Brazil, 76 percent in Mexico, 63 percent in Ecuador and 63 percent in Algeria.[28]

Urbanisation and the spread of market relations are not necessarily the same as the growth of wage labour.[29] People worldwide have been leaving the countryside at a much greater rate than the growth of stable livelihoods for them in modern sectors of the economy. This is especially true in countries where economic growth is slow or negative. Thus wage employment fell in absolute terms in several African countries during the 1980s,[30] and half the non-agriculture workforce of Africa is self-employed.[31] Even in China, with its rapid rate of accumulation, the employed working class has expanded more slowly than economic growth.[32] But in general, the slowness of job growth should not be identified with "deindustrialisation".[33]

There has been growth of wage labour in much of the Global South but it has been spasmodic, a product of the chaotic ups and down of capitalist industrial growth. And in very many cases, any growth in modern industry with "formal" employment has been overshadowed by what has been happening in the "informal" sector of very small businesses. The joint share of informal and small business activities of non-agricultural employment in Latin America as a whole rose from 40 percent in 1980 to 53 percent in 1990,[34] while in Brazil half the occupied urban population were not "formal employees", although more than half of the informal workforce were wage workers.[35]

In India growth has been even more concentrated in the informal "unorganised" sector, without workplace rights, while 40 percent of the urban population is self-employed—working in family businesses, usually without their own premises, or as vendors, rickshaw drivers, cart pullers and the like.[36] In China too the informal sector has mushroomed—with the number of urban workers not officially classified and doing things "in the informal sector (such as street vending, construction, and household services)" growing by 79 million between 1995 and 2002. By 2002 they amounted to 40 percent of urban employment.[37] In addition to—and often merging into—those in the informal sector, there are everywhere those denied any opportunities for employment by modern capitalism: the unemployed who typically make up 10 percent or more of the workforce in Third World cities.[38]

The failure of regular employment in the cities to absorb the vast influx of labour from the countryside follows from the logic of capitalism. Competition on a global scale has caused capitalists to turn to "capital intensive" forms of production which do not require massive numbers of new workers.

The Runaway System

Marx described very well the process by which the informal sector grows, looking at British society 150 years ago:

...The additional capital formed in the course of accumulation attracts fewer and fewer labourers in proportion to its magnitude. The old capital...repels more and more of the labourers formerly employed by it.[39]

This dynamic produces a "stagnant" component of "the active labour army" with "extremely irregular employment":

Its conditions of life sink below the average normal level of the working class; this makes it at once the basis of special branches of capitalist exploitation...characterised by maximum of working time, and minimum of wages... Its extent grows, as with the extent and energy of accumulation the creation of surplus-population advances.[40]

In general, the suffering of a very large chunk of the urban masses in Third World countries comes not from being super-exploited by large capital, but from the fact that large capital does not see a way of making sufficient profits out of exploiting them at all. This is most clearly the case in much of sub-Saharan Africa. After squeezing wealth out of the continent during the period from the onset of the slave trade to the end of empire in the 1950s, those who run the world system (including local rulers who move their own money to Europe and North America) are now prepared to write off most of its people as "marginal" to their requirements—except in the all-important local enclaves where raw materials, especially oil, are to be found.

The relation of the formal and informal sectors

The unevenness of industrial expansion and the mushrooming of the informal sector can lead to conclusions about the incapacity of workers to organise and fight that very much parallel the orthodoxies about "precariousness" in the old industrial countries. It is assumed on the one hand that those workers with stable jobs in the formal sector are privileged labour aristocrats—as one report on north east Brazil puts it, to "be formally employed is almost a privilege, since less than half of those who want such a situation are in fact 'enjoying' it".[41] At the same time it is assumed that those in informal sectors suffer from "social exclusion" and are not capable of self-organisation.

Working in the formal sector certainly has advantages over working in the informal sector. In India workers in the "organised sector" get paid a good deal more (30, 40 or even 100 percent) than those in the "unorganised sector".[42] In China, workers in large-scale industry were provided until the late 1990s with the "iron rice bowl" of a guaranteed income plus certain housing, sickness and pension benefits—all things denied to people migrating from the countryside to seek jobs.

Employers have not, however, provided such things out of the goodness of their heart. They need a certain stability in their labour force, particularly when it comes to skilled workers who they do not want to be poached by rivals during times of boom.[43] In many industries, the more stable and experienced a workforce, the more productive it is. Capital is prepared to concede higher wages to certain of the workers in those industries because by doing so it is able to make more profits out of them. Hence the apparent contradiction—some sections of the world's workers are both better paid than others, and more exploited. But by the same token, workers in the formal sector have the capacity to fight back against capital in a way which it fears.

The growth of the informal sector rarely means the destruction of the formal one. The informal workforce in Brazil's most important industrial city, São Paulo, grew by nearly 70 percent in the 1990s, but the number of "formal" workers employed in the private sector still remained more than four times higher than the number of "informal" workers.[44] It is wrong, as people like Paulo Singer did, to write of "deproletarianisation".[45] Rather what is happening is a restructuring of the workforce, with the hiving off by big firms of some tasks (usually relatively unskilled and therefore easily performed by a floating workforce) to small firms, labour-only contractors and the supposedly self-employed.

Far from the growth of the informal workforce benefiting the workforce in the formal sector, it has been accompanied by an increased exploitation of workers in this sector—and in many cases by a deterioration in wages and conditions. This has been most marked in Africa, where the scale of the decline in real wages for those with jobs in the 1980s was so great as to beggar belief. A report in 1991 told of:

> a sharp fall in real wages...an average 30 percent decline between 1980 and 1986... In several countries the average rate has dropped 10 percent every year since 1980... On average the minimum wage fell 20 percent over that period.[46]

In Latin America real industrial wages fell by more than 10 percent in the 1980s, while they did so in the formal sector in India in the late 1990s.[47]

The use of the informal sector to batter workers in the formal sector has led to the widespread assumption that informal sector workers are powerless. But capital faces a problem here too. The more it relies on them, the greater their potential capacity to resist its demands. In India those parts of the informal sector that have been taking on work from the formal sector—"intermediate goods producing activities in the unorganised sector, eg basic chemicals, non-metallic mineral products, metal products, and equipment sectors, have witnessed rises in wages as well as productivity"—indicating that "workers' bargaining power in these segments is not as bad as it is made out to be".[48]

The phenomenon of casual employment is by no means new in the history of capitalism. Casual employment has often played an important role in certain industries. And forms of contract labour are very old—it was common in the textile factories of the industrial revolution. In the mines in both the US and Britain in the 19th century overseers or foremen ("buttymen") would recruit workers and pay them out of a sum given to them by the mine owners. Such casual workers may not always have felt themselves to be part of the working class. They were often detached from the struggles of other sections of that class for years, even decades, at a time. Yet the potential for struggling within those sections was always there, and when it turned into reality the struggle could be very bitter, with an almost insurrectionary tinge.

Frederick Engels observed precisely this development in 1889 when London's dockers struck for the first time. He wrote:

> Hitherto the East End had been in a state of poverty-stricken stagnation, its hallmark being the apathy of men whose spirit had been broken by hunger, and who had abandoned all hope...

And now, this gigantic strike of the most demoralised elements of the lot, the dock labourers, not the regular strong, experienced, relatively well-paid men in steady employment, but those who have happened to land up in dockland, the Jonahs who have suffered shipwreck in all other spheres, starvelings by trade, a welter of broken lives heading straight for utter ruin... And this dully despairing mass of humanity who, every morning when the dock gates are opened, literally fight pitched battles to be first to reach the chap who signs them on, that mass haphazardly thrown together and changing every day, has successfully combined to form a band 40,000 strong, maintain discipline and inspire fear in the powerful dock companies...[49]

Engels' point is very important in the 21st century. Internationally there have been three decades of defeat and demoralisation for workers right across the world. This bred a fatalism about the possibility of fighting, which was reflected in a mass of studies which depicted the suffering of the poor and the oppressed, showing them always as victims, rarely as fighters. Thus there are masses of materials sponsored by the International Labour Organisation on "social exclusion"—a theme which suits the bureaucrats who run such bodies. Themes like the "casualisation" and "feminisation" of the workforce become stereotyped, academic ways of dismissing possibilities of struggle—even if some of those carrying through the studies try to escape from the paradigm in which they are trapped. This tendency to see the urban poor and the permanent workers as two separate groups hermetically sealed off from each other is particularly prevalent among NGO activists.

The reality is more complex. Slum districts themselves are rarely homogenous in their social make up. Permanent workers live in them alongside casual workers, the poorest sectors of the self-employed, the unemployed and even some sections of the petty bourgeoisie. Mike Davis tells how:

The traditional stereotype of the Indian pavement-dweller is a destitute peasant, newly arrived from the countryside, who survives by parasitic begging, but as research in Mumbai has revealed, almost all (97 percent) have at least one breadwinner, 70 percent have been in the city at least six years... Indeed, many pavement-dwellers are simply workers—rickshaw men, construction labourers, and market porters—who are compelled by their jobs to live in the otherwise unaffordable heart of the metropolis.[50]

Leo Zeilig and Claire Ceruti point out that recent research on Soweto in South Africa shows that "in 78.3 percent of households there was a mix of adults who were employed, self-employed and unemployed". They conclude that:

> the South African township and slum might be viewed as a meeting point for trade unionists, university students, graduates, the unemployed and informal traders. Though the spectre of unemployment affects all layers of society, these groups are not permanently cut off from each other and can be found in the same household supporting each other.[51]

The picture is similar for El Alto, the satellite city of the Bolivian capital, La Paz. It contains hundreds of thousands of mainly indigenous Ayama people who have moved to the city from the countryside or closed down tin mines, and whose efforts to somehow make a living for themselves are characteristic of the informal sector in such cities everywhere in the Third World. Yet El Alto is also "the principal industrial zone of the La Paz region",[52] with 54 percent of the region's industrial workforce and an increase of 80 percent in the numbers employed in industry in the last ten years. What is significant is "the combination between 'informality' and/or small businesses based on family labour on the one hand and the degree of incorporation of the labour force in wage labour in productive tasks on the other", so that neighbourhood forms of organisation have a class (as well as an indigenous) content.[53]

Under these circumstances, struggles by workers have the capacity to act as a focus for all discontents of the great majority of those living in the slums. So in South Africa a series of protests and riots over the delivery of basic services created an atmosphere in which:

> the public sector general strike in June 2007 was the largest strike since the end of apartheid, pulling many people into trade union action for the first time. The potential cross-fertilisation of these struggles—of community and workplace—does not live only in the mind of activists, but, as the survey suggests, expresses the real household economy of contemporary South Africa.[54]

In Bolivia, El Alto was at the centre of the near uprisings that drew together miners, teachers, peasants and indigenous organisations to overthrow two governments in 18 months. In Egypt late in 2006 a strike of 24,000 workers in the Misr Spinning factory in Mahalla al-Kubra:

> triggered a wave of workers' protests across Egypt, crossing different sectors of the economy and industries, from Mahalla to Kafr al-Dawwar to Shibin al-Kum, from spinning and weaving to cement to the railways and underground and public transport workers. The strike wave went from the public sector to the private, to the civil service, from the old industrial areas to the new towns, in all provinces. It went from the textile sector to engineering, to chemicals, to building and construction, to transport to services. The strikes had a wide impact also, reaching sectors which do not have a culture of protest, such as teachers, doctors, and civil servants, and even to slum-dwellers such as those from Qala'at al-Kabsh and the villagers from Al-Atsh.[55]

Such examples show that the working class in the Third World is not condemned to the divisions and passivity emphasised by social exclusion and NGO accounts. The incessant tearing apart of old patterns of economic and social by capitalism as it restructures itself on a world scale does not simply cause suffering. It also creates the potentiality for resistance that can find sudden expression when people least expect it.

There is, in fact, a pattern of such struggles going back to the first impact of capitalist industrialisation in such countries, recorded, for instance, in the collection *Peasants and Proletarians* edited by Cohen, Gutkind and Brazier 30 years ago.[56] There are innumerable examples from recent decades to bear out that picture. We must expect many more as economic crisis interacts with climate change and crises of food security throughout the rest of this century.

Fragmentation, bitterness and revolt

But it is also important to recognise that people's bitterness against poverty and oppression can burst out in other ways. The fragmentation of people's life experiences in the world's slums all too often leads to different groups turning on each other, as Mike Davis says:

Those engaged in informal-sector competition under conditions of infinite labour supply usually stop short of a total war of all against all; conflict, instead, is usually transmuted into ethnic, religious or racial violence. The godfathers and landlords of the informal sector (invisible in most of the literature) intelligently use coercion, even chronic violence to regulate competition and protect their investments...

The reality of such developments cannot be denied by anyone who has read accounts of the interethnic and Sunni-Shia riots that periodically paralyse the Pakistan city of Karachi, of the history of attacks on the Chinese populations of Malaysia and Indonesia, or of the wave of attacks on Zimbabwean refugees in the very South African cities described by Leo Zeilig and Claire Ceruti.

The city of Mumbai provides a graphic example of how the mood can shift. A semi-spontaneous upsurge from below by the workers in the city's textile mills in 1982 developed into one of the biggest prolonged strikes in world history, lasting a year, involving hundreds of thousands of workers and dominating the political life of India's commercial and industrial capital as it built networks of support going right back into the villages from which many of the workers had originally come.[57] During the strike there was unity between the different religious and caste groups that make up the mass of Bombay's lower classes. But the strike was defeated. In the aftermath Shiv Sena, a political organisation built by turning the local Marathi speakers against other groups and then Hindus against Muslims, rose to a dominant position in wide areas of the city. This culminated in murderous riots against the Muslim population in 1992-3.

Unity in struggle had created a sense of solidarity which then exerted a pull on the vast mass of the informal workers, self-employed, the unemployed poor and the impoverished sections of the petty bourgeoisie. The defeat led to the sectional attitudes and communal conflicts of the petty bourgeoisie influencing the self-employed, the unemployed and wide layers of workers.

This was a vivid example of how there are two different directions in which the despair and bitterness that exist among the "multitudes" in the great cities of the Third World can go. One direction involves workers struggling collectively and pulling millions of other impoverished people behind them. The other involves demagogues exploiting the sense of hopelessness, demoralisation and fragmentation to direct the bitterness of one section of the impoverished mass against other sections. That is why the working class cannot simply be seen as just another grouping within "the multitude" or "the people", and of no intrinsic importance for the struggle against the system. Nor can workers' struggles be seen by those who organise them as important simply because of their economic content. Their struggles are important precisely because they have the capacity to provide a direction for all the bitterness among the mass of people otherwise without hope as they try to survive in the slums of the world's megacities.

The peasantry

The development of the capitalist form of production has cut the life-strings of small production in agriculture; small production is irretrievably going to rack and ruin... We foresee the inevitable doom of the small peasant...[58]

So wrote Engels in the mid-1890s. The massive growth of the world's cities over the last half century has vindicated much of the reasoning behind Engel's statement. The peasantry is as absent today from North West continental Europe as it was from England in Engels' day. But the shrinkage globally has been much slower than Marx and Engels expected. Peasants still amount to about a third of the world's population. The reality, across much of Latin America, as in nearly all of Africa and South and East Asia, is that hundreds of millions of individual small farmers are clinging on to the land which they own or rent. They find themselves caught again and again in a vice, as rising prices for energy and fertiliser inputs squeeze them from one side and competition from capitalist farms with modern equipment presses them on the other. And the discontent bred by this can still make the peasantry an important political fact in major countries in the Global South. Even in Latin America, where the peasantry shrank by half between the 1960s and the 1980s,[59] it has been peasant-based rebellions against capitalism that have caught the imaginations of people around the world, with the Zapatistas in southern Mexico, the MST landless workers' movement in Brazil and a big section of the movement which swept Evo Morales to the presidency of Bolivia in 2006.

The Runaway System

These movements have led many activists to adopt what are sometimes called "neo-populist" views.[60] These see the peasants as the agent of social change, or at least a component in the agency of the "multitude". And sometimes the future of world food production is also seen as lying with them, since food production per hectare is often greater on small peasant plots than on larger holdings.[61]

But missing from this recognition of the persistence of the peasantry as a force, even if a declining one, is the way in which it has been changed profoundly by capitalism, although not necessarily in the way which Marx and Engels expected. Hamza Alavi and Teodor Shanin pointed out in the late 1980s that "two alternative forms of agricultural production" had developed within capitalism—on the one hand "farming based on wage labour", and on the other "a form of organisation of production based on the family farm which is incorporated into the capitalist mode of production". In this second form, "The peasant economy is structurally integrated within the capitalist mode of production" and "surplus value is extracted from the peasant through the agency of commercial capital and credit institutions" and "contributes to capital accumulation—but outside the peasant economy from which it is drawn".[62]

The peasantry that has been drawn into the circuits of capitalism in this way is not a homogenous group, but differentiated internally on the basis of size of landholding, ownership of equipment and levels of debt. At one extreme are those who have managed, by one means or another, to transform themselves into petty agricultural capitalists, at the other the landless labourers. Between them lies a bigger or smaller layer of those who rely on family labour, perhaps employing wage labour occasionally, perhaps supplementing their household incomes by agricultural labour for others.

Labour outside agriculture can be important for the poor and middle peasants. Figures from 15 developing countries in the 1980s showed non-agricultural income amounted 30 to 40 percent of total rural household income; in China it increased from 10 percent in 1980 to 35 percent in 1995[63] and "acquiring non-agricultural jobs has become crucial to avoiding the fate of peasant life and escaping rural poverty";[64] in Egypt 25 percent of rural household income came from "wages outside the village" in the 1980s.[65]

Not all peasant households are integrated into the wider economy in the same way. For many there are only the most menial forms of wage labour. But a minority may establish links with those in privileged positions—delivering support for politicians, doing favours for big landowners or moneylenders, manipulating supposedly traditional family, clan or tribal networks. A differentiation arises between peasant households as struggles over land are tied into the conflicts in the wider economy, at a local, a national or even a global level.[66]

Such differentiation means that what are conventionally described as "peasant movements" do not have a single automatic trajectory of opposition to capitalism and the ruling classes. The leadership in peasant movements often comes from those who have been most successful in enlarging their holdings and accumulating enough capital to employ labour power rather than sell it. They have sufficient freedom from daily toil and sufficient connections to wider society to take the initiative when it comes to mobilising others. Hamza Alavi noted long ago that peasant revolts tend to be led by middle peasants, not poor peasants or landless labourers.[67] The penetration by capitalism of the countryside means that it can, in fact, be the petty agricultural capitalists who head peasant movements, putting forward demands like lower prices for fertilisers that benefit themselves disproportionately.

That is not the only direction in which revolts from the countryside can go. The differentiation of the peasantry often means that the middle and poor peasants are under pressure from those who will use political connections to drive them from the land—caste Hindu landowners in India, local party cadres in China, chiefs connected to state apparatuses in Africa, soya barons in Brazil. The result can be uprisings directed against the petty agrarian capitalists and not led by them. But such uprisings then have to confront the forces of the state, which try to isolate them in particular localities, relying upon the very way in which the peasant household gets a livelihood—by labouring to produce a harvest from its own plot of land—to disperse the protests. So the Zapatista insurgency rocked the Mexican state, but that did not prevent the state effectively sealing the movement off in the Lacandon jungle where it remains isolated a decade and half later. The various Maoist movements of dalits (the former "untouchables"), tribal peoples, the landless labourers and poor peasants in

The Runaway System

India are annoying to Indian capitalism, but so long as they are restricted to remote country areas no more annoying than a gnat bite is to a healthy adult.

Yet the very penetration of the countryside by capitalism makes it more possible than ever before for links between the poorer sections of the peasantry and the urban workers. For it means that the poor peasant households have, through migration, family members in the cities. Just as workers' struggles can provide a focus for the bitterness felt by all the groups who live in the slums of the cities, so too they can do so for the hundreds of millions who still toil on remote patches of land. But whether that possibility becomes an actuality depends on workers fighting to win with demands that reach out to the poorer layers in the towns and countryside alike.

Who can overcome?

It is the very development of capitalism that shapes and reshapes the lives of those it exploits, creating the objective circumstances that can turn a disparate mass of people who sell their labour power into an increasingly self-conscious class "for itself". This class is the potential agent for challenging the chaotic and destructive dynamic of capitalism because capitalism cannot do without it. The mistake of Mouffe and Laclau—and thousands of other sociologists, philosophers and economists who write that the working class has lost its central place within the system—is that they do not grasp the elementary point made by Marx. The system is a system of alienated labour that has taken on a life of its own, and capital cannot survive without more labour to feed it, just as the vampire cannot survive without fresh supplies of blood.

There have been phases in the history of the system when it has had the means to bind the mass of people to it, either by repression or by keeping them relatively content. Hitler on the one hand and Stalin on the other did seem to rule on the basis of mass repression during what the Belgian-Russian revolutionary Victor Serge called the "midnight in the century".[68] It was possible for a British prime minister, Harold Macmillan, to tell people they had "never had it so good", and for most workers to concur, even if grudgingly, during the 1950s. I have tried to show that the dynamic of the system is going to make it difficult for capitalism to cement its control permanently over the mass of people by either means.

Its very restlessness means that it cannot allow those it exploits to remain in any degree of contentment for any great length of time. As the runaway system lurches from boom to slump and tries to boost profits and write off debts in a wild attempt to lurch back again it dashes the very hopes of a secure life that it has encouraged in the past. It insists the mass of the people have to work longer for less, to accept they must lose their jobs because bankers lost their heads, to resign themselves to hardship in old age, to give up their homes to the repo men, to go hungry on peasant plots so as to pay the moneylender and the fertiliser supplier.

People will react against this. Some were already doing so as I wrote these words. The last spurt of the mid-1990s onwards finance-fuelled boom saw spontaneous riots against rising food and energy prices in a score of countries. The first months of its new recession saw protests, riots and strikes against its effects. It could not be otherwise. All such movements can provide people with the conditions for learning for themselves about the potentialities of class struggle against the system. And the interaction of recurrent crises—economic, military, ecological—is repeatedly going to create conditions that breed further discontent even if capitalism does somehow finally emerge from the present crisis intact.

It bears repeating again and again that the wealthiest society in human history, the United States, operated over the last three decades before the current crisis broke by pushing down the living standards of those who labour within it. That too was the pattern of Japan from the early 1990s on. They are examples which those who rule over Western Europe have set out to emulate, and any success they have will create similar pressures on those presiding over capital accumulation in the newly industrialising societies of East and South East Asia. That does not necessarily mean there might not be spells in which some parts of the system might seem better than in the recent past to many who live within them. Such was the case in the mid to late 1980s and the mid to late 1990s, and it may well happen again. But in the "runaway world" of capitalism in the 21st century they cannot last long, and the crises that bring their sudden end can raise discontent to massive levels.

Lenin laid out conditions that he saw as necessary for society to enter a "pre-revolutionary crisis". Two are going to be fulfilled again and again in this century. The ruling class will not be able continue with things in the old way. And the mass of people will not feel able to put up with things in the old way. These two elements have produced very important social upheavals in the decades since the demise of the long boom—from Iran in 1979 and Poland in 1980-81, through to Russia in 1989-91, to Indonesia in 1998, to Argentina and then Venezuela and Bolivia in the years after 2001. The escalation of crisis in October 2008 led President Sarkozy of France to warn fellow rulers of the danger of "a European 1968". Whether his warning was right or wrong in the short term, we will see massive social upheaval repeatedly in the decades ahead. But what has so far been lacking has been a third element Lenin focused on, the subjective one: a political current able to win people in their masses to the notion of a reorganisation of society and prepared to take decisive action at key moments in leading people to fight for it.

The absence of such a current is itself a product of objective processes, some of which are described in this book. The last great wave of insurgency against the system in the late 1960s and early 1970s failed to break through.[69] Restructuring of the system through crises disorganised many of the forces involved in that insurgency just as defeat demoralised the left. The demoralisation was made more profound by the way the great majority of those on the left worldwide identified with the societies of the old Eastern bloc, societies which had, in fact, been absorbed into the system's dynamic of competitive accumulation and which suffered more than most from the crisis of the state capitalist phase of the system.

It was as if much of the left had to be born afresh when the latest phase of insurgency began to take off with the Chiapas rebellion in Mexico and a wave of public sector strikes in France in 1995, the demonstrations against capitalist globalisation of 1999-2001 and the movement against the Iraq war in 2002-3. But being born afresh also meant having to learn afresh. Typically, activists talked about fighting globalisation or neoliberalism, not capitalism. But the runaway system has itself created the objective conditions for yet another shift.

As I write this, the sheer scale of the crisis facing the world system is forcing even those who run the system to talk about capitalism, and having to recognise that Marx had something to say about it long before Keynes. Many of the new generation of activists have begun to study his writings and many of the older generation suddenly find they have an audience to pass what they have learnt on to.

That in itself does not guarantee that the subjective element will arise to make sure that the next great revolts against the system are not contained by it. For that to happen, those who study capitalism have to become an integral part of a movement of those who suffer from it. What we can say with certainty is that without such a movement the world by the end of this century is going to be intolerable for the majority of those who live in it. As the young Marx put it, "Philosophers have interpreted the world in many ways. The point is to change it."

Notes

Introduction
1   For a summary of the various attempts to measure happiness, see Iain Ferguson, "Capitalism and Happiness", *International Socialism*, 2:117, 2008.
2   *Washington Times*, 24 October 2008.
3   Bank of International Settlements, *Annual Report*, June 2007.
4   Quoted in Randall E Parker, Introduction, *Economics of the Great Depression* (Edward Elgar, 2007), px.
5   Quoted in as above, p95.
6   Interviewed in Randall E Parker, *Economics of the Great Depression*, p95.
7   Alfred Marshall, *The Principles of Economics*, 8th edition (London, 1936), p368.
8   Joan Robinson, *Further Contributions to Economics* (Oxford, 1980), p2.
9   See, for instance, Gillian Tett, "Curse of the Zombies Rises in Europe Amid an Eerie Calm", *Financial Times*, 3 April 2009.
10 Karl Marx, *Economic and Philosophical Manuscripts of 1844*, http://www.marxists.org/archive/marx/works/1844/manuscripts/labour.htm
11 Karl Marx and Frederick Engels, *Collected Works*, Volume 34 (London, Lawrence and Wishart, 1991), p398.
12 Karl Marx and Frederick Engels, *Manifesto of the Communist Party*, available at http://www.marxists.org/archive/marx/works/1848/communistmanifesto/ch01.htm
13 Put together by Engels from manuscripts Marx left in an incomplete state.
14 Also edited by Engels after Marx's death.
15 Available today as the *Grundrisse*, *Theories of Surplus Value*, and Marx's *Notebooks for 1861-3*.
16 This is the basis of the so-called "transformation problem".
17 Willem Buiter, *Financial Times*, 17 September 2008.
18 Arun Kumar provides a very useful account of how the conventional figures provide a distorted view of India, in "Flawed Macro Statistics", in *Alternative Economic Survey*, India 2005-2006 (Delhi, Daanish, 2006).

Chapter One: Marx's Concepts
1   Usually called "horticultural societies" by anthropologists.
2   Adam Smith, *The Wealth of Nations*, Book One, Chapter 4, available at http://www.econlib.org/library/Smith/smWN.html; see also David Ricardo, *On the Principles of Political Economy and Taxation* (Cambridge, 1995), p11.
3   Karl Marx, *Capital,* Volume One (Moscow, Progress Publishers, 1961), pp35-36.
4   It has, however, been partially recognised by some dissident mainstream economists belonging to the so-called Austrian school. So the conservative enthusiast for the "free market" Friedrich August von Hayek put consider-

able emphasis on the physical distinctiveness of commodities which cost the same price in his account of the business cycle. See, for example, his *Prices and Production* (London, 1935).

5   Followers of Piero Sraffa (1898-1983), an Italian economist at Cambridge University who did not see his own system as departing from Marx's, though people like Ian Steedman have used hiswritings in this sense.

6   This was the conclusion arrived at by "Analytical Marxists" like G A Cohen and Eric Olin Wright. See, for instance, G A Cohen, "The Labour Theory of Value and the Concept of Exploitation", in Ian Steedman and others, *The Value Controversy* (London, Verso, 1981), pp202-223.

7   Adam Smith, *The Wealth of Nations*, Book One, Chapter 5, available at http://www.econlib.org/Library/Smith/smWN.html

8   Marx, *Capital*, Volume One, p39.

9   As above.

10   Some translations into English use the archaic word "aliquot" for proportionate, adding considerably to the difficulty of Marx's work for new readers.

11   Karl Marx, "Letter to Kugelman" (11 July 1868), in Karl Marx and Frederick Engels, *Collected Works*, Volume 43 (New York, 1987).

12   Marx, *Capital*, Volume One, p75.

13   The use of the word "embodied" sometimes causes confusion. For clarification, see Guglielmo Carchedi, *Frontiers of Political Economy* (London, Verso, 1991), pp100-101.

14   See also I I Rubin, *Essays on Marx's Theory of Value* (Montreal, Black Rose, 1990), p71.

15   This is not always immediately obvious from Marx's exposition in Chapter One of *Capital*. This involves him analysing the commodity in abstraction from other features of the capitalist system which he deals with later. Competition is taken for granted, since commodity production assumes the competitive sale of commodities, but there is no account at this stage of its further impact. In the same way, Chapter One does not deal with capital although Marx later insists that it is only in a capitalist society that "being a commodity is the dominant and determining characteristic of its products" (*Capital*, Volume Three, Moscow, Progress Publishers, 1974, p857). For a fully rounded exposition of how competition between capitals subordinates each of them to the law of value, see *Capital*, Volume Three, p858; and Marx's posthumously published manuscript, "Results of the Direct Production Process", Karl Marx and Frederick Engels, *Collected Works*, Volume 34, pp355-466, available at http://www.marxists.org/archive/marx/works/1864/economic/index.htm

16   Marx, *Capital*, Volume One.

17   As above, p72.

18   As above, p74.

19   Figures for biggest 2,000 companies from "The Big Picture", http://www.Forbes.com, 4 September 2008.

20   Adam Smith, *The Wealth of Nations*, Book One, Chapter 8.

21   As above.

22   It was one of the points with which Marx disagreed with Ferdinand Lassalle, and it also caused him to write a pamphlet directed to an English working class audience, *Wages, Price and Profit*.

23   Karl Marx, *Wage Labour and Capital*. A slightly different translation to that used here is to be found at http://www.marxists.org/archive/marx/works/1847/wagelabour/ch02.htm

24 Karl Marx, *Grundrisse* (London, Penguin, 1973). Also available at

25 Marx, *Capital*, Volume One, p409.

26 So the chapters in *Capital* on manufacturing and machinery fall within the section of the work entitled "The Production of Relative Surplus Value", *Capital*, Volume One, pp336-504.

27 Marx, *Capital*, Volume One, p411. There is a minor ambiguity in Marx's work as to whether the intensification of the labour without any changing of technique amounts to "relative" or "absolute surplus value", since a passage on page 410 seems to imply the latter, and this is how some people read Marx. The point has no wide significance. I prefer the "relative surplus value" option since it is invariably combined with the introduction of machinery which, as Marx points out repeatedly, usually increases rather than diminishes the burden on the worker—and produces a different sort of resistance to that produced by extending the working day.

28 Marx, *Capital*, Volume One, p410.

29 As above, p411.

30 Engels, "Socialism: Scientific and Utopian," in Marx, Engels and Lenin, *The Essential Left* (London, Unwin Books, 1960), p130. There is sometimes confusion among Marxists about this. Some contend competition cannot be constitutive of capital since Marx's method in Volume One of *Capital* is to arrive at the general laws of the system by abstracting from the impact of competition over the distribution of surplus value between the different units of the system. Competition then supposedly belongs to the sphere of distribution, not that of production. But the competition is between producing units. It arises from the fact that their interaction with each other is not planned. This then imposes on each the general features of the system Marx analyses in Volume One. Without it there would be no reason for the individual capitals to abide by the law of value, even if some of the necessary effects of competition express themselves in the sphere of distribution. As Marx puts it, "The inner law [of value] enforces itself only through their competition, their mutual pressure upon one another." Hence it is absurd for some theorists to claim that the notion of capital does not include the notion of many competing capitals; the concept of capital presupposes commodity production. It is similar to substituting input-output tables relating particular industries to each other for the competition between capitals and then claiming to have a model of capitalist society, as do the "Ricardian" critics of Marx's theories.

31 Marx, *Capital*, Volume One.

32 "Valorisation" is the French translation of the German term used by Marx, *Verwertung*. "Valorisation" in French means an expansion in the value of something (eg a company share). But the general English meaning of the word is different, meaning simply "fixing the price or value of a commodity, etc, especially by a centralised organised scheme" (*Shorter Oxford English Dictionary*, Third Edition). This usage leads to confusion with the very different concept of "realisation" (ie getting the monetary value of commodities), which is how the term valorization is used in the English translation of the *Grundrisse* by Martin Nicolaus. All this is confusing for newcomers to Marx's writings—and encourages an academicist tendency to dense, often nearly unintelligible, expositions of Marx's analyses.

33 Marx, *Capital*, Volume One, p751.

34 As above, p716.

35 This is something David Harvey slips into in his books *The New Imperialism* (Oxford, 2005) and *A Short History of Neoliberalism* (Oxford, 2007).

Chapter Two: Marx and His Critics

1   Leon Walras, *Elements of Pure Economics* (London, George Allen, 1954 [1889]), p242.
2   As above, p372.
3   Alfred Marshall, *The Principles of Economics*, 8th edition (London, 1936) p109.
4   "Interview with Kenneth J Arrow", in G R Feiwel (ed) *Joan Robinson and Modern Economic Theory* (London, Macmillan, 1989), pp147-148.
5   Meaning "desirability".
6   Irving Fischer, "Is 'Utility' the Most Suitable Term for the Concept it is Used to Denote?" *American Economic Review*, Volume 8 (1918), pp335-7.
7   For a series of articles discussing this problem and the failure of different marginalist economists to deal with it, see J Eatwell, M Milgate and P Newman (eds), *Capital Theory* (London, Palgrave, 1990). The article by L L Pasinetti and R Scazzieri, "Capital Theory: Paradoxes", pp136-147, provides a useful and relatively accessible summary of the arguments. See also Joan Robinson, *Economic Philosophy* (London, Watts, 1962), p60.
8   Joan Robinson, *EconomicPhilosophy*, p68.
9   A Marshall, *The Principles of Economics*, p62.
10 "Two sets of incommensurable collections of miscellaneous objects cannot in themselves provide the material for a quantitative analysis", John Maynard Keynes, *General Theory of Employment, Interest and Money* (London, Macmillan, 1960), p39.
11 J M Keynes, *General Theory of Employment, Interest and Money*, p39.
12 Although it is a version in which the wage is the measure of value, rather than Ricardo's version, where it is labour performed.
13 J M Keynes, *General Theory of Employment, Interest and Money*, p41.
14 As above, pp213-214.
15 Marx, *Capital*, Volume One, p858.
16 A rise in the price of basic consumer goods will cause workers to pay more, so raising the price capitalists have to pay for their labour power in the form of wages. Of course, in reality, none of this happens without struggles between different capitalists and between capitalists and workers.
17 This whole argument for Marx's position is put simply and at length in Andrew Kliman, *Reclaiming Marx's Capital* (Lexington Books, 2007) pp149-175.
18 See Ian Steedman, *Marx after Sraffa* (London, New Left Books, 1977); for an influential debate on the issue see Ian Steedman and others, *The Value Controversy* (London, Verso, 1981). See in the same collection, Geoff Hodgson, "Critique of Wright: Labour and Profits", pp75-99. For the mainstream account of Marx, see P A Samuelson, "Understanding the Marxian Notion of Exploitation: A Summary of the So-Called Transformation Problem between Marxian Values and Competitive Prices", *Journal of Economic Literature*, 9:2 (1971), pp399-431.
19 Ben Fine, "Debating the 'New' Imperialism", *Historical Materialism*, 14:4 (2006), p135.
20 As above, p154.
21 For a fuller and very influential account of this critique, with mathematical presentations, see Paul Sweezy, *The Theory of Capitalist Development* (London, Dennis Dobson, 1946), pp115-123; see also G Carchedi, *Frontiers of Political Economy*, (London, Verso, 1991) pp90-92; A Kliman, *Reclaiming Marx's Capital*, pp45-46.

22 P Sweezy, *The Theory of Capitalist Development*, pp115 and 128.

23 Miguel Angel Garcia, "Karl Marx and the Formation of the Average Rate of Profit", *International Socialism*, 2:5 (1979); Anwar Shaikh, "Marx's Theory of Value and the 'Transformation Problem'", in Jesse Schwartz (ed), *The Subtle Anatomy of Capitalism* (Santa Monica, Goodyear, 1977).

24 This is an argument I accepted and spelt out in my book *Explaining the Crisis* (London, Bookmarks, 1984), pp160-162.

25 They have formulated what are known as "temporal" interpretations of Marx.

26 For various presentations of this argument, using mathematical examples, see G Carchedi, *Frontiers of Political Economy*, pp92-96; A Kliman, *Reclaiming Marx's Capital*, pp151-152; Alan Freeman, "Marx without Equilibrium", MPRA Paper no.1207 (2007) available at .de/1207/1/MPRA_paper_1207.pdf

27 This interpretation of Marx on this point is known as the "single system interpretation". Some of those who hold to it also accept, like me, the temporal interpretation, with the combination of both being known by the cumbersome (and somewhat offputting) phrase "The Temporal Single System Interpretation" or TSSI.

28 G Carchedi, *Frontiers of Political Economy*, pp96-97.

29 Marx, *Capital*, Volume One, p44.

30 This is essentially the account provided by Bob Rowthorn in *Capitalism, Conflict and Inflation* (London, Lawrence and Wishart, 1980) pp231-249. Except that Rowthorn sees training as taking place mainly via the state and therefore, for him, outside of capitalism. Carchedi sees training as adding to the value of labour power, but does not explain how this transfers into the final product (Carchedi, *Frontiers of Political Economy*, pp130-133). Alfredo Saad Filho and P Harvey both strongly reject the interpretation I have put here because "it conflates education and training with the storing of up of labour in machinery and other elements of constant capital"—see Alfredo Saad Filho, *The Value of Marx* (London, Routledge, 2002), p58. For Harvey, "Skilled labour creates more value in equal periods of time than does unskilled labour because it is physically more productive, and there is no reason to suppose that any determinate relationship exists between this increased physical productiveness and the physical productivity of the extra labour needed to produce the skill"—P Harvey, "The Value Creating Capacity of Skilled Labor in Marxian Economics", *Review of Radical Political Economy*, 17:1-2, quoted by A Saad Filho, in *The Value of Marx*). But what Harvey is assuming is that there is some way of measuring the comparative physical productivities of labour that might be producing quite different products, ie that you can equate the value of commodities by comparing their use values. This leaves him (and A Saad Filho) open to the very objection made by Böhm-Bawerk.

31 G Carchedi, *Frontiers of Political Economy*, p133.

Chapter Three: The Dynamics of the System

1 John Stuart Mill, *Principles of Political Economy* (London, 1911), p339.

2 See L Walras, *Elements of Pure Economics*, p381. For Jevons, see Eric Roll, *A History of Economic Thought* (London, Faber, 1962), p376.

3 Anwar Shaikh, "An Introduction to the History of Crisis Theory", in Bruce Steinberg and others (eds), *US Capitalism in Crisis* (New York, Union of Radical Political Economics, 1978), p221. Also available at http://homepage .newschool.edu/~AShaikh/crisis_theories.pdf

4 Luca Pensieroso, "Real Business Cycle Models of the Great Depression; A

Critical Survey", Discussion Papers 2005005, Université Catholique de Louvain, 2005, pp3-4, available at http://www.ires.ucl.ac.be/DP/IRES_DP/2005-5.pdf; see also Randall E Parker, *Economics of the Great Depression*, p29.

5   Marx, *Capital*, Volume One, pp110-111.

6   As above, p111.

7   This, for instance, is the argument of Pavel V Maksakovsky, in *The Capitalist Cycle* (Leiden, Brill, 2004).

8   Marx, *Capital*, Volume Three, pp239-240.

9   The most prevalent recent version has probably been that expounded by the radical American economists Paul Baran and Paul Sweezy in their book *Monopoly Capital* (London, Penguin, 1968). They see capitalism's problem as lying in a growing "surplus" which cuts the buying power of the masses and produces a secular trend to stagnation. A somewhat similar position is expounded by Joseph Steindl, *Maturity and Stagnation in American Capitalism* (New York, Monthly Review, 1976). See my critique of these positions in my book, *Explaining the Crisis*, pp148-154. See also Michael Bleaney, *Underconsumption Theories* (London, Lawrence and Wishart, 1976); Anwar Shaikh, "An Introduction to the History of Crisis Theory", in Bruce Steinberg and others (eds), *US Capitalism in Crisis* pp229-231.

10   The rest of this section is a paraphrase of the argument in Pavel V Maksakovsky, *The Capitalist Cycle*.

11   Interpretations of Marx's analysis which saw things simply in terms of disproportionality were prevalent among reformist socialists in the first decades of the 20th century. See Paul Sweezy, *The Theory of Capitalist Development*, p156.

12   This paragraph is a very condensed summary of the first four chapters of Volume Two of Marx's *Capital* (Moscow, Progress Publishers, 1984).

13   Marx, *Capital*, Volume Two, p100.

14   Marx, *Capital*, Volume Three, p432.

15   As above, p495.

16   See, for example, "In Praise of Hyman Minsky", *Guardian*, 22 August 2007.

17   Named after an Italian American fraudster of the early 1920s. There is an early account of such a scheme in Charles Dickens's *Martin Chuzzlewit*, written in 1844-5.

18   Marx, *Capital*, Volume Three, p383.

19   As above, p384.

20   As above, p249.

21   F A Hayek, *Prices and Production* (London, George Routledge, 1935), pp103-104.

22   See the quotes from Nigel Lawson in William Keegan, *Mr Maudling's Gamble* (London, Hodder & Stoughton, 1989), p55.

23   Leon Trotsky, "Report on the World Economic Crisis and the New Tasks of the Communist International", *The First Five Years of the Communist International*, Volume One (New York, Pathfinder, 1972).

24   W Keegan, *The Spectre of Capitalism* (London, Radius, 1992), p79. On the socialist left the Marxist account was rejected in the 1970s by Andrew Glyn, Bob Sutcliffe, John Harrison, Paul Sweezy and others. For a full account of the views of these "Marxist" critics of Marx's, see my book *Explaining the Crisis*, pp20-30.

25   For instance, those who accept the theories of monopoly associated with Baran and Sweezy; the Sraffian, neo-Ricardian current of Harrison, Steedman, Hodgson, Glyn and others; also critics of the Sraffians such as Bob Rowthorn.

26 Marx, *Capital*, Volume Three, pp236-7.

27 As above, p237.

28 As above, p245.

29 See, for instance, John Stuart Mill, *Principles of Political Economy*, Book 4, Chapters 4 and 5, available at http://socserv2.socsci.mcmaster.ca/~econ/ugcm/3ll3/mill/prin/book4/bk4ch04

30 Eric Hobsbawm, *Industry and Empire* (London, Penguin, 1971), p75.

31 Marx's rejection of Ricardo's explanation makes nonsense of Robert Brenner's assertion that Marx's theory rests on a "Malthusian" assumption that "productivity can be expected to fall". See Robert Brenner, "The Economics of Global Turbulence", *New Left Review*, 1:229 (1998), p11.

32 Marx, *Capital*, Volume One, p612.

33 Marx also uses another concept, the "value composition of capital" to describe the ratio of investment in means and material of production to the cost of labour power (or, in his terminology, the ratio of constant capital to variable capital, or c/v). Marx then defines the organic composition of capital as the value composition "in so far as it determined by the technical composition". Fred Moseley argues this distinguishes changes in the organic composition from changes in the value composition due to alterations in the cost of either means of production or labour power. See Fred Moseley, *The Falling Rate of Profit in the Postwar US Economy* (London, Macmillan, 1991), pp3-6. See also the discussion at http://ricardo.ecn.wfu.edu/~cottrell/ope/archive/0211/0092.html. By contrast, Ben Fine and Lawrence Harris in *Rereading Capital* (London, Macmillan, 1979, pp58-60) argue that the "value composition of capital is the ratio of the current value of the means and material of production consumed to the current value of labour power consumed". The point is that the current value of the capital consumed is not necessarily the same as the value of the original investment—indeed this is a point we will deal with later, and the value of consumed capital will tend to be less than the value of invested capital, as increased productivity reduces the socially necessary labour needed to produce each unit of capital.

34 I Steedman, *Marx After Sraffa*, p64; compare also pp128-29.

35 Andrew Glyn, "Capitalist Crisis and the Organic Composition", *Bulletin of the Conference of Socialist Economists*, 4 (1972); Andrew Glyn "Productivity, Organic Composition and the Falling Rate of Profit: A Reply", *Bulletin of the Conference of Socialist Economists*, 6 (1973).

36 Susan Himmelweit, "The Continuing Saga of the Falling Rate of Profit: A Reply to Mario Cogoy", *Bulletin of the Conference of Socialist Economists*, 9 (1974).

37 Robert Brenner, *The Economics of Global Turbulence* (London, Verso, 2006), footnote, pp14-15.

38 Gérard Duménil and Dominique Lévy, *The Economics of the Profit Rate* (London, Edward Elgar, 1993).

39 Nobuo Okishio, "Technical Changes and the Rate of Profit", *Kobe University Economic Review*, 7 (1961), pp85-99.

40 For Marx's argument with a numerical example, see *Capital*, Volume One, pp316-317.

41 For more on this argument, with a simple numerical example of my own, see my book *Explaining the Crisis*, pp29-30.

42 For a general mathematical proof of this argument, see, for instance, N Okishio, "A Formal Proof of Marx's Two Theorems", *Kobe University Economic Review*, 18 (1972), pp1-6.

43 See, for example, the arguments of Hodgson, Steedman, Himmelweit, Glyn, Brenner, and Duménil and Lévy.

44 This point was made by Robin Murray in a reply to an attempt by Glyn to use a "corn model" to disprove the falling rate of profit (see Robin Murray, "Productivity, the Organic Composition and the Rate of Profit", *Bulletin of the Conference of Socialist Economists*, 6, 1973). It has since been amplified by the temporal single-system school of Marxist economists.

45 Robert Brenner, after rejecting Marx's theory of the tendency for the rate of profit to fall on the basis of Okishio's argument, then puts forward an account of his own which rests precisely on the way in which capitalists who have invested a lot in fixed capital in the past see their prices undercut and their profits threatened by capitalists who have invested more recently with cheaper or technologically more advanced fixed capital. Having accepted Okishio's position on one page, Brenner provides his own refutation of Okishio a few pages later—and does not realise he has done so. See Robert Brenner, *Economics of Global Turbulence*, pp14-15 and 28-31.

46 Marx, *Capital*, Volume Three, p231.

47 Exceptional cases will be when completely new lines of production emerge with low organic compositions of capital but with a level of production and investment capable of absorbing a lot of accumulated surplus value. But these exceptions will soon be gripped by the tendency for their organic compositions to rise.

48 Marx, *Capital*, Volume Three, p241.

49 Marx's argument is contained in Volume Three of *Capital*, pp239-240 and p252. Ever since Marx's time there have been debates between various schools of Marxists who see the crisis as originating in the rate of profit or in the disproportion between different sectors of production and the rate of profit. In these passages Marx sees the tendency of the rate of profit to fall as clashing with the pursuit of the capital's selfexpansion, so producing disproportionalities and a periodic lag of effective demand behind global output. Confusion arises because Marx did not finish Volume Three of *Capital*, leaving behind a sometimes fragmentary manuscript which Engels tried to put into some order. It is then all too easy for people to quote from one page without relating it to what appears on other pages.

50 Rudolf Hilferding, *Finance Capital* (London, Routledge, 1981), pp93 and 257.

51 Otto Bauer was responding to an argument about the breakdown of capital from Rosa Luxemburg (discussed further on) which was very different to that of Henryk Grossman.

52 Henryk Grossman, *The Law of Accumulation and the Breakdown of the Capitalist System*, (London, Pluto, 1992), p76. See also Rick Kuhn, *Henryk Grossman and the Recovery of Marxism* (Champaign, IL: University of Illinois Press, 2006), pp224-234. Grossman based his argument, in part, on a passage in Volume Three of *Capital* (p247), where Marx writes that, "a portion of the capital would lie completely or partially idle (because it would have to crowd out some of the active capital before it could expand its own value), and the other portion would produce values at a lower rate of profit, owing to the pressure of unemployed or but partly employed capital... The fall in the rate of profit would then be accompanied by an absolute decrease in the mass of profit, since the mass of employed labour power could not be increased and the rate of surplus value raised under the conditions we had assumed, so that the mass of surplus value could not be increased either."

53 Henryk Grossman, *The Law of Accumulation and the Breakdown of the*

Capitalist System, (London, Pluto, 1992) p191.

54 See Rick Kuhn, *Henryk Grossman and the Recovery of Marxism*, pp138-148.

55 Henryk Grossman, *The Law of Accumulation and the Breakdown of the Capitalist System*, (London, Pluto, 1992) p76. Also Rick Kuhn, *Henryk Grossman and the Recovery of Marxism*, p85.

56 See, for instance, Marx, *Capital*, Volume Three, p241.

57 Marx, *Capital*, Volume One, p360.

58 As above, p356.

59 As above.

60 For a very good presentation of this argument, see "Marx's Theory of Value", in Michael Kidron, *Capitalism and Theory* (London, Pluto, 1974), pp74-75.

61 K Marx and F Engels, *The German Ideology*, in Marx and Engels, *Collected Works*, Volume 5, p52.

62 See John Bellamy Foster, *Marx's Ecology* (New York, Monthly Review, 2000); Paul Burkett, *Marx and Nature: A Red and Green Perspective* (London, Palgrave, 1999).

63 Marx, *Capital*, Volume One, p177.

64 Marx, *Capital*, Volume Three, p792.

65 As above, p793.

66 Marx, *Capital*, Volume One, pp506-508.

67 Marx, *Capital*, Volume Three, p793.

68 F Engels, *The Dialectics of Nature*, in Marx and Engels, *Collected Works*, Volume 25, p461.

69 As above, p462.

70 As above, p463.

71 Marx, *Capital*, Volume One, p233.

72 Marx and Engels, *Communist Manifesto*, available at http://www.marxists.org/archive/marx/works/1848/communistmanifesto/ch01.htm

73 There were a few exceptions in the 20th century, most notably Joseph Schumpeter in his *Capitalism, Socialism and Democracy* (London, Allen & Unwin, 1943), but they nearly always owed a debt to Marx for their approach, even while trying to adjust his findings to justify capitalism rather than damn it.

74 For this reason, Marx does not only describe the law of value as functioning in an abstract model of commodity production in Chapter One of Volume One of *Capital*, but also as it functions at a more concrete level through the interplay of capitals in the chapter "Distribution Relations and Production Relations" in Volume Three of *Capital* (pp857-859).

Chapter Four: Beyond Marx: Monopoly, War and the State

1 Quoted in D M Gordon, "Up and Down the Long Roller Coaster", in Bruce Steinberg and others (eds), *US Capitalism in Crisis*, p23.

2 See "Figure 2: Net Returns on Capital in the UK, 1855-1914", in A J Arnold and Sean McCartney, "National Income Accounting and Sectoral Rates of Return on UK Risk-Bearing Capital, 1855-1914", November 2003, available at http://business-school.exeter.ac.uk/accounting/papers/0302a.pdf

3 See the accounts in Gareth Stedman Jones, *Outcast London* (Harmondsworth, Penguin, 1991).

4 Frederick Engels, "Preface to the English Edition" (1886) in Marx, *Capital*, Volume One, available at http://www.marxists.org/archive/marx/works/1867-c1/p6.htm

5 For details and sources, see my book *Explaining the Crisis*, p52.

6 See, for Germany, G Bry, *Wages in Germany 1871-1945* (Princeton, 1960),

p74; A V Desai, *Real Wages in Germany* (Oxford, Clarendon, 1968), pp15-16 and p35.

7   See the detailed account of the trend of working hours in the 20th century inBKHunnicutt,*Work Without End*(Philadelphia,Temple, 1988).
8   Edward Bernstein, *Evolutionary Socialism* (London, ILP, 1909), pp80 and 83.
9   As above, p219.
10 R Hilferding, *Finance Capital*, p304.
11 As above.
12 As above, p325.
13 As above, p366.
14 As above, p235.
15 As above, pp289-290.
16 As above, p294.
17 As above.
18 See William Smaldone, *Rudolf Hilferding* (Bonn: Dietz, 2000), p105.
19 M Salvadori, *Karl Kautsky and the Socialist Revolution, 1880-1938* (London, Verso, 1979), p171.
20 From Karl Kautsky, "Imperialism and the War", *International Socialist Review* (November 1914), available on www.marxists.org
21 J A Hobson, *Imperialism: A Study* (New York, 1902), available at http://www.econlib.org/library/YPDBooks/Hobson/hbsnImp.html
22 For details see Barry Eichengreen, *Globalised Finance* (Princeton, 2008), p34.
23 Norman Angell, *The Great Illusion* (Toronto, McClelland & Goodchild, 1910), p269, available at http://ia350610.us.archive.org/1/items/greatillusionstu 00angeuoft/greatillusionstu00angeuoft.pdf
24 Nigel Harris, "All Praise War", *International Socialism*, 102 (2004).
25 Ellen Meiksins Wood, "Logics of Power", *Historical Materialism* 14:4 (2006), p23.
26 As above, p22.
27 Michael Hardt, "Folly of our Masters of the Universe", *Guardian*, 18 December 2002.
28 N I Bukharin, *Imperialism and World Economy* (London, Merlin, 1972), available at .marxists.org/archive/bukharin/works/1917/imperial/index.htm
29 V I Lenin, *Imperialism: The Highest Stage of Capitalism* (London, 1933 [1916]). Lenin's book was published before Bukharin's and is better known. But Bukharin actually wrote his book first.
30 As above, p24.
31 As above, p60.
32 As above, p108.
33 As above, p69.
34 As above, Chapter 7, "Imperialism, as a Special Stage of Capitalism".
35 Nicolai Bukharin, *Imperialism and World Economy*, Chapter 10, "'Reproduction of the Processes of Concentration and Centralisation of Capital on a World Scale".
36 Nicolai Bukharin, *Economics of the Transformation Period* (New York, Bergman, 1971), p36.
37 Nicolai Bukharin, *Imperialism and World Economy*, pp124-127.
38 Rosa Luxemburg and Nicolai Bukharin, *Imperialism and the Accumulation of Capital* (Allen Lane, 1972), p267.
39 See, for instance, Ellen Meiksins Wood, "Logics of Power: A Conversation with David Harvey," in *Historical Materialism*, 14, no 4, p23.
40 Figures from H Feis, *Europe: The World's Banker: 1879-1914*, quoted in M

Kidron, "Imperialism: The Highest Stage But One", in *International Socialism*, 9 (first series, 1962), p18.

41 The argument and the figures for this are provided by M Barratt Brown, *The Economics of Imperialism* (Harmondsworth, Penguin, 1974), p195.

42 For one of the first recognitions of this limitation of too literal applications of Lenin's theory, see Tony Cliff, "The Nature of Stalinist Russia" (1948), in T Cliff, *Marxist Theory after Trotsky* (London, Bookmarks, 2003), p117.

43 V I Lenin, *Imperialism: The Highest Stage of Capitalism*, Chapter 3, "Finance Capital and the Financial Oligarchy".

44 Nicolai Bukharin, *Imperialism and World Economy*, p114.

45 Nicolai Bukharin, *Imperialism and the Accumulation of Capital*, p256.

46 As above, p267.

47 Rosa Luxemburg, *The Accumulation of Capital* (London, Routledge, 1963).

48 Rosa Luxemburg, *Accumulation of Capital, An Anti-Critique*, in Rosa Luxemburg and Nikolai Bukharin, *Imperialism and the Accumulation of Capital*, p74.

49 Nicolai Bukharin, *Imperialism and the Accumulation of Capital*, p180.

50 As above, p224.

51 See the discussion in Chapter Three earlier.

52 Henryk Grossman, *The Law of Accumulation and the Breakdown of the Capitalist System*, p98.

53 Figures from Colin Clarke, "Wages and Profits", *Oxford Economic Papers*, 30 (1978), p401.

54 See "Figure 2: Net Returns on Capital in the UK, 1855-1914", in A J Arnold and S McCartney, "National Income Accounting and Sectoral Rates of Return on UK Risk-Bearing Capital, 1855-1914", *Essex University Working Paper*, 2003.

55 For a full exposition of Marx's various views on the state, see Hal Draper, *Karl Marx's Theory of Revolution: State and Bureaucracy* (New York, Monthly Review, 1979).

56 Graph available at http://www.econlib.org/library/Enc1/GovernmentSpending.html

57 For a forceful criticism of this view, see Justin Rosenberg, *The Empire of Civil Society* (London, Verso, 1994).

58 This was an important point made by Colin Barker in discussing various versions of the "capital derivation" theories of the state in his articles, "The State as Capital", *International Socialism*, 1 (1978); "A Note on the Theory of the Capitalist State", *Capital and Class*, 4 (1978).

59 Marx abstracted from the existence of many capitals in competition from each other in the early parts of Volume One of *Capital*, in order to avoid confusing the general dynamic of the system and its units with the continual ups and downs caused by the particular impacts of capitals on each other (eg oscillations of prices around their values). But this did not mean that he held that capitalism could exist simply as a single capital not facing competition. In the same way, it can be useful for some purposes to treat the abstract features of the capitalist state, but the concrete capitalist state does not exist in isolation from other states and the interplay of capitals. Marx recognised this when in his original plan for *Capital* the volume to deal with the state was due to appear after the volumes dealing with the interplay of different capitals in the circulation process, the distribution of surplus value between different capitals, the rate of profit, rent and so forth.

60 Ellen Meiksins Wood, "Logics of Power", p25. Even David Harvey, who

accepts there is an economic rationale to imperialism, writes at one point of "territorial and capitalist logics of power"! as distinct from each other. See David Harvey, *The New Imperialism*, p29.

61 See "Two Insights do not Make a Theory", *International Socialism*, 100 (first series, 1977).

62 My limited knowledge of these debates is indebted to a paper presented at the November 2005 conference organised by *Historical Materialism* in London. See Oliver Nachtwey and Tobias ten Brink, "Lost in Transition—the German World Market Debate in the 1970s", *Historical Materialism*, 16:1 (2008), pp37-71. For some of the key writers see Wolfgang Mueller and Christel Neusuess, "The 'Welfare State Illusion' and Contradictions between Wage Labour and Capital"; Elmer Alvater, "Some Problems of State Interventionism"; Joachim Hirsch, "The State Apparatus and Social Reproduction", in John Holloway and Sol Piccioto (eds), *State and Capital, A Marxist Debate* (London, Edward Arnold, 1987).

63 This is a summary of her argument provided by Nachtwey and Brink based on her "Kapitalakkumulation im Weltzusammenhang", in H-G Backhaus (ed), *Gesellschaft, Beiträge zur Marxschen Theorie* 1 (Frankfurt/Main, 1974).

64 This description of states negotiating on behalf of national capitalisms contrasts with his argument that the military adventures of the US state have not had any economic role (a point he made, for instance, in his contribution to the discussion on imperialism at the *Historical Materialism* conference in London in November 2007).

65 Frederick Engels, *On the Decline of Feudalism and the Emergence of National States*, in Marx and Engels, *Collected Works*, Volume 26, pp556-565.

66 V I Lenin, *The Right of Nations to Self Determination*, in V I Lenin, *Collected Works*, Volume 20 (Moscow, Progress Publishers, 1972), p396, available at http://www.marxists.org/archive/lenin/works/1914/self-det/ch01.htm

67 Heide Gerstenberger, *Impersonal Power: History and Theory of the Bourgeois State* (Leiden, Brill, 2007) brings out very clearly the difference between the precapitalist state and the modern state, but confuses things by lumping together absolutist and fully capitalist states like that of Britain in the 18th and well into 19th century as "ancien regimes". See the review of her book by Pepijn Brandon, *International Socialism*, 120 (2008).

68 For a much fuller development of this argument, see my article "The State and Capitalism Today", *International Socialism*, 2:51(1991), pp3-57, available at http://www.isj.org.uk/?id=234

69 Volume Two of Marx's *Capital* spells out the relation between the three forms once productive capitalism has established itself.

70 Neil Brenner, "Between Fixity and Motion: Accumulation, Territorial Organization and the Historical Geography of Spatial Scales", University of Chicago, 1998, available at http://sociology.as.nyu.edu/docs/IO/222/Brenner.EPd.1998.pdf

71 For an account of this, see W Ruigrok and R van Tulder, *The Logic of International Restructuring* (London, Taylor and Francis, 1995), p164.

72 For a useful discussion on the literature about these networks, see J Scott, *Corporations, Classes and Capitalism* (London, Hutchinson Educational, 1985).

73 Costas Lapavitsas, "Relations of Power and Trust in Contemporary Finance", *Historical Materialism*, 14:1 (2006), p148.

74 Costas Lapavitsas, "Relations of Power and Trust in Contemporary Finance", p150.

75 V I Lenin, *Imperialism: The Highest Stage of Capitalism*, p60.
76 Claus Offe, *Contradictions of the Welfare State* (London, Hutchinson, 1984), p49.
77 Antonio Gramsci, *Selections from Prison Notebooks* (New York, International Publishers, 1971), p170.
78 What are sometimes called "ruling blocs".
79 All quotes from Karl Marx, the first draft of *The Civil War in France*, in Marx and Engels, *Collected Works*, Volume 22, p483, available at http://www.marxists.org/archive/marx/works/1871/civil-warfrance/drafts/ch01.htm
80 It is this view which enables Harvey to see privatisation as a form of "accumulation by dispossession" of productive activities "outside of capitalism". See David Harvey, *The New Imperialism*, (Oxford University Press, 2005) p141.
81 In countries like Italy or Brazil this could be half of total productive investment; in the case of the United States arms expenditure was equal to total productive investment for long periods of time.
82 Marx, *Capital*, Volume Three, pp862-863.
83 Karl Marx, "Transformation of Money into Capital", *Manuscripts of 1861-3*, in Marx and Engels, *Collected Works*, Volumes 30 and 33, available at http://www.marxists.org/archive/marx/works/1861/economic/ch19.htm
84 R Hilferding, *Finance Capital*.
85 This, for instance, is the position implied by Fred Moseley in his study of the rate of profit in the US when he excludes the state sector from his calculations—see his *The Falling Rate of Profit in the Post War United States Economy*.
86 Marx, *Capital*, Volume Two, p97.
87 Frederick Engels, "Socialism Scientific and Utopian", in *Marx, Engels, Lenin, The Essential Left*, pp71-72.
88 Karl Kautsky, *The Class Struggle* (also known as "The Erfurt Programme"), Chapter Four http://www.marxists.org/archive/kautsky/1892/erfurt/ch04.htm
89 Leon Trotsky, *The First Five Years of the Communist International*, Volume One (New York, Pathfinder Press, 2009).
90 Marx, *Capital*, Volume One, p78.
91 Tony Cliff, *The Nature of Stalinist Russia*. Cliff was drawing out the implication of Bukharin's account in *Imperialism and the World Economy*.

Chapter Five: State Spending and the System

1 See Marx's comments on Smith in this regard in Karl Marx, *Theories of Surplus Value*, Volume One (Moscow, nd), pp170 and 291.
2 "Productive and unproductive labour is here throughout conceived from the standpoint of the possessor of money, from the standpoint of the capitalist, not from that of the workman", as above, p155.
3 As above, p156.
4 Marx, *Capital*, Volume One, p192.
5 Guglielmo Carchedi, *Frontiers of Political Economy*, p40.
6 According to Enrique Dussel, Marx's argument in his notebooks is that "unproductive labour" will, "with only minor exceptions, only perform personal services". Enrique Dussel, *Towards An Unknown Marx* (Routledge, 2001), p69.
7 Marx, *Theories of Surplus Value*, Volume One, p170.
8 Marx, *Capital*, Volume Three, p293.
9 Jacques Bidet, *Exploring Marx's Capital* (Leiden, Brill, 2007), pp104-121.
10 Marx, *Capital*, Volume Three, p296.
11 Marx, *Capital*, Volume Two, p137.

12   See Table F.1, in Anwar Shaikh and E A Tonak, *Measuring the Wealth of Nations* (Cambridge University Press, 1996), pp298-303.

13   Fred Moseley, *The Falling Rate of Profit in the Post War United States Economy*, p126.

14   Simon Mohun, "Distributive Shares in the US Economy, 1964-2001", *Cambridge Journal of Economics*, 30:3 (2006), Figure 6.

15   Michael Kidron, "Waste: US 1970", in *Capitalism and Theory*, pp37-39.

16   Alan Freeman, "The Indeterminacy of Price-Value Correlations: A Comment on Papers by Simon Mohun and Anwar Shaikh", available at http://mpra.ub.unimuenchen.de/2040/01/MPRA_paper_2040.pdf

17   Guglilmo Carchedi, *Frontiers of Political Economy*, pp83-84.

18   Michael Kidron, "Waste: US 1970", in *Capitalism and Theory*, p56.

19   Marx, *Theories of Surplus Value*, Volume One, p170.

20   Karl Marx, *Grundrisse*, pp750-751.

21   The *Grundrisse* was not published in English until 1973.

22   Michael Kidron, "International Capitalism", *International Socialism* 20 (first series, 1965), p10, available at http://www.marxists.org/archive/kidron/works/1965/xx/intercap.htm. Carchedi recognises the different effect of production of nonreproductive goods (which he calls "non-basic", using the terminology of the Ricardians he is criticising) on the dynamic of accumulation without explicitly drawing Kidron's conclusion about the rate of profit. "Non-basics cannot", he writes, "be the transmission belt through which value changes in the previous production process are carried into the next one"—G Carchedi, *Frontiers of Political Economy*, p83.

23   Michael Kidron, *Capitalism and Theory*, p16.

24   Michael Kidron, "Capitalism: the Latest Stage", in Nigel Harris and John Palmer, *World Crisis* (London, Hutchinson, 1971), reprinted in *Capitalism and Theory*, pp16-17. For a longer exposition of this insight which takes up criticisms from Ernest Mandel, see my *Explaining the Crisis*, pp39-40 and 159-160.

25   Henryk Grossman, *The Law of Accumulation*, pp157-158.

26   T S Ashton, *The Industrial Revolution* (London, Oxford University Press, 1948), pp112-113. They did then have to enforce on them their own discipline of work, timed by the clock. See E P Thompson, "Time and Work-Discipline", in *Customs in Common* (London, Penguin, 1993), pp370-400.

27   For a development of this argument with historical references, see Suzanne de Brunhoff, *The State, Capital and Economic Policy* (London, Pluto, 1978), pp10-19.

28   See Lindsey German, *Sex, Class and Socialism* (London, Bookmarks, 1989), pp33-36.

29   T H Marshall, *Social Policy* (London, Hutchinson, 1968), pp46-59.

30   Ann Rogers, "Back to the Workhouse", *International Socialism* 59 (1993), p11.

31   *Hansard*, Parliamentary Debates, 17th February, 1943, Col 1818.

32   Quoted in T H Marshall, *Social Policy*, p17.

33   Notoriously, the attack on public sector employment, Robert Bacon and Walter Eltis, *Britain's Economic Problem: Too Few Producers* (New York, St Martin's, 1976).

34   Marx's term in *Capital*, Volume One, p349.

35   If they are counted as part of constant capital, this is a peculiar form of constant capital that can walk away from the firm and work elsewhere, and in some interpretations this leads to the view of skilled workers as in some way possessors of their own "human capital" and a part of their wages is viewed as a "return" on this capital. It should be added, however, that disputes over

this question can be in danger of turning into pure scholasticism, since in any case the costs of training add to the investment costs of a firm. At the same time, insofar as training is generalised across the system as a whole, it increases average labour productivity and so serves to reduce the value in terms of socially necessary labour of each unit of output—and in doing so reduces the gains accruing to the individual capitalist from undertaking the training.

36   The "free rider" problem: see, for instance, Mary O'Mahony, "Employment, Education and Human Capital", in R Floud and P Johnson, *The Cambridge Economic History of Modern Britain*, Volume Three (Cambridge University Press, 2004).

37   Assuming the labour they train is going to end up as productive labour.

38   See Richard Johnson, "Notes on the Schooling of the English Working Class 1780-1850", in Roger Dale and others (eds), *Schooling and Capitalism* (London, Routledge & Kegan Paul, 1976), pp44-54. See also Steven Shapin and Barry Barnes, "Science, Education and Control", in the same volume, pp55-66.

39   For a full account of developments in the major industrial countries of the time, see Chris McGuffie, *Working in Metal* (London, Merlin, 1985).

Chapter Six: The Great Slump

1   Charles Kindleberger, *The World in Depression 1929-39* (London, Allen Lane, 1973), p117. See also Albrecht Ritschl and Ulrich Woitek, "What Did Cause the Great Depression?", Institute for Empirical Research in Economics, *University of Zurich Working Paper 50*, 2000, p13.

2   See the estimates for GNP in Angus Maddison, "Historical Statistics for the World Economy: 1-2003 AD", available at: http://www.ggdc.net/maddison/Historical_Statistics/horizontal-file_03-2007.xls

3   For a much more detailed account of the spread of the crisis, with sources, see my *Explaining the Crisis*, pp55-62.

4   See figures given in Fritz Sternberg, *The Coming Crisis* (London, Victor Gollancz, 1947), p23; Lewis Corey, *The Decline of American Capitalism* (London, Bodley Head, 1935), p27. Available at http://www.marxists.org/archive/corey/1934/decline/ch05.html

5   Quoted in R Skidelsky, *John Maynard Keynes*, Volume 2 (London, Macmillan, 1994), p341.

6   Quoted in W Smaldone, *Rudolf Hilferding*, p105.

7   See, for instance, Randall E Parker, *Economics of the Great Depression*, p14.

8   See the summary of the Austrian view by Randall E Parker, *Economics of the Great Depression*, pp 9-10. See also F A Hayek, *Pure Theory of Capital* (London, Routledge and Keegan Paul, 1941), p408, and *Profit, Interest and Investment* (London, Routledge, 1939) pp33, 47-49, and 173. For a very good contemporary exposition of Hayek's position see John Strachey, *The Nature of Capitalist Crisis* (London, Victor Gollancz, 1935), pp56-82.

9   Figures given by Corey in *The Decline of American Capitalism*. Robert Brenner and Mark Glick, "The Regulation Approach: Theory and History", *New Left Review*, 1:188 (1991), argue that wages rose sharply in the years before the Crash, but the graph they provide from S Lebergott, *Manpower in Economic Growth* (New York, McGraw-Hill, 1964) only suggests a rise of about the same level as Corey's figures.

10   Michael A Bernstein, *The Great Depression* (Cambridge University Press, 1987), p187. He adds that for the population as a whole it rose 13 percent, and for the top 1 percent of the non-farm population the figure was 63 percent.

11   Robert J Gordon, "The 1920s and the 1990s in Mutual Reflection", paper

presented to economic history conference, Duke University, pp26-27 March, 2004.

12 Alvin Hansen, *Full Recovery or Stagnation* (London, Adam and Charles Black, 1938), pp290-291. Hansen's figures were for 1924-29.

13 Simon Kuznets, *Capital in the American Economy* (Oxfor University Press, 1961) p92.

14 Joseph Gillman, *The Falling Rate of Profit* (London, Dennis Dobson, 1956), p27.

15 Joseph Steindl, *Maturity and Stagnation in the American Economy* (London, Blackwell, 1953), p155 and following.

16 Alvin Hansen, *Full Recovery or Stagnation*, p296.

17 As above, pp296 and 298.

18 See the calculations in Lewis Corey, *The Decline of American Capitalism*, Chapter 5.

19 As above, p170.

20 Barry Eichengreen and Kris Mitchener, "The Great Depression as a Credit Boom Gone Wrong", Bank of International Settlements, Working Papers No137, September 2003. Available at http://www.bis.org/publ/work137.pdf?noframes=1

21 L Corey, *The Decline of American Capitalism*, p172. Compare also Gillman, pp129-130.

22 Barry Eichengreen and Kris Mitchener, "The Great Depression as a Credit Boom Gone Wrong".

23 See, for instance, the account given by E A Preobrazhensky in *The Decline of Capitalism* (M E Sharp, 1985), p137.

24 See, for instance, Robert J Gordon, "The 1920s and the 1990s in Mutual Reflection".

25 C Kindleberger, *The World in Depression 1929-39*, p117.

26 Marx, *Capital*, Volume Three, p473.

27 Alvin Hansen, *Economic Stabilization in an Unbalanced World* (Fairfield, NJ, A M Kelley, 1971 [1932]), p81.

28 C Kindleberger, *The World in Depression 1929-39*, p117.

29 Milton Friedman and Anna Schwartz, *The Great Contraction 1929-33* (Princeton University Press, 1965), p21.

30 John Strachey's 1935 account of these contradictory arguments still makes powerful reading today. See Strachey, *The Nature of the Capitalist Crisis*, pp39-119. For interviews with past and present mainstream economists putting forward different interpretations, see the two volumes by Randall E Parker, *Reflections on the Great Depression* (Edward Elgar, 2002) and *The Economics of the Great Depression*.

31 J M Keynes, *General Theory of Employment, Interest and Money*, p164.

32 As above, p59.

33 As above, pp161-162.

34 As above, pp135-136 and 214.

35 As above, p219.

36 As above, p316.

37 As above, p221. For Keynes's account of the "marginal efficiency of capital" and its tendency to "diminish", see pp135-136, 214, and especially, 314-324. For a comparison of Keynes's position with Marx's, see Lefteris Tsoulfidis, "Marx and Keynes on Profitability, Capital Accumulation and Economic Crisis", available at http://iss.gsnu.ac.kr/upfiles/haksuo/%5B02-2005%5DLefteris%20Tsoulfidis.pdf

38   Hayek's recognition of the physical as well as the value character of production
     distinguishes his writings from those of most of the rest of the marginalist neo-
     classical school. He admits the importance of Marx in developing such ideas.
     See F A Hayek, *Prices and Production*, p103. This provides him with certain
     insights missing in Keynes, despite the much more reactionary conclusions
     Hayek draws. He was too honest for many of his disciples, who can't accept
     the implication that crises are inevitable.

39   F A Hayek, *Prices and Production*, quoted in Strachey, *The Nature of the
     Capitalist Crisis*, p108.

40   See the calculations in Joseph Gillman, *The Falling Rate of Profit*; Shane
     Mage, "The Law of the Falling Rate of Profit: Its Place in the Marxian
     Theoretical System and its Relevance for the US Economy" (PhD thesis,
     Columbia University, 1963, released through University Microfilms, Ann
     Arbor, Michigan); Gérard Duménil and Dominique Lévy, *The Economics of
     the Profit Rate* (Edward Elgar, 1993), p254; Lewis Corey, *The Decline of
     American Capitalism* gives figures for the 1920s only.

41   For profitability before 1914, see Tony Arnold and Sean McCartney, "National
     Income Accounting and Sectoral Rates of Return on UK Risk-Bearing Capital,
     1855-1914", Essex University Working paper, November 2003, available at
     http://www.essex.ac.uk/AFM/Research/working_papers/WP03-10.pdf. For
     profitability before and after the First World War, see Ernest Henry Phelps
     Brown and Margaret H Browne, *A Century of Pay* (London, Macmillan,
     1968), pp412 and 414; tables 137 and 138.

42   Theo Balderston, "The Beginning of the Depression in Germany 1927-30",
     Economic History Review, 36:3 (1985), p406.

43   Calculations from Joseph Gillman, *The Falling Rate of Profit*, p58; Shane
     Mage, "The Law of the Falling Rate of Profit", p208; and Gérard Duménil
     and Dominique Lévy, *The Economics of the Profit Rate*, p248 (figure 14.2).

44   These are to be found in Marx, *Capital*, Volume 3, part V.

45   This is interpreting Grossman's account as showing how capitalism is driven
     to extreme crises, not to a breakdown from which it has no escape. See Rick
     Kuhn, "Economic Crisis and Social Revolution", School of Social Science,
     Australian National University, February 2004, p17.

46   E A Preobrazhensky, *The Decline of Capitalism*, pp33 and 29. Preobrazhensky
     was, however, vague as to how this impeded recovery from the crisis. Like many
     Marxist economists of the first decades of the 20th century he did not pay much
     attention to the passages in Marx on the tendency of the rate of profit to fall.

47   Michael Bleaney, *The Rise and Fall of Keynesian Economics* (London,
     Macmillan, 1985) p47.

48   Charles Kindleberger, *The World in Depression 1929-39*, p272.

49   Figures given in Fritz Sternberg, *Capitalism and Socialism on Trial* (London,
     Victor Gollanz 1951), p353; Arthur Schweitzer, *Big Business in the Third
     Reich* (Bloomington, Indiana University Press, 1964), p336.

50   Arthur Schweitzer, *Big Business in the Third Reich*, p335.

51   See Chapter Four.

52   Chris Harman, *Explaining the Crisis*, p71.

53   Fritz Sternberg, *Capitalism and Socialism on Trial*, pp494-495.

54   A D H Kaplan, *The Liquidation of War Production* (New York, McGraw-
     Hill, 1944), p91.

55   As above, p3.

56   John Kenneth Galbraith, *American Capitalism* (Transaction Publishers, 1993),
     p65. The view that the depression only really ended with the war is accepted by

most of the mainstream economists interviewed in Parker's two volumes.

57 The view of Paul Sweezy and Paul Baran in the US, of the editorial team of
    New Left Review in Britain, the left wing of European social democracy, and
    of the great majority of academic Marxists.

58 Trotsky had developed this notion in the 1930s, and it continued to be
    accepted by supposedly "orthodox" Trotskyists until the collapse of the
    USSR in 1991—and in a few cases even afterwards.

59 M Reiman, *The Birth of Stalinism* (London, Taurus, 1987), pp37-38, provides
    an account of the crisis based on internal documents.

60 As above, p89.

61 Joseph Stalin, *Problems of Leninism*, quoted in Isaac Deutscher, *Stalin*
    (London, Oxford University Press, 1961), p328.

62 Stalin, quoted in E H Carr and R W Davies, *Foundations of a Planned
    Economy*, Volume One (London, Macmillan, 1969), p327.

63 E A Preobrazhensky, *The Decline of Capitalism*, p166.

64 Lewis Corey, *The Decline of American Capitalism*, p484. His concept of de-
    cline did not rule out short periods of growth, but with "shorter upswings"
    and longer "depressions".

65 John Strachey, *The Nature of Capitalist Crisis*, pp375-376.

66 E A Preobrazhensky, *The Decline of Capitalism*, p159.

67 Leon Trotsky, *The Death Agony of Capitalism and the Tasks of the Fourth
    International* (1938), available at http://www.marxists.org/archive/trotsky/
    1938/tp/index.htm

Chapter Seven: The Long Boom

1   I use the term "Western" as short for "Western style", in contrast to the
    "Eastern bloc" countries.

2   Albert Fishlow, "Review of Handbook of Development Economics", *Journal
    of Economic Literature*, Volume XXIX (1991), p1730.

3   Monetary measures were included in the conventional Keynesian tool kit,
    although Keynes had been sceptical about their efficacy.

4   J M Keynes, *General Theory of Employment, Interest and Money*, pp135-136,
    214, 219 and 376.

5   As above, p376.

6   As above, p378.

7   Robert Skidelsky, *John Maynard Keynes*, Volume 2, p60.

8   Generally called "orthodox Keynesianism" or "the post-war synthesis"

9   J Robinson, *Further Contributions to Economics*.

10 J Strachey, *Contemporary Capitalism* (London, Gollanz, 1956), p235.

11 As above, p239.

12 The most recent is Dan Atkinson and Larry Elliot, *The Gods that Failed*
    (Bodley Head, 2008).

13 See, for instance, Will Hutton, *The State We're In* (Jonathan Cape, 1995).

14 Graham Turner, *The Credit Crunch* (Pluto, 2008). Turner looks to a mixture
    of the ideas of Keynes and the pre-war monetarist Irving Fisher.

15 Gérard Duménil and Dominique Lévy, *Capital Resurgent: Roots of the
    Neoliberal Revolution* (Cambridge, Harvard University Press, 2004), p186.

16 David, Harvey, *A Brief History of Neoliberalism*, p10.

17 R C O Matthews, "Why has Britain had Full Employment Since the War?",
    Economic Journal, September 1968, p556.

18 Meghnad Desai, *Testing Monetarism* (London, Frances Pinter, 1981), p76.
    See also Robert Brenner, *The Economics of Global Turbulence*, p94.

19 Ton Notermans, "Social Democracy and External Constraints", in K R Cox (ed), *Spaces of Globalisation* (Guildford Press, 1997), p206.

20 Michael Bleaney, *The Rise and Fall of Keynesian Economics* (London, Macmillan, 1985), p101.

21 P Aglietta, *Theory of Capitalist Regulation* (London, New Left Books, 1979), p165.

22 Robert Brenner and Mark Glick, "The Regulation Approach: Theory and History", *New Left Review*, 1:188 (1991). For my own, earlier, criticism of the Regulation School, see *Explaining the Crisis*, pp 143-146.

23 See Gérard Duménil and Dominique Lévy, *The Economics of the Profit Rate*, Figure 14.2, p248. For various interpretations of the rate of profit in these decades, see Shane Mage, "The Law of the Falling Tendency of the Rate of Profit"; Joseph Gillman, *The Falling Rate of Profit*; William Nordhaus, *Brookings Papers on Economic Activity*, 5:1 (1974); Victor Perlo, "The New Propaganda of Declining Profit Shares and Inadequate Investment", *Review of Radical Political Economics*, 8:3 (1976); Martin Feldstein and Lawrence Summers, "Is the Rate of Profit Falling?", *Brookings Papers* 1:1977, p216; Robert Brenner, *The Economics of Global Turbulence*; Fred Moseley, *The Falling Rate of Profit in the Post War United States Economy*; Anwar Shaikh and E A Tonak, *Measuring the Wealth of Nations*. Different ways of measuring are used, and the figures differ somewhat from each other, with some showing a long-term decline and some a dip in the mid 1950s. But none of them show a fall to the level of the first three decades of the 20th century, or to the level of the late 1970s.

24 Shane Mage, "The 'Law of the Falling Rate of Profit'", p228.

25 Michael Kidron, "A Permanent Arms Economy", *International Socialism*, 28 (first series, 1967), available at http://www.marxists.org/archive/kidron/works/1967/xx/permarms.htm

26 For a longer discussion on the analyses of Baran, Sweezy and Steindl, see the Appendix, "Other Theories of the Crisis", in my book *Explaining the Crisis*.

27 Michael Bleaney, *The Rise and Fall of Keynesian Economics*, p104.

28 Mage argues that it rose 45 percent 1946-60. See "The Law of the Falling Tendency of the Rate of Profit", p229; Gillman argues that the ratio of the stock of fixed capital to labour employed more than doubled between 1880 and 1900, but grew by only 8 percent between 1947 and 1952; Duménil and Lévy show the capital-output ratio for the US nearly doubling between 1945 and 1970, but quadrupling for West Germany, France and Britain combined (Duménil and Lévy, *Capital Resurgent*, Figure 5.1, p40). They also show (p144) output per unit of capital invested (the "productivity of capital") as falling by about a third in the last two decades of the 19th century for the US, but remaining more or less fixed from 1950 to 1970—this ratio tends to move in the inverse direction to the organic composition.

29 See Michael Kidron, *Western Capitalism Since the War* (London, Weidenfeld and Nicolson, 1968). For earlier versions of a "permanent war economy" theory, see the article by T N Vance (also known as Walter Oakes) in Hal Draper (ed), *The Permanent Arms Economy* (Berkeley, 1970).

30 John Kenneth Galbraith, *The New Industrial State* (Princeton University Press, 2007), p284.

31 As above, pp33-34.

32 As above, p2.

33 E Alvater and others, "On the Analysis of Imperialism in the Metropolitan Countries", *Bulletin of the Conference of Socialist Economists* (Spring 1974).

Notes

34 K Hartani, *The Japanese Economic System* (Lanham, Lexington Books, 1976), p135.

35 Miyohai Shonoharu, *Structural Changes in Japan's Economic Development* (Tokyo, Kinokuniya Bookstore Co, 1970), p22.

36 Robert Brenner, *The Economics of Global Turbulence*, p94.

37 The phrase used by Tony Cliff.

38 Kidron estimated that this resulted in a total transfer of value to the developed countries in 1971 of over $14 billion dollars—Michael Kidron, *Capitalism and Theory*, p106.

39 See Anwar Shaikh, "Who Pays for the 'Welfare' in the Welfare State?", *Social Research*, 70:2, 2003, http://homepage.newschool.edu/~AShaikh/welfare_ state.pdf

40 For Britain, see, for instance, *Social Trends* (1970), which showed that the vast bulk of increasing educational expenditure was concentrated in these areas, while primary education expenditures hardly grew at all.

41 James O'Connor, *The Fiscal Crisis of the State* (Transaction Publishers, 2001), p138.

42 Figures from Alex Nove, *An Economic History of the USSR* (London, Allen Lane, 1970), p387.

43 See the figures in V Cao-Pinna and S S Shatalin, *Consumption Patterns in Eastern and Western Europe* (Oxford, Pergamon, 1979), p62.

44 Figures from Alex Nove, *An Economic History of the USSR*, p387. Angus Maddison's more recent calculations suggest the output of the USSR grew about three-fold between 1945 and 1965, slightly faster than the 19 states he includes in Western Europe and more than 50 percent faster than the US. http://www.ggdc.net/maddison/Historical_Statistics/horizontal-file_03-2007.xls

45 *Pravda*, 24 April 1970.

46 This was a key insight of Tony Cliff in "The Nature of Stalinist Russia" [1948], reprinted in *Marxist Theory After Trotsky*, pp80-92.

47 D W Conklin, "Barriers to Technological Change in the USSR", *Soviet Studies* (1969), p359.

48 Josef Goldman and Karel Korba, *Economic Growth in Czechoslovakia* (White Plains, NY, International Arts and Sciences Press, 1969).

49 Branko Horvat, "Business Cycles in Yugoslavia", *Eastern European Economics*, Volume X, pp3-4 (1971).

50 Raymond Hutchings, "Periodic Fluctuation in Soviet Industrial Growth Rates", *Soviet Studies*, 20:3 (1969), pp331-352. The unevenness from year to year is shown clearly in Madison's figures for GDP, see horizontal-file_03-2007.xls

51 F Sternberg, *Capitalism and Socialism on Trial*, p538.

52 For details, see my book, *Class Struggles in Eastern Europe 1945-83* (London, Bookmarks, 1988), pp42-49.

53 *New York Times*, 5 July 1950, quoted in T N Vance, "The Permanent War Economy", *New International*, January-February 1951.

54 M Kidron, "Imperialism: The Highest Stage but One", in *Capitalism and Theory*, p131.

55 J Stopford and S Strange, *Rival States, Rival Firms* (Cambridge University Press, 1991), p16.

56 For a succinct account of the role played by Israel as a tool for imperialism see John Rose, *Israel, The Hijack State* (London, Bookmarks, 1986), available at http://www.marxists.de/middleast/rose/

57 See the fascinating account of how Malay nationalists used ethnic riots against the country's Chinese minority to stage a "coup" committed to the

path of "state capitalist" development of industries under their own control—Kua Kia Soong, "Racial Conflict in Malaysia: Against the Official History", *Race & Class*, 49 (2008), pp33-53.

58   World Bank, *World Development Report*, 1991, pp33-34

59   For summaries of these arguments, see I Roxborough, *Theories of Underdevelopment* (London, Macmillan, 1979), Chapter 3; Nigel Harris, *The End of the Third World* (Harmondsworth, Penguin, 1987) and R Prebisch, "Power Relations and Market Forces", in K S Kim and D F Ruccio, *Debt and Development in Latin America* (South Bend, Notre Dame, 1985), pp9-31.

60   I Roxborough, *Theories of Underdevelopment*, pp27-32.

61   A Gunder Frank, "The Development of Underdevelopment", *Monthly Review*, September 1966.

62   As Roxborough points out, Gunder Frank "never claimed to be a Marxist", *Theories of Underdevelopment*, p49.

63   P Baran, *The Political Economy of Growth* (Harmondsworth, Penguin, 1973), p399.

64   P Baran, *The Political Economy of Growth*, p416.

65   A Gunder Frank, *Capitalism and Underdevelopment in Latin America* (Harmondsworth, Penguin, 1971), pp35-36.

66   Despite Baran's preparedness to criticise certain features of Stalin's rule, he quoted Stalin favourably himself and accepted Stalinist claims about the USSR's agricultural performance and living standards that were completely false. See, for example, P Baran, *The Political Economy of Growth*, p441.

67   Nigel Harris, "The Asian Boom Economies", *International Socialism*, 3 (1978-9), p3.

68   Lenin, *Imperialism*, Chapter 4, "The Export of Capital".

69   Leon Trotsky, *The Third International After Lenin* (New York, Pioneer, 1957), p18.

70   Leon Trotsky, *The Third International After Lenin*, p209.

71   See the comparison of Italian and Argentinian growth rates in M A Garcia, "Argentina: El Veintenio Desarrollista", in *Debate*, 4 (1978), p20.

72   "Argentina", *Citta Future Anno Vi*, 1 (Rome, nd), p3.

73   Figures given in Geisa Maria Rocha, "Neo-Dependency in Brazil", *New Left Review*, 2:16 (2002).

74   *Economist*, 29 March 1986.

75   Press release summarising a report for the World Bank by Benno Ndulu, *Facing the Challenges of African Growth*, available at http://web.worldbank.org/WB SITE/EXTERNAL/COUNTRIES/AFRICAEXT/0,,contentMDK:21121869~menu PK:258658~pagePK:2865106~piPK:2865128~theSitePK:258644,00.html

76   Bill Warren, "Imperialism and Capitalist Industrialization", *New Left Review*, 1:81 (1973).

77   As above.

78   As above.

79   As above.

80   Leon Trotsky, *The Third International After Lenin*, p209.

Chapter Eight: The End of the Golden Age

1   For details see, for instance, Robert Brenner, *The Economics of Global Turbulence*, pp139 and 146. For a contemporary attempt to analyse the inflation of 1970, see "Survey: The Economy", in *International Socialism*, 46 (first series, 1971).

2   *Guardian*, 26 September 1983.

3   Joan Robinson, *Further Contributions to Economics*, p36.

4   Quoted in the *Guardian*, 15 September 1994.

5   Frederic Lee, "The Research Assessment Exercise, the State and the Dominance of Mainstream Economics in British Universities", *Cambridge Journal of Economics*, Volume 31: 2 (2007).

6   William Keegan, *Mrs Thatcher's Economic Experiment* (Harmondsworth, Penguin, 1984), p126.

7   William Keegan, *Mr Maudling's Gamble* (London, Hodder and Stoughton, 1989), p144.

8   As above, pp103 and 127.

9   As above, p173.

10   See R W Garrison, "Is Milton Friedman a Keynesian?" in M Skousen (ed), *Dissent on Keynes* (New York, Praeger, 1992), p131.

11   H H Happe, in M Skousen (ed), *Dissent on Keynes*, p209.

12   J R Schumpeter, *Capitalism, Socialism and Democracy*, p103.

13   Schumpeter had tried to explain why expansion took place at different speeds at different points in the history of capitalism by reference to "long waves", based upon the differing tempos of innovation. But since innovation depends on the wider dynamics of the system, it is hardly an explanation of the latter. For a long discussion on these matters see my book, *Explaining the Crisis*, pp132-136.

14   Ton Notermans, "Social Democracy and External Constraints", in Kevin R Cox, *Spaces of Globalisation*.

15   Companies will often do their best to understate their profits to governments, for tax reasons, and to workers, in order to justify low wages; they also often overstate their profits to shareholders, in order to boost their stock exchange ratings and their capacity to borrow.

16   Thomas Michl, "Why is the Rate of Profit still Falling?", Jerome Levy Economics Institute, Working Paper 7, September 1988.

17   Anwar Shaikh and E Ahmet Tonak, *Measuring the Wealth of Nations*.

18   Ufuk Tutan and Al Campbell, "The Post 1960 Rate of Profit in Germany", Working Paper 05/01, Izmir University of Economics, Turkey.

19   Edwin R Wolf, "What's Behind the Rise in Profitability in the US in the 1980s and 1990s", *Cambridge Journal of Economics* 27 (2003), pp479-499.

20   Piruz Alemi and Duncan K Foley, "The Circuit of Capital, US Manufacturing and Non-financial Corporate Business Sectors, 1947- 1993", September 1997, available at http://homepage.newschool.edu/~foleyd/circap.pdf

21   Gérard Duménil and Dominique Lévy, "The Real and Financial Components of Profitability", 2005, p11, available at http://www.jourdan.ens.fr/levy/dle2004g.pdf

22   Robert Brenner, *The Economics of Global Turbulence*, p7.

23   Fred Moseley, "The Rate of Profit and the Future of Capitalism", *Review of Radical Political Economics* (May 1997), available at http://www.mtholyoke.edu/~fmoseley/RRPE.html

24   Gérard Duménil and Dominique Lévy, "The Real and Financial Components of Profitability".

25   Andrew Glyn and Bob Sutcliffe, *British Capitalism, Workers and the Profits Squeeze* (Harmondsworth, Penguin, 1972).

26   Bob Rowthorne, "Late Capitalism", *New Left Review*, 1:98 (1976), p67.

27   Ernest Mandel, *Late Capitalism* (London, New Left Books, 1975), p179.

28   Martin Wolf, *Fixing Global Finance* (New Haven, Yale University Press, 2009) pxii.

29   For a summary of the evidence, see my book, *Explaining the Crisis*, pp123-124.
30   Victor Perlo, "The New Propaganda of Declining Profit Shares and Inadequate Investment", pp53-64. For a damning recent refutation of the view that increased wages were the cause of falling profit rates see Robert Brenner, *The Economics of Global Turbulence*, p139.
31   M N Baily, "Productivity and the Services of Capital and Labour", *Brookings Papers on Economic Activity*, 1981:1.
32   *Bank of England Quarterly Bulletin*, 1978, p517.
33   *Financial Times*, 3 March 1977.
34   Thomas Michl, "Why Is the Rate of Profit Still Falling?" *Colgate University Working Paper, 1988*.
35   Edwin Wolff, "What's Behind the Rise in Profitability in the US in the 1980s and 1990s?" *Cambridge Journal of Economics*, 27:4.
36   Figures for non-residential business capital given in H Patrick and H Rosowski (eds), *Asia's New Giant* (Washington, Brooking Institution, 1976), p112.
37   As above, pp11-12 and 55.
38   As above, p8.
39   David Halberstam, *The Best and the Brightest* (London, 1970), p78.
40   US Department of Commerce figures are given in Joseph Steindl, "Stagnation Theory and Policy", *Cambridge Journal of Economics*, 3 (March 1973).
41   For a longer discussion on this, see my book, *Explaining the Crisis*, pp137-140.
42   Robert Brenner points repeatedly in *The Economics of Global Turbulence* to the way in which German and Japanese industry was able to be profitable at the expense of US industry—although, as we have seen earlier, he does not relate this to Marx's account of falling profit rates.
43   M N Baily, "Productivity and the Services of Capital and Labour".
44   The argument is Baily's—though he does not, of course, present it in Marxist terms as referring to the way concrete labour inside the US has to be evaluated in terms of abstract labour on a world scale.
45   For exceptions, see Tony Cliff, *Russia: a Marxist Analysis* (London, International Socialism, 1964); and Chris Harman, "Prospects for the Seventies: The Stalinist States", *International Socialism*, 42 (first series, 1970).
46   E Germain (Ernest Mandel) *Quatrieme International*, 14 (1956), 1-3 (my translation).
47   Ernest Mandel, "The Generalised Recession of the International Capitalist Economy", *Inprecor*, 16- 17 (1975).
48   See the *Report on Draft Guidelines for Economic and Social Development*, given by the then Soviet prime minister, N Ryzhkov, to the 27th Congress of the CPSU, March 1986.
49   Abel Aganbegyan, *Pravda*, 5 April 1988.
50   J Knapp, *Lloyds Bank Review*, October 1968, p9. Quoted in Chris Harman, "Prospects for the Seventies: The Stalinist States". These figures were based on official Eastern bloc sources at the time; American estimates showed growth rates in the USSR as being between two thirds and three quarters of the Soviet estimates, but with the same downward trend. For other estimates and a discussion on the different figures, see B Kostinsky and M Belkindas, "Official Soviet Gross National Product Accounting", in CIA Directorate of Intelligence, *Measuring Soviet GNP, Problems and Solutions*, Washington, 1990.
51   *Finansy* SSSR, 28/69.
52   Solzhenitsyn's short story *For the Good of the Cause* provides a graphic sense of the frustration and bitterness this caused to those involved in producing.
53   H Liebenstein, "Allocative Inefficiency v. 'X-Inefficiency'", *American*

Notes

Economic Review, June 1960.

54   Robert S Whitesell, "Why Does the USSR Appear to be Allocatively
      Efficient", *Soviet Studies*, 42:2 (1990), p259.

55   V Selyunin, *Sotsialistischeksaya Industria*, 5 January 1988, translated in
      Current Digest of the Soviet Press, 24 February 1988. See also A Zaichenko,
      "How to Divide the Pie", *Moscow News* 24, 1989. See also the figures from
      Narodnoe Khoziiaistvo SSR, in Mike Haynes, *Russia: Class and Power
      1917-2000* (London, Bookmarks, 2002).

56   Marx, *Capital*, Volume One, pp648-652.

57   "An Open Letter to the Party", published in English as Jacek Kuron and
      Karol Modzelewski, *A Revolutionary Socialist Manifesto* (London,
      International Socialists, nd), p34.

58   Batara Simatupang, foreword to *The Polish Economic Crisis* (London,
      Routledge, 1994).

59   Barana Simatupang, *The Polish Economic Crisis*, p3.

60   As I wrote in 1977, bringing together the analyses of Tony Cliff and Kuron and
      Modzelewski, "The Polish crisis is an expression of something much greater.
      The era in which the state could protect national capitalism from the direct
      impact of world crisis is drawing to an end. Discussion on 'state capitalism'
      needs to give way to discussion of the world system of state capitalism... Each
      national state capitalism is more and more sucked into a chaotic, disorganised,
      world system where the only order is that which is provided by the crises and
      destructiveness of the world market itself"—Chris Harman, "Poland: Crisis of
      State Capitalism", *International Socialism*, 94 (first series, 1977).

61   Chris Harman, *Class Struggles in Eastern Europe*, p332.

62   Report of meeting of USSR Council of Ministers by D Valavoy, *Pravda*, 19
      September 1988. All reports from the Soviet press are from the monitoring
      service unless indicated otherwise.

63   *Pravda*, 6 February 1989.

64   Soviet TV report of 17 January of a Council of Ministers meeting, *BBC
      Monitoring Reports*, February 1989.

65   *Moscow News*, 25 October 1989.

66   *Izvestia*, 22 October 1988.

67   *Pravda*, 31 October 1989.

68   I Adirim, "A Note on the Current Level, Pattern and Trends of
      Unemployment in the USSR", *Soviet Studies*, 41: 3 (1989).

69   *Trud*, 12 January 1989.

70   *Tass*, 25 October 1989.

71   Maddison's figures show Japanese GNP overtaking that of the USSR in
      1987, see maddison/Historical_Statistics/horizontal-file_03-2007.xls

72   Figures given by Costas Kossis in "Miracle Without End", *International
      Socialism*, 54 (1992), p119.

73   Figures from Angus Maddison, given in Takeshi Nakatani and Peter Skott,
      "Japanese Growth and Stagnation: A Keynesian Perspective", University of
      Massachusetts Working Paper 2006-4, February 2006, available at
      http://www.umass.edu/economics/publications/2006-04.pdf

74   World Development Indicators database, World Bank, 1 July 2007.

75   Costas Kossis, "Miracle Without End". Maddison's figures suggest it was
      just over 40 percent of the US size in 1992.

76   Stefano Scarpetta, Andrea Bassanini, Dirk Pilat and Paul Schreyer, "Economic
      Growth In The OECD Area: Recent Trends At TheAggregate And Sectoral
      Level", *Economics Department Working Papers No 248*, OECD/2000.

77 Figures given by Robert Brenner, *The Economics of Global Turbulence*, p8.
78 Figures given by Arthur Alexander, *Japan in the Context of Asia* (Baltimore, Johns Hopkins University, 1998).
79 Costas Kossis, "Miracle Without End", p118.
80 Arthur Alexander, *Japan in the Context of Asia*, figure 2.
81 Productivity in manufacturing, judged to be the most efficient sector of the economy, was variously estimated at 75 percent to 80 percent of the US figure.
82 Rod Stevens, "The High Yen Crisis in Japan", *Capital and Class*, 34 (1988), p77.
83 As above, pp76-77.
84 Karel van Wolferen, "Japan in the Age of Uncertainty", *New Left Review*, 1:200 (2003).
85 Costas Lapavitsas, "Transition and Crisis in the Japanese Financial System: An Analytical Overview", *Capital & Class*, 62 (1997).
86 Karel van Wolferen, "Japan in the Age of Uncertainty".
87 Figures given by Gavan McCormack, "Breaking Japan's Iron Triangle", *New Left Review*, 2:13 (2002).
88 Regrettably, some left wing commentators with a quite justified distaste for the Japanese ruling class also imply that if it had been more "Western" in its approach to competitiveness, things would have turned out differently. See, for example, R Taggart Murphy, "Japan's Economic Crisis", *New Left Review*, 2:1 (2000).
89 Fumio Hayashi and Edward C Prescott, "The 1990s in Japan: A Lost Decade", September 2001, available at: http://www.minneapolisfed.org/research/prescott/papers/Japan.pdf
90 As above.
91 Paul Krugman, "Japan's Trap", May 1998, available at http://web.mit.edu/krugman/www/japtrap.html
92 Richard Koo, *The Holy Grail of Macroeconomics* (Wiley, 2008).
93 Gavan McCormack, "Breaking the Iron Triangle".
94 Fumio Hayashi and Edward C Prescott, "The 1990s in Japan: A Lost Decade".
95 For India, see, for instance, Vivek Chibber, *Locked in Place* (Tulika Books and Princeton University Press, 2004), p252; for China, the official figures show a halving of the growth rate for 1976-8 compared with the early 1950s and the mid-1960s—see Justin Yifu Lin, Fang Cai and Zhou Li, "Pre-Reform Economic Development in China", in Ross Garnaut and Yiping Huang, *Growth Without Miracles* (Oxford University Press, 2001), p61.
96 See graph in World Bank, *World Development Report* 1991.
97 A de Janvry, "Social Disarticulation in Latin American History", in K S Kim and D F Ruccio, *Debt and Development in Latin America* (South Bend, University of Notre Dame Press, 1986), p49.
98 D F Ruccio, "When Failure becomes Success: Class and the Debate over Stabilisation and Adjustment", *World Development*, 19:10 (1991), p1320.
99 A de Janvry, "Social Disarticulation in Latin American History", p67.
100 K S Kim and D F Ruccio, *Debt and Development in Latin America*, p1.
101 A Fishlow, "Revisiting the Great Debt Crisis of 1982", *Working Paper 37*, Kellogg Institute, University of Notre Dame, May 1984, p106.
102 IMF, quoted in A Fishlow, "Revisiting the Great Debt Crisis of 1982", p108.
103 Figures given in A A Hoffman, *Capital Accumulation in Latin America* (1992).
104 Report by the Techint group of companies, June 2001—see http://www

.techintgroup.com

105 *Financial Times*, 13 July 1990.

106 UNCTAD *Handbook of Statistics*, 2002.

107 J Stopford and S Strange, *Rival States, Rival Firms*, p8.

108 Figure given in Romilly Greenhill and Ann Pettifor, *HIPC: How the Poor are Financing the Rich*, a report from Jubilee Research at the New Economics Foundation (April 2002), available at http://www.jubilee2000uk.org

109 "Trade Makes US Strong", www.ustrade.org

110 M C Penido and D Magalhaes Prates, "Financial Openness: The Experience of Argentina, Brazil and Mexico", *CEPAL Review* 70 (2000), p61.

111 As above, p60.

112 Paula R De Masi, "The Difficult Are of Economic Forecasting", *Financing and Development*, International Monetary Fund, December 1996. See http://www.imf.org/external/pubs/ft/fandd/1996/12/pdf/demasi.pdf

113 World Bank figures, see http://lnweb90.worldbank.org/ECA/eca.nsf/General/1F68871C993E5A5485 256CDB0058A048?OpenDocument

Chapter Nine: The Years of Delusion

1 Ben Bernanke, Speech to the Eastern Economic Association, Washington DC, February 20, 2004, available at http://www.federalreserve.gov/BOARD-DOCS/SPEECHES/2004/20040220/default.htm

2 Philip Thornton, *The Independent*, 1 November 1999.

3 Précis in the US government publication, Monthly Labor Review Online, of an article by W Michael Cox and Richard Alm in the 1999 Annual Report of the Federal Reserve Bank of Dallas, available at http://www.bls.gov/opub/mlr/2000/06/precis.htm

4 This is based on my personal recollection of debating with Desai at LSE and Minford at Cardiff University at the time.

5 *Financial Times*, 11 September 2001.

6 See, for instance, "US Recession May Have Ended Before It Began", *Financial Times*, 1 March 2002.

7 World Bank, *World Development Indicators*.

8 For further discussion on this, see my response, "Misreadings and Misconceptions" to Jim Kincaid, "The World Economy—A Critical Comment", in *International Socialism*, 119 (2008).

9 Marco Terrones and Roberto Cardarelli, "Global Imbalances, A Saving and Investment Perspective", *World Economic Outlook*, International Monetary Fund, 2005, Chapter Two (Fig. 2.1) available at http://www.imf.org/external/pubs/ft/weo/2005/02/pdf/chapter2.pdf

10 David Kotz, "Contradictions of Economic Growth in the Neoliberal Era", *Review of Radical Political Economy*, 40:2 (2008).

11 Fred Moseley, "Is The US Economy Headed For A Hard Landing?", available at http://www.mtholyoke.edu/~fmoseley/#working

12 Kerry A Mastroianni (ed), *The 2006 Bankruptcy Yearbook and Almanac*, Chapter 11, available from http://www.bankruptcydata.com/Ch11History.htm

13 Joseph Stiglitz, *The Roaring Nineties: Why We're Paying the Price for the Greediest Decade in History* (Harmondsworth, Penguin, 2004).

14 Gareth Dale, *Between State Capitalism and Globalisation* (Peter Lang, 2004), p327.

15 R Honohan and D Klingebiel, quoted in Charles Goodhart and Dirk

Schoenmaker, "Burden Sharing in a Banking Crisis in Europe", available at http://www.riksbank.com/pagefolders/26592/2006_2artikel3_sv.pdf

16 See the OECD report on these questions, "Government Policies Towards Financial Markets", Paris 1996, available at http://www.olis.oecd.org/olis/1996doc.nsf/3dce6d82b533cf6ec125685d005 300b4/a3cde538b08dc983c12563a20050fa59/$FILE/ATTKJYQH/09E6067 7.doc

17 Fred Magdoff, "The Explosion of Debt and Speculation", *Monthly Review*, 58:6 (2006), p5.

18 Stefano Scarpetta, Andrea Bassanini, Dirk Pilat and Paul Schreyer, "Economic Growth in the OECD Area: Recent Trends at the Aggregate and Sectoral Level", OECD Economics Department Working Papers 248 (2000), p26.

19 Figures supplied by Robert Brenner at the Historical Materialism Conference, London 2007.

20 Table from Stefano Scarpetta, Andrea Bassanini, Dirk Pilat and Paul Schreyer, "Economic Growth in the OECD Area: Recent Trends at the Aggregate and Sectoral Level".

21 As above, p30.

22 For mainstream economic discussions on the increased rate of depreciation due to computerisation, see Stacey Tevlin and Karl Whelan, "Explaining the Investment Boom of the 1990s", *Journal of Money, Credit and Banking*, 35 (2003); for an earlier discussion on the shortening of the lifetime of fixed capital and thus of increasing depreciation rates, see Martin S Feldstein and Michael Rothschild, "Towards an Economic Theory of Replacement Investment", *Econometrica*, 42:3 (1974), pp393-424. They suggest "a significant change in the average expected age of new non-farm investment...from 19.8 years in 1929 to 15.3 years in 1963."

23 Total labour compensation, including employers' social security and pension contributions and imputed labour income for selfemployed persons. For figures, see http://ocde.p4.siteinternet.com/publications/doifiles/812007131G25.xls .There would seem to be problem with using these figures to compare labourshares from country to country, as opposed to over time, since other data indicate a much higher share of capital accumulation in Japan than in the US and Western Europe.

24 Chuck Collins, Chris Hartman and Holly Sklar, "Divided Decade: Economic Disparity at the Century's Turn", *United for a Fair Economy*, 15 December 1999.

25 See the graph in G Duménil and D Lévy, *Capital Resurgent*, p46.

26 International Labour Organisation figures, available from www.ilo.org/public/english/bureau/inf/pr/1999/29.htm The figures given by various sources vary considerably, depending on how they count parttime working and whether they take into account unpaid overtime measurements. Other figures, based on reports from firms, show a bigger rise than do the ILO figures.

27 BBC report, 5 September 2005.

28 Anwar Shaikh, "Who Pays for the 'Welfare' in the Welfare State?"

29 Table from Duane Swank and Cathie Jo Martin, "Employers and the Welfare State", *Comparative Political Studies*, 34:8 (2001), pp917-918.

30 Figures from US Department of Labor, Organization for Economic Cooperation and Development. There are discrepancies with the ILO figures

for individual countries, but the same overall pattern between countries.

31 Productivity per worker in France was only 70 percent of that in the US, but productivity per hour worked is 5 percent higher—figures for the year 2000 from EU, Ameco data base, given in Olivier Blanchard, "European Growth over the Coming Decade", September 2003. See http://www.mit.edu/files/1779

32 Details from Stefan Bornost, in "Germany: The Rise of the Left", *International Socialism*, 108 (2005).

33 Stephen Broadberry, "The Performance of Manufacturing", in Roderick Floud and Paul Johnson, *The Cambridge Economic History of Modern Britain* (Cambridge, 2004), p59; Office of National Statistics, *Monthly Digest of Statistics*, July 2007, Table 7.1.34 For greater detail, see Chris Harman, "Where is Capitalism Going: Part Two", *International Socialism*, 60 (1993), pp98-101.

35 Chen Zhan, editor of *The China Analyst*, June 1997.

36 Ching Kwan Lee, "'Made in China': Labor as a Political Force?", University of Montana, 2004, available on http://www.umt.edu/Mansfield/pdfs/2004LeePaper.pdf

37 For the full story see the issues of the *China Daily* (Beijing) for the second week of August 2005.

38 C Guidi and W Chuntao, Survey of Chinese Peasants, quoted in Yang Lian, "Dark Side of the Chinese Moon", *New Left Review*, 2:32 (2005), available at http://www.newleftreview.net/NLR26606.shtml

39 *South China Post*, quoted in M Hart Landsberg and P Burkett, "China and the Dynamics of Transnational Accumulation", paper given at conference on "The Korean Economy: Marxist Perspectives", Gyeongsang National University, Jinju, South Korea, 20 May 2005, p24.

40 Figure given by Martin Wolf, in *Fixing Global Finance* (New Haven, Yale University Press, 2008), p165.

41 Steven Barnett and Ray Brooks, "What's Driving Investment in China?", IMF Working Paper 265 (2006), available at http://ideas.repec.org/p/imf/imfwpa/06-265.html

42 As above.

43 Jahangir Aziz and Li Cui, "Explaining China's Low Consumption: The Neglected Role of Household Income", *IMF Working Paper 181* (2007), available at http://www.imf.org/external/pubs/ft/wp/2007/ wp07181.pdf

44 As above.

45 From Jahangir Aziz and Steven Dunaway, "China's Rebalancing Act", *Finance and Development*, IMF, 44:3 (2007) available at http://www.imf.org/external/pubs/ft/fandd/2007/09/aziz.htm

46 Figure quoted in M Hart Landsberg and P Burkett, "China and the Dynamics of Transnational Accumulation", p5.

47 Quoted by J Kynge, *Financial Times*, 23 September 2003.

48 *Financial Times*, 4 February 2003.

49 Quoted in *Financial Times*, 18 November 2003.

50 Jonathan Anderson, "Solving China's Rebalancing Puzzle", *Finance and Development*, IMF, 44:3 (2007), available at http://www.imf.org/external/pubs/ft/fandd/2007/09/anderson.htm

51 Ray Brooks, "Labour Market Performances", in Eswar Prasad (ed), *China's Growth and Integration in the World Economy* (IMF, 2004).

52 The "secondary sector" includes construction, water, electricity generation,

etc, as well as manufacturing.

53 Steven Barnett and Ray Brooks, "What's Driving Investment in China?" p5.
54 Phillip Anthony O'Hara, "A Chinese Social Structure of Accumulation for Capitalist Long-Wave Upswing?", *Review of Radical Political Economics*, 38 (2006), pp397-404. But as with all calculations of profit rates, there can be doubts as to the accuracy of the statistics he bases his calculations on—particularly since his figures indicate a decline in the rate of exploitation, which hardly fits in with the declining proportion of wages and consumption in GNP shown in Jahangir Aziz and Li Cui, "Explaining China's Low Consumption: The Neglected Role of Household Income".
55 Figures given in Jesus Felipe, Editha Lavina and Emma Xiaoqin Fan, "Diverging Patterns of Profitability, Investment and Growth in China and India during 1980-2003", *World Development*, 36:5 (2008), p748.
56 Zhang Yu and Zhao Feng, "The Rate of Surplus Value, the Composition of Capital, and the Rate of Profit in the Chinese Manufacturing Industry: 1978-2005", paper presented at the Second Annual Conference of the International Forum on the Comparative Political Economy of Globalization, 1-3 September 2006, Renmin University of China, Beijing, China.
57 Quoted in J Kynge, *Financial Times*, 23 September 2003. See also Steven Barnett, "Banking Sector Developments", in Eswar Prasad (ed), *China's Growth and Integration in the World Economy*.
58 Steven Barnett and Ray Brooks, "What's Driving Investment in China?", p17.
59 Sebastian F Bruck, "China Risks Caution Overkill After Bear Prudence", *Asia Times*, 26 March 2008.
60 Quoted in Jahangir Aziz and Steven Dunaway, "China's Rebalancing Act".
61 Thomas Lum and Dick K Nanto, "China's Trade with the United States and the World", CRS report to Congress, January 2007, available at http://digitalcommons.ilr.cornell.edu/cgi/viewcontent.cgi?article=1017&context=key_workplace
62 China's share of global output was estimated at 10.9 percent, the US's at 21.4 percent. See Selim Elekdag and Subir Lall, "Global Growth Estimates Trimmed After PPP Revisions", *IMF Survey Magazine*, 8 January 2008.
63 See *Financial Express*, 30 April 2004, available at www.financialexpress.com
64 Petia Topalova, "India: Is the Rising Tide Lifting All Boats?", *IMF Working Paper,* WP/08/54, March 2008, available at www.imf.org/external/pubs/ft/wp/2008/wp0854.pdf
65 A Banerjee and T Piketty, "Top Indian Incomes, 1922-2000", *World Bank Economic Review*, 19:1, pp1-20, quoted in Petia Topalova, "India: Is the Rising Tide Lifting All Boats?"
66 Abhijit Sen and Himanshu, "Poverty and Inequality in India: Getting Closer to the Truth", *Ideas*, 5 December 2003, available at http://www.networkideas.org/themes/inequality/may2004/ie05_Poverty_WC.htm. There has been a very long discussion on how to interpret the official figures in various articles in the *Economic and Political Weekly*.
67 Figure for 1992 from Abhijit Sen, *Force*, 20 April 2004.
68 Abhijit Sen, *Force*, 20 April 2004.
69 Sukti Dasgupta and Ajit Singh, "Manufacturing, Services and Premature De-Industrialisation in Developing Countries," Centre for Business Research, *University Of Cambridge Working Paper 327.*

Notes

70   Figures given in Ministry of Labour and Employment, "India, Informal Sector In India , Approaches for Social Security".
71   "Labour Shortage Threat to Indian Call Centre Growth", UNI 2006, http://www.uni-ilc.org/docs/Labour%20shortage%20threat%20to%20Indian%20call%20centre%20growth.pdf

Chapter Ten: Global Capital in the New Age

1   WTO *Annual Reports*, 1998 and 2008.
2   UNCTAD *Investment Brief*, Number 1 (2007).
3   UNCTAD *World Investment Report* 2008 and International Monetary Fund, *World Economic Outlook*, October 2008, Database: Countries.
4   Multinational firms (eg ITT, Ford, Coca-Cola) had existed in the prewar period. But they were not generally based upon integrated international research and production. So the British subsidiary of a US car firm would generally develop and market its own models independently of what happened in Detroit. Insofar as there was international organization of production, it was by firms based in the metropolitan countries controlling the output of foodstuffs and raw materials in the Third World, as for instance Unilever or Rio Tinto Zinc did.
5   *Financial Times*, Survey: World Banking, 22 May 1986.
6   A Calderon and R Casilda, "The Spanish Banks Strategy in Latin America", *CEPAL Review* 70, 2000, pp78-79.
7   As above, p79.
8   UNCTAD press release, available at http://www.unctad.org/Templates/webflyer.asp?docid=2426&intItemID=2079&lang=1
9   See, for a prime example of how such nonsense could become a fashionable commodity just before the last world recession, Charles Leadbetter's much hyped book of the late 1990s, *Living on Thin Air* (Harmondsworth, Penguin, 2000).
10 Quoted in the *Financial Times*, 20 June 1988.
11 *Business Week*, 14 May 1990.
12 V Forrester, *The Economic Horror* (London, Polity, 1999), pp18-19.
13 Naomi Klein, *No Logo* (London, Flamingo, 2000), p223.
14 John Holloway, "Global Capital and the National State", in Werner Bonefeld and John Holloway, *Global Capital, National State and the Politics of Money* (New York, St Martin's Press, 1995), p125. Holloway does at one point recognise that productive capital is less mobile than money capital, but then goes on to ignore the effect of this distinction on the relations between capitals and states.
15 Speech to Congress, 6 March 1991.
16 N Harris, *The End of the Third World* (Harmondsworth, Penguin, 1987), p202.
17 Scott Lash and John Urry, *The End of Organised Capitalism* (London, Polity Press, 1987).
18 Suzanne de Brunhoff, "Which Europe Do We Need Now? Which Can We Get?" in Riccardo Bellofiore (ed), *Global Money, Capital Restructuring, and the Changing Patterns of Labour* (Cheltenham, Edward Elgar, 1999), p50.
19 D Bryan, "Global Accumulation and Accounting for National Economic Identity", *Review of Radical Political Economy*, 33 (2001), pp57-77.
20 Alan M Rugman and Alain Verbeke, "Regional Multinationals and Triad

Strategy", 2002. See http://www.aueb.gr/deos/EIBA2002.files/PAPERS/
C164.pdf. For an important analysis of the "core firms" which have the
most influence in national economies, see Douglas van den Berghe, Alan
Muller and Rob van Tulder, *Erasmus (S)coreboard of Core Companies*
(Rotterdam, Erasmus, 2001).

21 Gordon Platt, "Cross-Border Mergers Show Rising Trend As Global
   Economy Expands", *Global Finance*, December 2004.

22 Sydney Finkelstein, "Cross Border Mergers and Acquisitions", Dartmouth
   College, available at http://mba.tuck.dartmouth.edu/pages/faculty/syd.finkel-
   stein/articles/Cross_Border.pdf

23 Tim Koechlin, "US Multinational Corporations and the Mobility of
   Productive Capital, A Sceptical View", *Review of Radical Political
   Economy*, 38:3 (2006), p375.

24 As above, p376.

25 As above, p374.

26 Riccardo Bellofiore, "After Fordism, What? Capitalism at the End of the
   Century: Beyond the Myths", in *Global Money, Capital Restructuring and
   the Changing Patterns of Labour* (Edward Elgar, 1999), p16.

27 Tim Koechlin, "US Multinational Corporations and the Mobility of
   Productive Capital, A Sceptical View", p374.

28 W Ruigrok and R van Tulder, *The Logic of International Restructuring*
   (London, Routledge, 1995).

29 M Mann, "As the Twentieth Century Ages", *New Left Review*, 214 (1995),
   p117.

30 Mary Amiti and Shang-Jin Wei, "Service Offshoring, Productivity and
   Employment: Evidence from the United States", *IMF Working Paper*
   WP/05/238, p20.

31 Tim Koechlin, "US Multinational Corporations and the Mobility of
   Productive Capital, A Skeptical View", p378.

32 Martin Neil Baily and Robert Z Lawrence, "What Happened to the Great
   US Job Machine? The Role of Trade and Offshoring", paper prepared for
   the Brookings Panel on Economic Activity, 9-10 September 2004, p3.

33 Alan M Rugman, *The Regional Multinationals* (Cambridge, 2005).

34 Alan M Rugman and Alain Verbeke, "Regional Multinationals and Triad
   Strategy".

35 Michaela Grell, "The Impact of Foreign-Controlled Enterprises in the EU",
   Eurostat 2007, http://epp.eurostat.ec.europa.eu/cache/ITY_OFFPUB/KS-SF-
   07-067/ EN/KS-SF-07-067-EN.PDF

36 Georgios E Chortareas and Theodore Pelagidis, "Trade Flows: A Facet of
   Regionalism or Globalisation?" in *Cambridge Journal of Economics*, 28
   (2004), pp253-271.

37 As above.

38 Figures from UNCTAD, *World Investment Report 2005*, Annex, Table B3.

39 See "Pentagon Takes Initiative In War Against Chip Imports", *Financial
   Times*, 27 January 1987.

40 *Financial Times*, 12 September 1990.

41 Article reprinted in *International Herald Tribune*, 17 December 1996.

42 Robert Brenner, *The Economics of Global Turbulence*, pp206-207.

43 For an excellent account of the Argentinian economy in this period, see
   Claudio Katz, "El Giro de la Economía Argentina", Part One, available at
   http://www.aporrea.org/ imprime/a30832.html

44 Dick Bryan, "The Internationalisation of Capital", *Cambridge Journal of*

Economics, 19 (1995), pp421-440.
45 Mark E Manyin, *South Korea-U.S. Economic Relations: Co-operation, Friction, and Future Prospects*, CRS Report for Congress, July 2004. See http://www.fas.org/man/crs/RL30566.pdf which contains a fascinating list of the clashes between the US and South Korean governments as each seeks to advance the economic interests of the firms operating from its national territories.
46 This, essentially, is the argument of William Robinson in *The Theory of Global Capitalism* (Baltimore, Johns Hopkins, 2004).
47 Marx, *Capital*, Volume Three, p248.
48 Henry Kissinger, *Diplomacy* (New York, Simon & Schuster, 1994), pp809 and 816.
49 *Weekly Standard*, 7 September 1997.
50 Project for the New American Century, *Statement of Principle*, 7 June 1997.
51 Fred Magdoff, "The Explosion of Debt and Speculation", p5. Net physical investment by non-farm, non-financial corporate business in the US in 2006 amounted to $299 billion, the US military budget to $440 billion.
52 *Iraq Study Group Report*, 2006, available at http://www.usip.org/isg/iraq_study_group_report/report/1206/index.html

Chapter Eleven: Financialisation and the Bubbles That Burst

1   Gideon Rachman, *Financial Times*, 29 January 2007.
2   Chris Giles, *Financial Times*, 5 February 2008.
3   Nouriel Roubini's Global EconoMonitor, 7 September 2008, available at http://www.rgemonitor.com/blog/roubini/
4   *Financial Times*, 29 January 2009.
5   Chris Giles, *Financial Times*, 29 January 2009.
6   Andrew Glyn, *Capitalism Unleashed* (Oxford University Press, 2007), p52.
7   These figures are based on Robert Brenner's calculations. Other estimates, for instance by Martin Wolf in the *Financial Times* (28 January 2009), arrive at a figure of 40 percent for the mid-2000s.
8   Michael Mah-hui Lim, contribution at conference on Minsky and the crisis, *Levy Institute Report*, 18:3 (2008), p6.
9   Sebastian Barnes and Garry Young, "The Rise in US Household Debt: Assessing its Causes and Sustainability", *Bank of England Working Paper* 206 (2003), Chart Four, p13, available at http://www.demographia.com/db-usdebtratio-history.pdf
10 World Bank, *Global Development Finance* (2005).
11 Robin Blackburn, *Banking On Death, Or Investing In Life* (London, Verso, 2002); *Age Shock : How Finance Is Failing Us* (London, Verso, 2007).
12 Andrew Glyn, *Capitalism Unleashed*, p69.
13 Martin Wolf, *Financial Times*, 15 January 2008.
14 Figures as given in Robert Brenner, *The Economics of Global Turbulence*, p282.
15 Named after an Italian American fraudster of the early 1920s. There is an early account of such a scheme in Charles Dickens's *Martin Chuzzlewit*, written in 1844-5.
16 Chris Harman, "Where is Capitalism Going?", *International Socialism*, 58 (1993).
17 Michel Aglietta, "A Comment and Some Tricky Questions", *Economy and Society*, 39 (2000), p156. The discussion between Aglietta and Boyer was indicative of a situation where the Regulation School's effort to explain the

long-term trajectory of capitalism comes adrift. For a comment on it, see John Grahl and Paul Teague, "The Regulation School", *Economy and Society*, 39 (2000), pp169-170.

18   For a full explanation see Dick Bryan and Michael Rafferty, *Capitalism with Derivatives* (Palgrave, 2006), p9.

19   Thomas Sablowski, "Rethinking the Relation of Industrial and Financial Capital", paper given to *Historical Materialism* conference, December 2006.

20   "Immeltdown", *Economist*, 17 April 2008.

21   *Financial Times*, 6 September 2001.

22   As above.

23   As above.

24   *Financial Times*, 15 September 2007.

25   Speech opening the London HQ in Canary Wharf in 2004.

26   "Flow of Funds Accounts of the United States, Second Quarter 2007", Federal Reserve statistical release, p106, table R102. See http://www.federalreserve.gov/RELEASES/z1/20070917/

27   Marco Terrones and Roberto Cardarelli, "Global Imbalances: A Saving and Investment Perspective", *World Economic Outlook*, International Monetary Fund, 2005, p92.

28   "Corporates are Driving the Global Savings Glut", *JP Morgan Research*, JP Morgan Securities Ltd., 24 June 2005. See www.securitization.net/pdf/JPMorgan/GlobalSavings_24Jun05.pdf

29   Dimitri Papadimitriou, Anwar Shaikh, Claudio Dos Santos and Gennaro Zezza, "How Fragile is the US Economy?", *Strategic Analysis*, The Levy Economics Institute of Bard College, February 2005.

30   Speech at the *Historical Materialism* conference, London, November 2007.

31   *Financial Times*, 22 January 2008.

32   Martin Wolf, *Financial Times*, 21 August 2007.

33   Martin Wolf, *Financial Times*, 22 January 2008.

34   Marx, *Capital,* Volume Three, p458.

35   Adair Turner, "The Financial Crisis and the Future of Financial Regulation", The Economist's Inaugural City Lecture, 21 January 2009, available at http://www.fsa.gov.uk/pages/Library/Communication/Speeches/2009/0121_at.shtml

36   Martin Wolf, "A Week Of Living Perilously", *Financial Times*, 22 November 2008.

37   Martin Wolf, *Financial Times*, 23 November 2008.

38   *Financial Times*, 3 February 2009.

39   Quoted in *Financial Times*, 7 January 2009.

40   *Financial Times* editorial, 16 September 2008.

41   Quoted on *Financial Times* website, 29 January 2008.

42   John Gapper, "Davos and the Spirit of Mutual Misunderstanding", *Financial Times*, 30 January 2009.

43   I heard him speak at the University of London's School of Oriental and African Studies (SOAS) in late January 2008.

44   Larry Elliot and Dan Atkinson, *The Gods that Failed* (Bodley Head, 2008)

45   I shared a platform at a fringe meeting at the National Union of Students conference in 2000 with one of its leading figures who criticised me for talking of "anticapitalism" on the grounds that neither of us had "an alternative to capitalism".

46   Gérard Duménil and Dominique Lévy, "Costs and Benefits of Neoliberalism: A Class Analysis", in Gerald A Epstein, *Financialisation and the World*

Economy (Edward Elgar, 2005), p17.

47 James Crotty, "The Neoliberal Paradox: The Impact of Destructive Product Market Competition and 'Modern' Financial Markets on Nonfinancial Corporation Performance in the Neoliberal Era", in Gerald A Epstein, *Financialisation and the World Economy*, p86.

48 François Chesnais, *La Mondialisation du Capital* (Syros, 1997), p289.

49 As above, p74. The passages from Chesnais are translated by me.

50 As above, p297.

51 As above, p304.

52 Peter Gowan, *The Global Gamble* (London, Verso, 1999), pp13-14.

53 Will Hutton, *The State We're In* (Jonathan Cape, 1995); William Keegan, *The Spectre of Capitalism* (Radius, 1992).

54 See, for example, Engelbert Stockhammer, "Financialisation and the Slowdown of Accumulation", *Cambridge Journal of Economics*, 28:5, pp719-774; Thomas Sablowski, "Rethinking the Relation of Industrial and Financial Capital"; Till van Treeck, *Reconsidering the Investment-Profit Nexus in Finance- Led Economies: an ARDL-Based Approach*, see http://ideas.repec.org/p/imk/wpaper/01-2007.html; Andrew Glyn, *Capitalism Unleashed* (Oxford University Press, 2007), pp55-65.

55 James Crotty, "The Neoliberal Paradox: The Impact of Destructive Product Market Competition" and "Modern Financial Markets on Nonfinancial Corporation Performance in the Neoliberal Era", in Gerald A Epstein, *Financialisation and the World Economy*, p91.

56 He raised the argument at a conference on Finance and Financialisation at University of London's SOAS in May 2008 and at the Marxism event in London in July 2008. See the paper available at http://www.soas.ac.uk/economics/events/crisis/43939.pdf

57 The one reference by Marx to "secondary exploitation" is when he writes that "the working class is swindled" by the moneylender and also by the "retail dealer who sells the means of subsistence of the worker"—Marx, *Capital*, Volume Three, p596.

58 Samantha Ashman made this point forcefully at Lapavitsas's presentation of his paper at the SOAS Financialisation conference. He had, she pointed out, confused the different levels of abstraction with which Marx had analysed capitalism. It should be added that, carried to its logical conclusion, Lapavitsas's argument would undermine the central stress in Marxist political economy on exploitation at the point of production, since there are all sorts of consumer payments that could be designated as "direct exploitation"—tax payments, rents for domestic accommodation, the elements in shopping bills that go to retailers' and wholesalers' profits, the payments made to privately owned public utilities.

59 Sebastian Barnes and Garry Young, "The Rise in US Household Debt: Assessing its Causes and Sustainability", *Bank of England Working Paper*, 206, 2003.

60 Dick Bryan and Michael Rafferty, *Capitalism with Derivatives*, pp32-33.

61 Engelbert Stockhammer, "Financialisation and the Slowdown of Accumulation", pp719-741.

62 James Crotty, "The Neoliberal Paradox: The Impact of Destructive Product Market Competition and 'Modern' Financial Markets on Nonfinancial Corporation Performance in the Neoliberal Era", in Gerald A Epstein, *Financialisation and the World Economy*, p82.

63 Figure given in Robert Brenner, *The Economics of Global Turbulence*, p215.

The figure for Britain was much larger.

64 Robert Milward, "The Service Economy", in Roderick Floud and Paul Johnson, *The Cambridge Modern Economic History of Britain*, Volume Three, p249.

65 Gérard Duménil and Dominique Lévy, "The Neoliberal Counterrevolution", in Alfredo Saad Filho and Deborah Johnston (eds), *Neoliberalism, A Critical Reader* (London, Pluto, 2005), p13.

66 Robert Brenner, *The Economics of Global Turbulence*, p186.

67 Marx, *Capital*, Volume Three, p504.

68 The case for this interpretation of the shift is well made by Robert W Parenteau, "The Late 1990s" US Bubble: Financialisation in the Extreme", in Gerald A Epstein, *Financialisation and the World Economy*, p134.

69 Makato Itoh and Costas Lapavitsas, *Political Economy of Money and Finance* (London, Macmillan, 1999), p60. They also point out that this is clear from Marx's treatment of the issue in Volume Two of *Capital*, although at points in Volume Three he ascribed these functions to different groups of capitalists.

70 Thomas Sablowski, "Rethinking the Relation of Industrial and Financial Capital".

71 Interview on *Today* programme, BBC Radio Four, 23 January 2009. See http://news.bbc.co.uk/ today/hi/today/newsid_7846000/ 7846519.stm

72 Michel Husson, "Surfing the Long Wave", *Historical Materialism* 5 (1999), available at http://hussonet.free.fr/surfing.pdf

73 This was the position of Engelbert Stockhammer, in "Financialisation and the Slowdown of Accumulation"; reiterated in "Some Stylized Facts on the Finance-Dominated Accumulation Regime", in *Competition & Change*, 12:2 (2008), pp184-202; Duménil denied the relevance of profitability in conversation at the SOAS conference on Financialisation in May 2008 and in his presentation at the *Historical Materialism* conference in November 2008.

74 Gérard Duménil and Dominique Lévy, *Capital Resurgent*, p201.

75 Ben Fine, "Debating the New Imperialism", *Historical Materialism*, 14:4 (2006), p145.

76 Friedman's initial academic fame rested on research that claimed to show that too low a money supply had caused the crisis of the early 1930s. He turned his conclusions upside down when it came to the crises of the 1970s and 1980s, blaming them on too great a money supply. The crisis of September-October 2008 led some of his followers to hark back to his original research.

77 George Soros, *Financial Times*, 29 January 2009. See also Martin Wolf, *Financial Times*, 27 January 2009.

78 Bank of England Stability Report, October 2008, quoted in the *Guardian*, 28 October 2008. The January 2009 estimate of losses originating in the US was $2.2 billion (*Financial Times*, 29 January 2009).

79 See charts accompanying Martin Wolf, "To Nationalise or Not to Nationalise", *Financial Times*, 4 March 2009.

80 See, for example the articles in the *Financial Times* by Wolfgang Muenchau, 24 November 2008; Jeffrey Sachs, January 27 2009; Samuel Brittan, 30 January 2009.

81 Paul Krugman, "Protectionism and Stimulus", available at http://krugman.blogs.nytimes.com/2009/02/01/protectionism-andstimulus-wonkish/

82 Nicolas Véron of the Bruge think tank quoted in *Financial Times*, 5 February 2009.

83 See Gillian Tett and Peter Thal Larsen, "Wary Lenders Add to Introspection", *Financial Times*, 30 January 2009.
84 Gideon Rachman, "Economics Upstages Diplomatic Drama", *Financial Times*, 30 January 2009.
85 John Gapper, "Davos and the Spirit of Mutual Misunderstanding".
86 Peter Temin, "The Great Depression", in S L Engerman & R E Gallman, *The Cambridge Economic History of the United States, Volume Three, The Twentieth Century* (Cambridge, 2001), p305.
87 As above, p306.

Chapter Twelve: The New Limits of Capital

1   Charles Dickens, *Hard Times* (Harmondsworth, Penguin, 1969).
2   F Engels, *The Condition of the Working Class in England*, in Marx and Engels, *Collected Works*, Volume 4, p343.
3   For brief histories of the science, see John W Farley, "The Scientific Case for Modern Anthropogenic Global Warming", *Monthly Review*, July-August 2008; Jonathan Neale, *Stop Global Warming, Change the World* (London, Bookmarks, 2008), p17; Spencer Weart, "Timeline: The Discovery of Global Warming", http://www.aip.org/history/climate/timeline.htm
4   James Hansen and others, "Target Atmospheric CO_2", quoted in Minqi Li, "Climate Change, Limits to Growth, and the Imperative for Socialism", *Monthly Review*, 60:3 (2008), p52.
5   George Monbiot, "Environmental Feedback: A Reply to Clive Hamilton", *New Left Review*, 2:45 (1997); See also Jonathan Neale, *Stop Global Warming*, p24.
6   Summary of conclusions, in *Guardian*, 30 October 2006.
7   Jonathan Neale, *Stop Global Warming*, p179.
8   John Vidal, *Guardian*, 20 December 2006.
9   George Monbiot, *Guardian*, 2 December 2008.
10 Quoted by John Vidal, *Guardian*, 20 December 2006.
11 George Monbiot, *Guardian*, 8 May 2007.
12 Clive Hamilton, "Building on Kyoto", *New Left Review*, 45 (May–June 2007).
13 Figures from Jonathan Neale, *Stop Global Warming*, p71.
14 George Monbiot, "Environmental Feedback: A Reply to Clive Hamilton", *New Left Review*, 45 (May–June 2007).
15 Stern quoted by John Bellamy Foster, Brett Clark and Richard York in "Ecology: The Moment of Truth", *Monthly Review*, 60:3 (2008), p5.
16 Fiona Harvey, "Eco-Groups Fear an Opportunity Lost", *Financial Times*, 14 March 2009.
17 *Guardian*, 11 March 2009.
18 *Observer*, 15 February 2009.
19 Marx, *Capital*, Volume One, Chapter 10, "The Working Day", Part 5, "The Struggle for the Working Day", available at http://www.marxists.org/archive/marx/works/1867-c1/ch10.htm#S1
20 As above.
21 All figures from Jonathan Neale, *Stop Global Warming*, pp28-29 and 157.
22 David Adam, "Climate Change Causing Birds to Lay Eggs Early", *Guardian*, 15 August 2008.
23 For a summary of the various calculations about peak oil, see Energy Watch Group, "Crude Oil Supply Outlook", October 2007, EWG-Series No 3/2007.
24 As above, p44.
25 As above, p18.

26 John Bellamy Foster, "Peak Oil and Energy Imperialism", *Monthly Review*, 60:3 (2008).

27 *Report of the National Energy Policy Group*, May 2001, p181, available at http://www.whitehouse.gov/energy/National-Energy-Policy.pdf

28 John Bellamy Foster, "Peak Oil and Energy Imperialism".

29 The extent to which the price rise was a result of the approach of peak oil is open to debate—some ascribe the rise to this, others to speculation that big oil producing nations were keeping oil in the ground so as to raise its price. For an argument that it was due to war, political instability, currency rates and speculation, see Ismael Hossein-Zadeh, "Is There an Oil Shortage?", available at http://www.stateofnature.org/isThereAnOilShortage.html

30 See, for example, Robert Bailey, "Time to Put the Brakes on Biofuels", *Guardian*, 4 July 2008; Jonathan Neale, *Stop Global Warming*, pp101-103.

31 See, for instance, Javier Blas, "The End of Abundance: Food Panic Brings Calls for a Second 'Green Revolution'", *Financial Times*, 1 June 2008; for an apocalyptic view of what is happening, see Dale Allen Pfeiffer, "Eating Fossil Fuels", *From the Wilderness*, 2004, available at www.fromthe wilderness.com/free/ww3/100303_eating_oil.html

32 Their arguments on this point were reliant on the findings of the pioneering organic chemist Liebig, whose writings both Marx and Engels studied. See John Bellamy Foster, *Marx's Ecology* (New York, Monthly Review Press, 2000), pp147-170.

33 Shelley Feldman, Dev Nathan, Rajeswari Raina and Hong Yang, "International Assessment of Agricultural Knowledge, Science and Technology for Development. East and South Asia and Pacific: Summary for Decision Makers", IAASTD (2008), available at http://www.agassessment.org/docs/ESAP_SDM_220408_Final.pdf

34 World Bank, "World Development Report 2008: Agriculture for Development" (2007), p7, available at http://go.worldbank.org/ZJIAO-SUFU0

35 The term is that of the Harriet Friedman—see, for instance, "The Political Economy of Food", *New Left Review*, 2:197 (1993), pp29-57.

36 Javier Blas, "The End of Abundance: Food Panic Brings Calls for a Second 'Green Revolution'."

37 World Bank, 2007, "World Development Report 2008: Agriculture for Development", p7, available at http://go.worldbank.org/ZJIAOSUFU0

38 Javier Blas, "The End of Abundance: Food Panic Brings Calls for a Second 'Green Revolution'."

39 For a longer analysis of the crisis and its possible implications, see Carlo Morelli, "Behind the World Food Crisis", *International Socialism*, 119 (2008).

40 Javier Blas, "Warning of 'Food Crunch' with Prices to Rise", *Financial Times*, 26 January 2009.

41 Report produced by Chatham House, quoted in *Financial Times*, 26 January 2009.

42 See, for instance, Aditya Chakrabortty, "Secret Report: Biofuel Caused Food Crisis", *Guardian*, 4 June 2008.

Chapter Thirteen: The Runaway System and the Future for Humanity

1 By Alex Callinicos in the column he writes for *Socialist Worker*.

2 Details of the report first appeared in the *Observer*, 22 February 2004. The full report is available on http://www.stopesso.com/campaign/Pentagon.doc

Chapter Fourteen: Who Can Overcome?

1   John H Goldthorpe, David Lockwood, Frank Bechhofer and Jennifer Platt, *The Affluent Worker in the Class Structure* (Cambridge, 1971), p6.

2   C Wright Mills, *The Causes of World War Three* (New York, Simon and Schuster, 1958).

3   Herbert Marcuse, *One Dimensional Man* (London, Routledge & Kegan Paul, 1964). http://www.marxists.org/reference/archive/marcuse/works/onedimensional-man/index.htm

4   Ernesto Laclau and Chantal Mouffe, *Hegemony and Socialist Strategy: Towards a Radical Democratic Politics* (London, Verso, 1985), p82.

5   M Hardt and A Negri, *Empire* (Cambridge, Harvard, 2001), p53.

6   D Filmer, "Estimating the World at Work", Background Report for World Bank, *World Development Report 1995* (Washington DC, 1995), available at http://www.monarch.worldbank.org

7   See, for example, my calculation for the size of the new middle class in Britain, in my article, "The Working Class After the Recession", *International Socialism*, 33 (1986).

8   UNDP *World Development Report 2009*, Table 21. Similar figures to those of the UNDP are provided in the CIA Year Books. The figures provide a similar geographic distribution of industrial work to Filmer, with over 300 million industrial workers in the old industrial economies and a similar total in the BRIC countries.

9   "Introduction", in R Baldoz and others, *The Critical Study of Work: Labor, Technology and Global Production* (Philadelphia, Temple University Press, 2001), p7.

10 US Federal Reserve figures, available at http://www.federalreserve.gov/re-leases/G17/Revisions/20061211/table1a_rev.htm

11 US Department of Labour provides UN figures for 2006 available at http://www.dol.gov/asp/media/reports/chartbook/2008-01/chart3_7.htm. According to World Bank figures the United States accounted for 23.8 percent of the world's manufacturing output in 2004, and over two decades the US share had barely dipped. The annual average since 1982 was 24.6 percent, while China's share for 2004 was 9 percent and South Korea's 4 percent. Quoted in the *International Herald Tribune*, 6 September 2005.

12 The CIA Year Book provides a figure nearly twice that for the old industrial countries alone, no doubt because of a wider definition of what constitutes the industrial sector.

13 Figures given by C H Feinstein, "Structural Change in the Developed Countries in the 20th Century", *Oxford Review of Economic Policy*, 15:4 (1999), table A1.

14 R E Rowthorn, "Where are the Advanced Economies Going?", in G M Hodgson and others, *Capitalism in Evolution* (Edward Elgar, 2001), p127.

15 As above, p127.

16 As above, p127.

17 *Guardian*, 5 June 2002.

18 Office for National Statistics, *Living in Britain 2000*, Table 3.14, available at http://www.statistics.gov.uk

19 All the figures are from "Employed Persons by Occupation, Sex and Age", available at ftp://ftp.bls.gov/pub/special.requests/lf/aat9.txt

20 Manuel Castells, "The Network Society: From Knowledge to Policy", in

Manuel Castells and Gustavo Cardoso (eds), *The Network Society* (Baltimore, Center for Transatlantic Relations, 2006), p9.

21   Bill Dunn, *Global Restructuring and the Power of Labour* (London, Palgrave Macmillan, 2004), p118.

22   Kate Bronfenbrenner, "Uneasy Terrain: The Impact of Capital Mobility on Workers, Wages, and Union Organising", The ILR Collection, 2001, available at http://digitalcommons.ilr.cornell.edu/cgi/viewcontent.cgi?article =1001&context=reports

23   Raymond-Pierre Bodin, *Wideranging Forms of Work and Employment in Europe*, International Labour Office report 2001.

24   As above.

25   Robert Taylor, "Britain's World of Work: Myths and Realities", ESRC Future of Work Programme Seminar Series, 2002, available at http://www.esrc.ac.uk/ESRCInfoCentre/Images/fow_publication_3_tcm6-6057.pdf

26   These figures are from the Office for National Statistics' *Social Trends 2001*, p88. Kevin Doogan, *New Capitalism? The Transformation of Work* (Cambridge UK, Polity, 2008) provides a similar picture to these figures.

27   These are very rough calculations, given the problems of counting the number of workers in the often massive sectors of national economies. But Filmer's figures, those of UNDP and those of the CIA all suggest a pattern similar to this.

28   All figures are for 2005, from UNDP, *Human Development Report 2009*, Table 5.

29   A failure to see this leads some to vastly exaggerate the growth of the working class that has resulted from globalisation and urbanisation. So in a much quoted paper, Richard Freeman has written of an "effective doubling of the global labour force (that is workers producing for international markets) over the past decade and a half, through the entry of Chinese, Indian, Russian and other workers into the global economy". This has supposedly changed the "global capital/labour ratio by just 55 percent to 60 percent of what it otherwise would have been". There is a triple error here. It assumes that those labouring in the former USSR, China and India were not doing so as part of the world system until the early 1990s, and that their whole workforces are now workers employed by capital. There is, however, a big difference between the workforce in its totality and those who are wage workers. In 2001 the non-agricultural workforce of the developing and transition economies was 1,135 million (figures from *Summary of Food and Agricultural Statistics*, Food and Agriculture Organisation of the United Nations, Rome 2003, p12). But by no means all the non-agricultural workforce workers. Self-employment as a proportion of the non-agricultural workforce is 32 percent in Asia, 44 percent in Latin America and 48 percent in Africa (*Women and Men in the Informal Economy*, International Labour Organization, 2002). And only a proportion of those who seek work as wage workers succeed in getting employed in the formal sector in modern industry. Most are in very low productivity jobs, often working for firms with only a couple of workers.

30   International Labour Office, *African Employment Report 1990* (Addis Ababa, 1991), p3.

31   International Labour Office, *Women and Men in the Informal Economy*, 2002.

32   See Chapter Nine for details; see also Ray Brooks, "Labour Market Performance and Prospects", in Eswar Prasad (ed) *China's Growth and*

Integration in the World Economy (IMF, 2004), p58, Table 8.5.

33   A mistake made, for instance, by Mike Davis in *Planet of Slums* (London, Verso, 2006).

34   Figures from PRELAC *Newsletter* (Santiago, Chile), April 1992, diagram 3.

35   Paolo Singer, *Social Exclusion in Brazil* (International Labour Office, 1997), Chapter 2, Table 7, available at http://www.ilo.org

36   Figures in J Unni, "Gender and Informality in Labour Markets in South Asia", *Economic and Political Weekly* (Bombay), 30 June 2001, p2367.

37   Ray Brooks, "Labour Market Performance and Prospects", Eswar Prasad (ed), *China's Growth and Integration into the World Economy*; for further analysis of the Chinese urban workforce, see Martin Hart-Landsberg and Paul Burkett, "China, Capitalist Accumulation, and Labor", *Monthly Review*, 59:1 (2007).

38   UNDP, *World Development Report 2009*, Table 21.

39   Marx, *Capital*, Volume One, p628.

40   As above, p643.

41   P Singer, "Social Exclusion in Brazil", International Labour Office, 1997, Chapter 2, p14.

42   See, for instance, the figures given in J Unni, "Gender and Informality in Labour Markets in South Asia", *Economic and Political Weekly* (Bombay), 30 June 2001, Tables 19, 20 and 22, pp2375-2376. There are, of course, situations in which a sudden demand for labour can only be met from the informal sector, leading to wage rates temporarily above those in the formal sector. The same phenomenon occurs, for instance, with "lump" labour in the building industry in Britain.

43   For an account by employers of why they employ permanent workers, see H Steefkerk, "Thirty Years of Industrial Labour in South Gujarat: Trends and Significance", *Economic and Political Weekly* (Bombay), 30 June 2001, p2402.

44   Paulo Singer, *Social Exclusion in Brazil*, Chapter 2, table 10.

45   As above, p17.

46   International Labour Organisation, *African Employment Report 1990*, p34.

47   Rajar Majumder, "Wages and Employment in the Liberalised Regime: A Study of Indian Manufacturing Sector", 2006, available at http://mpra.ub.unimuenchen.de/4851/

48   As above.

49   F Engels, "Letter to Bernstein, 22 August 1889", in Marx and Engels, *Collected Works*, Volume 48 (London, 2001).

50   Mike Davis, *Planet of Slums*, p36.

51   Leo Zeilig and Claire Ceruti, "Slums, Resistance and the African Working Class", *International Socialism* 117 (2008), available at http://www.isj.org.uk/index.php4?id=398&issue=117

52   "Informo de Desarrollo Humano in la Region del Altiplano, La Paz y Oruro", PNUD Bolivia, 2003, quoted in Roberto Saenz, "Boliva: Critica del Romanticismo Anti-Capitalista", in *Socialismo o Barbarie*, 16 (2004). My translation.

53   As above.

54   Leo Zeilig and Claire Ceruti, "Slums, Resistance and the African Working Class".

55   From a pamphlet on the strike by two Egyptian activists, Mustafa Bassiouny and Omar Said, translated by Anne Alexander in *International Socialism*, 118 (2008).

56 Robin Cohen, Peter C W Gutkind and Phyllis Brazier, *Peasants and Proletarians: the struggles of Third World workers* (New York, Monthly Review Press, 1979).

57 H van Wersch, *The Bombay Textile Strike 1982-1983* (OUP, 1992), pp45-46; Meena Menon and Neera Adarkar, *One Hundred Years One Hundred Voices* (Kolkata, Seagull Books, 2004).

58 F Engels, *The Peasant Question in France and Germany* [1894], in Marx and Engels *Collected Works*, Volume 27, pp486 and 496.

59 Adam David Morton, "Global Capitalism and the Peasantry in Mexico", *Journal of Peasant Studies*, 34:3-4 (2007), pp441-473.

60 For criticism of "neo-populism" see, for instance, Terence J Byres, "Neo-Classical Neo-Populism 25 Years On: Déjà Vu and Déjà Passé, Towards a Critique," *Journal of Agrarian Change*, 4:1-2 (2004).

61 See, for instance, Keith Griffin, Azizur Rahman Khan and Amy Ickowitz, "Poverty and the Distribution of Land," *Journal of Agrarian Change*, 2:3 (July 2002).

62 Hamza Alavi and Teodor Shanin, Introduction to Karl Kautsky, *The Agrarian Question*, Volume 1 (Zwan, 1988), ppxxxi-xxxii.

63 Danyu Wang, "Stepping on Two Boats: Urban Strategies of Chinese Peasants and Their Children", in *International Review of Social History*, 45 (2000), p170.

64 As above.

65 S Rodwan and F Lee, *Agrarian Change in Egypt* (Routledge, 1986).

66 For an account of recent research on these questions, see Pauline E Peters, "Inequality and Social Conflict Over Land in Africa", *Journal of Agrarian Change*, 4:3 (2004).

67 Hamza Alavi, "Peasants and Revolution", *Socialist Register* 1965, pp241-277, available at http://socialistregister.com/socialistregister.com/files/SR_1965_Alavi. pdf

68 Although even then a degree of consent from quite wide layers of the population was obtained as a result of economic growth.

69 For an account of the insurgency and an explanation for its failure, see Chris Harman, *The Fire Last Time* (London, Bookmarks, 1998).

Glossary

Absolute surplus value: The increase in surplus value that occurs when working hours are increased without a parallel increase in pay.

Abstract labour: What all particular acts of labour have in common under capitalism; is measured in terms of the proportion each constitutes of the total socially necessary labour time expended in the economy as a whole.

Austrian School: Version of bourgeois economics which tends to see economic crises as inevitable, but necessary for continued economic growth. Best known figures Friedrich August von Hayek and Joseph Schumpeter.

Autarchy: Attempt to cut an economy off from trade links with the rest of the world.

Baran, Paul: Marxist theorist who argued that development was only possible in Global South through a break with capitalism. Collaborator of Paul Sweezy.

Bauer, Otto: Austrian Marxist of first third of 20th century who followed a policy of trying to reform capitalism.

Bernstein, Edward: "Revisionist" critic of revolutionary Marxism within German socialist movement at beginning of 20th century.

Bills: Documents issued by banks and other capitalist firms that act as IOUs as they grant each other credit.

Böhm-Bawerk, Eugen von: One of the founders of neoclassical economics, wrote best known critique of Marx's work.

Bortkiewicz, Ladislaus von: Polish economist at beginning of 20th century who carried through a serious examination of Marx's work but rejected some of its crucial findings.

Bretton Woods: Venue of the conference that set up the post World War Two financial system based on gold and dollars. Name given to that system until its collapse in 1971.

BRICS: Initials standing for Brazil, Russia, India, China and South Africa.

Bukharin, Nicolai: Bolshevik leader and economist theorist; executed by Stalin in 1938.

Capitals: Term often used to describe economically competing units of capitalist system (whether individual owners, firms or states).

Centralisation of capital: Tendency for capital to pass into fewer and fewer hands through takeovers, mergers, etc, so that whole capitalist system is under direct control of fewer competing capitals.

Chicago School: Followers of Milton Friedman and monetarism.

Circulating capital: *see* Fixed capital.

Clark, John Bates: American economist, one of the founders of neoclassical economics.

Cliff, Tony: Palestinian born Marxist resident in Britain through second half of 20th century; developed theory of state capitalism and, in a rudimentary form, of the permanent arms economy.

Commercial capital: Investment aimed at making a profit from the buying and selling of goods as distinct from their production. Sometimes called merchant's capital.

Commodity: Something bought and sold on the market. Commodities are commonly called "goods" in English.

Concentration of capital: Growth in size of the individual competing capitals that make up the capitalist system.

Concrete labour: Refers to the specific characteristics of any act of labour—what distinguishes, for example, the labour of a carpenter from that of a bus driver.

Constant capital: Marx's term for a capitalist's investment in plant, machinery, raw material and components (in other words, the means of production), denoted by c.

Corey, Lewis: Also known as Louis Fraina, an early member of the American Communist Party who later wrote an important Marxist analysis of the slump of the 1930s.

CPSU: Communist Party of the Soviet Union, ruling party within USSR. Its general secretaries—Stalin, Khrushchev, Brezhnev, Andropov, Chernenko and finally Gorbachev—ran the state.

Credit crunch: When buying and lending seizes up in the banking system and the wider economy.

Cultural Revolution: Political turmoil in China in the late 1960s and early 1970s.

Davos: Swiss ski resort where World Economic Forum of leading industrialists, financiers, government ministers and economists takes place each year.

Dead labour: Term used by Marx to describe commodities made in the past but used in production in the present.

Deficit financing: The method by which a government pays for the excess of expenditure over receipts from taxation by borrowing.

Deflation: A fall in prices, normally associated with impact of economic crisis.

Department One: Section of economy which is involved in turning out equipment and materials for further production (called by mainstream economists "capital goods").

Department Two: Section of economy concerned with turning out goods which will be consumed by workers (sometimes called "wage goods").

Department Three: Section of economy which turns out goods which will not be used as means and materials of production, and which will not be consumed by workers either—in other words the section that turns out "luxury goods" for consumption by the ruling class, armaments and so on. Sometimes referred to as Department 2a.

Dependency theory: Theory very widespread in 1950s and 1960s which held that dependence of Third World economies on advanced economies prevented economic development.

Depreciation of capital: Reduction in the price of plant, machinery and so on during their period of operation. This can be due to wear and tear, or to the "devaluation" of capital (see below).

Derivatives: Financial contracts designed to allow investors to insure themselves against future changes in prices. Derivatives trading developed as a means of speculating on interest or exchange rates, and then into a form of financial gambling on changes in markets in general.

Devaluation of capital: Reduction in the value of plant, equipment and so on as technical advance allows a greater amount to be produced with a given quantity of labour time.

Euromoney (Eurodollars): Vast pool of finance, denominated in dollars but held outside the US, which grew up in late 1960s and 1970s, beyond the control of national governments.

Eurozone: Currency union of 16 European Union states which have adopted the euro as their sole legal tender. It currently consists of Austria, Belgium, Cyprus, Finland, France, Germany, Greece, Ireland, Italy, Luxembourg, Malta, the Netherlands, Portugal, Slovakia, Slovenia and Spain.

Exchange value: Term used by Smith, Ricardo and Marx for worth of commodities in terms of other commodities. *See* Value and Use value.

Expenses of production: Spending which capitals have to undertake to stay in business, but which does not materially expand the output of commodities (for instance, spending on marketing goods, advertising, protecting plant and machinery).

Fiat money: Form of money that has no intrinsic value apart from a guarantee from a government, eg tokens such as notes and coins made of cheap metal. Stands in contrast to monetary medium made of or exchangeable for material with value in its own right, such as gold or silver.

Fictitious capital: Things like shares and real estate investments that are not part of the process of production but which provide the owners with an income out of surplus value.

FDI: Foreign Direct Investment, investment by a firm in one country which gives it more than 10 per cent of ownership of a firm in another country. Investment that does not give that level of ownership or control is called portfolio investment.

Finance capital: Capital in the financial as opposed to productive and sales sectors of the economy. Often used to imply that financiers are the real power in the economy as a whole.

Financialisation: Growth of the financial section of the economy and its influence. Often the term implies this is detrimental to capital in other sectors.

Fiscal measures: Tax and spending undertaken by governments.

Fischer, Irving: Leading neoclassical economist in US in first third of 20th century.

Fixed capital: Capital invested in plant and equipment which last for several cycles of production. Contrasts with circulating capital, which is invested in things that are used up in each cycle of production and have to be replaced for the next one, ie raw materials, components and labour power.

Fordism: Term sometimes used to describe capitalism from 1920 to mid-1970s. Implies supposed cooperation between firms in mass production industries with unions to keep up wage rates.

Formal sector: Jobs in which workers have legal employment rights.

Friedman, Milton: Conservative free market economists who believed state could stop crises by correct control of money supply. Inspired "monetarist" policies of Margaret Thatcher in early 1980s.

Galbraith, John Kenneth: American economist of the post-war decades critical of unrestrained free markets.

GDP: Gross Domestic Product, measure of the market value of all final goods and services made *within* the borders of a nation over a year.

GNP: Gross National Product, as GDP but also includes the net income from overseas investment.

Gold standard: System under which states tied the value of their national currencies to quantities of gold and paid off debts to each other with it. States broke with it during World War One and from the early 1930s to the end of World War Two. Operated in modified form under post-1945 Bretton Woods system that collapsed in 1971.

Golden Age: Term sometimes used for long boom in the decades following the Second World War.

Great Depression: Term used for period of crises in the 1870s and 1880s, and again for slump of the 1930s.

Grossman, Henryk: Polish-Austrian Marxist activist and economist of first half of twentieth century.

Hansen, Alvin: One of leading mainstream US economists of middle third of 20th century, converted to Keynesianism by crisis of 1930s.

Hayek, Friedrich August von: Conservative economist who opposed attempts of state to mitigate impact of economic crises, claiming this could only make things worse. Admired by Margaret Thatcher.

Hilferding, Rudolf: Published pioneering work on impact of finance and monopoly on capitalism, but later served as finance minister in Weimar Republic and opposed revolutionary socialism.

Hobson, J A: British liberal economist of beginning of 20th century, argued that imperialism suited finance but not the rest of capitalism.

Human capital: Term used by mainstream economists to describe the skills employees gain from education and training.

ILO: International Labour Organisation, a United Nations agency dealing with labour issues.

IMF: International Monetary Fund, international body dominated by old industrial countries (particularly the US) which, along with the World Bank, lends money to countries in economic difficulties in return for them accepting tight controls over their policies.

Import substitutionism: Attempt to speed up industrialisation by blocking imports and providing protected market for local capitalists.

Informal sector: Jobs where workers do not have formal employment rights.

Jevons, William Stanley: British economist of 1860s-70s, a founder of neoclassical economics.

Kautsky, Karl: Most prominent Marxist at beginning of 20th century, later opposed revolutionary approach.

Keynesianism: Economic doctrine based upon ideas of the British economist of the inter-war years, J M Keynes. Holds that governments can prevent recessions and slumps by spending which is greater than their income from taxation (so-called "deficit financing").

Kidron, Mike: Marxist economist resident in Britain in second half of 20th century who further developed theory of permanent arms economy out of ideas of T N Vance and Tony Cliff.

Labour power: Capacity to work, which is bought by capitalists by the hour, day, week or month when they employ workers.

Labour theory of value: View developed by Marx (on basis of ideas of previous thinkers such as Smith and Ricardo) that there is an objective measurement of the value of goods, which is ultimately responsible for determining their prices. This is the "socially necessary" labour time needed to produce them—in other words, that across the system as a whole, using the prevailing level of technique, skill and effort. For Marx's own accounts of the theory, see *Wage Labour and Capital*, *The Critique of Political Economy* and chapter one of *Capital*, Volume One.

Leverage: Borrowing to magnify the buying power of small cash payments for shares, property and other assets.

Liquidity: Having cash in hand (or assets that can be easily turned into cash) to meet claims that fall due or, in the case of a bank, meet withdrawal requests.

Luxemburg, Rosa: Polish-German Marxist, leader of revolutionary opposition in Germany to First World War, murdered by counter- revolutionaries in January 1919.

Macroeconomic: Referring to economy as whole, as opposed to "microeconomic" relations between individual elements within it. "Macroeconomics" is a branch of mainstream economics concerned with trying to guide national economies.

Marginalism: Another name for neoclassical economics.

Marshall, Alfred: British economist of late 19th and early 20th centuries and a key figure in neoclassical economics.

Menger, Carl: Austrian economist, one of the founders of neoclassical economics.

Mercantile or **merchant capital:** Investment aimed at making a profit without engaging in production, for instance in the buying and selling of goods.

Mercosur: A regional trade agreement between some Southern American states (Argentina, Brazil, Paraguay and Uruguay).

Microeconomic: *see* macroeconomic.

"Military Keynesianism": Term used for economic impact of rising military expenditure paid for out of government debt during Ronald Reagan presidency in 1980s US.

Minsky, Hyman: Non-orthodox mainstream economist of mid-20th century who recognised inevitability of speculative booms and busts for capitalism.

MITI: Ministry of Internation Trade and Industry, powerful Japanese government agency.

Monetarism: Doctrine which holds crises cannot be solved by governments increasing their spending to more than their tax income. Increasing the supply of money, this holds, will simply lead to higher prices. Under the name the quantity theory of money, this was the orthodoxy in bourgeois economics before the rise of Keynesianism in the 1930s, and became fashionable again in the mid-1970s.

"Monetary measures": Attempt to regulate economy, preventing inflation and countering recessions by government contraction or expansion of amount of money that is circulating.

Money capital: Money held with the intention of increasing its value, either as part of the process of productive investment, or through lending to others.

Moral depreciation of capital: Loss of value of plant and capitals as it becomes obsolescent in the face of rapid technological advance.

NAIRU: Non-Accelerating Inflation Rate of Unemployment, see Natural Rate of Unemployment.

Natural Rate of Unemployment: Level which free market economists decided was necessary for capitalism to avoid accelerating inflation. Also called NAIRU—Non-Accelerating Inflation Rate of Unemployment.

Neoclassical economics: Dominant school in bourgeois economics since the end of the 19th century. Believes value depends on the "marginal" satisfaction people get from goods, and justifies profit as a result of the "marginal productivity of capital". Also known as "marginalism".

Neoliberal: "Liberal" is term used in continental Europe meaning "free market", so neoliberal means a return to free market economic measures. Used by some people on left to refer to attacks on workers' conditions and welfare benefits. Also sometimes used to describe period from mid-1970s to present.

"New Classical" School: School of free market economics which developed in 1980s; holds that a market economy will stay in equilibrium unless subject to external forces or interference by state, monopolies or trade union action.

NICs: Newly Industrialising Countries of 1960 to 1980s, like South Korea, Brazil, Taiwan.

Nomenklaturists: Those holding high up, privileged positions in state and industry in old Eastern Bloc countries before 1989-91.

Non-productive consumption: The use of goods in ways which serve neither to produce new plant, machinery, raw materials and so on ("means of production") nor to provide for the consumption needs of workers. The use of goods for the consumption of the ruling class, for advertising and marketing or for arms, all fall into this category.

Non-productiveexpenditures: Expenditures undertaken by capitalists or the state over and above what is necessary for the production of commodities (includes spending on consumption of the ruling class, on its personal servants, on the '"expenses of production" and so on).

OECD: Organisation of Economic Cooperation and Development. Organisation of the established industrialised countries with an important research arm.

Oil shock: Sudden increase in price of oil, especially as a result of the Arab-Israel war of October 1973.

Okishio's theorem: Theory which claims to disprove Marx's tendency of the rate of profit to fall.

OPEC: Organization of the Petroleum Exporting Countries, a cartel currently made up of twelve countries: Algeria, Angola, Ecuador, Iran, Iraq, Kuwait, Libya, Nigeria, Qatar, Saudi Arabia, the United Arab Emirates, and Venezuela.

Organic composition of capital: Ratio of the value of investment in plant, machinery, raw materials and so on ("means of production") to the value of expenditure on employing productive labour. Using Marxist terminology, this is the ratio of constant capital to variable capital, or c/v. See also Technical composition of capital.

Organised sector: Term used in India for formal sector, ie where workers have legal working rights.

Pareto, Vilfredo: Italian neoclassical economist at turn of the 20th century, who supported Mussolini's rise to power.

Plaza Accord: 1985 Agreement by Japan and Germany to allow the value of their currencies to rise so as make it easier for the US to export.

Ponzi scheme: A fraudulent scheme which pays profits to old investors out of money collected from new investors.

Preobrazhensky, Evgeny: Russian Bolshevik activist and economist, executed by Stalin in 1937.

Private equity funds: Investment vehicle where rich individuals come together to buy shares in companies in order to make a profit.

Productive expenditures: Spending which is necessary if commodities are to be produced and surplus value created (spending on the means and materials of production on the one hand, and on workers' wages on the other).

Productive labour: Labour which contributes to the creation of surplus value.

Profits, mass of: Total profits of a particular capitalist. Measured in pounds, dollars and other currency.

Profit, rate of: Ratio of surplus value to capital invested. Measured as a percentage. Denoted as s/(c+v).

Profit share: Proportion of total output of a firm or country that goes in profits, as opposed to wages.

Rate of exploitation: Ratio of surplus value to wages (strictly speaking only the wages of workers who produce commodities should be counted). It can be expressed another way, as the ratio of the time the worker spends producing surplus value for the capitalist, compared to the time he or she spends on producing goods equivalent to his or her living standard. Also called rate of surplus value, that is, the ratio of surplus value to variable capital, and depicted as s/v.

Realisation: Term used by Marx to describe the successful sale of produced commodities so as to achieve a profit.

"Regulation" theorists: French school of economists influenced by Marxism who periodise 20th century capitalism into Fordist and post-Fordist phases.

Relative surplus value: Increase in surplus value obtained when time it takes for workers to produce the equivalent of their own wage is reduced, so causing a greater portion of their working time to go to the capitalist.

Rentier: Old fashioned term describing someone who lives off unearned income such as rent or dividends.

Reserve army of labour: Pool of unemployed workers used by capital to keep down the wages of those with jobs and who are able to be drawn into industry with the periodic expansion of production.

Ricardo, David: Political economist of first decades of 19th century, developed labour theory of value and an important influence on Marx's ideas.

Robinson, Joan: Radical Keynesian economist of middle third of 20th century, broke with neoclassical school but rejected Marx's theory of value.

Samuelson, Paul: Major populariser of the mainstream synthesis of neoclassical and Keynesian ideas through his economic textbook in post-war decades, and adviser to the Kennedy government in the US.

Say's law: Supposed law that holds there cannot be any general overproduction of goods because each time someone sells something someone else buys it.

Schumpeter, Joseph: Austrian economist of first half of 20th century. Supported capitalism but rejected idea that it developed smoothly, coined phrase "creative destruction".

Smith, Adam: Most important political economist of latter part of 18th century. Distorted presentations of his ideas now constitute apologies for capitalism, but a critical use of many of his concepts was important to Marx.

Socially necessary labour time: Labour time needed to produce a certain good, using average techniques prevailing throughout economy and working at average intensity of effort. Determines the amount of abstract labour—and therefore value—embodied in a commodity.

Social wage: Term used to describe welfare, health and other benefits supplied through the state which improve workers' living standards.

Solvency: Ability of firms or individuals to pay off all debts providing they have time to turn their own assets into cash.

Sraffa, Piero: Cambridge economist who refuted basic contentions of orthodox bourgeois economics, the "neoclassical" marginalist school. His followers tend to base themselves on Ricardo rather than Marx and reject the Marxist theory of the falling rate of profit, and usually see crisis as arising when wages cut into profits. They are often known as "neo-Ricardians", although Sraffa regarded himself as in the Marxist tradition.

Strachey, John: Best known purveyor of Marxist interpretations of slump of 1930s in Britain, Labour Party minister in the late 1940s and Keynesian apologist for right wing Labour ideas in 1950s.

Surplus value: Marx's term for excess value produced by the exploitation of workers. It forms the basis for the profit of the individual capitalist plus what he pays out to others in the form of rent, interest payments and taxation (plus what he spends on "non-productive activities"). Denoted by s.

Sweezy, Paul: American economist who wrote a pathbreaking account of development of Marxist ideas in 1940s (*The Theory of Capitalist Development*) and, with Baran, an account of mid 20th century capitalism in 1960s (*Monopoly Capital*).

Tariffs: Taxes on imports, designed to raise their price and so make it easier for local producers to dominate markets.

Taylorism: Technique of so-called "scientific management", based upon time and motion studies of every act of labour. Spread through industry in the early 20th century.

Technical composition of capital: Physical ratio of plant, machinery, raw materials and so on ("means and materials of production") to total labour employed. When this ratio is measured in value terms rather than physical terms, it becomes the "organic composition of capital".

Terms of trade: The relative prices of a country's exports to imports. An improvement to the terms of trade means a country has to pay less for the products it imports.

Tigers: Term used for East and South East Asian industrialising economies.

Transformation problem: Problem which arises when the attempt is made to move from Marx's account of capitalism in terms of value to the prices at which goods are actually bought and sold. Many economists have claimed it is impossible to solve the problem, and that therefore Marxist economics must be abandoned.

Triad: The three major parts of the industrialised capitalist world, ie North America, Europe and Japan.

Trusts: Associations of industrial concerns which collaborate to carve up markets and force up selling prices.

Turnover time of capital: Time taken from beginning of production process to final sale of goods.

UNCTAD: United Nations Conference on Trade and Development, a development agency and important source of economic statistics.

Under-consumptionism: Theory which blames capitalist crisis not on the law of the falling rate of profit, but on the alleged inability of capitalism to provide a market for all goods produced within it. The first versions of the theory were put forward by early 19th century economists such as Jean Charles Léonard de Sismondi, but it has been developed since both by Marxists (from Rosa Luxemburg to Paul Baran and Paul Sweezy) and by Keynesians.

Use value: Immediate useful qualities of a commodity. See Exchange Value.

Glossary   401

Valorisation: Term used in some translations of Marx's capital for the self-expansion of capital, based on the French translation of the German word *Verwertung*.

Value: Amount of abstract labour contained in a commodity; determines its exchange value and, after some redistribution of surplus value between capitalists, its price. *See* Exchange Value.

Value composition of capital: Ratio of constant to variable capital, differs from organic composition by taking into account changes due to other factors as well as change in technical composition.

Vance, T N: American economist who developed theory of "permanent war economy" in 1940s and 1950s.

Variable capital: Marx's term for capital invested in employing wage labour. Denoted by v.

Volcker, Paul: Head of US Federal Reserve in the late 1970s and 1980s.

Volcker shock or Coup: Sudden increase in US interest rates in 1979.

Walras, Léon: French economist of latter part of 19th century; a founder of neoclassical economics.

World Bank: See International Monetary Fund.

WTO: World Trade Organisation, international agency that aims to promote free trade and neoliberal agenda.

World Bank: See International Monetary Fund.

WTO: World Trade Organisation, international agency that aims to promote free trade and neoliberal agenda.

Index

and 1960s; compared with Italy 188; economic and political crises of 1970s 218; crisis of 2001-2 224

Arms expenditure, US during long boom 198; variations between states during long boom 198; in 1990s and early 2000s 234; China 2009 327; Russia 2009 327; US 2009 327; US 2009 327; and dynamic of system 131; effect on organic composition of capital 234

Arrow, Kenneth, on limits of mathematical model of market 43

Asian crisis of 1997-8 9, 242; panic among commentators 230; role of IMF in helping Ford and GM acquire Korean firms 266

Asian Tigers, growth as fast as Stalin's USSR 218 *see also* Asian crisis

Atkinson, Dan 163 *see also* Elliot, Larry

August 2007 credit crunch 8

Austrian school 194; and slump 145; and restructuring through crises 232 *see also* Hayek, Friedrich August von; Schumpeter, Joseph

Autonomy of state 110-112

Bail outs, in 1980s and 1990s 233; Chrysler 1979 233; 2008-9 291, 300

Baker, James 274

Baldoz, Koeber and Kraft, quoted 332

Balkan Wars of 1990s, role of different imperialist interests in 270

Banks, role in capitalist production 63-4, 87; failures in US in 1931 149; nationalisations in Japan, Scandinavia, in 1990s 234; Spanish and French in Latin America 240; crash of September-October 2008 277-8 290; estimates of losses in 2008 300

Bank of International Settlements 7; on failure of economic forecasts 9

Banking capital 63

Banking crises, before 2003, costs to governments of bail outs 234; *see also* Credit crunch

Banking mergers, international 255

Bankruptcies and crises 67, 76

Bankruptcy Year Book, quoted on increased frequency of bankruptcies 233

Baran, Paul 165, 190, 218; version of dependency theory, quoted 186-7; misinterprets Lenin on economic development 187

Bauer, Otto 77; claimed refutation of Rosa Luxemburg 100

Bear Stearns bank, taken over by Morgan Chase 277

Bellofiore, Riccardo, on Foreign Direct Investment 261; on "privatised Keynesianism" 288

Bermuda 221

Bernanke, Ben, on lack of an explanation for Great Depression 9,145; on decline in economic volatility 229

Bernstein, Edward, revisionist arguments of 89

Bernstein, Michael, quoted 146

Bevan, Aneurin 135

Bhopal disaster 308

Biofuels and food shortages 322

Bismarck, Otto von, provides pension 88; nationalisation of railways 115

Blackburn, Robin, on pension funds 280

Blair, Tony, and climate change 310

Bleaney, Michael 165, on Keynesianism and long boom 164

Blind Shaft, Chinese film about miners 245

Boeing/McDonnell Douglas merger, role of state in facilitating 265

Boer War, and panic over fitness of working class 134

Böhm-Bawerk, Eugen von 41, 50, 51, 67; critique of Marx on value and price 48

Boom, of 1920s, and contradictions within 144, 146; short-lived of mid to late 1980s 194; of 1980s 283; of 1990s 283

see also Long boom

Boyer, Robert 296; quoted (with Aglietta, Michael) on asset bubbles and US boom of 1990s 283

Braunmuhl, Claudia von 104-5; on the state and world market 104

Brazil 218, 221; growth in 1970s 188; in period 1965-80 219; "miracle"

European Union, combined
  manufacturing output 333
Exchange rates, and role of state 265;
  and distribution of surplus value
  between capitalist classes 266
Exchange value 23, 25; in Adam
  Smith 22
Expenditures that do not contribute to
  accumulation 128-9 *see also* Waste,
  Leaks
Explaining the Crisis (Chris Harman)
  14, 16
Exploitation 28-35; and accumulation
  37; rate of 38; and impact on rate
  of profit 72-73
Export barrier 204
Export of capital *see* Capital exports
Export oriented development 219; and
  growing debt 219
Exports, role in German and Japanese
  economies 171

Family wage 132
Famine, Irish 40
Farmers, small, number in 21st
  century 322
Federal Reserve 8, 149 *see also*
  Volcker, Paul; Greenspan, Alan;
  Bernanke, Ben
Fertilisers in USSR 177; and global
  food output 321
Fetishism of commodities 33, 65; and
  alienation 28
Feuerbach, Ludwig, on alienation and
  religion 13
Fiat money 27
Fictitious accumulation 299
Fictitious capital 65; and
  intensification of boom-slump
  cycle 66
Filmer, Deon, study of world
  workforce 331-2
Finance and "financialisation"
  theories, 292-298
Finance capital 90-92; Hilferding on
  89-92; Lenin on 98; Bukharin on
  98; and interests of productive
  capital 293-4, 297, 298; during
  years of slump and long boom 279
Finance in recovery of 1980s 283;
  blamed for deterioration of
  system 293-5

Finance Capital (Rudolf Hilferding)
  90-91
Finance, speculation and the crisis,
  65-67; impact on workers
  budgets 279-80
Financial bubbles, and demand for
  output of real economy 287; in
  Japan late 1980s, reason for 214
Financial assets, global, and global
  output 1980-2005 278
Financial capital, national dimension
  to 259
Financial corporations, US, growth in
  valuation of 278
Financial crisis, of 1907 92; increased
  frequency of 280; of 2007-8 11
Financial flows, international flows
  of in 1980s, 1990s and early
  2000s 279
Financial industry, investment as share
  of total investment, US and
  Britain 295
Financial institutions 63; and the
  expansion of credit 64
Financial instruments 286
Financial labour 123
Financial protectionism 301-2
Financial system, origin of 63
Financial Times, praise for letting
  Lehman Brothers go bust 291
Financialisation 277-292, as
  temporary motor to world
  economy 289
Financialisation theory 292-8, 299,
  385, 386
Fine, Ben, on academicisation of
  Marxism 48; on fog of markets
  caused by financialisation 299
First World War 89
Fiscal measures 149, 162 *see also*
  Keynesianism
Fischer, Irving, on problem with word
  "utility" 43; optimism after Wall
  Street Crash 144; monetarist
  explanation for slump 145
"Flexible production" 261
Food, and capitalism 320-322; crunch,
  threat of 322; price rises of 2007-8
  320; security 322; production and
  population growth in 20th
  century 320-21
Ford 284; River Rouge plant 152;

factories in Germany during Second World War 269; closure of Dagenham Assembly plant 259

Ford, Henry 35

"Fordism", theory of 164; critique of 164

Foreign Direct Investment, destinations 183; stocks, concentrated in developed countries 263; shares of different state 263; flows 1982-2006, growth of stock 1950-2007 255; not mainly on new productive capacity 261; low proportion of total US investment in recent decades 260

Formal employment 339

Former USSR, growth in 1990s 225

Forrester, Viviane quoted 258

Foster, John Bellamy 81; on peak oil 318

Fragmentation among slum dwellers 344-5

France, fall in industrial production in slump 143; economic output 1940s to 1970s 161; during long boom 170; cuts in public expenditure 240; imperialism in Africa after decolonisation 185; conflicting interests with US in Africa and Middle East 274

Frankenstein's monster 85

Free labour, partial negation of 175

"Freeing" of labour 40

Freeman, Alan, on unproductive labour 127

Freeman, Richard, figures on global workforce, critique of 390

Friedman, Milton 300; popularity of ideas after crisis of mid 1970s 192; denounced as Keynesian 194

Fukuyama, Francis, and "end to history" 258

G8 meeting in Rostock 2007 309

Galbraith, John Kenneth 202; on planning during long boom 168-9

Garcia, Miguel Angel 49

General Electric, reliance of finance for profits 284-5

General Motors, and financial profits 284; in crisis in 2009 290

General Theory of Employment,

Interest and Money (John Maynard Keynes) 149

George Bush senior, on New World Order 258

Georgian attack on Ossetia, 2008, 319; role of US 274

German capitalism, economic growth and profits in 1990s and early 2000s 240

German Ideology (Marx and Engels) quoted 81

German unification, economic effects 239

Germany, industrial output in 1920s 144; beginning of crisis in 1928 148; fall in industrial production 1929-33 143; economic recovery of mid and late 1930s 155; seizure of western Poland 156; state planning during two world wars 115; West Germany during long boom 164, 170; economic output 1947-70 161; increase in share of global output 198; unemployment 1957, 1960 172; East Germany, crisis of 1953 179; unification, economic effects 239, and Croatian Independence 270; Social Democrat-Green government 240; fall in real wages 240; world's biggest exporter 239

Ghana 185

Giddens, Anthony 325

Gillman, Joseph 146

Global character of capital's destructiveness in 21st century 316

Global crisis, national solutions to in 1930s and today 302-3

Global Gamble, The (Peter Gowan) 293

Global South 18, 91; in long boom 182-201; state capitalism and economic growth 190; economic growth, unevenness of 189; and end of long boom 217-225; impact of collapse of Keynesian and Stalinist economic models 217-8; terms of trade 218; negotiations with multinationals 222; debt 223; inability of poor countries to attract investment 222 *see also* Third World, Emerging markets

"Globalisation" 258, 260, 261, 264, 266, 267, 277, 281, 298, 301, 325,

expenditure on 131; and turnover time of capital 235; under state capitalism 117-119; in long boom and after 164, 195-7; and end of long boom 200; and Japanese crisis of 1990s 216; and restructuring through crisis 232; in China in 1990s and early 2000s, estimates 248; and wages and crisis 76

Rational expectations theory 194

Raw material barrier 204

Raw material, and empire before World War One 97; cheapening during long boom 165

RBS Nabisco takeover of late 1980s 279

Reagan, Ronald, economic policy 194

Real business cycle theories 56

Real wages, rise at end of 19th century 88; *see also* Wages, United States, Germany, Long Boom

Realist school of international relations 103

Recessions, growth, during long boom 165; of mid 1970s, explanations for 191-2; of 1980s and 1990s 224; of 2001-2, 287; panic among commentators 230; loss of manufacturing jobs 332; of 2008-9 spread to China and India 291; of 2008-9 and cutbacks in green investments 313-4

Recycling of oil funds, and growth of finance 281

Reform, economic, in Communist countries 176

Regional character of many multinationals 262-3

Regulation School 164

Reification 28

Reiman, Michael 158

Relative surplus value 34

"Rentiers" 92, 98, 114; "power of" 294; "euthanasia of" 162

Reproduction of labour power and productive labour 135-7

Reserve army of labour 137-8

Restructuring of capital, in slump, war and long boom 164; in 1980s, 1990s and early 2000s 224, 234-5; limited economic effects of 235; and working class 335; across national borders, and growth of

finance 281

Revisionist controversy 89

Ricardo, David 12, 24, 25, 43, 46; development of ideas of Adam Smith 22; theory of value 30; gap in his theory of value 47; theory of falling rate of profit 69; followers of 23

Rio Earth Summit 1992 309

Robinson, Joan, on support for economic orthodoxy by those with power 11; on persistence of neoclassical theories that have been refuted 44; on "Bastard Keynesianism" 162; on changed message from apologists for capitalism 192

Roosevelt, Franklin D 154

Roubini, Nouriel 300; quoted 277

Rows between governments in crisis of 2008-9 302

Rowthorn, Bob, quoted 333; on wages as cause of declining profits 197

Royalties, and role of state 266; on seeds 322

Rugman, Alan M, on non global nature of big multinationals 262

Russia 327; Tsarist, industrial development 187; slump of 1990s, scale of 210; in 1989-91 351 *see also* USSR

Sablowski, Thomas, on difficulty of separating financial and industrial capitalists 298

Sachs, Jeffrey, and shock therapy 210

Samuelson, Paul, text book 10; critique of Marx on value and price 48; quoted on end of business cycles 191

Sao Paulo, Brazil, size of formal and informal workforces 340; *Economist* calls it "a Detroit in the making" 188

Sarkozy, Nicolas, warns of danger of "a European 1968" 351

Saudi Arabia 183

Savings & Loans, bail out 233

Say, Jean-Baptiste 55

Say's law 57

Schroeder, on "internal modernisation" 240

dynamic 118; Germany and Japan in 1930s 155; during long boom 170; militarised 172; Japanese directed to global market competition 171; Stalinism and Keynesianism as its ideological correlates 302; and limits to accumulation within a national economy 201, 206; and state capitalists 115-19

State capitalist trusts, in Bukharin's theory 95-6

State directed, monopoly capitalism and war 156; industrialisation, in India 251

States, economic management during First World War 154; role in supplying labour power in long boom 172; expenditure, US, 1800-1980 103; revenues as arising from surplus value 113-14; comparable to profit, interest and rent 112; share in national output, Japan in early 2000s 216; theories that see as external to capitalist economic system 103-4, 112; little attention to in *Capital* 88; role in integrating mass of people into system 110-11

States and capitals, structural interdependence 110; difficulties of break between them 112, 113, 114; relationship left unresolved by Marx 102; in Lenin's theory 93-5; in the era of "globalisation" 264-70

Steedman, Ian 48; alleged refutation of Marx on falling rate of profit 71

Steindl, Josef 146

Stern report 309; suggestions tailored to profitability 312

Stern, Todd 313

Stockhammer, Engelbert, and finance and real investment, quoted 295

"Stop-go" policies 164

Strachey, John 64, 158, best known writer on Marxist economics in Britain in 1930s 163; decides Keynes is right 163; and "end of imperialism" 164

Strikes, air traffic controllers in US, defeated 238; miners in Britain, defeated 239; Egypt, 2006 344; South Africa, 2007 343; Soviet miners of 1989 209; Mumbai

textile strike 1982-3 345

Strong, Benjamin 145

Subprime mortgages 286

Sub-Saharan Africa, growth in 1960 189; debt burden 279; much of it marginal to global capital 224, 340

Subsidy to advanced countries from Third World through migration 173

Subsistence farmers 21

Summers, Larry, and "the new paradigm" 229

Surplus value 29, 31-5; relative 34; *see also* Absolute Surplus Value, Relative Surplus Value

Sweezy, Paul 48; on transformation of values into prices 48

Syria 185

Taiwan 218, 242

Taleb, Nassim Nicholas, cheered at Davos for attack on bankers 292

Taylor, F W 34

Taylorism 35; and assembly line 35

TechNet 220

Technical advance, and the organic composition of capital 70-1

Technical composition of capital 69, 71; and organic composition of 73

Telecoms investment boom of late 1990s 285

Temin, Peter, on Smoot-Hawley Act 302

Temporary contracts, Britain 337

Tett, Gillian, on Zombie banks, 12, 354

Thailand 221, 242; per capita growth in 1960s 189

The means of production, ownership of 29

The new working classes of the "Third World" 336-339

Theory and Practice of Socialism, The (John Strachey) 163

Third World 18; economic growth during long boom 161, multinationals 220-1, 257 *see also* Global South

Three Mile Island 308

"Thrombosis in crisis" 153

Tiananmen Square protests of 1989 244

"Tiger cubs" 242

"Tigers" 242; after Asian crisis 282

Tipping points 308, 327

Tonk, Ertugrul Ahmet 126, 195-7

332; arms spending 2005 234; balance of trade 198; trade and budget deficits in 2000s 273; blows to hegemony, 274; overseas hegemony and crisis of 2007-9 327; nationalises Freddy Mac and Fanny Mae 277; sources of oil 319; world's biggest manufacturing country 332-3

Unproductive expenditures, and the dynamic of the system 129; and boom of 1920s 146-7

Unproductive labour, and waste production 127; scale of in US 126

Urbanisation in 20th and 21st centuries 337; and growth of wage labour, 336

US capitalism's interest and climate change 317

Use value 23; in Adam Smith 22

Use value and exchange value 108, 176; and crisis 59; under military competition 117

USSR, character of economy after 1929 158; economic mechanisms established in 1928-9 157-9; accumulation and consumption 177, 204; bureaucracy substitutes itself for capitalist class 157; slave labour 176; and law of value 176, 204; economic growth 1950-70s 175; seen as model for Third World development 186; imperialism in Eastern Europe 181; Competition with West, Brezhnev on 203; causes of waste 177; consumer goods appear by 1960s 175; as world's second economic power 211; productivity and competition with US 180; agricultural problems 176; cyclical fluctuations in growth 178, 204; from Stalin to Gorbachev 115; growth rates long term decline 203; growing dependence on foreign trade 207; stagnation of 1980s 202-3; crisis of late 1980s, causes and scale of 181, 207-8; compared with Japanese crisis of 1990 217; why market reforms were not the answer 210-12; inflation of late 1989 and early 1991 208; revolts of national minorities 208; collapse of 234

"Valorisation" 37

Value added in schools 135

Value 25, 32, 33; substance of 26; and prices 46-50; during crises 60-1; Marx on productivity and 27; and technical advance 27

Vampire-like character of capitalism 84

Variable capital 38, 70

Venezuela 221, 351; and US oil 319

Vietnam 184, 185; French withdrawal 182

Vietnam War 327; and cost to US 271,198

Village industries 243

Vitro 221

Volcker "coup" 296

Volcker, Paul, raises interest rates 1979 296

von Bortkiewicz, Ladislavs, on transformation of values into prices 48-9

Wade, Robert, calls for greater regulation 292

Wage controls 178

Wage labour in USSR 158

Waged employment, fall in several African countries 339

Wages, and development of crises 60; rises in US in 1920s 145; not cause of low profits in 1970s 197; of US workers in 1970s 197; Japan in 1980s 213; real fall in Germany in early 2000s 237

Wall Street crash 143

Walras, Léon 42; ignores problem of time 42; economic crises 56

War and surplus value 156

War on terror and arms spending 234; failures in 327

Warren, Bill, theory imperialism as advancing economic development 189-90

Wars, waged by US in Global South 271, 273; hot, waged in Third World 268

"Washington Consensus" 221

Waste expenditure 234; in US, 1970 127; and accumulation 129-30; a

contradictory role 132
Waste production 126
"Weightless economy" 332; myth of 257
Welfare expenditure, productive and unproductive 137; as proportion of GDP in different countries 1975-95 (table) 238
Welfare provision, early development in Britain 134; development in 20th century 135; during long boom 164; costs in Western Europe and US 174; cuts to 137
Welfare state and needs of capital 135
Wolf, Martin 197; on Thai crisis of 1997 as a "blip" 242; quoted on financial crises 280; quoted on "deleveraging" 290; on role of US household borrowing in keeping global economy going 288
Wolff, Edwin 195-6, 195, 197
Women, married, entry into employed workforce during long boom 173
Wood, Ellen Meiksins 112; on imperialism as caused by politics, not capitalist economics 93; state not instrument of appropriation under capitalism 104
Woolworths in UK goes bust 291
Work measurement and payment schemes 137
Workers, number in world according to Deon study 331; as proportion of workforce in US 334
Working class, in classical Marxism 329-30; theories of decline of 330-1; global size of 331; global distribution of 337; unevenness within 330; relation of the formal and informal sectors 338-344
Working day, legal limits on 33, shortening in 20th century 33; lengthening of 33
Working hours, decline in first part of 20th century 89
Working year, different countries, 2004 239; United States, 1973-98 236
Workplace and community 343
World accumulation, 1970-2004 232
World Bank, endorsement of state planning in 1950s and 60s 186
World growth 1961-2003 231
World Trade Organisation,

negotiations, states and corporate interests 266
World Trade Organisation 17
WorldCom, bankruptcy 233
Wright Mills, C 331

X-efficiency 169, in West and in USSR 204

Yeltsin, Boris, and dissolution of USSR 210

Zapatistas 346, 348
Zeilig, Leo, and Ceruti, Claire, on South African township 343
Zombie banks 11

Printed in the USA
CPSIA information can be obtained
at www.ICGtesting.com
JSHW011912291024
72607JS00003B/9